To Renew Books
PHONE (925) 258-2233

To See
and See
Again

To See
and *See*
Again

A LIFE IN IRAN AND AMERICA

Tara Bahrampour

FARRAR, STRAUS AND GIROUX

NEW YORK

Farrar, Straus and Giroux
19 Union Square West, New York 10003

Copyright © 1999 by Tara Bahrampour
All rights reserved
Distributed in Canada by Douglas & McIntyre Ltd.
Printed in the United States of America
Designed by Abby Kagan
First edition, 1999
Third printing, 1999

Library of Congress Cataloging-in-Publication Data
Bahrampour, Tara.
To see and see again : a life in Iran and America / Tara
Bahrampour.—1st ed.
    p.   cm.
ISBN 0-374-28767-8 (alk. paper)
1. Bahrampour, Tara.   2. Iranian American women—Biography.
3. Iranian Americans—Biography.   4. Political refugees—United
States—Biography.   5. Oregon—Biography.   6. Tehran (Iran)—
Biography.   I. Title.
E184.I5B35   1999
979.5'0049155—dc21   98-27360

Grateful acknowledgment is made for permission to reprint "The
Tent" by Jelaluddin Rumi. Originally published in *Open
Secret: Versions of Rumi* by John Moyne and Coleman Barks.
Copyright © 1984 by Threshold Books, 139 Main Street,
Brattleboro, VT 05301

For Mama and Baba

To See
and See
Again

❖

JUST BEFORE I TURNED TWELVE, MY FAMILY DROVE TO OREGON to outrun the spring. Every time it looked like we were going to stay in one town, the weather would warm up and my father would pluck us out of the life we were considering and swing us back north on the highway. I think that deep down he believed that acknowledging the change of seasons would mean admitting we were in America to stay. So from January to March the days got shorter instead of longer and the backseat windows grew colder as we slipped off the golden piecrust of California, wound through muddy mountains, and descended into a gorge where evergreens blocked out all but a strip of sky.

We traveled in a red Chevrolet Malibu whose trunk held four sleeping bags, five suitcases, a bag of shirts and jeans from J. C. Penney, and a sack of antique Persian tapestries. Before leaving Iran, my father had told us each to pack our favorite things in a suitcase, and I had put in my new Polaroid camera, my fifth-grade yearbook, and my yellow sweat suit. We'd bought the sleeping bags and jeans when we'd gotten to Los Angeles, and as for the Malibu, my parents had opened up the yellow pages a few days after we arrived and called up the first car dealership listed.

At the dealership, my mother bent toward us and pointed at a dark-haired couple and an older lady being led out to the parking lot. I heard a flash of Farsi, spoken loudly, as if they thought no one could understand. My mother is American, but she can spot Iranians immediately, even at a distance. She said a few days earlier the Department of Motor Vehicles had been packed with them, newly arrived and lining up to get their licenses, none suspecting that this red-haired, freckled woman had also just come out of Iran.

In the parking lot, crisscrossed strings of red, white, and blue triangles flapped under a cloudless sky. A long-haired man named Sonny led us along the rows of gleaming cars, their silver cursive "Malibu" logos giving them a wild, exotic aura. Sonny stopped to stroke a metallic red hood. "Seats five," he said, and looked at us appreciatively, as if to congratulate us on being a family of exactly five. "Come on, kids," he said. "Get in and show your mom and dad how much space you've got."

Normally, Baba being called "dad" would have made us laugh—it sounded so American. But that day in the car lot we didn't even look at each other. We were all watching Sonny. He pulled at the handle of the back door, it gave with a rich, oily click, and my brother and sister and I obediently climbed in.

"Well? How does it feel?" Sonny's red face filled the window; his voice boomed, bossy and cheerful, through the glass. Beyond him stood Mama and Baba—and at that moment they looked pale, almost translucent, as if the bright light glinting off the tops of the cars had leached something out of them. They seemed small and far away. So, as the plastic new-car smell wafted seductively around us, we smiled and waved and stretched out our legs in all the space we had.

We said goodbye to my grandparents, coasted down to Sunset Boulevard and merged onto the freeway. Three-year-old Sufi climbed over the front seat to sit on Mama's lap. Ali and I lay head to head on the backseat, our bare feet making shadowy prints on the glass as the power lines outside dipped down and up.

"How long does it take?" Ali called up. We liked to time our trips. The Caspian Sea took four hours, Qom took two, Esfahan took seven. We had driven in all directions from home, and we knew how long it took before the desert sloped up into mountains in the south and the tunneled-out rocks opened up onto the lush, rainy coastline in the north. On the way home, too, we knew when to look out for the gray sea of smog that hung over Tehran. But here, looking out the window didn't tell us a thing. It was all neat and identical and unfathomable.

"Well?" Ali said. He was nine, still small enough to stand leaning over the front seat. "How many hours?"

"That depends," Mama said, holding up the Triple-A map. "If we stop in San Luis Obispo it's about four hours, but if Santa Barbara looks nice we might stay there. And we want to see Santa Rosa, up near San Francisco." This was strange; we had never taken a trip that didn't have a destination.

Outside the window, huge swoops of roller coaster made us sit up. "Please, please, can we go?" we begged. A few years before, when Mama was making her first record album and we were staying in Hollywood, Baba and I had spent an afternoon riding that roller coaster. Now, for one mute, hopeful moment I watched the back of his head and willed his fingers to tighten around the wheel and swerve us into the exit lane.

"No, we're already late." He said it loudly and deeply—the stern-father voice he rarely used.

Mama turned and gave us a sympathetic smile, her eyes lost behind big round sunglasses. "There'll be other roller coasters," she said.

L.A. disappeared behind us.

Simply by coming to America, it was clear we had fallen behind. So we drove and drove, always trying to make it to the next town before it got too dark to look around. Whatever I wrote down in my new "Happy Days Diary" always turned out to be wrong. "Tonight we will stay in San Luis Obispo," I wrote—but we ended up in a Howard Johnson's in San Jose. "Tomorrow we are visiting Mama's friend in Berkeley"—but we detoured into San Francisco. So I began to take note of smaller details—the flavors of ice cream we'd had that day, the TV shows we'd watched in the motels, the Jack-in-the-Box drive-through SuperTacos that we'd eaten in the car, cranking down the windows and letting the taste of the salty beans and soggy lettuce mingle with the sweet, dry tree smell seeping down from the hills.

Each week in Iran, when the international *Time* and *Newsweek* had come out, Mama would drive us to the Hilton Hotel and send me in with a handful of toumans. I would come back out, deliver the magazines to the car, and then, sitting in traffic, watch Mama read about America. Now, in America, Baba became similarly addicted to TV, but he was more obsessed. As the waitress at a roadside diner set our plates down in front of us, Baba would suddenly look at his watch and cry, "Wrap it up!" and we'd hold our food-filled napkins closed as we raced down the freeway.

"The news, the news!" Baba clicked the buttons on the motel TV, frowning at the lag time before the picture bloomed over the screen. All at once, Peter Jennings's face appeared and his voice blasted painfully down onto our beds.

"We're not deaf," I said, peeling the tissue off my grilled cheese sandwich, feigning indifference.

"Shhhhh!" Baba answered.

We watched the whole broadcast turned up high. During the ads, Baba frantically flipped through the other channels, trying to find Tehran, as if any second the revolution might be over and we could go back home, if only we didn't miss the news segment that told us so.

We stopped in every town Mama had heard was nice—Palo Alto, Petaluma, Santa Rosa, and back down to Sausalito. In the motels we watched *Roots*. The show probably lasted no longer than four or five days, but it seemed to run endlessly, being—apart from the news—the only scheduled event in our lives. Every night at eight o'clock it began with the recap of the previous day's scenes and we snuggled down under our blankets—Mama and Baba in one double bed, Ali and I in the other one, and Sufi switching between us. In Iran, Baba had never paid much attention to TV. But now he talked about *Roots* all the time. His favorite part was when the African prince of the jungle is captured, put in chains, and taken to America, where he is

forced to change his name. At different times of the day Baba would
stand up and throw back his shoulders, his round nose flaring, his
eyes wild. "Kunta Kinte," he'd bellow, thumping himself on his
smooth bare chest. "My name is Kunta Kinte!"

On the news, the Shah and the Queen were also in transit. After
spending a few weeks in Egypt they flew to Morocco, where they sat
on a hotel patio in flare-leg pants, looking exhausted, as the newscasters speculated about where they might go next. Meanwhile, the
Ayatollah Khomeini was on his way from Paris to Iran. I recognized
his black-turbaned, white-bearded face from the placards that I'd seen
carried down the street during demonstrations in Tehran, and I remembered his voice from contraband tapes at my cousin's house.
Now, as we watched him step off his plane in Iran and be greeted by
an exultant crowd, Baba said his arrival might end the confusion that
had followed the Shah's departure. So we did not cash in the return
half of our Swissair tickets and Baba did not talk about looking for a
job. Instead, we settled into a motel run by an Iranian and his German
wife on the edge of Highway 101, just below the turnoff to the San
Quentin prison.

In Santa Rosa a man named Fat Morrie led us past wooden houses
and lawns and oak trees with swings, past two girls my age with
barrettes clipped to the left side of their hair, walking along the
sidewalk. I had known American girls at my international school in
Tehran—cool blondes who told dirty jokes and showed off their
butt-hugging Dittos, which, they pointed out, could only be bought
in the United States. Those girls had mostly bothered each other.
The non-American majority had diluted them. But I was alone now,
and I shrank down, hoping the girls wouldn't see me. I was suddenly
embarrassed to be driving around with my family instead of out walking with a friend.

"This might be your junior high next year," Mama said brightly,
looking back from the front seat. She pointed at a high chain-link
fence surrounding a flat beige building with a "Home of the Cou-
gars" sign over the entrance. I stared blankly at the vista of wire and
concrete. Compared to my school in Iran, with its tall, shady trees
and graceful brick buildings, this looked like a jail. I did not want it

to be my school. It was not fair that I should be singled out just because I was the oldest, while Sufi and Ali got to look blissfully out the other window, her preschool and his elementary school still only existing in dream bubbles.

"If we're not staying in America, then why do we have to buy a house?" I asked.

Mama sighed. "We've got to live somewhere while we decide what to do, don't we? We can't stay in motels forever. And you know, you guys and I might stay in America a little longer when Baba goes back. Don't you want to go to school in the meantime?"

I supposed so. Every other time we'd visited America I had attended school. But we had never tried to buy a house just so we could go to school here for a couple of months. I waited for Mama to say something like, "This time it's different," or "We're here to stay now." But when she spoke again her voice drifted. "Who knows? Even if we all go back to Iran we could still buy a house here. It could be waiting for us, just in case."

We got out of the car and stared up at a big old brown-shingled house with a peaked roof.

"This place is practically a mansion," Fat Morrie said, coaxing the key into the lock. The middle of his button-up shirt gaped open over his hairy stomach. "Seven bedrooms at a hundred and ninety thousand—unbelievable."

Ali and Sufi and I ran in ahead. We rocked on the owners' chairs, stroked the colored soaps in their bathroom, and stared at the framed pictures of their children. In a room that smelled of flowers and wood, I found twin beds with cream-colored comforters and a little built-in bench by the window. I sat down to wait for my parents.

"So, are you going to be working in this area?" Fat Morrie's voice echoing down the hall sounded like a friendly American uncle's.

A short pause, then Mama's voice. "We're not sure yet. We're just looking around."

"Oh, Santa Rosa's great for families," Fat Morrie said. "What line of work are you in, anyway?"

Another pause, in which I almost jumped up and ran out to answer. *He's an architect and she's a singer. She makes albums in Los Angeles, and she works at CBS Records in Tehran. He used to teach at the university but now he's opened his own office, and he's just built us a big house of our own that's almost ready to move into.*

But these things weren't exactly true right now, so I didn't come out and say them.

"Architecture," Baba finally said. "I'm a professor at Tehran University."

Now Fat Morrie paused. "Well, you know, if you don't have jobs here you might need more than that ten percent down you were talking about."

I stuck my head out the door. "Can I have this room?" I waved them in and flung myself onto one of the white beds. "See, when I have a friend spend the night she can sleep on that bed." Baba nodded, squinting around the sunny room.

We ended up putting an offer on an A-frame house in Corte Madera. We still lived at our motel, but every day we drove by the house and Mama and Baba pointed up and told us how they were going to remodel the attic into a master bedroom. As soon as we moved in, Grandma would send us Yip, our dog, whom we had brought over from Iran and left for her to take care of. In the meantime, Baba bought me an old blue Schwinn for thirty dollars and Mama signed us up for school.

I'd been out of school almost four months, but the year was not over. I was still in sixth grade. A freckled girl named Tami was assigned to show me around, and my teacher, a hoarse-voiced lady with thick glasses, gave me multiple-choice tests and told me that I seemed to have kept up just fine.

Sitting with Tami on a picnic bench, I bit into my bologna sandwich and thought back to lunchtime at my school in Tehran. Everyone's mothers would make their lunches, and for a while I had been able to convince my Taiwanese friend Shih-Fang to exchange her stacked metal tins of sticky rice and pork for my peanut butter and jelly sandwiches. We ate each other's food gleefully, each sure the other was crazy to switch, until eventually she realized hers really was better and stopped trading. But lunch was still full of wonders: dried strips of mango brought by my Indian friend Malika; empanadas from my Argentine friend Cristina; spring rolls from Bayette, whose American father had met her Vietnamese mother when he'd gone to Vietnam with the Army. Sixth grade in Iran had been the first year of middle school. We'd had electives, and a science class with a real laboratory, and a walrus-mustached social studies teacher named Mr. Pulford, who was all excited about Sir Thomas More and Machiavelli. In Corte Madera, sixth grade was still elementary school, with one teacher for all subjects, but I hoped that the following year the electives and the Renaissance would resurface, and that once they did I would be back where I was before I'd lost Mr. Pulford.

And then we couldn't have the house.

"The owners are selling it to someone else," Mama explained. We had not been the first bidders. We had put in an offer in the hopes that the first people would back out. "It looked like they were going to," Mama said. "But they changed their minds."

I wondered if this meant that we had not been good enough. Had we been scrutinized and found undeserving? Or had we been too slow—maybe that extra day in Santa Rosa had delayed us just enough to miss this house. Now we drove slowly by it again, gazing up as we passed. I had barely looked at it before, but now I wanted that house more than anything. *Let us get it, let us get it, let us get it,* I mouthed.

I had tried this silent praying once before, the night we had picked up our new car in Los Angeles. During the ride back to my grandparents' house my chest had gone tight and I had started to bargain: *I miss Iran,* I wrote in my diary. *I miss the cats. I miss the house. I miss school. I miss my friends.* I would never tease Sufi or Ali again or ask for another toy if we could only swing back around, reverse the last ten days, and go back to Iran.

"Pack your bags," Baba said the next morning. "We're leaving."

I caught my breath and looked up from my book. "What about school?"

"We'll find you a new school," he said, again in that uncharacteristic father-to-child voice.

"Where?"

"Wherever we go."

"Well, why not here?" I asked. "You said we were staying."

"Someone else got our house." He shrugged, as if it was out of his hands.

"Then why don't we find another one?"

But he didn't answer. So I packed my bag, including among my possessions two Narnia books whose dark blue "Neil Cummins Elementary School" stamps stared accusingly up at me as I zipped my suitcase. Mama said not to worry about it because it was the weekend and there was no way to give them back. But I worried anyway. When everyone went back to school on Monday my desk would be empty. There would be no explanation. The overdue slips would come, my teacher's dry voice would inform the librarian of my disappearance, and the two books, like me, would be marked down as missing.

Leaving Corte Madera so unexpectedly, I felt I had not foreseen something I should have. When we'd first gotten to Los Angeles we had kept driving past a big signboard on Sunset Boulevard that said "Maps to the Stars." I thought it must be a fortune-telling technique, a mapping of my stars, and I had meant to ask my parents to stop for a consultation with the blond woman in the purple tank top and sunglasses who sat by the sign. In the end, though, I had forged ahead without consulting her; and I must have miscalculated, because here we were, moving again. *Don't check out books*, my stars would have told me; *don't start on those math problems, don't make friends*. But up here there was no star map to tell us these things, and so, guideless, we slammed the car trunk closed, hitched my bike to the back, and joined the morning traffic.

❖

The Soft Garden

WHEN BABA WAS A BOY IT TOOK ALL DAY TO DRIVE FROM ONE
end of his family's property to the other. For errands around the
village they went on horseback, but for longer trips he and his father
would climb into the back of their big black Dodge and be ceremoniously chauffeured over all the land they owned, sending up clouds
of dust from the dirt road which until then only horses and camels
had traveled.

"The servants would stand along the running boards and then jump off and wave as we drove away," Baba used to tell us, his eyes glowing. "We would drive past the rivers and farms, and in each village our driver would stop and all the men there would line up to kiss our hands."

As Baba talked, the sunbaked mud walls of the village, the rows of poplar trees, and the distant purple mountains would take shape in my mind. The men in camel-hair hats and woven cloth slippers would stand in the road with one hand on their chests in a gesture of respect as my grandfather Agha Jan emerged from the massive car. A fedora rested on Agha Jan's slicked-back hair, a square mustache punctuated his round Mongolian face, and his bushy eyebrows cut together sharply as he nodded to the men. Baba himself would stand as straight as his father, shoulders back, eyebrows raised, eyes lowered, as the villagers lined up. "Esfandiar-khan," they called him—a lord, although he was only nine—and after they kissed his father's hand they bent to kiss his too. Then they kissed the ends of their own fingers and touched them to their foreheads, chins, and chests, finally looking upward with a sigh as if they'd touched heaven.

The way Baba told it, nothing in the world today could ever be as good as those early days. On summer days he and a couple of cousins would head into the hills to hike, fish, shoot rabbits and swim in the river. Returning through the village, where everyone knew them, they would stop to greet other children, joining a ball game before going home to a leisurely meal with the family. Even breakfast in those days was a magical event. Every morning in the whitewashed mud farmhouse, Baba and his six brothers and sisters would awake to the sounds of roosters and cowbells and workers singing in the darkness on their way to the fields. Inside the house, the tea water simmered in a big brass samovar as the servants moved from room to room, getting the day started. The night before, the maids would have milked the cows, boiled the milk, and set it out in the cold desert air, and when they brought the large copper pans inside, the cream lay fixed in a thick, white layer for the children to fight over. The family sat around a big cloth on the floor and feasted on hard-boiled eggs, flat bread, honey, walnuts and quince jam, as an oil lamp in the center spread soft light over everything.

My grandfather was born without a last name. Nobody in Iran had one until the 1920s when Reza Shah, the last Shah's father, decreed that everyone must choose a surname. But even after Baba's father picked out a name for our family, people rarely addressed him by it. The family called him Agha Jan, which literally means "Beloved Sir." Other people called him Haji-khan, because he had journeyed to Mecca as a young man. That was long before he married Baba's mother, back when making the Haj still meant a two-week camel caravan to Abadan and a ten-week boat ride around the triangle of Arabia, during which anyone who got sick was thrown overboard so as not to contaminate the other pilgrims.

Being a Haji only added to the respect Agha Jan had already accrued through his wealth and connections. He owned a large number of villages (Baba never knew exactly how many), and received a percentage of all the crops produced by the villagers. In return, he provided them with medicine, schools, and mosques, as well as food and shelter. When merchants from nearby towns went on holy pilgrimages to Qom or Mashhad or Mecca, they brought him their bags of silver coins and he became their bank. If anyone had a problem—a land dispute, a sick child, a neighbor who used too much of the communal water—he became their judge, sipping his tea and frowning and deciding what should be done. Politicians running for local office also came to Agha Jan because if he agreed to support a candidate and told all his villagers to vote for him, that person would win.

To Western eyes, Agha Jan would not have looked particularly rich or powerful. In public he wore rough wool suits; at home he simply wore pajamas. Like everyone else in the village, he owned almost no furniture—the family slept and ate on the floor. He did not force his wives and daughters to stay inside the house and he did not enforce separate men's and women's quarters as many people still did, but male guests were always shown to a specific room where Agha Jan awaited; they were never led through the rooms used by the family.

Agha Jan was deeply religious. He had endured many hardships—he had lost his parents when he was still young, his first three children had died of diseases and then his first wife had become barren, which was why he had taken my grandmother Aziz, a mullah's daughter, as a second wife. His misfortunes had strengthened his faith, and his preferred method for tackling a question or a problem was to open his worn leather Qoran to a random page and follow whatever advice he found there.

My mother likes to say that Baba grew up with four mothers—his own mother, Aziz; Aziz's mother; the woman who was his wet nurse; and Agha Jan's first wife, Wife-of-Agha Jan, who had her own room in the house and was loved and respected by everyone except Aziz, who was jealous and made bitter remarks about her "low, villagey ways."

Baba, the youngest child, was adored and indulged. His sparkling black eyes and the quick, engaging smile that teased the dark mole above his lip made even strange women stop in the street to hug and kiss him. Surrounded by so much affection, he never felt unloved by his gruff father, although the old man might yell and chase the children with a stick if their playing interrupted his nap.

Baba did not pay much attention to religion. He played tricks on the little mullah with thick glasses whom Agha Jan brought over twice a week to teach the Qoran to the children, and he avoided the mosque as much as he could, especially on mourning days.

"They would tell us to fast and pray, and force us to sit in the mosque for hours," Baba remembered. "Everyone would be crying about the martyrs and gathering like black crows around those dusty graves. I just wanted to go outside and play, so I would climb over all the women to get to the door and they would reach out and pinch me for stepping on them."

For Aziz, going to the mosque was more of a social event than a spiritual one. She would walk over to the mosque, talk a little with the other women, and come home furious about the mullah's hour-long discussion about "which hand to eat with and which hand to wipe yourself with." Ranting about how they were making a fool of her, she would swear that she wasn't going back anymore, but she always did.

It fell to Aziz to care for Baba's material needs. "Don't you see anything, old man?" she would say to Agha Jan. "All the other children have bicycles and Essie is sad. You have to buy him one." Aziz also insisted that the family go live in the nearest town during the cold months so Baba and his brothers and sisters could be close to school.

Aziz was more modern than her husband. She had been a young wife when Reza Shah had established a new law banning chadors; upon hearing the news, she had thrown hers off, put on a European dress and hat, and hurried out for a walk. She was a firm believer in a secular, preferably foreign, education for her sons (at age fifty she would teach herself to read and write in order to send them letters when they went abroad). But she also relied upon ancient traditions to help run her household. If someone fell ill she drew symbols and letters on an egg, blew on it, and then tapped it on the patient's forehead to break the evil spell of sickness. If that didn't work, she made cuts in the back of the sick person's neck to let the bad blood drain away. Certain problems required experts—when someone lost a key, Aziz called for the key finder, a woman who came to the house and chanted something against the jinns who had hidden the key. Or, if a strange thump was heard from an unused storage room, Aziz called a jinn catcher, who went alone into the room—no one dared follow—and came out a little later to announce that all the jinns had been banished.

But Aziz's remedies had no effect when her sixteen-year-old son Khosrow began to feel tired and sick all the time. So she put her faith in modern medicine and convinced Agha Jan to buy a house in Tehran, where the best doctors were. She also brought along her crazy uncle Dai-Hossein, who had tried to kill himself three times already—in the hopes that the Tehran doctors could do something for him.

The new house in the city was three stories high, with the bottom floor reserved for servants brought in from the village. There were nine servants in all, plus a tenth man whose job was to watch over Dai-Hossein and chain him to a radiator every night so he wouldn't kill himself or anyone else. There was the driver, the cook, the gardener and his wife (although the city garden was barely as big as the village chicken yard), two young maids, handpicked by Aziz from among the prettiest girls in the village—"so when my children wake up in the morning they will see beautiful faces"—and two retired old servant women, brought along for sentimental reasons, who spent the days begging family members for cigarettes. Finally, there was the old poet who taught everyone the Qoran and who specialized in making up poems about how wonderful Baba and his sisters and brothers were.

The neighbors laughed. It showed what villagers they were, with all these people lining up to see them off in the morning and greeting them when they came home.

Later, when the family moved to a bigger, newer house off Amirabad Avenue, they decided that the first house had been a bad-luck house. First it had caught fire and burned out an entire side of one floor. Then Dai-Hossein had escaped and run to the outskirts of town, where his body was found the next day floating in a well. Worst of all, in that house Khosrow only grew sicker, despite the family's best efforts. They made Parviz, the third son, get rid of his beloved pet pigeons because an old lady had said that playing with pigeons caused people to die. They forbade Baba to play in the mud because another old lady said that touching mud made people die. They brought in a turbaned old man who scattered beads on the floor to read Khosrow's fate, and who sat mumbling to himself as the top doctors conducted their examinations and drank tea and whispered together. Khosrow had a fever in his heart, they said, and nothing they knew of could cure it.

After Khosrow died, Aziz cried inconsolably for months and went to the graveyard in South Tehran every day. Agha Jan retreated to the village to be comforted by his first wife. The older children felt guilty, responsible, perhaps, for the various bad-luck omens that might have brought about their brother's death. But Baba and Massi, the sister closest to his age, had passed the months of Khosrow's illness playing outdoors with the gang of cousins and servant children who lived nearby. If anything, they came away with an almost rebellious determination to preserve their happiness through any catastrophe.

When Baba was in high school in Tehran he used to go to the Iran-America Cultural Association for American novels and glossy brochures about the United States. Since 1953, when the oil was nationalized and taken away from British control, the American association and its Soviet counterpart had been giving out free literature to any Iranian who walked into their office. The American pictures were bigger and shinier than the Russian ones; and in any case, no picture, however beautiful, could dispel the Iranians' fear of the Soviet Union. Baba remembers *The Siege of Stalingrad* showing at a local theater and the audience hurling ripe tomatoes at the screen. Huge and close, the Soviet Union seemed to lie in wait to take over Iran and make Iranians stand in line for bread like the Russians did.

America was different. In the movies Baba stood in line to watch every Friday, he saw an America full of beautiful women and big cars. America had John Wayne, Gregory Peck, and Gary Cooper, all dubbed into Farsi; and Baba and his friends dreamed of going there. It was not educational or professional opportunity that Baba wanted. Neither he nor his brothers would ever need to worry about job skills; Agha Jan's property could easily support them throughout their lifetimes. America was alluring simply because it was America, the land of cowboys and gangsters and Esther Williams in a silvery bathing suit.

Baba's older brothers Parviz and Jamsheed had already joined the wave of wealthy young Iranians going to college in America, and Baba wanted so badly to follow them that after graduating from high school he refused to take the Tehran University entrance exam. Agha Jan didn't see the point of all his sons spending so much money to attend school in a place so far away from their family, but Aziz understood their desire for adventure. "Open your eyes, old man," she said to Agha Jan. "Can't you see Essie wants to go to America like his brothers? You have to send him." And, as he increasingly did as he got older and Aziz got bolder, Agha Jan threw up his hands, cast his eyes heavenward and gave in.

Baba left Iran in the summer of 1958. He departed like the old-time travelers, with his money sewn into the lining of his coat; just to be safe he wore his coat into the airplane rest room, where after staring for a minute at the mystifying chair, he finally climbed on top of it and squatted over the opening as he always had. In Germany he boarded a propeller plane that crossed the flat ocean and wended slowly down over the mountains and forests of a green land that went on and on without stopping.

To Baba, everything in America was magical. In the Washing-

ton, D.C., airport, he walked by a door that opened on its own, and
he jumped back in terror before being rescued by his brothers. At the
supermarket he marveled at the coldness of the milk and at the butter
that came whipped in a jar or wrapped in paper in neat yellow bricks.
But most amazing were the girls. They walked down the street in
shorts. They smiled at Baba for no reason. In Iran, he had once asked
a girl he saw every day on the bus to meet him after school; she had
agreed, and then at the appointed time, she had sent her brothers
instead. They had surrounded Baba and punched and kicked him
until a policeman rescued him, rode him home on the front of his
bicycle, and demanded ten toumans not to tell Baba's parents.

But in America, when Baba said hello to a beautiful blonde, she
said hi back. "Let us go to a movie," he said haltingly, and after she
heard his broken English she was even nicer to him. They kissed in
the dark theater, oblivious to the movie, until the girl glanced back
and said, "Oh, my brother's here." Baba jumped up. Then his eyes
fell upon a young boy sitting a few rows back, smiling and licking an
ice-cream cone. This was the brother. America was even better than
Baba had dreamed.

Baba was accepted into an agriculture program at Cornell University,
but when he found out it required him to work on a farm for a year,
he told his brother Jamsheed that he had come to America to get
away from raising goats, and the two of them boarded a Greyhound
bus for California. They enrolled in school at Berkeley, where Jamsheed decided to study economics and Baba chose medicine—until
an Iranian friend explained, "To be a doctor takes eleven years of
school, Essie-jan. You're good at drawing. Why don't you study
architecture?"

The brothers moved into an apartment above LaVal's Pizza. Baba
took up ceramics and photography, and he and tall, wavy-haired Jamsheed found girlfriends among each fall's new crop of freshmen. During college, Baba did not pay much attention to events taking place
back in Iran, and he was unaware of the turmoil erupting in his own
parents' house. In his junior year of school, the Shah signed a land
reform bill that wiped out Iran's feudal system and dissolved Agha
Jan's empire. The Shah was photographed handing rolled-up land

deeds to the villagers, and the large areas that had been tilled under Agha Jan became small patches owned by individuals. In America, Baba felt only mild ripples of this upheaval. His family stopped sending money, but by then he was almost done with his studies. He earned the rest of his tuition by waiting tables at the Faculty Club, and after graduation he got a drafting job at a small architecture firm in Oakland.

People sometimes ask in an awestruck voice how my parents "ever got together," as if some mysterious factor must have been responsible for a boy from Iran marrying a girl from Los Angeles in 1965. But it was not so strange. By the time my parents met, Baba had decided against the Iranian way of marriage. On his one college visit back to Iran the women in his family had plied him with hints and suggestions. *You know, you're handsome and American-educated; you could marry anyone. Dai Mohsen-khan's youngest daughter is a very good girl; you should take her as your wife. Go to their house next week and see her; they'll be expecting you.* But it never occurred to Baba to let his family select his wife, although that is how all his brothers and sisters except for Massi eventually married. After seven years in America, where his relationships were "full of tears and crying and declarations of love," he could not imagine getting married any other way.

Whenever I asked either of my parents how they got together, they always mentioned Mama's jeans. Mama's roommate had considered Baba her own discovery, and had invited him to drop by one afternoon. The roommate offhandedly introduced him to Mama, who was stretched out on the couch in a pair of tight new blue jeans. Her red hair was pulled back, setting off her deep brown eyes, pretty mouth, and pale, freckled skin. As soon as the roommate left the room for a minute, Baba made his move.

"You want to go to Carmel with me on Sunday?" he asked.

"Sure," Mama said.

"I'll pick you up at five in the morning."

Back in the days when Baba was sitting in Tehran movie theaters and dreaming about the land of cowboys and gangsters, Mama was growing up in a split-level house in the soft glow of Hollywood's periphery. Her father had a psychoanalytic practice in Beverly Hills, and although the location gave her childhood a tinge of glamour, Mama describes it as "a regular old fifties growing up. Dad worked, Mom stayed at home. There was Christmas; there was golf; there was going to the beach; there were the parties where Dad served the drinks and Mom played the piano." Mama spent her days going to ballet classes, camp and cotillion, hiking in the nearby canyons and eating hot dog dinners in front of the TV with her younger brother.

It was not until high school that she began to sense that something was missing. Part of this started at home, where, as perfect as they might have seemed from the outside, her parents were slowly discovering how mismatched they were. They had married young—he was a thin, shy pre-med student at Stanford and she was a vivacious Berkeley freshman with long dark hair, a dazzling smile, and a determined-looking jaw that masked her under-confidence. She had grown up without much money in a wealthy town in Northern California, and later she always talked about how she had envied the girls who came to school in the luxurious cashmere sweaters she could not afford. Marrying a doctor from a prosperous family made Grandma feel included in a world she had always longed to be part of, and in the early years of the marriage she was full of exuberance. But gradually it faded. Grandma began to complain that Grandpa was "more comfortable with psychoanalytic interpretation than with simple emotional expression." Mama remembers Grandma slowly retreating into the only role she felt suited for—wife and mother—while Grandpa sat at the head of the table, thoughtfully discussing Freud with his children while testing the dinner plates to see if they had been properly warmed.

By the time Mama was in high school her parents seemed to disagree about everything. Grandma came down with an ulcer and began what would be a thirty-year litany of grievances along the lines of: "Well, he's a good provider but he can't understand the most basic things about people." Grandpa, on the other hand, was frustrated by Grandma's "block against exploring mankind's darker sides." During the Cuban missile crisis he developed an intense interest in the apocalypse. To Grandma, all this doom and gloom seemed designed to arrive just as she was about to give birth to their third child. "Why can't we be like other people?" she asked irritably. "No one else I know has to plot the course of radioactive fallout during dinner."

The missile crisis had a different effect on Mama. Sixteen years old and believing that the world could end any day, she conceived an urgent desire to see as much as she could of the world beyond the warm, eucalyptus-scented hills of Los Angeles. Her imagination was fueled by the Italian art films she watched at the theaters on Wilshire Boulevard, and she developed a romantic idea of an outside world of sophisticated women living exciting, passionate lives. The missile crisis only heightened her impatience to see this world. Walking dreamily out of an Antonioni movie one day, Mama made a pledge to herself that for the rest of her life she would say yes to everything that came her way.

She and a school friend decided that after graduation they would go to Italy. They saved up money from part-time jobs and had just bought their tickets when, without warning, her friend's parents whisked their daughter off to Australia to evade the imminent nuclear disaster. So Mama went on her own. She lived in an Italian *pensione*, accompanied a group of student Communists to Hungary, and sailed to a Greek island with a boy she had met on the ship from New York. After six months she returned to attend college at Berkeley, where she dated a civil rights activist and a series of boys much like the ones she had known in high school—until the day her roommate brought over the boy from Iran.

It was not by mistake that Mama was perched on the couch in her new stretch jeans that afternoon when Baba walked in. She had seen him driving around town with no shirt on and the windows rolled down and she had thought he was cute. When he asked her to go to Carmel with him at five in the morning, the fact that she had a date planned for the night before did not daunt her. She said yes right away.

Whenever Mama talked about that first date, her eyes would soften and a little smile would play on her lips. Baba's black-and-white Nash Rambler glided up the dim street, he opened the door for her, and by the time the sun spilled over the eastern mountain ridge they were coasting through the velvety yellow hills of the Almaden Valley.

There remains just one photograph from that day, copied and en-larged, so it has a bright but misty quality, like the sun breaking through fog. Mama is sitting in front of the Mission Carmel in a straight skirt and sandals, her loose red hair framed by a powder-blue scarf. Her eyes are tired but she is smiling, and something about her expression makes it easy to understand what Baba liked in her—a kind of openness, as if she were ready for anything that might happen.

Later she joked that that first date should have warned her about what she was getting into; this was an excursion to the most distant place they could go to in one day. But that kind of adventure was precisely what she was looking for, and in this foreign architect whose warm eyes and slightly asymmetrical nose gave his handsome face an easy informality, she saw a spontaneous energy that promised to take her beyond the world she had grown up in.

After three more dates he showed up at her door one night and said, "How would you like to live with me?"

Mama said yes immediately. It was 1964, and they knew of no other unmarried couple who lived together, although a year or two later most of their friends would start doing it. Mama says she and Baba were not trying to set a trend; they were simply blind to ev-erything but each other. They found a little cottage in Oakland shrouded by trees, although Mama continued to pay her thirty-five-dollar rent at Peggy's and kept a few dresses in the closet for when her grandparents visited from down the street.

Back in L.A., her parents complained that she was never home when they called. Her father awkwardly warned her about the repu-tation of a girl who has lived with a man who doesn't end up marrying her; she shrugged it off. Her father had always encouraged her to trust her impulses, and in any case she was prepared for either out-come. She would marry Baba or move on to something else—either way, she would be experiencing the world.

She bought a Persian cookbook and skipped classes to prepare elaborate meals. They drank wine and read poetry late into the night. One evening, a few months into it, he said, "I'd marry you in a second if I thought you could live in Iran."

She did not stop to think about whether or not it would work. They drove down to Los Angeles to tell her parents, whose only request was that they be allowed to throw a big wedding. Only a few of their Berkeley friends attended. The guest list was mostly comprised of her parents' friends, who drank champagne and whispered about how attractive the couple was, and how young, and how, after all, Mama could always get a divorce and come back home.

My parents ended up going to Iran by mistake. They had planned only to go to Europe, to attend Baba's family's first—and only—vacation abroad. It was summer, and Jamsheed had driven Aziz, Agha Jan, and his sisters Massi and Homa from Tehran to Geneva, where Parviz joined them from Washington and Baba and Mama flew in from California.

Massi, a tall, striking woman with flashing dark eyes, spotted Mama in the bathroom of the Geneva train station and guessed who she was. After triumphantly hurrying her out to the snack bar to meet the rest of the family Massi took her new sister-in-law aside. "You—baby?" she said, pointing at Mama's stomach, rounding her hands out in front of her own stomach and raising her eyebrows in a question.

"Not yet," Mama said.

Massi made a circle with her thumb and index finger and poked her other index finger in and out of it. "You—Essie—kaput?"

Thinking "kaput" meant finished, Mama smiled and shook her head. "No, no. No kaput."

"No kaput?" said Massi. She looked at her sister and mother and repeated it to them. "Essie and Karen, no kaput!"

Later, Mama found out "kaput" meant condom. The Iranian women she met were preoccupied with babies—either with having them or with not having them—and one of the objectives of the European trip for Massi and Homa was to get birth-control pills, which were not yet available in Iran.

Their other objective was shopping. In each country, my aunts and grandmother spent large segments of the day at department stores. Mama had imagined her in-laws to be a more cosmopolitan version of her own parents, whose luxurious European vacations revolved around sightseeing and fine dining. But except for shopping excursions, Baba's family rarely went out. They did not visit tourist sites, and most of their meals consisted of bread, butter and jam on the hotel room floor—as much a factor of habit as of frugality. Mama and Baba followed them from shop to shop, but after a couple of weeks, desperate to be alone together, they decided to spend a few days in Venice and meet the family in Istanbul. They left most of their money and belongings with the family for safekeeping and enjoyed Venice so much that they stayed an extra day. When they arrived at the Istanbul hotel the proprietor handed them a note.

Sorry, we couldn't wait. We went back to Iran.

—Jamsheed

The family had left an hour earlier.

Although they had only a couple of dollars between them, they decided not to telegram Mama's parents for money. It would have been embarrassing; moreover, they could not even afford a hotel for the days it would take for money to arrive. So they went to the Iranian Consulate.

"Here is enough money for food and a train to Erzerum," said the consul general, a sympathetic young Iranian Turk. "From Erzerum you can catch a bus into Iran. You can send the money back to me once you get there."

The family's house in Tehran was not as Baba had left it. Most of the servants had returned to the village. Wife-of-Agha Jan, Baba's beloved stepmother, had died several months earlier, although in Europe no one had mentioned it to Baba for fear of upsetting him. But the family was as hospitable as ever, and when it became clear that Baba was going to be stuck in Iran for a few months while he waited to see if he would be drafted, he and Mama moved into an apartment at the top of the family home.

Soon after they arrived, Baba's sisters and female cousins pulled Mama into a bedroom to compare breasts. "Who has the best ones?" they asked eagerly, turning it into a contest. Mama spoke no Farsi, and, not wanting to offend, she undid her shirt along with everyone else. They all looked around for a minute and then buttoned their shirts back up. The reason, Mama guessed later, had to do with an old tradition. In the old days, when a man could not see his wife before the wedding, his female relatives had only to go to the bathhouse to see everything about her. If her looks pleased them, they could take their investigation further: greeting her with kisses on the mouth to see if her breath was sweet, stroking her head affectionately to make sure her hair was really her own. But Essie had married without any advice or approval, even after Jamsheed had written a letter warning him not to, because "surely Karen has dated before." Later Massi reported to Baba that Mama's were among the two sets of breasts voted as the best. The other set belonged to the cousin the family had hoped he would marry when he came back from America—in other words, he'd made a wise choice on his own but the choice they had made had been good too.

The household settled into a comfortable routine around Agha Jan, who, too old to dominate the family as he once had, sat on the floor puffing on his water pipe and drinking tea. Mama sat with him and read poetry books in English; he smiled at her through the haze of smoke and paid her small compliments through intermediaries. It was hard for the rest of Baba's family to find much wrong with Mama. She was good-humored and polite and clearly in love with their son. Unable to communicate with her beyond single words and pantomimes, they treated her with a bemused mix of condescension and respect ("See, she knows how to sew!" Massi gushed. "Exactly like an Iranian woman!") injected with an occasional tinge of disapproval ("Just look at how much she likes Essie," Aziz's sister whispered in a scandalized voice, as if there was something commendable but also something incautious about a woman who liked her husband so much). In any case, Baba made it clear from the beginning that he would not tolerate any of the heckling so often leveled at daughters-in-law, and that if they attempted even so much as a criticism of the way Mama peeled oranges he would refuse to listen.

In general, though, they were less concerned with her flaws than with her virtues. Being foreign, she was considered an expert on anything Western. She was the one who deciphered the instructions on the Valium and birth-control pills from Europe; and if someone was sick she was often called upon to give a diagnosis, which everyone would listen to with respectful nods.

She was also the expert on chic. Had an Iranian woman tried to go around in the miniskirts and sleeveless blouses Mama had bought for the trip to Europe, her father and brothers would most likely have locked her up in her room. But the fact that Mama's wardrobe raised no objections from Baba, coupled with Agha Jan's obvious affection for her, resulted in a kind of amnesty for everyone. Her in-laws initially explained her outfits to outsiders as "the way American women dress," but soon the younger women in the family were taking Mama's clothes to the tailor and asking for exact copies. As for Agha Jan, he hardly noticed the sartorial changes in his household, which in any event coincided with the advent of miniskirts in Tehran later that year. The only comment he made was to Baba, one night when his bachelor cousins had invited him out for the evening. "Never be like the men who go out at night," he said. "Karen is too good a girl to leave alone at home."

In the meantime, even as the women consulted Mama about birth control, they could not refrain from asking her every few days if she was pregnant. As the months passed, their questions intensified. My parents had already decided to go to New York so Baba could get a master's degree and Mama could finish her bachelor's degree; but for now they were stuck where they were. Baba couldn't go to school or even work in Iran until he found out about the draft. In the meantime, having nothing much to do, the two of them decided that having a baby might not be such a bad idea, and soon Mama was able to give the women the answer they wanted.

❖

"TARANEH-JAN!"

"*Naz!*"

"*Janam!*"

A crowd of strange, shrieking women surrounds us. It is late at night and we are hot and sticky. On the plane, my baby brother Ali slept on Mama's lap, but since I'm three I got my own seat. Mama drew me a picture of the world with all its countries and us flying above it, from America to England to Iran. When we landed, Baba picked me up to walk down the airplane steps, and I am still in his arms when the women in the airport run up to us, screaming. I want a glass of water, but the women are talking so much that no one can hear me, and I can't understand what they're saying. One of them pinches my cheek hard, and I turn my head toward Baba's shoulder, but the fingers follow.

"Taraneh, Taraneh!" That is my Iranian name, which I've only heard my uncle Jamsheed use, the time he visited us in New York. Everyone else calls me Tara. When I was born, in Los Angeles, Baba

was still in Iran, and he told Mama over the phone that he wanted
to name me Sheefteh, which means "charmed" in Farsi. But Mama
said I should have a name that Americans could pronounce. Mama
says I can be Taraneh in Iran and Tara in America and never feel
strange in either place.

But I feel strange at this airport with the screaming women. I am
tired and want to go back to my room in Brooklyn. Instead, we are
bundled into a car and driven to a place where all of us sleep on the
floor and mosquitoes buzz around us; but I am glad because the other
people are gone and it is just us four again.

In our new house I have a big iron bed and a backyard with a little
L-shaped pool of water. On the floor above us lives Aziz, my grandmother, who sometimes comes down to sit in the backyard with me.
Above Aziz lives my uncle Dadash and his family. His wife, Leila-
khanoum, has black curly hair and long pearly fingernails. She doesn't
speak any English, and neither do their two children, who are ten
and eleven. But Dadash speaks a little. He is very thin, with slicked-
back hair and a tiny black mustache. His voice is soft, but his whole
body goes stiff whenever I run by him.

"Don't go so fast down the stairs," he calls out in careful English.
"You will fall."

"American girls run down the stairs all the time," I answer back,
and he gets a look on his face as if he smells something bad. But I
know he is not mad, because when we visit him upstairs he kisses me
and lets me go into his bedroom and play with the fur-headed shaving
brushes on his dresser.

At night we go to people's houses where everyone speaks Farsi. I
whisper in English to Mama and Baba, who bend their heads and answer
softly back. The other grown-ups grab me and hug me and pinch my
cheek so hard that it feels bruised. They give me plates of smelly green
stew, which I don't eat until Mama scrapes all the green off the meat and
cuts it up and says "There, now it's just like steak in America."

One night, when Mama is tucking me into bed, I tell her I am
homesick.

She gives me an odd look. "How can you be homesick? This is
our home."

After that night Mama starts letting me bite her. If I am upset about something she pushes up her sleeve and I sink my teeth into her freckled arm, leaving a football-shaped tooth mark. For a few months whenever I am mad I get to bite her. It makes me feel better, even if she is not the thing I am mad at.

But when Baba tucks me in I forget to be homesick. "Once upon a time," he begins, "there was a king who was sad because he had no children." I close my eyes and see the king, who finally has a baby but it has strange white hair, so he abandons it in the desert. A magic bird called the Simorgh takes the baby to her mountain nest and raises it to be the great white-haired King Zal, who returns to the land of men but always carries a feather from the Simorgh, who will come to help him whenever he is in trouble. The story never ends, but runs on into the next night and the next, with all the characters appearing and vanishing and reappearing. A dead prince can be revived with a potion; a beautiful princess can turn out to be a wicked old lady; an evil, horned *deev* can seem to die but return a few nights later as a cat. But I am never scared. Baba's fingers are long and dry, and as I lie in the dark they circle my hand like the wing of the Simorgh.

The first couple of summers after we move to Iran, Mama takes me and Ali on trips to America. I can't wait to go. In America no one pinches my cheek or screams in my ear or tells me I should be speaking Farsi by now. I hate when my relatives say that; and even when I do understand them I sometimes look at them blankly as if I don't. Then they get mad and tell Baba that I should learn my own father's language.

In Los Angeles, Ali and I watch cartoons and eat all the candies and ice cream that Iran doesn't have. We go swimming in Grandma and Grandpa's pool and Grandma gives us boxes of toys and clothes that our uncle Doug and aunt Laurie have grown out of. Mama's old friends from high school work in the music industry, and on one trip she buys a guitar and starts writing songs. Then, when I am five, we stay in America so long that I start kindergarten, and on the first day our teacher tells us to draw pictures of our parents. That is easy; I've done it a hundred times—orange crayon for Mama's hair, black crayon for Baba's—until a blond girl named Jenny looks at my picture and shakes her head.

"Your father can't have black hair."

"Why not?"

"No one really has black hair. It's probably just very dark brown."

"No, it's not," I insist. "It's black."

But Jenny shakes her head and I can't prove it. Baba is in Iran, and Mama says we can't go back right now because there is too much snow for the airplanes to fly. So we live in an apartment near Grandma and Grandpa and Laurie and Doug, and Ali and I stay with them at night while Mama sings in clubs. Ali has his third birthday party at their house and gets leather boots and a mini-briefcase, just like Baba. He keeps asking when we are going to see Baba again. I want to see him too, and I write "I miss you very very much" on the back of my school picture to send him. I know that we are going back to him as soon as the planes can fly, but Ali doesn't understand this, and he plays "Baba" all the time, walking off to work in his boots and carrying the toy briefcase in his hand.

In the spring we go back to Iran. The moment we walk through the airport's glass doors Baba grabs us all at once and holds us in a big, tight hug. Mama and Baba are kissing and we are all smiling and laughing, and he scoops me and Ali up in each of his arms so I can touch the mole on his forehead and his thick bangs that fall forward, as black as I remembered. "Wait till you see our new house," he says. He drives us to an apartment that he's decorated with rugs and pillows and tapestries. He shows me and Ali our rooms, but we are too excited to sleep and we stay up all night, telling him about America and showing him his presents and being glad to be back in our own family again.

❖

We've lived in Iran four years and I still don't like the green stew, which is called *ghormeh-sabzi*. I don't like most Iranian food, although Ali loves it and eats bowl after bowl. I like kabob, though, because I can see exactly what's in it—meat.

At school I have to hide my food. The Parthian School is up in the mountains north of Tehran, too far away for me to go home at lunchtime the way Iranian children do. Parthian's tall brick building looks strange standing alone in the middle of a village that is all tiny houses and huge old trees, but every weekday a fleet of buses carries several hundred English-speaking children up there from all over the city. Each Saturday, the first day of the week, we sit in rows on the cafeteria floor so the headmistress can give speeches about how, as the "future elite of this country," we have "tremendous responsibilities to shoulder." We don't listen to her. But we have to listen to Miss Jane, her red-faced assistant, because she watches us eat lunch. We are served enormous mounds of rice or noodles—including *ghormeh-sabzi*—and afterward we have to bring our empty plates to an inspector, who puts his hand under our coats to make sure we aren't hiding anything. My friend Pamela and I fill Kleenexes with spaghetti, hoping they won't break before we can slip out into the yard and throw it to the cats.

I skip school often. Baba teaches at the university and supervises research projects in all different parts of Iran. We load up the car with suitcases and fruit and a red Coleman thermos filled with water, because once we leave Tehran we can't drink from sinks. Driving through the desert, Mama makes up stories about the Jell-O Monster who goes to Sand Land and is always in danger of melting until at the last minute he is rescued by the Sand Monster. By the time it gets dark we feel like Sand Monsters ourselves because our hair is dusty and our throats are dry and there is only a little puddle of warm, plastic-tasting water at the bottom of the thermos.

Baba doesn't dress like my friends' fathers. Instead of suits, he wears blue jeans and sweaters. He wears his hair long and shaggy, and when he drives he puts a terry-cloth tennis band around it—unless we go to Turkoman land, up in the top corner of Iran, where Chinese-looking men in black curly hats lay red carpets out in the sun. There, Baba gets his own lamb's-fleece hat, wide at the top and narrow at the bottom, and he stands in the middle of the market, lights a Winston cigarette from the red-and-white box, and blows a stream of smoke out. He looks toward the northern mountains and tells us that in a few years we will start visiting other countries, like Afghanistan and Egypt and Turkey, but for now we get in our car and turn back toward the green hills of the Caspian Sea. The sun falls slowly into the trees. "Don't wake Mama up," Baba whispers, and we are all quiet as he steers us toward a cool, dark tunnel in the mountain.

Baba always gives me and Ali the job of spotting our destination. Driving to Qom, the holy city, we must find the golden dome. "There it is," we cry from the backseat, pointing at white flecks in the sand, but Baba laughs and shakes his head. Finally, when we pass over the last ridge of mountains, we recognize the flat brown town with the glinting onion in the center. "The golden dome!" we yell, triumphant that we have saved ourselves from going thirsty in the desert.

We check into a little hotel in the middle of town and go walking through the crowded bazaar. I pick out glittery material for Mama to make me a princess outfit and I also choose dark fabric to take to the tailor's. Tomorrow we are going to the golden dome, the shrine of Massoumeh, and, since I'm almost seven, I am too old to go in without a chador. In a tiny shop in an alleyway, the tailor drapes the fabric over my head and cuts it in a circle around my ankles, muttering as his long shears chomp through the cotton. "In the morning it will be done," he says gruffly, and folds his body onto a tiny bench behind an old black sewing machine.

"Coming?" Baba says to Mama in the morning.

"You guys go; I've seen it already." She looks up from the bed, where she's stretched out with a book. She always brings a pile of books on our trips, and afterward they sit in the back of the car until the pages turn brittle and the covers fade and fall off. Now she smiles and waves us out the door.

The clouds hang in shreds like wet tissue paper in the sky. In the fresh morning air, the scent of *sohan*, Qom's special pistachio brittle, mingles with the exhaust of idling buses whose conductors yell, "Tehran! Tehran!" We walk along the crowded sidewalk, past a row of open-front shops where mullahs in turbans and brown robes finger their worry beads, young men sell cigarettes and gum from boxes, children beg their mothers for sweets, old women buy prayer candles, and younger women inspect the soaps and the silverware and the animal-shaped pottery. A donkey hee-haws under its load of cloth sacks, and a beggar on the ground tells us that God is great, echoing the calls of *"Allahu Akbar!"* that drift out over the wall of the shrine.

In the little shop in the alleyway, the tailor drapes my new chador over my head. I want to keep it on, but Baba and the tailor are speaking Farsi too fast for me to get a word in. The chador gets folded and wrapped tightly in newspaper and Scotch tape. In Tehran only some girls and women wear chadors, and I never do. Today I am wearing a red T-shirt with plaid pants, and I stick out like a bright strawberry in this street full of black clothes.

We walk along a brick wall, and stop at the point where women in chadors are going in and out of an archway. Baba opens my chador and holds it out—a half circle of cloth as tall as I am—and I pull the straight part over my head and let the sides hang down to my ankles. But the harder I clutch it under my chin, the more the top slides off my head, and it is not until a clump of women push through the portal, their chadors expertly held in place, that I see how to wear mine. I gather up the right side and pull the extra material from the left side across to my right armpit, where it stays secure and gives me a free arm. The women don't notice me copying them; they are too busy crowding around a wooden door, bending down or standing on tiptoe as they press their lips onto the carved wood. Baba says they're kissing it to make their wishes come true, and Ali wants to kiss it too, but Baba says not to because it is covered with germs.

The inner courtyard is tiled with flat marble slabs, and people are walking back and forth or standing over them. "Each one has a person buried underneath," Baba says, pointing at the Farsi calligraphy engraved on the slabs. "Over there, under that arch, is Agha Jan's."

I have only seen my grandfather Agha Jan in pictures. He died while we were still in New York and Mama was pregnant with Ali; when they heard the news, Mama and Baba put aside their list of Persian-hero names like Som and Zal and named Ali after Baba's father. Ali and I want to go see his burial spot, but Baba says there are a bunch of people sitting on it right now. We continue on up to a big arched doorway and put our shoes on a shelf next to other people's shoes. Then we step into the shrine.

Glass chandeliers hang from the high, vaulted ceilings. The walls are pale green. Our stockinged feet slide over cool marble that is almost translucent, like sea water under glass. This is the burial place of Massoumeh, the sister of a man named Emam Reza. Massoumeh was only seven or eight when she died while her family was traveling through Qom, so they buried her here. I want to see Massoumeh's coffin, but too many people are pushing for me to see anything besides a big cage with thick silver bars. Everyone is crying and moaning, especially the women on the other side of the cage. One of them ties a scrap of cloth on to one of the bars and slips a damp green five-touman bill through: it falls onto a pile of crumpled money inside the cage. Baba says the woman is asking for a favor from Massoumeh, and that many sick people come here hoping that Massoumeh will make them or their families better. I can see some of those sick people—an old man with a tangerine-sized lump weighing down his forehead; a small boy whose eyes are gummed up with tears; a man with no eyes, holding his wooden stick close.

"Don't touch," Baba reminds us as we circle through the chambers. The walls echo back the broken wails of women we cannot see, the crowd sweeps us from room to room, and when we stop for a second I stare up at a giant chandelier with blood-red glass cupped around the lights like flower petals. Suddenly my fingers slip out of Baba's. A forest of men's legs closes in. Holding my chador up like a battering ram, I push through, trying to find Baba's blue jeans; but something grabs my arm and starts pulling me sideways. It must be someone who has seen me in my black chador and mistaken me for another girl. Fear races through me as I lose my footing and am swallowed into the crowd.

"Did you get lost?"

I can breathe again. It is Baba's hand that has mine, with Ali on the other side of him. We are back at the entrance, and Baba gives us our tennis shoes. I sit down to put mine on, relieved and exhilarated, as though I've just been on a roller coaster. As Baba teaches Ali how to tie his shoes the Iranian way, with a loop and a knot in the right string and another loop and knot in the left string, I lean back and look up. The arched entryway to the shrine is inlaid with tiny diamond- and teardrop-shaped mirrors that twinkle and sparkle like a giant tiara. It is only after my eyes have adjusted to the glitter that I begin to see what lies there. It is a reflection of the outside world, shattered into fragments and remade in miniature so you have to look really hard to find any one object. I squint my eyes and keep still and there, as Ali tightens the knot on his shoe, I see it—a thousand rain-slicked courtyards, a thousand pools of shimmering water, and, deep inside the diamonds, a thousand calligraphed tombs with tiny pilgrims holding bottles of rose water over them. I keep looking, trying to see myself in the mirrors. But every time I move a little bit the reflection changes.

Cutting off the road from Qom to Esfahan, we head west across the rocky desert. After a while the road begins to slope up; the dry tumbleweed is replaced by green fields and cypress trees; and old, crumbling walls mirror the jagged line of mountains above.

We bump slowly down a dirt road that leads to a small village of mud-walled houses, turn into a gate in a brick wall and drive up through a garden. Then we pass through another gate and roll up to a yellow brick house with a long front porch—my uncle Dadash's farm.

On the porch, a hunched figure in a long dress and pajama pants whisks a stickless broom back and forth. When she sees us she does not straighten up, but puts her hand on her crooked back and squints, opening her caved-in mouth in greeting.

Kobra has worked for the family since before Baba was born. Her leathery face is carved into hatch marks so deep that her eyes and mouth just look like slightly bigger slits. Her nose droops down to her top lip, and out of the front of her scarf fall thick bangs that are white at the top and tangerine-colored the rest of the way down. She folds her arms in front of her chest and hobbles toward us, still bent at the waist, her stockinged feet pushed halfway into a pair of plastic flip-flops.

"Hi, how are you, how is everyone?" Baba says, looking behind the house to see if there are any other cars parked there.

"*Bah, bah,* Esfandiar-khan with his wife and children. Khanoum!" Kobra calls into the house. "They have arrived!" She reaches a gnarled hand toward Ali's head and Ali ducks and runs behind Mama, peeking back out around her legs. "*Ey sheitan!*" she chuckles, "the little devil wants to play games with me." She turns to Baba. "Kha-noum is here. And your sister, and Roya-khanoum. Agha went to Tehran with Javad-khan." Agha means sir and Khanoum means madam, and my Farsi is good enough now to know that Kobra is talk-ing about Dadash and his wife, Leila-khanoum, and their kids, Roya and Javad. Although they live upstairs from us in Tehran most of the year, they come to their farm during summers and school holidays.

Baba frowns. "I told my brother we were coming yesterday or today."

Kobra shrugs. "Maybe Javad-khan had tests for school. *Enshallah* they'll be back soon."

Leila-khanoum hurries out of the house to greet us, and a servant boy with closely cropped hair drags our suitcases out of the car. They are as big as he is, but he uses the weight on each side to balance himself.

Kobra beckons me over.

"Congratulations!" she whispers in my ear. "You have gone to Qom. Did you put in a prayer to Hazrat-e Massoumeh for me?"

Unsure what she means, I nod.

"You did a good thing," Kobra whispers. "Now I will call you Qomi-Taraneh. And what did you wish for yourself?"

I look at her blankly.

"*Vai,*" she says. "The first time a person steps through the doors of the shrine, whatever he wishes will come true. Didn't you know that?"

How could I know? No one told me about making wishes before we went to Qom. I stand in the garden, weighing my new knowledge. Suddenly all the preparations—the buying of the chador, the taking off of the shoes, the walk through the shrine—have a meaning I didn't know about. My stomach feels empty because now I will never be able to step through those gates for the first time and get my wish.

"With those clothes she went to the shrine?" Another old lady, with a gold front tooth, appears at the door, brushing chopped green dillweed off her hands. She drops her eyes down to my T-shirt and my short pink skirt.

"They made a chador for her, no?" Kobra says. "Go bring it."

The old ladies follow me into the entryway and watch as I unzip a suitcase and pull out my new chador.

"*Bah, bah, mashallah!*" Their wrinkles deepen into smiles when I hold it out. Kobra rubs the cloth between her crooked fingers. "What a good Moslem you are," she says, draping the chador over my head. "So small, and already visiting Hazrat-e Massoumeh."

I tuck the sides of the chador behind my ears. "I'm not a Moslem," I tell her.

The old ladies are silent for only half a second before Kobra says, "What talk is this? Of course you are. Your father and mother are both Moslem, so what else would you be?"

"*Voh*, if you weren't Moslem how could you go into the shrine?" says the gold-tooth lady in a scandalized voice.

"My father is Iranian and my mother is American," I say.

"Your mother is American; she is also Moslem," Kobra says.

Gold-tooth nods and adds, "Her name is Zohreh."

"Her name is Karen," I say. I run into the house to find Baba.

Baba and Ali are sitting with their legs under the *korsi*, the table everyone sits around from the first fall frost to the last cold spring night. It is a low, wide square with soft bedrolls and long pillows on all four sides and a heavy quilt laid over the top. Under the table is a big metal plate filled with red-hot embers and covered with gray ash to make sure no one's feet get burned. If I push myself down and stretch my legs I can feel the rim of the plate. But I never go all the way under, and I never spend the night beneath the quilt on the side as Leila-khanoum does, because Baba told me that when he was little a boy fell asleep under the *korsi* and suffocated.

I go and stand beside Baba, who is reading a Tintin book to Ali.

"Baba, why didn't you tell us we were supposed to make a wish at the golden dome?"

He looks up. "Where did you hear that?"

"Kobra told me."

"I didn't know that. Why don't you come sit under the *korsi* and you can make a wish right now."

Making a wish under the *korsi* doesn't mean anything, but I slide under the quilt and onto Baba's lap and listen to him finish the book. His English sounds funny when he reads out loud—he says each word extra-forcefully, no matter how little or big it is.

"I can still hear you shouting, 'We're falling into the sea!'—Ha ha ha ha ha ha!" The Thompson twins splash into the water and the story ends. I lean over onto Baba's lap and roll my finger back and forth over the stubble that he lets grow out on his face whenever we travel. "Baba," I say, "what was the worst thing that happened to you when you were little?"

He smiles and rolls his eyes. I ask this all the time. He tells us the story of when he was ten and he fell off a donkey and broke his arm. The village grocer, who was also a bonesetter, put his arm in a cast for six months and when they took the cast off, his arm was shriveled down to the bone and completely paralyzed. So the grocer put black leeches on his arm. "If they had decided to suck," Baba adds, "my arm would not be here now." Finally, in the Tehran bazaar, an old man with a turban shook his head at the grocer's handiwork and gave Baba a rope and pulley, and after six months of exercises his arm came back to life.

"What else bad happened?" I ask, vainly hoping for a hidden story we have never heard.

"Nothing else happened to me," Baba says. "But I can tell you some bad things that happened to my father, Agha Jan. When he was a little older than you guys, he was kidnapped. He used to go to school in a different town from where he lived, and he would walk home on a lonely road across the desert. One day a group of bandits saw him walking, and they saw that he was wearing an expensive robe, so they threw him over a horse and galloped away. Then they sent a message to his father, saying 'We have your son and if you don't give us such and such amount of money we will kill him.' "

"And so he gave them the money," Ali finishes with a flourish of upturned palms.

Baba shakes his head. "No, he didn't. His father told the messenger, 'That boy you have? He's not my son; go ahead and kill him. My son would never let himself be captured.' The bandits were so impressed with his father's bravery that they let Agha Jan go."

"Hah, I bet those bandits never came back again," Ali says.

"Well, maybe not those bandits," Baba says. "But in those days the countryside was full of different bandits. That was how Agha Jan's father died. There was one famous bandit named Rajab-Ali. He had a hundred men on horses, and he used to go around to different villages and demand food and carpets and other nice things. People in the villages would give it to him so he'd leave them alone. Agha Jan's father was the only one who said no to the bandits, but Rajab-Ali knew he had nice carpets and lots of wheat, so he sent his men to request them again. At that time Agha Jan's father was forty-eight years old, but he had white hair and a white beard, like Zal. And he had an eye disease, so he couldn't see very well. When he heard the bandits were coming he started yelling for people to help him, but the villagers had all run away in fear. So he went up to a tower of his house and shot at the bandits until he ran out of bullets. He cried out for his daughter-in-law, 'Ghamar! Ghamar! Bring my bullets!'— and when he heard someone coming up the steps he said, 'Did you bring the bullets?' But it wasn't Ghamar on the steps; it was one of the bandits who had gotten into the house. The bandit said, 'Here, Haji, this is your bullet,' and when Ghamar came up she found him there, fallen forward over his gun."

"Where was Agha Jan?" Ali asks.

"In the next village, taking care of his father's land. It's a good thing he wasn't there or they could have shot him too."

"Or he could have saved his father," I say.

"Who knows?" Baba says. "After the bandits left, the villagers ran and told Agha Jan what had happened. Agha Jan swore he would chase and find Rajab-Ali, and all the police and Agha Jan's friends spread out to look for him. It took two or three years, though. Rajab-Ali was a Lor—"

"What's that?" Ali and I ask.

"Lors are a tribe that occupy Loristan, in the mountains. That's where they finally found his hideout. The police announced that he was captured and that whoever had anything against him should come to the town of Borujerd to see him hang. So Agha Jan went. They used to hang criminals on high platforms in the town square, and a big crowd gathered to watch. Right before they were going to hang him, Rajab-Ali looked around the crowd and with tears in his eyes said, 'Isn't there one man here who can step forward and save my life?' Agha Jan could have done it because it was his father who had been killed. He always said afterward that he almost stepped forward, but at that moment he remembered his father's kind old eyes and he couldn't."

We ask for more stories, but Baba shakes his head and jumps out

of his chair. Ali and I chase him from room to room until we find
him on the living-room floor with his arms spread out and his eyes
rolled back.

"He's dead, he's dead!" we cry, although the corners of his lips are
trying not to smile.

"What are you saying? Get up!" The shocked voice of my aunt
Homa-khanoum makes us look up. She is Baba's oldest sister, a delicate, doll-like aunt with a soft voice that makes everyone stop and
listen. Her auburn hair is tied back in a small ponytail, but people in
the family say that when she was young she used to let it stream
behind her as she galloped through the mountains on horseback.
Then she got married and had five children and started praying all
the time.

"Never say these things," she says reproachfully, biting her bottom
lip and patting the couch for Baba to come sit beside her. He grins
up at her from the floor and reaches his arms up over his head. Ali
takes a running start, gives a yell and leaps over his stomach.

"Eh! But have you gone crazy?" Homa-khanoum grabs Ali's arm
and pulls him over to the couch. "If you jump over a person lying
on the ground, that person will die!"

"Oh, leave them alone," Baba says. In English, he adds, "Don't
listen to that stuff."

"You shouldn't teach them these things," she says to Baba. Then,
to no one, she says, "I am going to pray." Homa-khanoum always
prays like this, in the middle of everything. My grandmother Aziz
usually slips away and sets up her rug on the bedroom floor, bending
stoutly forward and straightening up, arms out, palms up, never
flinching or looking at anyone. But Homa-khanoum is a wide-awake
prayer. She washes her hands and feet at the kitchen sink, unfolds
her white prayer scarf and light blue chador and prays right at the
dining table while we keep on talking. Her hands rise up in front of
her face and her voice murmurs words too low to hear—but when
Baba makes a funny face she gets louder and says, "I can see that
Esfandiar is making jokes and thinks I can't see him," which makes
us laugh more.

In the kitchen Leila-khanoum fries the greens, adds the onions, and
stirs in the yellow spice that she scoops out of a huge square glass

jar. I kneel on the floor with her as she pounds on slabs of meat with a metal hammer until flecks of red flesh fly all around us. When she is finished, she goes to the refrigerator and hands me a cold potato cutlet to eat and tells me to go help the old women who are sitting around a huge mound of *baghali*—fava beans. I sit on the floor beside them, shifting my legs to avoid pinning down the chadors that drape like cobwebs from their heads to their elbows to their knees as their hands dart out to grab the beans.

Only Kobra doesn't wear a chador—she is like one of the family, sitting in her usual position on her haunches, with her pajama-clad knees drawn up to her ears and her long arms reaching out around the sides. Her twisted fingers split open the large pods, slice each bean in half and push out the tender green core. "*Akh*," she says, stopping for a minute to wave a long fava pod at us. "*Baghali* always remind me of when the Aal came to Wife-of-Agha Jan."

"Ooh, if you talk about that I'm leaving," Leila-khanoum interrupts. "I'll have bad dreams." She puts the pot of rice down and starts out toward the door. But Kobra is going to tell the story anyway, and Leila-khanoum can't help staying.

"Well, it's good Roya is not here," she says, looking around as if her daughter might appear at any moment. "If she hears such stories she won't even go into the bathroom alone."

I sit up proudly. I am not afraid of Kobra's stories—not even if they are about the Aal, a tall, bird-headed monster-woman with yellow hair.

"It was a long time ago, and Wife-of-Agha Jan was still young," Kobra begins, and the flat vowels and trilled consonants of her village accent are like the chirp of a sparsely feathered black-and-orange bird. "I was sitting in the garden with a big bag of *baghali*, when all at once I heard everyone screaming and yelling. I ran over and asked what had happened, and they told me: The Aal had come to Wife-of-Agha Jan's room and stolen her liver!"

"Oooh," says the gold-tooth lady, biting her bottom lip with her gold tooth. "Why did they do that bad thing, leaving her alone right after she had given birth?"

"What do I know?" Kobra says. "But somehow she was alone for a few minutes. The Aal is sneaky and knows when to come. And so, on that day, it came, stole her liver and ran off."

Leila-khanoum leans in and whispers, "You know it's not true?" I nod. When Baba was little he believed all the stories the servants told—about talking animals, and people at the bathhouse with little hairy tails, and Jews who kidnapped Moslem children to drain the oil out of them and sell it in their shops. "If they catch you," the servants warned, "they'll stick pins in you and chant 'Mohammadoo! Mohammadoo!' until they collect all your oil in a pot." Walking to school, Baba and his sister Massi looked straight ahead and took fast, petrified strides past the Jewish houses. Baba says they didn't know any better.

"Yes," Kobra continues. "Everyone ran out, and they got Wife-of-Agha Jan's liver back just before the Aal could throw it into the well. Otherwise she would have died."

"Thank God," Leila-khanoum mumbles softly, and I look up at her, wondering if she really does believe it after all.

"But didn't she have knives under her bed in case the Aal came?" says the gold-tooth lady. "Metal to keep the evil spirits away? Or— *vai!* God forbid her baby was switched with a jinn! Jinn babies stay small and die soon."

"*Akh*, what talk," Kobra snaps. She frowns, and hundreds of new wrinkles appear. "That baby became a regular boy. He died of *abeleh*, like his two brothers."

What is *abeleh*? I start to ask Leila-khanoum, but she waves her hand backward and says it is something that used to kill people in the old days.

"And then," Kobra finishes in a low voice, "no matter what she tried to do, Wife-of-Agha Jan never had another child."

She slaps her palms together in a "finished" motion and all the women shake their heads and click their tongues in a whispery chorus.

Kobra pushes her pile of beans into the center and looks around at the other piles. She reaches over and pinches my cheek. "Eh, what a good girl you are! *Mashallah!*"

"*Mashallah*," echoes the gold-tooth old lady.

Mashallah. People always say it, and I used to think it just meant "good for you." But Baba told me it also means "may God not do it." May God not take this child away, or make him sick or weak; may God not leave him prey to the jinns who want to replace him with his twin, a jinn child who looks and sounds just like him but never gets any bigger, and dies before he can grow up.

Baba once had an eighteen-year-old brother, a two-year-old sister, and three half brothers who all died before they could grow up. Mama and Baba say that jinns are not real, and that we have vaccinations now that keep children from dying, but the old ladies still seem worried. *Mashallah*, say the slanty-eyed old ladies in our family who wear black dresses and armors of red-gold necklaces, and who bend down to stroke our faces and run their hands through our hair. Whenever we speak or smile or wear new clothes—anything that is good—we get a *mashallah* and fingers laid on us to make sure the evil eye does not swoop down to take our goodness away.

Mama is not in the bedroom. She is not outside where she sometimes reads in front of the green-black swimming pool. I slip out of the garden, down to the bottom of the rocky driveway, and out the gate to where the white dust of the donkey trail is pitted with hoof marks. Two cows wander past the baked-mud, rounded-roof ruin of an old fort; beyond them, the alfalfa fields glimmer with sharp, bright dragonflies. I cut across a field and run over the hard dips of plowed earth until I see Mama. She is walking under the poplar trees in her big straw hat and a long-sleeved shirt. Mama has to wear a hat because she has white, freckled skin that never gets tan like the rest of us. I wish I had freckles too, and sometimes I use Mama's eyeliner to draw them across my nose and cheeks.

"Hi, Big T," Mama says when I catch up to her. "You want to come down to the river?"

Her clear young American voice melts away the shrill Farsi mutterings of the old ladies. I slip my warm hand into her cool one and tell her that Leila-khanoum taught me to cook something called *coo-coo* and Kobra told us about the Aal and the liver.

Mama laughs. "Oh I've heard those stories of Kobra's."

"Really?" I say. "Like what else?"

"Oh, something about how when she was young she was in the yard and she got invited to some genies' wedding."

"You mean jinns?"

"Yeah, jinns. She said they had a wedding in the attic with fancy costumes and food, and she almost got up to dance with them but then she looked down and saw they had hooves instead of feet. And I guess maybe horns too. Do jinns have horns? Anyway, Kobra said she ran out of there just in time."

"In time for what?"

"I'm not sure," Mama says. "Did she say what happens to you if you hang around genies too long?"

"No," I say. "But you know what else Kobra said? She thought we were Moslem."

"Oh, did she say that?" Mama pushes up her jeans to stick her feet in the water. "Well, actually, she's right."

"But you said we were nothing."

"We *are* nothing. But officially we're Moslem. Agha Jan asked me to convert when I was pregnant with you. He was very religious, and he asked us to get married a second time because he wanted me to become Moslem. That way you guys would come out Islamic."

"Didn't he care that you married Baba the first time without being Moslem?"

"No, but he wanted to make sure that you would be."

I have seen pictures of Mama and Baba's first wedding, with "Bel Air Hotel" inscribed in gold underneath the swans and the accordion player and the blurred rice flying past Mama's white veil. Now Mama tells me that in the second wedding she wore a black chador. The only guests were Aziz and Agha Jan, and the only gift was a large red carpet that Agha Jan brought for the ayatollah who performed the ceremony. Mama had to say in Arabic that there was no God but Allah and that Mohammad was his prophet; and after she said it three times she got her Islamic name, Zohreh.

That night I ask Baba about it, and Homa-khanoum says she remembers lending a chador to Mama for the occasion.

"And you came out Islamic," Homa-khanoum adds. "That is why you can put on a chador and go with your Baba to the golden dome. A girl who was not a Moslem would not have been able to go. In fact," she adds, lowering her voice, "a few years ago, people in Qom killed a foreigner they caught sneaking into the shrine of Massoumeh."

"Oh, but that would never happen to us," Mama says quickly.

"No," Homa-khanoum says, "because you are Moslem. But Karen-jan, remember the first time you went to the shrine of Emam Reza in Mashhad? Taraneh, some men stopped your mother at the entrance. She was wearing a chador, but they said, 'No foreigners,' and your Baba had to yell at them and say, 'This is my wife, how dare you say she's not a good Moslem?' Then they had to let her in. But if she had not been Moslem, God only knows what would have happened."

"Nothing would have happened," Baba says.

But Homa shakes her head, as if to say it's better to be safe.

The next day we load up the car to go back to Tehran. Everyone comes outside to see us off, and Baba gets into the driver's seat and lets the Jeep's brake slip with a clank.

Suddenly, Homa-khanoum runs out of the house, waving her arms.

"Wait, wait!" she cries. "Get out and kiss the Qoran!" Baba laughs and pulls up the brake again.

"*Bismillah al-rahman al-raheem,*" Homa-khanoum chants as she holds a book over our car.

"What's she doing?" I ask.

"Making us go under the Qoran so we'll get home safely without crashing into anything," Baba says. He peels off his T-shirt and wraps it around his head to keep his hair out of his face.

Homa-khanoum says, interrupting her chanting to smile at Baba's bare chest, "*Ey,* what a dervish."

People in the family call Baba a dervish all the time because he does things they don't, like letting his hair grow long and wearing sandals to dinner parties without worrying about what people will think. Of course, Baba isn't a real dervish. He showed me a real one in Qom—a man in a dirty *aba* cloak and a fez, whose eyes looked like they had been gouged out. His head was tipped up toward the sun and he was singing loudly, and people came up and dropped coins into his *kashkool,* the half-moon-shaped gourd that dervishes hold by a chain. People give money to dervishes because they are special holy men who don't have a home but wander from place to place, singing stories and telling fortunes and bringing good luck to those who are kind to them.

We coast through the little stream between Dadash's house and the other houses. Five or six villagers who are watering their cows stand aside and raise their hands to say goodbye. We wave back and Baba slows down so the dust won't rise in their faces. And then we are out where the road becomes asphalt and there is just the rocky land and the toothy mountains in the distance. Faster, faster, Ali and I say, and we glide into the opposite lane and shoot past one, two, three cars. Mama clutches the door handle until her fingers turn white; but then she lets go and starts peeling an orange to pass around. Soon we are far from the village, barreling through the desert, the only car on a straight road with nothing to crash into.

⁜

"Are you Japanese?"

I laugh, and the shopkeeper realizes he is wrong. My wavy brown hair, light skin, and slightly flat-lidded eyes are a mix of a lot of things, but I'm not Japanese. On my mother's side I am English, Irish, Scottish, Swedish, and German. My father's side is harder. Agha Jan's family is said to have come from the Qashqais, a nomadic tribe that moves between the mountains and the plains of the southern province of Fars. Baba says that is why even the old ladies in our family go out every evening for a brisk stride around the block, with the blood of the nomads pumping through their legs. On Aziz's side, three Turkoman brothers moved to the Zagros Mountains, between Esfahan and Arak, a hundred and fifty years ago; one of them became her grandfather. It is their northern blood that gave Baba, Dadash, Massi, Homa-khanoum, and Parviz their straight hair, dark eyes and smooth, honey-colored skin.

"I'm half Iranian and half American," I answer in Farsi.

"Ah, *do-rageh*," he says, nodding. *Do-rageh* means two-veined, or two kinds of blood in one vein, and whenever people say it I think of my two bloods swirling together like a two-colored lollipop.

"Here, have a chocolate." The shopkeeper hands me a hard candy with little pictures of grapes and oranges on the foil wrapping— *shokolat* in Farsi, even though there's nothing chocolatey about it. Then he catches sight of Mama. "Hah," he says, answering the question he was about to ask me. "I see it is your mother who is American."

Mama smiles politely.

"Khanoum," he says. "I have one question. Which is better? Iran or America?"

Everyone always asks her this.

"Both are good."

The shopkeeper tosses his head back and flaps Mama's answer away with his hand. "Come on, khanoum; tell the truth. It's better over there. I mean, look how hard we work, and what do we get? Will I ever get rich here? There's no chance of it! But I have heard that in America, if a man opens up a shop, he can buy a car within two years."

"Maybe," Mama says. "But some things really are better in Iran."

"Like what?" the shopkeeper says, but he doesn't stop to listen to her answer. "Iran is small, Iran is nothing. With your permission, khanoum, I must remind you that America is big and has everything."

"But Iran is good too," Mama says. She never takes sides.

Iranians are usually surprised at how well Mama speaks Farsi. She has an American accent that won't go away no matter how many times we repeat something to her, but she knows a lot more words than I do. When I was little I didn't worry about knowing them, but now that I'm starting second grade I have to worry. After lunch at school I'll have to go to a class called Quick Farsi, which is for students who are behind their grade in Farsi. I imagine a young, soft-spoken blond woman will be my teacher, translating every Farsi word into English. But when I walk in on the first day an old Iranian lady with gold chains hanging from her glasses says, *"Befarmaeed benshineed, bacheha,"* and then launches into the fastest Farsi I have ever heard. Everyone takes out a piece of paper and starts to write. The teacher talks on, and soon I can't see her or anyone else because my eyes are brimming with tears.

After a while things get better—my teacher still doesn't speak English, but she gives me a first-grade book and explains the work slowly enough so I can understand. Every day I learn a new letter, and soon I start looking forward to learning the next day's Farsi letter, like the breaking of a secret code. But I still don't like to speak it. If I am

going somewhere by myself, like to the corner store, I ask Mama for
the word for thumbtacks or cardboard and then walk quickly down
the half block, carefully repeating it in my head before it disappears
like salt between my fingers.

My uncles Parviz and Jamsheed speak English to us because they
studied in America, but some of our other relatives say that Ali and
I should speak better Farsi. They say we might if we did more *deed-o-
baz-deed*, which means "seeing and seeing again." They do it all the
time, going over to each other's houses every day to sit and drink tea
and talk. Then the next day they go to someone else's house. Baba
says all that visiting can get boring, and he tells anyone who asks that
Ali and I will pick up Farsi on our own time.

My Farsi life swims darkly below my English life. It surfaces whenever
I talk to anyone who is not from my school or my immediate family.
The more I speak it, the more I notice I've picked up words I don't
remember having learned. In fact, there are some words I only know
in Farsi, words my family uses no matter which language we are
speaking. *Khash-khash* is a hard green oblong pod the size of my fist,
which Ali and I split open to shake out handfuls of white seeds that
pop between our teeth like tiny pearls. *Toot* is a musky purple or white
berry that grows on trees, and *joob* is the trench between street and
sidewalk that carries water through the city, getting slower and
blacker the further south it goes. A *ghallian* is a hoopskirt-shaped glass
jar with a tall carved wooden top and a bowl of coals and a thin hose
coming out the side. The old men who visit Dadash use it for smoking tobacco, or sometimes for *taryak*, which looks like chocolate but,
we are repeatedly warned, is not.

Some people's names mean things. Dadash means "big brother"
—our Dadash's real name is Abdollah, but everyone, including his
own mother, calls him Dadash. Aziz has a real name too—Saltanat.
Aziz simply means "dear." Some people are called the thing they do,
like the *ashghali* who comes to our house to collect the *ashghal*—the
garbage; and the *nafti*, who wheels his oil-cart down the street, yelling
"*Naft!*" in a high creaky voice.

I understand the Farsi of my relatives better than that of other
Tehranis because Baba and his family still have a trace of the slow,
flat-voweled accent of the village.

"*Vali een bacheh* kheili *koochik-e*," says my father's cousin, a broad-faced woman with dyed bronze hair who holds me at arm's length as she looks me up and down. "This child cannot be eight years old; she's not big enough!" It's true; I am almost a head shorter than everyone else in my class. I don't mind. I like it when the teacher tells me to get in the front of the line and lead the class down the hall, and I like being chosen to play Mary in the school Christmas pageant; most kids are cows and sheep, while I get to ride on the back of the boy who plays the donkey taking me to Bethlehem.

But Mama doesn't like it when people call me small. "I was the same height when I was eight," she says, which is not true—in her third-grade class picture she is just as tall as the other kids—but it satisfies the relatives.

"Ah, and you grew up to be a good size" the bronze-haired lady says. "It must be the way Americans are."

"Karen-jan, tell me," another of Baba's cousins asks. "*Kodoom bacheh ra beeshtar doost daree?*" Which child do you like better?

"I like them both the same," Mama answers.

"Oh, but you must like one better," the cousin insists. "You must like Ali better, because he's a boy. Or maybe you like Taraneh better because she looks like you."

"No," Mama says, her Farsi simple and definite. "*Har-do-ta ra doost daram.*" I like them both.

They don't believe her. But they indulge her. With an Iranian woman they might push for an answer; with Mama they just give her a kiss and say *Joon-e-delam* and *Ghorbanet beram*, the same way they do to me and Ali. I know these words like song lyrics, although it is a long time before I think to ask Baba what they mean—that we are the souls of their hearts and that they would die for us.

We had to move back into our old basement apartment underneath Aziz after the ceilings in our new apartment fell down. Baba promised Mama it would only be for a short time. Our old apartment used to be his family's servants' quarters—half sunk into the ground, with one door leading up to the front alleyway and another door leading out to the garden and the back alleyway. All the houses on the street are like this, with the buildings attached together in a row and the gardens separated by brick walls.

Mama says she doesn't want to live in four dark rooms with crumbling walls and huge shiny cockroaches, but Baba reminds her that it is rent-free and that we are saving up to build our own house. In the meantime, the fact that we have no real living room and no real furniture is a good excuse not to do too much *deed-o-baz-deed*.

"Real furniture" would be the gilded chairs and coffee tables that my aunt Massi calls "Louis-quatorze" and that most of my Iranian relatives have in their houses. We don't have these. We just have plain wooden beds, big velvet pillows that Mama sewed to make a couch, and lots of colorful *kilims* and carpets on the floor. I like our apartment, though. The archways between the rooms turn it into a cozy cave, and our old Russian samovars sit in the corners like golden pets with smooth round stomachs. Ali and I pull out their gun-shaped spigots and point them at invisible witches as we creep over the large rugs. We have to be careful because the witches are always watching us. Sometimes in the pockets of our clothes from America we find little white tags that say "Inspected by Number 6" or "Inspected by 14," and I tell Ali that we are being inspected by numbered witches and that he'd better do what I say or the witches will get mad.

But in real life it's not easy to get into trouble at our house. Mama and Baba don't make us eat all the food off our plates or take naps the way parents do in books, and there is nothing in the house that we are not allowed to play with. When we invent a game called Primary School in Africa, which involves dressing Ali in all the suits and ties in Baba's closet, Mama just asks if he's sure he's not too hot and if we want some lemonade. Maybe if we were English she would be different. In my English storybooks the children hardly ever see their parents, let alone go into their closets, and they never play the Running-Around Game that we play, with Baba running through the house in his underwear and me and Ali chasing him and trying to grab the waistband. But English children have other kinds of fun. Simply by living in England, they end up in enchanted forests and criminal lairs and boarding schools, which are enough reason for me to wish I were English. I practice the English accent of my schoolteachers, and I dress in a white shirt and a navy-blue sleeveless dress that look like the uniforms in my St. Clare's boarding school books. But when I tell Mama I want to go to boarding school, she just smiles and says she'd miss me too much.

The only thing that Ali and I are not allowed to do is to go into Mama's room when she is meditating. She sits on the bed, cross-legged, eyes closed, and Baba keeps us away from her door and makes us tiptoe around for twenty minutes. When Baba and Mama do yoga, though, Ali and I don't tiptoe. We laugh at them, and when they stand on their heads we try to tip them over.

Baba comes home from work to the sound of American rock-and-roll music. Mama and Ali and I are sitting in a sea of fabric and felt, with the radio turned up high. Baba picks up the green dinosaur puppet Mama is making us and his eyes soften. "You guys have a nice mama," he says, wrapping his arms around her shoulders and kissing her head. She closes her eyes and smiles. Baba says we are lucky because Mama knows special American things to do—like going to see *The Wizard of Oz* or having a Halloween party or making a big turkey dinner, to which Ali and I invite our Taiwanese friends who have never had Thanksgiving before. And it is because Mama is American that we always buy a Christmas tree from the street vendors and decorate it with homemade decorations and a glittering silver star from IranSuper, the big market that sells cornflakes and Vienna sausages and other foreign things.

But Mama also does things that even other American mothers don't do. No one else, Iranian or American, has birthday parties like ours. About thirty kids come for the whole day, and at my Little House on the Prairie party the guests get hand-sewn pink bonnets and aprons just like the ones on the show on English-language TV. Mama ties her flowered Russian scarf around each guest's face, spins her around a few times, hands her the broomstick, and dashes over to grab the rope of the homemade papier-mâché Mrs. Oleson piñata. The blindfolded players swing the stick through the air, but Mama always jerks the rope just before they can hit it.

Another thing Mama does that other American mothers don't is songwriting. She sits on her bed next to a reel-to-reel tape recorder, humming and nodding and scribbling in her notebook. A friend of Mama's once asked if Baba and his family minded that she sang. The friend was American too, but her Iranian husband and his family wouldn't even let her go out by herself in Tehran, let alone fly to Los Angeles to sing in public like Mama does. Baba's relatives don't always approve of women singing—one of his cousins has a voice so beautiful it makes people cry, but her father won't let her sing in front of anyone outside the family. Baba doesn't know much about American music and he can't really sing on key, but he wants Mama to do what she likes, even if it's different from what Iranian women do. I heard that when we first moved to Iran, Aziz came downstairs and asked Baba why his wife let the house get so messy, but Baba just took her gently by the arm, led her to the door, and told her that this was our house and we wanted to be comfortable in it. By now the relatives are used to Mama doing strange things, and they don't ask why she sits with the guitar on her bed and sends tapes of her voice to America. My cousin Niki only asks, "Don't you get sad, being all alone in your room like that?"—because Niki hates being alone.

It's different with my uncles' wives—Iranian women whom the family helped pick out. Everyone watches to see how they serve tea and how their rice turns out. If they make a mistake, like walking in front of Aziz instead of letting her go first, everyone whispers about them. But Mama is like a child performing adult tasks—if she doesn't get them right it's okay because she's foreign; and if she does get them right, they praise her lavishly, talking over her head as if she still doesn't understand them. "*Bah bah*, see what a rice Karen has made us," Homa-khanoum says when Mama has soaked the rice overnight, washed and steamed it, and covered the pot lid with a towel until the grains fall apart in long, separate fingers. "*Mashallah!*—she did it exactly like an Iranian woman."

And even though Mama leaves Baba in Iran for months at a time, and even though in Los Angeles she sings in front of studio executives and long-haired male musicians, the Iranian relatives still call her *zaeef-o-najib*—weak and modest—to compliment her.

Mama does do a few things the relatives do not approve of, like letting us go out the door. In Iran, everything is behind high walls. Walking down the street, they're all you can see—brick if they're old; concrete or marble if they're new. You never know what's inside. Our garden has a tiled driveway, a family of cats, a canopy of sour-grape vines, and a small wading pool with a hose to water the trees and cool the hot tiles; but from the street all you see are a few branches hanging over the top of the bricks. It's only when we go in or out of the garden gate that someone outside, passing at just the right moment, might catch a glimpse of our lives. According to Dadash, even that is too much. Just on the other side of the wall, he says, lurk "kidnappers, thieves, dogs, and other bad things."

Ali and I love dogs and we want to see what the other bad things are. We slip down to the bottom of the garden and climb up the woody grape plant to sit cross-legged on top of the wall that looks out over the back alleyway. All we can see are other three- or four-story apartment buildings and their gardens. But directly across the alleyway from us is a gap—an empty lot that has become a *kharabeh*.

If there were an English word for *kharabeh* it would mean "the broken place." It is a maze of tiny huts built from mud and wooden crates and scraps of corrugated siding. The *kharabeh* is also surrounded by a wall, but this wall is crooked and scraggly, with bits of rock filling the holes between the bricks. The warped wooden door always hangs open, and no one seems to have warned the *kharabeh* children about the bad things outside. They drift in and out of the entrance, the girls with their tangly hair and the boys with their heads shaved like boys in the village. The older ones carry the babies in ragged slings, and the younger ones play in the street until their bare feet turn black from the dirt.

"Is that a kidnapper?" Ali asks, pointing at a small man walking down the alley toward us.

"No, that's a thief," I say. "Kidnappers are bigger than that."

Ali nods. The man passes by us.

"Eh! What are you doing up there?"

We turn around to see Dadash standing in the middle of the garden. The breeze is flapping his silk scarf against his charcoal-gray suit lapels, but it doesn't disturb his slicked-back hair. "What if someone sees you?" he says. "Get down right away!"

"Our mother said we could sit here," I say.

The furrow between his eyes deepens and his small black mustache shrinks to a dot. He unlatches the metal gate, scrapes it across the cement tiles, and walks back to his car, tucking the end of his scarf inside his jacket. Dadash is a very thin man, and his dark suits and fluttering scarves only make him look thinner.

"Any minute now you're going to fall," he says, easing his long body into the driver's seat.

Mama never said we could climb the wall, but if Dadash told her we were up here I know she would back us up. She doesn't like the way Baba's relatives are always telling us what not to do—*don't run, don't dirty your clothes, don't play in the rain, don't touch cats or dogs or caterpillars.* Mama lets us do all these, as well as some things they don't think to warn us against. Ali and I can ride bikes around the block by ourselves or walk alone to the corner store, where the merchant keeps a running tab for our candy and ice cream, just as his father did for Baba and Massi when they were little.

Mama even lets Ali run away from home sometimes. Whenever he gets really mad he goes into his room, packs some toys and clothes into a pillowcase, and stomps down the garden walkway and out the gate. We keep an eye on his shadow underneath the gate, and if he doesn't come back after a while, Mama decides that we need to go to the store for something. "Oh, you're back!" she says, pretending to be surprised when we open the gate and find Ali sitting there. He tells us he's decided to give us one more chance, and then we all walk out past Naneh, the tiny old lady in a black chador who stands all day in her doorway next door to the *kharabeh.*

"Khanoum, your boy was out on the street," Naneh says in her wheedling voice. "You'd better watch out a person thief doesn't steal him."

A person thief is the same as a kidnapper—a large, bald man in a black coat that he whips around children to steal them. If I ever saw a man like that I would run away, but I am not scared of Naneh. She is very small and very old, and she keeps her arms clamped to her sides to hold her thin chador around her chest. She never does anything to us, but when the *kharabeh* boys kick their dented plastic soccer ball past her she shrieks, "Get lost, little satans!" and flaps one arm of her chador at them.

"Khanoum," she says to Mama. "You should know that yesterday my sons beat me with sticks. May God forgive them."

"Oh, that's awful," says Mama, tsk-tsk-ing.

Naneh shrugs and looks up at the sky.

Naneh is half crazy; my Farsi is good enough to know that.

But I am even better at fake Farsi. Ali and I can make ourselves sound just like the Iranian TV broadcasters who string together unending chains of complicated words to announce the news. Deciphering them is impossible; instead, we make up Farsi-sounding sentences, keeping all the same pauses and inflections. Ali hums the opening music of the news. I frown, clear my throat, and round out my lips to produce the formal pronunciation I've only heard from newscasters and from Iranians reciting poetry.

"*Salaam, beenandegaan-e aziz* [Hello, dear viewers]. *Emrooz beest-o-chahaarom-e septaambr, va hala aghaz-e pakhsh-e akhbar* [Today is September twenty-fourth and this is the news]. *Behdaayyat-e maftanboolian, baad az forojamegaanha-ye khaghenaammat-e youstekarianhaa-ye ostobaran, dofarbiat-e nashenooshidan-e khabraw-mellayi, ghashebanfoor shodeh-and.*" It means nothing, but Ali starts to giggle and my voice breaks as I try to make my sentence as long as the ones on TV. On the real news, the second hand goes an entire minute and more before the final flourish of the sentence, but I always have to stop after about fifteen seconds. Ali picks up where I left off, putting his hand on his chin and starting with a long, pensive "*Ammaaaa . . .*" [However . . .]—before launching into the news.

The record people in America want Mama to make an album. Grandma calls from Los Angeles to say she'll bring the contract over herself. She has never been to Iran and this is as good a reason as any.

At the airport I sit on Baba's shoulders and stare eagerly over the sea of dark heads. It doesn't take long to spot Grandma. She is tall and thin, with chin-length blond hair, and when she sees me waving she smiles and waves back hard. Baba puts me down and I run up and hug her, and when she kneels down she smells like her perfumey bathroom in Los Angeles.

At home she unzips her suitcase and it lets out the smell of America and of airplanes. She pulls out a Barbie doll for me, a G.I. Joe doll for Ali, a tennis shirt for Baba and a dress and a book called *Fear of Flying* for Mama. "I got a whole new wardrobe for the trip,"

Grandma says, and the next morning she appears at the table in a silky shirt and drapey pants that make her look like a model.

After breakfast she stays in the kitchen with Mama.

"You didn't tell me you were pregnant," Grandma says.

"I know. I guess I thought you'd be disappointed."

"Well, you're right; I didn't expect it—now, of all times. You know, darling, you don't seem very excited about getting your record contract."

"I am, it's just that I had almost given up on getting one. And I've been busy here; we've been traveling a lot. We thought it was a good time to have a baby, before the kids get too old."

"Karen honey, your career is just about to take off. What are they going to say when you get off the plane like this?"

Mama laughs. "You don't like my shirt? It's from Shiraz. It's what women during the Qajar dynasty used to wear. I thought it would be perfect for maternity clothes."

"Honey, remember the cute jeans and halter top you wore when you sang at the Troubadour? That's how they know you. These clothes make you look so . . ." she struggles for a word and then sighs. ". . . so foreign."

Baba's relatives invite Grandma to their houses. They put fresh flowers around their living rooms and bring her tea and sweets and fruit, and say to each other that she's very chic and her clothes are of very good quality and it's clear that she comes from a high-up family in America. Grandma smiles and nods and calls Dadash "Dar-dash," which makes me and Ali giggle. Mama and Baba take her to a university party with Baba's colleagues, but most of them are Italian-educated and don't speak much more English than our relatives, and Grandma's main comment afterward is how short all the men at the party were. Grandma is five feet eight. The only other woman I know who is that tall is our maid, Fatimeh, who looks like a Gypsy, with colorful dresses and gold earrings and long, henna-red braids hanging down from under her scarf. She also has a tooth missing, which makes one side of her mouth look like a wolf's when she smiles.

While Mama goes to the supermarket, Grandma, Ali, and I play Go Fish and Concentration. We try to teach her Pasur, which all kids in Iran know, but Grandma keeps forgetting the rules. She also can't remember any of the Farsi we teach her. "Now, what did you say *panir* is?" she asks. "Is that milk?" We tell her it's cheese, but by the time we go into the kitchen to eat some she's forgotten it again. Fatimeh is in the kitchen cooking lunch and Grandma smiles at her and says, "*Salaam*," because that is a word she always remembers. Then she says, "*A que hora llega la señora a la casa?*"—and Fatimeh shakes her head and makes a clicking sound with her tongue and tells me to tell Grandma she doesn't speak English.

After we have shown Grandma all around Tehran we take her on a trip to Esfahan. We check into our usual hotel, the IranTour, an old villa with tall, flaking columns, overgrown gardens, brick walkways, and a large swimming pool. Grandma isn't staying with us. She's staying in the Shah Abbas, the fanciest hotel in town. It is a renovated old caravansary, with white arches and balconies and a courtyard with fountains and a traditional Iranian teahouse.

We pick Grandma up there and take her to all the famous sights in Esfahan, but she doesn't pay much attention to them. She's too busy telling us how mad she is at Grandpa. We eat dinner at her hotel and a fortune-teller in a tall white hat goes from table to table, reading the inside of people's coffee cups. He looks into Grandma's cup and says, "I see a dark, handsome man with a mustache, riding on a horse." Baba translates and Grandma listens carefully and tells us to remember all the details.

After dinner we go riding in one of the horse-drawn carriages lined up outside the Shah Abbas. This is something I have always wanted to do, but Mama and Baba said it was too expensive. Now, though, we all climb into the carriage and the driver clicks his tongue.

"Isn't this exciting?" Grandma says. But the ride moves too slowly and goes nowhere. I had always imagined the horse galloping, flying us out into the desert and the mountains, far beyond the tourists wandering around the antique shops in the lit-up square. But we clop primly past them, down one side of the square and up the other, ending in exactly the same spot where we started. An Iranian family looks up as we step down, and suddenly I am embarrassed. *We never really do this*, I want tell them; *we're Iranian too*. But they walk away.

On the way home we stop in Qom. Grandma ties a scarf awkwardly over her head but everyone still stares at the bright blond wave of hair falling forward. We can't take her to the shrine of Massoumeh because she's not Moslem, and we can't take her out for *kalepatcheh*, which is Baba's and Ali's favorite breakfast food. *Kalepatcheh* is lamb's head and feet in broth with the eyeball floating on top, and Mama says we can't possibly expect Grandma to eat it. Instead we go out for kabob and Grandma gets mad when we are crossing the street because the drivers go too fast and no one crosses at crosswalks. I love my Grandma, but no one can relax when she is here, and I am glad she is leaving at the end of the month because soon we will be seeing her in America, where she is not afraid of cars or lamb soups.

When Mama makes her album even Baba comes to America. We stay in a suite at the Sunset Marquis Hotel, one floor above the swimming pool and five minutes away from a store that sells red, white, and blue Popsicles. We walk to the store at night; the sidewalk glitters, and the Popsicles go down from cherry to lemon to blue raspberry by the time we get back. Ali and I go to school down the street, and on weekends we go to Grandma and Grandpa's house. Grandma is her old cheerful self again, dancing around the house and playing little tunes on the piano. We play airplane pilot and basketball with our nine-year-old uncle Doug, but our aunt Laurie is twelve now and spends most of her time with her friends. I walk by her room, trying to catch glimpses of the girls with long blond hair and braces talking together on the bed. I may not be able to have blond hair, but I can have braces and glasses like Laurie's friend Stephanie. I punch the lenses out of a pair of sunglasses and put them on, and I pull the handlebars off my Barbie bicycle and fit them over my teeth. I wear them whenever we go out, hoping people in the street will see the silver band and the stem sticking out of my mouth and think I have an extra-fancy set of braces.

Over the three months we are there we watch a lot of TV. One day the news says a serial killer is knifing people in Hollywood parking lots, and that the victims are black-haired, olive-skinned males. Ali says, "Hey, Baba has black hair," and we joke that he should be careful. Maybe we would really be scared if we heard that news in Iran. But the bad things that happen here happen to Americans, not to us. We can always get on an airplane and go back to Iran.

A few weeks after we do, Ali and I wake up to find Mama gone. Baba says she went to the hospital at three-thirty in the morning and had the baby. We all go to the hospital to see our new sister, which is what I was hoping for although Ali wanted a boy. Baba says that in the waiting room this morning he thought of the perfect name: Sufi.

When Mama brings Sufi home the relatives come over.

"*Ey naz*, look how blond she is," my aunt Massi says, stroking the smooth yellow down on Sufi's head. "She looks like a little American."

"Not at all," Aziz says, tipping her head up as she cradles Sufi in her arms. "This child is a little Iranian. Wasn't she born here, after all? And isn't she growing up in her father's land?"

I know that no matter what anyone says, Sufi is half Iranian and half American, just like me and Ali. But people are always trying to make us one thing or another.

❖

Chahar-shambeh-Souri, the eve of the last Wednesday before the Iranian New Year, falls on a cold March night. We troop around the block, looking under the drippy streetlights for anything that is not too wet to burn. The neighbors stand in the street and talk while the children run up and down, collecting cardboard boxes and broken tree branches and newspapers and piling them up in the street. When the piles run all the way down to the end of the alley, someone pours gasoline on them. A teenage boy lights a match, and fires erupt in a chain down the alley.

Leila-khanoum backs up and bunches her skirt around her thighs. "On all other days you must stay away from fire," she reminds us. She starts running and as she leaps over the first fire her black-stockinged legs and high-heeled shoes are outlined in a blazing aura. "Good job, good job," Dadash says, hopping through the fires behind her. Their children follow; then come two neighbor boys, holding hands and laughing; then a girl with rabbity front teeth and short hair whose father trots alongside as she yells into the flames.

"Each time you jump over the fire, say 'My yellow to you, your red to me,'" Baba says. "The yellow is all your sicknesses and bad things going into the fire, and the red is the healthy stuff of the fire going into you." He tells us it is an old tradition from the Zoroastrians, which is what Iranians were before they became Moslems.

My sadness to you, your joy to me. My weakness to you, your strength to me. Baba teaches us all the things to say and I hang back for a few minutes, watching the fire and repeating the phrases to make sure I don't confuse the yellow and the red.

A few days later it is Noruz, New Year's Day, which falls on the first day of spring. Everyone visits everyone else. We see their feet from the window at the top of Mama and Baba's bedroom—fathers and mothers walking by in suits and dresses and shiny shoes, and kids running ahead in frilly skirts and new sneakers. Haji Firouz, who is like a Noruz Santa Claus although he doesn't bring presents, dances up the sidewalk, and we crane our necks to see his red fez and painted-black face. Upstairs, the front doorbell buzzes again and again.

When we go up, Aziz's apartment is packed with all the aunts and uncles and cousins in fresh haircuts and new clothes. We turn on the radio and listen for the second counter to tick up to the moment that winter turns to spring. Just before noon, the new year begins and everyone gets hugs and kisses. The grown-ups give the kids crisp ten-touman bills, and soon I have a sheaf of pink money with different relatives' signatures and the new year's date inked in over the watermark of the Shah's head.

Leila-khanoum squeezes behind the chair where Ali and I are comparing our signed bills. "What are you doing back here? Come put something sweet in your mouth so you will have sweetness all year." She takes our hands and pulls us out to the *Haft-Seen* table, covered with seven things that start with the Farsi letter *seen*. Aziz has arranged them in a circle: the coins are *sekkeh*; the garlic is *seer*, the vinegar is *serkeh*, the apple slices are *seeb*. *Senjed* is a sweet, crunchy dried fruit, *sabzi* is a plate of green sprouted grass, and sumac is sumac in both languages. In the middle of the table are some things that don't start with *seen* but are always there at Noruz. Painted eggs. A mirror. A bowl of goldfish. A silver box of tiny four-leafed sweets that fit together like the tiles on a mosque.

"Here, eat." Leila-khanoum pushes a sweet onto my tongue and it crumbles into a soft, nutty paste.

Everyone has to spend Seezdeh-be-dar, the thirteenth day of the new year, outdoors. If you don't it's bad luck. We are going with Dadash's family and Aziz to a river in the mountains, and Aziz prepares big pots of rice and meat and chopped-up herbs to bring along.

But when we wake up in the morning it is raining.

"This is very bad," Aziz says, looking out the window at the dark sky and the rain dribbling off the trees.

"Take off your shoes," Dadash says. "We're not going anywhere."

"*Deh?*" Aziz says, sticking out her round chin and crossing her arms. "We have to go out. Otherwise the year will be bad."

"The year will be worse if we get colds for a month," Dadash says.

"My boy, since long before you were born I have always gone outside on Seezdeh-be-dar," Aziz says. "I will go today."

"You want to go sit by the river? Go. I'm staying here."

Eventually Dadash and Baba tack plastic tablecloths around the balcony and we eat our lunch there, so we are officially outside but we don't get wet. Aziz cheerfully scoops big mounds of lamb and dillweed rice onto the plates and fills up swirled pink-glass teacups with *doogh*, a salty yogurt-and-mint drink, to wash it all down. "We did a good thing," she says every few minutes, nodding at the wisdom of our choice. "We are outside, but not sitting with those unfortunates in the rain."

After lunch we put on our coats and take the plate of grass off the *Haft-Seen* table. Having grown for so long on Aziz's sunny windowsill, the grass no longer stands up in a straight tuft but droops over itself. Aziz tucks it under her coat and leads us out the front door.

"See," she says as we step out into the street. "Why do we need a river?" She points to the end of the alley, where other people are standing by the big *joob* that runs between street and sidewalk. It is gorged with rainwater, sticks, leaves, and paper, all swirling and rushing toward the south.

As we walk to the *joob* Naneh scurries over from her doorstep across the alley and tugs on Mama's sleeve. "Khanoum," she says.

"You should know that this morning my sons tied me to the ironing board and burned me."

Mama shakes her head. "You should tell someone," she says.

"God give me my death," Naneh mumbles, and she totters back to her door.

Ignoring Naneh, Aziz shoots a suspicious glance at the gathering of neighbors. She leads us over a metal grate to the other side of the *joob*, "so we won't be so crowded." The rain has stopped but large drops of water still drip off the trees, so Aziz stands under a large umbrella that Dadash holds out. She takes a handful of grass, whispers something under her breath, and tosses it into the water. Then she holds the grass out for each person to grab some.

"Will it go to the Persian Gulf?" Ali asks.

"It will," Aziz says. "With the sickness and the evil thoughts, all the grass will be carried away to Arabistan."

I take my grass and go stand on the little metal bridge to toss it over. But before I throw it in I notice, on the other side of the *joob*, the girl with short brown hair who was jumping over fires the other night. She is sitting on her haunches, tying blades of grass into knots.

"People whose names start with *alef*," she says, dropping a knotted strand into the rushing water. "People whose names start with *beh* and *peh*." She drops another one. She quickly goes through the Farsi alphabet and then ties some more knots.

"What are you doing?" I ask.

She looks up with big round eyes, and smiles over her rabbit teeth. "Making sure no one puts his evil eye on me." She gestures at her pile of knots. "People born on Saturday, people born on Sunday, people born on Monday. If I name everyone in the world they can't hit me with their bad thoughts."

I sit beside her and tie my own grass into knots. "Neighbors on the right, neighbors on the left," we say. "Neighbors in front, neighbors in back. Neighbors upstairs and neighbors downstairs and neighbors in the middle."

The girl, Gita, lives right across our front alleyway. She is not allowed out of her garden, but her gate is often halfway open and she stands there in a T-shirt, pajama pants and flip-flops, rearing her bike up like a horse. One day I go get my bike and bring it over and we ride in circles around her yard until we get hot and her older brother turns on the hose and makes a shower of droplets for us to ride through.

"Eh, don't make me wet!" cries Gita's mother, who is pinning sheets onto a clothesline. She has the same doe eyes as Gita and a long braid hanging down the back of her dress. She giggles and hops away from the spray of water, running behind the hanging sheets. "*Bitarbiat!* Ill-behaved boy!" Her plastic slippers make squishing sounds as she runs into the house.

We take off our shoes and follow her into the front room, where the paint on the walls is a faded eggshell blue, cracked and chipped down to beige and then to chalky white plaster. Sitting down on the floor, we lean back on carpet-covered pillows, the way people do in the village.

"How old are you?" Gita's mother asks me.

I tell her that I am nine and I have a six-year-old brother Ali and a one-year-old sister Sufi. I tell her I go to school in a far part of town; that is why I cannot come out to play until late. Gita and her brother lean in to listen. A grandmother wrapped in shawls goes to get a tray of tea, and when she comes back in, the lightbulb hanging from a cord makes her shadow run up and down the wall.

"Taraneh's mother is American," Gita's mother announces when Gita's father enters the room. He is carrying his bag from work, although he slipped off his shoes at the door like everyone else. He slides down onto a cushion, puts a sugar cube in the back of his mouth, and slurps the hot tea to cool it.

"Eh?" he says, his mustache puckering as he talks around the sugar cube. "Really? And your father?"

"Her father is the son of Saltanat-khanoum, across the street; the youngest brother of Abdollah-khan," Gita's mother says.

"Ah, I heard one of them had gotten a foreign wife." He looks at me for a second and says, "You don't look foreign."

I shrug proudly. "It's my mother who's foreign," I say in my best Farsi.

Gita cuts in. "Baba, Taraneh is allowed to ride her bike to the end of the alleyway. Can I too?"

"Is this true?" Her father looks at me with almost a wink.

I give him a worldly nod.

"Can I too?" Gita says.

"We'll see."

Gita gives me a delighted smile and hugs her knees.

After many promises of staying together and not going too far in either direction, Gita and I are allowed to play in the alley in the evenings. We speed up and down, swerving past Gita's brother and his friend, who buzz a remote-control police car along the tiny dried-out *joob*. Summer is almost here, and the warm air smells like honeysuckle as the purple sky folds into black. Gita's mother calls us in for tea.

"Was that your aunt who came over with the baby this afternoon?" she asks.

"No, that was my cousin."

"How old is she? Whose daughter is she? Is she the sister of the cousin with the motorcycle?" Accustomed to their questions, I rattle off the answers while I practice holding a lump of sugar in my mouth the way Gita and her family do. They can make it last through a whole cup of tea, talking and laughing as they slurp and swallow. But as soon as I take a sip, the hot tea runs to the back of my mouth and dissolves the sugar; and if I try to talk, the sugar catches between my teeth and gets crunched away.

"You have to keep them in three different parts of your mouth," Gita's grandmother says. "Sugar in one part, tea in another part, talk in another part."

"Is your father the man with the mustache and the gloves?" Gita's mother asks.

"No, that's his older brother," says her father. "That's Abdollah-khan, right?"

"Right," I say. "My father has longer hair and a rounder face."

"And your mother?" says Gita's mother.

"Oh, she has red hair and—what are those spots on the face?"

"This?" She puts her finger on the dark mole above her lip.

"No, lighter-colored." But I cannot think of the Farsi word for freckles.

"Do you have pictures of your family?" she asks.

I nod and wedge a new cube of sugar into the back of my mouth.

The next day I peel some photos out of an album and bring them over to Gita's. They are pictures Baba took, of us standing in the shallow waves of the Caspian Sea.

Gita's father balances the edges of the photographs between his fingers and looks carefully at each one.

"Oh, there's you," Gita says, leaning over his shoulder.

"Don't get your fingers on it," her father says, laying the picture on the carpet and holding the next one up to the light.

"Is that your mother?" Gita's mother asks. "How old is she?"

"Thirty-one."

"Eh, that's exactly my age," she says. She sorts through the stack to find a picture she has already looked at. "I was seventeen when I got married," she says. "How old was your mother?"

"Nineteen."

"And she has three children?" She looks back at the picture. "*Akh*, how young she looks."

I smile.

"It's because she is foreign," Gita's grandmother says, and everyone nods.

Later, I ring my doorbell and Mama buzzes me in. I slide down the banister and land where she is holding the door open.

"What are those?" she asks.

I hand her the pictures. "Gita's parents wanted to see them," I say.

She glances up the stairway and closes the door. "Why did they want to see these?" she asks, thumbing through the pictures and frowning. Behind her, Homa-khanoum and her tall, silver-haired husband Agha Vakili are sitting in our living room with Baba, holding cups of tea.

"They wanted to see what my family looked like," I whisper, suddenly embarrassed, although Homa-khanoum and Agha Vakili don't know English.

"You showed her parents *this*?" It is a picture of Mama in a blue bikini and a wide straw hat, with the ash-colored waves lapping at her stomach.

"It's a good picture."

Mama sighs. "You shouldn't have brought pictures of me in a bathing suit."

"Oh, they don't care. They didn't even notice."

But Homa-khanoum has noticed. She comes over and takes the pictures out of Mama's hand and stares hard at each one.

"What was she doing with these?" she asks.

"Nothing," Mama says quickly, but Homa-khanoum gives me a sharp look. "*Voh*, she took these over to the neighbors?" She stares at Mama's flat, white stomach in the photograph.

"It's okay, now we've told her not to," Baba starts to say, but Homa-khanoum interrupts him.

"Now it's going to get around that there are pictures of Agha Esfandiar-khan's foreign wife with no clothes, and that their kids are showing them around!"

I slip into my room and make a face at her from behind the wall, glad that Baba doesn't care about things like that. But later he comes into my room.

"Look, for showing your friends from school those pictures would be fine. But Gita's family is not used to seeing people in bathing suits. Gita's mother probably never goes swimming. Gita's not even allowed to go to your house, is she?" I shake my head. "A lot of girls aren't allowed to go by themselves to other people's houses. In fact, when I was little, there were girls in the village who never left their house alone until the day they got married. People like that might get upset if they see someone's mother in a bathing suit."

I don't answer. Baba usually just laughs when the relatives say not to do something. "You know," he says, "once Jamsheed and I were sitting on the roof with our shirts off and some girls in the building across the street saw us and started calling us the 'crazy sons of Haji-khan.' "

"But it's none of their business if you wanted to take your shirt off on your own roof. And anyway, how did they know who you were?"

Baba sighs. "They just knew. Those girls told everyone we were crazy and that we must be a bunch of Armenians, and Aziz got upset and told us not to take off our shirts anymore."

"Why Armenians?"

"That's what people say if you do something strange. Armenians drink wine and are more relaxed about things."

"But you drink wine."

"Yes, but I bet Gita's parents don't."

If Baba were like Dadash or Homa-khanoum, if he yelled and ordered me around, it would be easy not to listen. But he doesn't yell, and the gentleness in his voice makes everything worse. If Gita's parents knew about the wine in our kitchen I wonder if they would still let her go out in the street with me. Maybe they won't anymore, now that I have shown them the pictures of my mother with no clothes.

My face is hot and my throat is dry. I want to rush back and erase the day, go back to the morning when everything was still all right. Instead I sit in my room, dreading the next time I see Gita and her parents.

But the following day Gita is still allowed to play in the alley, and when it gets dark her mother calls us in for tea and her father hands me a sugar cube to drink through. No one even mentions the pictures. And yet, as I say goodnight and walk back across the dark alley, I can't help worrying that they're just being nice now. I wonder if they really feel sorry for me and figure it is Mama who has made me strange and indecent and Armenian.

❖

Every afternoon the English-language TV channel signs on with the national anthem and a big picture of the Shah's face. Then come the kids' shows, *Sesame Street*, *Scooby-Doo*, and *Land of the Lost*; then the news; and then the nighttime shows like *Donny and Marie*, *Charlie's Angels*, and *The Rockford Files*. There are no advertisements between the shows; instead they show a picture of a flower for a few minutes, or, lately, they show one of two songs—either Rod Stewart singing "You're in My Heart" or ABBA, all dressed in white, singing "Take a Chance on Me."

Once a week we watch a show called *Big Blue Marble*. It features two or three children from around the world and shows what they do all day. A Swedish boy goes grass skiing. An African girl makes pottery. "The world's a Big Blue Marble when you see it from out there," goes the song. "There" is outer space, and the idea is that from so far away you can't tell the difference between the people of the world.

At the end of the show, superimposed over the gray globe spinning on our black-and-white TV, is an address in America to write to if we want a pen pal. I write a letter, listing my hobbies as swimming, playing the piano (I just started taking lessons), stamp collecting, and horses. Mama and Baba have promised me a horse for as long as I can remember. It used to be that I would get one when I was ten, but as I got closer to ten it changed to twelve, and now it's fourteen. I'm starting not to believe them, even though they say they want to retire someday on a farm in San Luis Obispo, California, where I will get my horse and Ali will get the monkey he's wanted ever since he saw *Planet of the Apes*.

In the meantime, Ali and I collect stamps. We have several sources. The Stamp Shop on Takhte-Jamsheed Avenue sells pristine, expensive stamps from every country in the world, and we scrutinize their books for the rarest and most beautiful sets. Baba's cousin has a Swiss wife, and at their house we pounce on letters with the orange-and-black Helvetia stamps on them. At our house, letters come often from America; we each set apart at least a page in our books for them. Our friends Pamela, Anita, and Ravi Dar collect stamps too, and sometimes we spend entire afternoons negotiating trades at their house. Indian stamps have almost no value because the Dars have brought back so many from there. Mongolian stamps are especially valuable because we get so few of them. Ali likes the thick old Iranian stamps with pictures of Reza Shah or even the Qajar shahs on them; some are so old that they are hand-cut and smooth on the edges.

For my *Big Blue Marble* letter I stick on two stamps with the gold silhouette of the Shah's profile and drop it in the post box on Amirabad Avenue. Walking home, I imagine the letters I will soon be getting, with strange, colorful stamps of their own. My pen pal might send me tales of steamy, vaporous jungles, giant snakes, carts drawn by armadillos. Or perhaps I'll get someone who goes skating out on the frozen seas of Finland, or someone from the town in India that has a river full of dead people floating away. I know about that town from my friend Malika, who visits her Indian grandmother every year and brings back dried mangoes and elephant pendants. Most of my friends at school have at least one parent who is from somewhere else, and after holidays they come back with things we cannot get here. Cherry-flavored candies come from Germany; a box of shriveled strawberries comes from Israel; a pack of round Union Jack playing cards comes from London, where my half-English friend Nadia also buys halter-top bikinis. If I get a pen pal from there, I might ask her to send me a halter top.

My letter from *Big Blue Marble* finally arrives. I open it carefully, unfold the paper, and scan the page down to the filled-in blanks.

Your pen pal is: Becky Blakley.
From: Kentucky, U.S.A.
Please send your pen pal a letter soon. S/he is very excited to hear from you.

And it hits me. They think *I* am the exotic one. The *Big Blue Marble* people saw my name, saw that I lived in Iran, and matched me up with an American girl. It is an American show, and they are not linking up people from all different parts of the world; they are linking foreigners with Americans. Someone like me, writing from Iran, would never be matched up with a pen pal from a mysterious, fascinating land when the center of the *Big Blue Marble* is America.

As it is, I see plenty of Americans just by walking around Tehran. They are tall and blond, and everyone on the street stares at them. They walk in long strides and wear American clothes, which everyone knows are better than Iranian clothes. Foreign things are what people want, and that is why the sweaters at the bazaar have English words knitted into the patterns, and why so many shops have signs in English, and why the fancy restaurants serve chicken Kiev and cream of mushroom soup and french fries but not kabob. Iranian shopkeepers might claim that their clothes are as good as in America and Europe, but no one believes them; the only way to really have clothes that don't bleed or unravel or fade is to bring them from abroad.

I also see more Americans at school now that Ali and I have

switched to Community School, in South Tehran. It has a tree-shaded campus with old brick buildings and cheerful blue-painted windows, and teachers who put snapshots of us on the classroom wall and bring in tapes of their favorite songs from when they were in college. The high schoolers coach us in gymnastics, and when we see them on campus they wave and call out our names. Morning classes are in English and afternoons are in a different language—Farsi, for most students, since so many of us are Iranian or some mix of Iranian.

The principal, Mr. Burt, is from Florida. He has three sons—tall, skinny teenagers with sharp chins and long hair down to their shoulders. Ali and I have seen plenty of long-haired men in Los Angeles, but in Iran the Burt brothers look hilarious. We secretly follow them around the school courtyard to find out what they say, and at home we go into hysterics mimicking their deep-voiced American drawl. Even Mama and her American friends don't talk like that; Mama says that after a few months in Iran her English always starts to sound foreign because she speaks to so many non-Americans. But living in Iran has not made the Burt brothers sound any less American, and in the evenings we use the school directory to prank-call them.

One ring, two rings—my ear is crushed against Ali's so we can both hear.

"Hello?" (deep American-teenager voice)

"Hello?" (Ali's falsetto)

"Who is this?"

"Who is *this*?"

"I asked you first!"

"This is Ant and Bee."

"Hey, Austin, it's that faggot calling for you again."

Faggot! We hadn't heard that one before, and we gleefully mouth it to each other, smothering our giggles, trying to think of some way to keep our Burt brother on the phone. But he makes a loud hyena sound and hangs up, and we collapse on the floor.

My friend Connie is also from Florida, although she doesn't talk like that. I sit on her kitchen counter and she reaches over and opens the refrigerator.

"You want a Hi-C?" she says.

I reach for the purple can, unable to believe it. I have only seen

Hi-C in America; to drink it here is an unthinkable luxury. I pull the tab off and lift it to my lips, letting the sharp, sweet liquid trickle slowly over my tongue. "Did you bring these from America?" I ask.

"No," she says blithely. "We got them at the commissary."

The commissary is nestled within the American Embassy, and restricted to diplomats and military personnel. I have gone to the embassy—Mama and Baba sometimes play tennis there—but I have never seen the commissary. I imagine it to be a deep vault, filled with Oscar Mayer wieners and Wonder bread and Bubble Yum and guarded by a person behind a desk who can tell just by looking who is American enough.

Connie and her friends are American enough. They go to America for every vacation, and sooner or later—unlike us with our vague talk of farms and monkeys—they will all move back there. In the meantime they teach us jokes, sneaky ones—like "Repeat this African chant five times" or "Describe your hair in five ways"—that end up embarrassing whoever is listening. The Americans are daring and fun, but even their touch can be dangerous, like when they tap us on the arm, tell us we have cooties, and run away—leaving us, unsure what exactly we have contracted, to shake them off onto someone else.

The Americans also go steady. One day we hear that Jimmy Aikman and Barbara Ann Shaw are going together. All the Americans are in on it, as if it was a decision jointly made in some place like the commissary where the rest of us are not permitted. The rest of us watch, impressed, as Jimmy and Barbara Ann walk through the playground hand in hand. A few weeks later when they break up, the Americans are in on that too. Going together and breaking up, they are sophisticates. The rest of us might be friends with boys or even have crushes, but as for deliberate romance, we would have no idea how to go about it.

"I like coffee, I like tea! I like Shih-Fang to jump with me!"

We are jumping rope when Connie walks up, white-faced, her lips pressed together. "I hate Cathy," she announces.

"Why?" we ask.

But she shrugs and will not tell us. She hates Cathy and plays with us for a few days; then one day the two of them go off under the trees, best friends again. We continue our game, calling each other into the circling jingle, stepping aside to let each person in. Perhaps we do not have enough of a common ground to compete with each other. Or perhaps we—already odd and special in our walled-in school in South Tehran—have too much in common to worry about it. The Americans are only a minority because they feel themselves to be.

When the school year ends and the days get hot, Mama drives us up the parkway each morning to the German Club. Ali and Sufi and I sit in the backseat, our Popsicles melting over our hands as we sing along to the English-language radio station. The American deejay comes on and pretends to speak Farsi. "That was Paul Simon for you today, *kelly koob*, very good stuff, all right!!" One day he plays one of Mama's songs that she recorded on our last trip to Los Angeles, and he tells the listeners that "that was our very own, *kelly* marvelous, Karen Alexander!" Once a week, Casey Kasem's American Top Forty is on. Mama has never been on the Top Forty, but we are not waiting to hear Mama; we just want Casey Kasem to hurry up so we can hear what is number one before we leave the car. When we are away on trips we have all the time we need because Wolfman Jack on the American Armed Services station reaches far out into the provinces. But in the city the ride is never long enough, and sometimes we sit with Mama, sweating in the parked car with the flies buzzing and the street vendors trying to sell us gum as we wait to hear the most popular song in America.

Inside the German Club, the world cools down. We walk under the trees and past the director, who waves energetically from behind his desk on the pathway, his round stomach almost popping his shirt buttons off. We pass the blue metal swings and the wide circle of grass and the gurgling fountain and outdoor bar where megaphones on tall poles blare out the Bee Gees and Boney M as the grown-ups on the terrace nod their heads to the heavy disco beat. We joined the German Club because it is prettier and quieter than the American Club, which teems with the hundreds of American families who live in Tehran. The German Club is more like Community School, with people from all different countries, including a lot of Iranians and half-Iranians like us.

We find a shady spot by the swimming pool and Mama lays out towels and blows up Sufi's inner tube. Looking around to see which of our friends have arrived, Ali and I peel off our clothes and jump into the icy pool. At lunchtime, Baba arrives. He crashes through some butterfly laps and then joins us in the sun, where he is handed a cold glass of beer by tall, blond Wolfgang, the only German Club employee who is German. Baba sits back and shakes salt into his beer and says, "This is how the Russians drink it," and I lean over to lick the bitter foam on top. Then my friends call my name and I run over to the lawn to play hide-and-seek.

Baba says that in a couple of years we won't be going to the German Club anymore. "Soon we'll have our own German Club," he says mysteriously, and one day he takes us out in the car to show us.

We drive north up the parkway, but instead of going all the way up to the street that leads to the German Club, we turn off onto a pebbly, unpaved road. Baba stops the car in the middle of nowhere and Ali and Sufi and I jump out, our sandals crunching over an empty moonscape. All we can see is the high wall of the Alborz Mountains looming over us.

This patch of desert, Baba and Mama tell us, is going to be a new section of Tehran called Shahrak-e-Gharb, which means "Little City in the West." "It's being designed like neighborhoods in America, like Grandma and Grandpa's," Mama explains. "That means when we build a house and move in here you guys are going to be able to walk to school, because Community School has decided to move up here too."

This news is enough to sell me on living here. As it is now, I sit on the bus for an hour in the morning and two hours in the afternoon, idling my afternoon away in smoke and traffic. Baba starts talking about large lots, detached houses and local parks, but I am fixed on the idea of walking to school, until Baba mentions the other main attraction of our new house in Shahrak.

"It's going to have a pool," he says.

"Will it have a diving board?" I ask excitedly.

"Sure, anything you want."

"How about a slide?" asks Ali.

Baba nods.

"How about a slide from my room into the pool?" I ask, to see how far he will go.

But he just smiles and says yes, and my mind turns to horses and trampolines and every other thing I've ever wished for.

❖

Our maid Fatimeh leaves and we get a new maid named Soghra. She lives right across the alley from us, in the *kharabeh*. She has seven children, and sometimes she brings her youngest, a loud-voiced two-year-old boy, to crawl around on the floor with Sufi while we watch *Sesame Street*. Soghra makes up Farsi names for the characters—Big Bird is "Dadash Parandeh" [Big Brother Bird], and Mr. Hooper is "Haj Ramezan" because he looks like Ramezan, the little bald shopkeeper down our street.

Aziz tells Mama, "Karen-jan, you really shouldn't let the maid bring her kids over to watch TV. I've had a lot of experience and I'm telling you, if you let her bring one kid today, tomorrow she'll bring two and soon your house will be full of them. And it's not good to let them go so much without working; they forget their duties and they stop showing you respect."

But Mama and Soghra have much more fun together than other people do with their maids. Neither of them worries about *ta'arof*, the Iranian politeness ritual that involves trying to guess what people want before they ask for it, or acting like you don't want something when you really do. Mama and Soghra don't worry about who watches TV or who precedes whom into the room. They're usually too busy talking and painting pictures.

When Mama first asked Soghra to be her model, Soghra put her big hand over her mouth and giggled, "Why me? Why don't you paint the children?" But now they sit together every day, Mama dabbing at her paints, her eyes darting up and down as Soghra sits still on her chair and the laundry and dishes stay dirty.

At first Mama copied from pictures. Around the house I would find discarded photographs of old men from the village with green Magic Marker lines dividing them into thirds to get their proportions. Now she paints from life or makes up her own compositions, like the one of Qajar princes and turbaned mullahs on a backdrop of playing-card kings and queens. Mama and Baba worried a little about what the relatives would think of Mama painting mullahs, but when Aziz came downstairs and saw the kings-and-mullahs painting she immediately asked if she could have it. "Karen has become a painter," she said wonderingly, barely glancing at Soghra's son watching TV in her hurry to go upstairs and hang the painting.

Mama says Soghra's face is hard to capture even if you are looking right at her. From certain angles the tip of her nose looks like it has been bitten away by tiny mouths. "I caught *abeleh* when I was a girl," Soghra explains. "My mother told me not to, but I kept doing this." She claws her fingers vigorously up and down her cheeks. *Abeleh* means smallpox; and it has covered Soghra's face with pits that show up even more than they might if she didn't cinch her scarf so tightly around her head. Once Ali and I sneaked up behind her to whip her scarf off. It was harder to pull off than we had imagined—Soghra shrieked and struggled and tried to duck out from under us. But finally we grabbed it and ran from room to room, laughing. Soghra chased us, holding her hands on top of her head. We thought she was just screaming at us because she was Moslem and didn't want anyone to see her hair, but when she finally caught us and grabbed the damp scarf back we saw, at the top of her black braids, a circle of baldness. Then we looked at each other guiltily because Soghra hadn't wanted anyone to see it.

I know the baldness is from ringworm because Aziz's brothers and sister are also bald like that. Baba says they probably got it at the bathhouse when they were young. In the old pictures Aziz's sister was a beautiful, slender woman with high cheekbones and a regal stare. But she always wore a wig, and it is only now that she is old that she lets people see the sparse white strands sadly combed over her scalp.

Soghra has no wig, just the long braids that stick deceptively out from the bottom of her scarf. Mama says that the bald spot and pock-marks were probably the reason why, even though Soghra is so smart and nice and can recite poetry by heart, she had to marry a man who is a little retarded. I try to imagine what Soghra would have looked like if she had never gotten sick, but I can never see past her scarves and craters.

One day while Mama is painting I open a block of clay and start to make a cat. Soghra, sitting across from me, pinches a corner off the block and brings it to her lap. Soon she has placed a row of clay animals on the table: a cow, a calf, a horse, and a dog, all as small as pinky fingers. The horse is grazing, the cow and calf are talking to each other, and the dog is staring up quizzically, the way dogs do.

After that, Soghra makes animals every day. They stand on the table in various stages of dryness, and Baba and Mama tell us not to touch them but they keep picking them up and saying how great they are. Baba says he is going to talk to the university art department about having a show, and Soghra gives a little smile and says in that case she will make whole families of animals—mothers and fathers and rows of babies. She works on them every day, showing me how she rolls the clay into a fat cigar and then pulls and plucks at it until the animal emerges.

Soghra's daughters start coming to our house once a week so Mama can tutor them in English. I spy on them through the little cutout arch in the wall between my room and the living room, keeping quiet as Mama presses a book open and the two sisters in blue school tunics and trousers lean forward and read aloud.

"Hi, there," says a deep voice. I jump, and then beckon Baba in from the doorway so he won't make Soghra's daughters look up. "How are they doing?" he says. "As well as you in Farsi?" I shrug. Baba helps me with my homework from the fourth-grade Farsi book, which still has a lot of pictures and large text. It is in the fifth grade that the writing gets small and difficult, with all the calligraphed poetry to memorize. I have seen Soghra's second daughter, Maryam, walking to the local school reading a dog-eared copy of the fifth-grade book, her eyes darting left and right as she walks. She is a smooth-faced girl whose straight thick hair is orangey black, and she makes me shy. When I see her in the street I pretend not to notice.

Baba peers through the little window and I sit back on the carpet and dig my toes into the center diamond that is surrounded by flowers and vines. Little girls probably made this carpet; they are the only ones whose hands are small enough to hook such intricate designs into the loom. On a big carpet like this one, two or more girls may work at once, and that is why the flower on one side may not match its mirroring flower on the other side; it may be too big, or leaned over to one side, or a different kind of flower altogether. Dadash likes to bring home new carpets and show us how well matched they are. But I like the unevenness on my bedroom carpet.

A few years ago in Dadash's village I saw the rug-weaving girls. They worked in a mud-walled room between the sheep pen and the pigeon roost. A shaft of sunlight moved from left to right as the day passed, and their fingers pushed tendrils of yarn between the strings of the loom, filling the white space so fast that it was impossible to see what their hands were doing. I watched, fascinated, until Baba asked me if I wanted to try. He lifted me onto the wooden bench and one of the girls put a strand of yarn into my hand and pointed at where to push it through. It took me a few tries to loop it in evenly, and the girls waited as I did three or four strands. Then one of them pushed down hard on my looped yarns, and my little row became part of the plush flowerscape.

I wanted to stay longer, but Baba said the girls had a lot of work to do and lifted me up off the bench. Then, as we walked back through the garden, he said, "When I was a kid I used to watch the farm boys working. Sometimes I wished to be them. They had such strong muscles from working in the fields, and I used to feel ashamed because they were out there working and I wasn't."

I wished that day that I could be one of those rug girls. But then we left the village and I stopped wishing it. I guess Baba wished it more often than I did, because he lived in the village all through his childhood. He even had a milk-brother there, the boy whose mother had been Baba's wetnurse and had held Baba at one breast and her own son, Houshang, at the other one. The two boys grew up side by side, but Houshang had to work around the house while Baba got to go on trips to the nearby town. Houshang would run alongside the car and ask Baba to bring him back something from town, like a hat or a knife. Baba said he always felt bad that Houshang couldn't come and he always made sure to bring him the thing he wanted.

I walk with Baba down our alley, past the *kharabeh* boys who are laughing and kicking their plastic ball, down to Amirabad Avenue, where cars and pedestrians are separated by a row of tall plane trees and a *joob* full of gray rushing water. As we walk, the rich smell of roasting *chelo* kabob swirls up, overpowers the exhaust fumes, and fades into the smell of the greengrocer's fresh dill and scallions. We pass the knife sharpener, who sits on a wooden box at the corner, and I kick myself because I keep forgetting to bring along a knife so I can watch him sharpen it on the stone wheel that makes sparks fly. We sidestep the cigarette vendor and the dry-goods store, and go into the chicken shop, where metal cages are stacked to the ceiling, each with a white chicken inside.

"One?" the man says. "Killed?"

Baba nods.

"Plucked?"

Baba nods again.

A nervous squawking starts up behind me and I try to concentrate on the framed portrait of the Shah that hangs in every shop and office in the country. But no matter how hard I stare at the Shah I can't help feeling sorry for the chickens.

The man returns from the back room and hands Baba a white paper bundle; then we walk down another alleyway to the *sangaki*, the bakery that makes stone bread. It is my favorite bread, not just for the warm, clay-oven flavor but for how much fun it is to watch it being made. First the baker stretches a ball of dough out into a huge flat pancake; then he picks it up with an iron spatula taller than he is and slings it into a glowing cave full of smooth pebbles that go back so far that they disappear into the orange heat. After only a few minutes the bread is brown and bumpy and the baker reaches his long spatula in to retrieve it.

Walking home, Baba and I pull pieces off the steaming bread, avoiding the hot pebbles still stuck to it. As usual, there is a traffic jam on Amirabad Avenue. Everyone is honking at a man threading between the cars, pushing a donkey loaded with eggplants.

"When I was a boy," Baba says, "Amirabad was a dirt road. We used to play soccer on it."

"There weren't any cars?"

"Maybe one every few hours. And a few horses—they used to carry tanks of water to the houses before they had plumbing. In those days the water in this *joob* was as clean and clear as ice. And Amirabad ended only two blocks up, where Farah Park is now—horse races were held there, and everyone would go there to have picnics under the trees."

"What was beyond it?"

"Nothing. Desert. You could see the mountains perfectly. Like you can now from Shahrak." I look up the smoky street. It hasn't rained in months and the ridge of mountains barely shows above the buildings.

A car honks behind us and we move to the side. Dadash slows down his yellow Range Rover and nods to us as he turns down our alley. He gets out to open the gate and then heaves his big car through, frowning at the swarm of *kharabeh* boys who crowd around to peer in through his windows. *"Boro gom-sho!"* he yells. "Go get lost! *Bitarbiat!* Ill-behaved!" He gets out of the car and slowly pushes the green metal gate against the group of boys still trying to see into our garden.

As we pass the *kharabeh* Baba tells me that Soghra was happy to get a place here, because most *kharabehs* are in South Tehran, where the air and the *joobs* are dirtier than here and the streets are more crowded. In our neighborhood, which is sandwiched between the neat grid of North Tehran and the mazelike alleys of South Tehran, we might occasionally see a little boy pulling a huge one-wheeled cart or a *chadori* woman with her arms wrapped around a struggling goat. We might once in a while hear the clop-clop of a donkey or the nasal voice of an old man singing about the copper pots or brooms he is selling. But in South Tehran the donkeys and carts and voices multiply and echo off each other and float down every alleyway.

"This neighborhood has good schools for Soghra's children," Baba explains. But he also says the *kharabeh* is dangerous. "One bad rain is going to collapse the roofs down on their heads," he says. "And it's full of germs."

Baba might be a dervish who doesn't worry about who gets served first, but he never stops worrying about germs. When we go back into the house he takes me straight into the bathroom to wash my hands, and the warm water turns gray even though I haven't touched anything. There are germs all around—in the air and in the water and in the walls of the buildings we pass. Outside Tehran there are

even more germs; rural roadside bathrooms are smeared with diar-
rhea, and even though we don't drink the water in small towns, Mama
gets dysentery and Ali and Sufi and I get the white worms that wriggle
around in the toilet. We take pills that turn our faces yellow and we
pour purple chemicals into a tub of water to soak our fruits and vegetables. Later, when we eat them, the bitter tinge of medicine reminds
us of all the germs we've killed.

But there are always new ones to look out for. Ringworm starts at
the bottom of a bare foot and works its way up to the top of the
head; we are supposed to watch for ring shapes under our skin. Tape-
worm looks like a measuring tape and lives in the stomach; we'd know
it was there if we started becoming thin and hungry. *Saalaks* are a
kind of worm or bug that digs into people's cheeks and leaves deep,
coin-sized craters that look like someone has scooped out the skin
with a teaspoon. I am careful not to step barefoot into wet places or
let my mouth brush against water fountains, and I take all my worm
medicine and even memorize the rattlesnake-bite procedure in our
American first-aid manual. But I'm not sure how to guard against the
saalak that might already be crawling around under my skin. "Don't
worry," Mama says. "That never happens anymore. And anyway, if
it does, it's easy to cure—if you catch it in time."

One day I go into the backyard and find Soghra's daughter Maryam
talking to our dog Yip. We just got Yip a few months ago when Baba
finally said we could have a small dog even though half our relatives
might never set foot in our house again. Iranians say dogs are *najess*,
unclean. But Yip is clean. He is a black-and-brown miniature dachshund with a goatish beard who loves to play with us but cowers under
the bed whenever a stranger rings the doorbell. He doesn't hide from
Maryam, though; he just stares at her as she says, *"Bia, bia,"* in a soft,
cajoling voice.

"He doesn't understand Farsi," I say in Farsi. Maryam jumps in
surprise, her dark reddish hair fanning out as she wheels around.
"You've got to call to him in English." I teach her how to say, "Come
on, Yip," and she practices "come" and "Yip" until she gets the
short *u*'s and *i*'s that don't exist in Farsi. Yip must have been listening
to my lesson, because as soon as Maryam gets his name right he

leaps up and goes for her heels, barking like a battery-operated dog. Maryam runs screaming around and around our little L-shaped pool until Soghra sticks her head out the upstairs window to see what on earth is wrong.

After that Soghra starts bringing Maryam over more. We roller-skate or watch TV or play with my old Barbie airplane, using a toy globe to choose the countries that the Barbies travel to. Normally I don't play with Barbies anymore, but with Maryam it's fun, maybe because we're playing in Farsi and my Farsi is still babyish enough for Barbies. We make the Barbies talk like the crazy, high-voiced puppets on the Iranian TV children's shows, and we make them hike through the tall grass of Africa and tame the wild plastic horses we've set up for them. But our favorite game is still running away from Yip, seeing how many times around the pool it takes us before we catch up to him from behind.

"Maryam!" Soghra calls from our kitchen window. Maryam leaps up onto the ledge of the pool and Yip barrels past her, skidding around the corner on his spindly legs. "What sounds you make, Maryam-jan!" Soghra brings her hand up to her head. "Go home and bring me another scarf!"

"*Chashm*," says Maryam, which means eye, as in "May your footsteps tread on my eye." This is like "I'll sacrifice my life for you" or "I am your servant"—it's the polite way to talk in Farsi.

I scoop Yip up under one arm and go over to the ledge to wait. But then Maryam turns around and asks, "Do you want to come?"

An invisible hand grips my shoulder. Baba, of course, would say it was dangerous, but the hand belongs to Dadash. If he heard us from his third-story window his eyes would widen with displeasure and his voice would become tight and angry as he said, *Have you gone mad? Don't you set foot in there!*

But no one has heard. I shake the hand off—why should an imaginary Dadash tell me what to do? And how can I refuse to go to Maryam's house when she has invited me? "Sure," I say. I put Yip down and slip out the gate behind her.

It is almost dusk. Gusts of wind race between the buildings and lift my hair and my skirt. I follow Maryam across the alley, through the front opening of the *kharabeh* and into a passageway so narrow that the front doors on each side almost touch my shoulders—only they are not really doors, just openings with tacked-on cloths that ripple as we pass, releasing cracks of light and radio noises and the acrid smell of rice and burnt butter. Dried mud has flaked off the walls and its fine powder gets into my sandals and feels chalky between my toes. A rush of wind swirls it up to my face and I clamp my mouth shut and take light, raspy breaths.

Suddenly I feel a prick on my arm, and then an itch on my leg, and then I think I feel something land on my cheek. Seized with horror, I try to brush it off, but then I feel it on my finger, so I whip my hand away. My heart pounds as half-forgotten warnings rush back to me, my uncles' and aunts' mouths forming the words. *Filthy, deadly place; ah, why are you in there, Taraneh-jan? Just because we told you about germs, did you think they weren't real? Did you think we were being silly and you were being brave? We only tell you these things because we love you. And because they're true. People get sick and die; we have seen it and we know. Turn around before it's too late.*

We keep walking. The walls close in and I draw my shoulders together. Swift clouds blacken the sky, and even in this dim light I can feel the eyes of the boys Dadash kicks away from his car. They would recognize me, the girl who sits up on her wall and never comes down; only now I am here in the place where they live, with no gate to separate me from their eyes that stare into our garden and their hands that throw stones at our cats.

Halfway down the narrow passageway Maryam parts a curtain; I take her hand and we slip into blackness. She lights a match and cups a brittle glass flue over an oil lamp, and in its flickering light, the burnished outlines of a single room come into focus. Worn carpets cover the floor; I can feel the uneven earth beneath them. Cloth bundles are piled along one wall; schoolbooks and notebooks and pens are lined up along another wall. In one corner is a neat pile of bedrolls and a small gas burner and some pots, and on the ceiling are rolls of sheets which, unfurled, would create the partitions of a home.

"Could you help me?" Maryam says. I reach up to where she is pulling at a huge cloth bundle. It eases away from the wall, finally tipping out like a brick and plopping down between us. A mass of colored cloth spills onto the floor.

"*Bah, bah,*" I say, picking up a shred of turquoise gauze edged with silver thread. "How beautiful."

"They're my mother's old clothes from the village," Maryam says, pulling out another piece. "She cuts them up to patch things." We finger the swatches of fabric, holding them up to the oil lamp. "Look," she says, holding out a bright blue square. "This would make a perfect skirt for the Barbie-*ha*." (In Farsi, Barbie plus Barbie equals Barbie-*ha*.) "And look," she says, picking out a piece of red woven fabric, "this could be their rug on the airplane."

"Perfect," I say, pulling out a long stream of lightweight black fabric dotted with tiny flowers. "See, we can make them chadors too."

"Yes," she says. "I've been thinking they needed them for when they go to make the Haj." We giggle and start planning the Barbies' pilgrimage to Mecca.

"And what about *Mard-e Shish Million Dollari?*" Maryam says. The Six Million Dollar Man. "Can he go?" So Ali's Steve Austin and G.I. Joe dolls get added to the passenger list and we find them pieces of white cloth to wear over their heads like Arabs.

The wavering of the lamplight makes us look up. A breeze lifts the portal curtain, and behind it the sky is dark. Maryam grabs Soghra's scarf; we roll up the bundle and push it back into its spot. "Come on," she says breathlessly, pulling me to the doorway. But when we get outside I stop and point down at the dark splats of water in the dust.

The sky opens up. We stop and hold out our arms. It has not rained for so long we had almost forgotten about it. Drenched and laughing, we duck into an open doorway where a woman stands, her chador hanging loosely open over her dress, her face tipped up to the sky. As we huddle beside her she looks down and breaks into a smile. "We won," she says—and then I remember that today there was a soccer game and that if Iran won we might go on to the World Cup. The rain subsides and we hear jubilant honking from Amirabad and the circus music of celebration from a nearby radio. "Good for us," I say. And all of a sudden I know there is nothing to be afraid of here. The rain drenches our feet and a smell like hay rises from the ground and I breathe deeply to take it all in.

❖

Mama is turning into an Iranian. The other night we saw Sadaf, my second cousin, who is eleven, a little older than I am. She used to have straight hair down to her waist, but now it is short, like a boy's. "To make her grow," Sadaf's mother explained. "If all the energy keeps going into their hair, they stay as short as dwarves."

Now Mama thinks I should cut my hair too. Ever since I can remember she has been afraid that I will be a midget. I am smaller than anyone in my class, and she thinks that she didn't eat enough when she was pregnant with me. Once she even took me to the doctor to ask him. The doctor did not weigh or measure me; he just laid his fingers around my wrists and ran them up to my elbows and shoulders and said, "Don't worry. She will grow up to be exactly as tall as you."

But she worries anyway. "Who knows if it's true?" she says. "What if cutting your hair really does add an extra inch or two? It can't hurt to be on the safe side."

It can hurt. It has taken me two years to grow out my hair so I could have braids like Laura Ingalls in the *Little House* books and it's finally gotten long enough to wrap them over the top of my head like Laura does when she turns fourteen.

"Hair is dead," I say. "I can't believe you are falling for that stuff."

Mama looks embarrassed and says it is probably just an old wives' tale, but adds that after all there's no way to be sure.

Mama has an Iranian job now, too. She started it a few weeks ago, after we came back from Los Angeles, where Ali and I went to school for three months while she made another album. When we got back to Iran, Mama started taking cello lessons and working at CBS Records, listening to new songs from Europe and America and deciding what should be played in Iran.

Back in L.A., Mama's producers had wanted her to stay and promote her album, but Mama told us she was too excited to get back to Baba and to everything that is going on in Iran. Baba didn't come to America with us because he was busy setting up the new office he is opening with three other architects. It is almost ready, and on weekends we all go over to help paint the walls, nail up corkboard, and organize the furniture. One of Baba's partners is also an artist, and he designs a modern-looking logo for the firm. Boxes of pencils and erasers and rulers arrive, and by summer they are open for business.

Meanwhile, we go see our house in Shahrak almost every day. First it is just a hole in the ground. Then the workers pour the cement. Then a rust-colored skeleton rises up against the sky. Baba drives to Qom to pick out handmade bricks, and, guided by a taut string, the men lay rows of them, each a slightly different hue, until the outside of the house is smooth and dusty yellow. We walk up concrete blocks that will be stairs, careful not to fall into the spaces that are not yet walls or banisters. I tiptoe across the chalky floor of my room and stand by my window and look up at what will soon be my own private loft. Baba has drawn a little ladder into the design to show how I'll get up there.

"Imagine this street with tall, shady trees," he says, but it is hard because I still can't see the street. I can see my uncle Parviz's house, though; it is a one-story red one that will be finished before ours. By this time next year his family will be living right down the road from us and we will see them all the time. Massi's daughter Haideh goes to another international school that is also building a new campus in Shahrak, so we will see her a lot too. Now that Ali and Sufi and I speak better Farsi and my cousins speak better English, we've all started to play together more often, and I can't wait to go swimming with them in our new pool.

We drive away from Shahrak, and I look through the back window at the huge red disc of the setting sun. Our basement apartment has begun to feel temporary—like four rooms meant for a family who are waiting for their real home to hatch. In the meantime, Mama and Baba are always shopping. They return excitedly from the bazaar with tapestries and samovars and a set of antique iron gates, stashing it all in the closet for when we move. We speak in the future tense: we'll eat pancakes in the breakfast nook; we'll make a rec room out of the basement; on weekends we'll drive up to the villa Baba is building for us on the Caspian. Breakfast nook and rec room and villa are new words describing things we have never had before, and the idea of having them is like receiving a sudden inheritance.

Early one morning we wake up to the sound of explosions. They are muffled, with a dull rumbling between the blasts, and we hurry out through the dewy garden and unlatch the gate to see what all the noise is.

In a haze of dust, people are dragging clothes and bundles out of the *kharabeh*. A wrecking machine stands diagonally, its back in the street and its front in the *kharabeh*, like a hulking orange monster poking its nose into a house that is too small for it. Some of the huts have their roofs caved in, and their jagged walls stand tilted. I strain to see if Soghra's house is one of them, but the *kharabeh* looks different without its front wall, and I can't remember how far back their house was. I don't see any sign of Soghra or her children.

Two policemen stand at the *kharabeh* entrance, moving their arms like traffic controllers. "Hurry!" one of them barks at a woman who is running out with a sack under one arm and a baby under the other. A young man starts to go in, but with a slight backward tip of his head the policeman says, "You've gone in enough times."

"Excuse me, sir, but my family's belongings are in there."

"But what are you going to do with all this stuff?" The policeman gestures to the piles of clothes in the street, shakes his head, and closes his eyes, giving the young man a moment to slip inside.

From a doorway of a still-intact house further in, a woman screams out a stream of angry words. The other policeman calls out to her. "Mother, you have to come out. What are you staying for? Look, all your family is out here waiting for you. Do you want to be in there alone when the roof comes down on your head? What will your husband and children say?"

She lets out a flood of curses, but he keeps talking, laughing a little, like someone trying to reason with a child.

Baba shuts the gate. Ali and I stare at the back of it.

"The owner must be coming back," Baba says. "He was out of the country."

"But why does he want to kick them out?" I ask.

"I guess he wants to build something on the lot."

"Stupid owner!" Ali says angrily.

"Come on," Mama says. "You'll miss your bus." We get dressed, grab our schoolbags and hurry up the stairs to the front alley. There is no sign of bulldozers here. Our school bus is waiting at the end of the block, and Ali and I run and wave so the driver won't leave. We go to our usual seat, the last boy gets on after us, and someone starts singing, "Those were the days, my friend." Everyone joins in. We make up new verses and sing it over and over as the bus stumbles through the downtown traffic, and by the time we get to school the *kharabeh* has faded from my mind the way dreams do in the morning.

But when we get home Aziz calls down the stairwell. "Come see what they've done! Come see!" We go upstairs to her bedroom, where Dadash and Leila-khanoum are standing at the window. Even after what we saw this morning I am shocked when I look down.

The *kharabeh* is gone. In front of where it used to be is a new wall with mortar squeezed out messily between the bricks and a glinting padlock on the door. The sidewalk is covered with plastic tarps and cardboard boxes where the *kharabeh* people have set up tents.

"Dirt on his head," Aziz mutters as she looks out the window. "Son of a burnt father. God bring that son of Reza Shah his death."

Dadash's eyes widen. He checks behind a curtain to make sure no one is crouching there. "Don't say these things," he says in a low voice.

"Why?" I say. "Did the Shah ruin the *kharabeh*?"

"No," Dadash snaps. "What kind of talk is that?"

But I know that is what Aziz meant. She hates the Shah, and whenever she talks about him her voice is like lead.

"By God, he doesn't leave anyone alone. The gardens my father gave me for my wedding. The lands it took Agha Jan all his life to buy. All for these sons of burnt fathers to come and sweep up into their sleeves. For the people—hmph!" She bats her hand toward the window and makes a spitting sound. "Look! See what they do for the people. Snake venom! Gigolo!"

"Shhh," Dadash says.

I have never actually seen the Shah, but he looks at me from everywhere. He smiles in black-and-white from the first page of new

schoolbooks; he towers in bronze over street intersections; he is pro-
jected in full color onto the screen before every movie. He comes
through onto notebook paper when I scribble over coins, and, when
I hold paper money to the light, his square head, thick eyebrows, and
pear-shaped nose appear like magic in the empty whiteness. The
newspaper shows him waving to crowds, shaking hands with foreign
guests, saluting the Army, and, ski poles in hand, smiling jauntily out
from mirrored sunglasses on top of a Swiss Alp.

I have seen traces of his actual self. On a field trip to his air base
my fourth-grade class climbed inside his personal plane. We stared
at the wrinkled leather of the seat he had recently sat in. We touched
the control panel his fingers had recently touched. But that's as close
as I've ever gotten to seeing him.

The Queen, however, is going to visit our school. Community
School used to be a hospital, and a brass plaque outside a certain
classroom states that Her Royal Majesty was born inside it on Oc-
tober 14, 1938. Because of this, she is coming to visit, and for days
in advance we rehearse, filing into the playground and standing in
rows and being led off again. Our schedules are rearranged and an-
nouncements are sent home and a thousand metal chairs are stacked
up against the administration building.

On the appointed day, a helicopter lands on our soccer field in a
storm of brown dust. The Queen emerges, beautiful and white. Her
blouse is white, her skirt is white, her high heels are white, and so is
her big round hat. We sit on the metal chairs and a man with a
microphone tells us that the Queen gives money to artists and opens
homes for orphans and holds the hands of sick people in the hospital.
The children who have been chosen to dance for her step up in crisp
dresses and pants, and a little first-grade girl hands her a sheaf of
white flowers. The Queen dips her head gracefully and kisses the
girl's cheek, and it looks just like the stories in the Farsi schoolbooks
that say how much she loves us. And then I am thinking about
schoolbooks—a straight row of them on a dirt floor, with the pens
and pencils lined up neatly on the side—and I feel a catch in my
throat because I have remembered something I ought not to have
forgotten. What happened to those schoolbooks? When the walls of
the *kharabeh* crashed in, where were those blue-lined notebooks with

the neat letter strokes spelling out the names of Maryam and her sisters and brothers?

Soghra's family has set up a blue plastic tarp in our garden. I've been avoiding the backyard so I won't intrude on them. I have not seen Maryam since they knocked down the *kharabeh*, and I don't know what I would say if I did. She is living in a tent now, like the heroine of a novel. That makes me the weak, silly spoiled girl whom the story is not about. I am embarrassed because I have a house when she doesn't.

And then one day the tent is gone. They have found a new *kharabeh*, Baba says, in the southern part of town. Soghra will still be our maid, but now she will take the bus.

"That's not fair," Mama says. "What about the kids' schools?"

"They'll go to school in the new place," Baba says.

"But they have friends here," Mama insists. "And they're so smart. They were getting scholarships because they got to go to this school."

"I know," Baba says, shaking his head. "But they say the schools are getting better everywhere."

"How am I supposed to help them with their English?" Mama demands.

"And what about Soghra's show at the gallery?" I ask.

"Maybe she'll still have it; there's no reason why she shouldn't." But Baba says this in a sad way, and I know what he's not saying, that a few weeks ago Soghra had taken the animals home to the *kharabeh* to show her children, and that there was no way, in that day of falling ceilings and crashing walls, that those tiny creatures would have been saved.

❖

Whenever something big happens in the world I cut it out of *Kayhan International*, the English-language newspaper. I have all the articles on the jumbo jet collision in the Canary Islands, and all the stories about famous people who have visited Iran, like Lee Majors, the Six Million Dollar Man; Colonel Sanders in his white Kentucky Fried Chicken suit; and President and Mrs. Carter. Soon I have a whole scrapbook of celebrities and tragedies.

One day in late August, bold letters darken the front page.

"HOLOCAUST—377 burned alive in Abadan cinema arson." Shortly after a movie called *The Deer* began, someone locked the exit doors in the Rex Cinema in the southern town of Abadan and set it on fire. Hundreds of men, women, and children beat on the locked doors, but by the time the fire department arrived they were dead. No one knows who did it, but the government has blamed the fire on "saboteurs and religious extremists."

Soghra purses her lips and declares she will not let her children go to movies anymore. But Mama tells us not to worry—it won't happen here. Abadan is far to the south and very hot, and I wonder if Mama means that the fire started spontaneously from the heat there. But that would not explain the mysterious locked doors. Maybe she means that the Rex Cinema was showing an Iranian film, and that it would not happen in the English-language cinemas like the Goldis or the Ice Palace. But lately we've been going to Iranian cinemas too. When *Jaws* played in Farsi near our house we stood in line for an hour, buying lemonade off the street vendors while we waited.

Little by little, other news takes over the papers again. The pope dies and a new one is installed. National Iranian Radio and Television announces a plan to broadcast TV shows in color. We see *Close Encounters of the Third Kind* in a local theater and I add the fire articles to my scrapbook.

My friend Carla, who used to live here and went to nursery school with me, shows up one day with her family. Although her mother was my mother's best friend when I was four and five, we've only seen them once since they moved away. They are American, but after leaving Iran they moved to India and then to Afghanistan. Now Communists have taken over Afghanistan, so Carla's family is on their way to Egypt.

We take them to dinner at the German Club and Carla and I go off to play under the trees like we used to. She tells me about how the tanks arrived when she was at a baseball game and how she had to leave her puppy in the care of the gardener. She says a boy at her school told her that Egypt has stickers, which neither Afghanistan nor Iran has. The next morning, she and her family fly away.

School starts. I am in sixth grade, the first year of middle school, which means I have classes on a separate part of campus, and I get my picture in the big, hardcover yearbook instead of the paperback elementary school one. Middle-schoolers also get three electives, and I pick art, music, and typing. The typing teacher won't be here for another month, though, so I get a free period, and I feel like a high schooler, sitting in the courtyard and reading a book while everyone else is in class.

Sometimes I stay late after school and go home on the five o'clock bus. It follows main roads instead of going all the way up to each kid's alley like the regular bus does. I get off on Shah Reza Avenue, near the entrance to Tehran University, where a bronze Reza Shah statue sits on a horse. He stares darkly out at the students, frowning at their jeans and leather jackets as if to say they should be wearing soldiers' uniforms, like he is. But I like the way the college students look, shaggy and glamorous, especially the girls with their long hair and high-heeled boots. That is how I plan to look when I'm in college, although I'll be in America. Tehran University's classes are in Farsi, which I only take now for one period a day because Community School is geared toward going to college in America. But in the crisp fall afternoon, walking past the rows of stores where the students are shopping for textbooks, I can get the feeling of college, and I can get the feeling of what Shahrak is going to be like next year, when I am twelve and really walking home alone.

At first I don't connect the college students with the newspaper articles. The paper says that university classes are opening late this year due to the demonstrations and unrest. I haven't seen any unrest, but soon after I read that article I start hearing about fires at cinemas, banks, and liquor stores. These are not like the Abadan fire; these happen at night when no one is there. Riding the school bus in the morning, we see blackened walls and smashed windows; the next day, the same buildings are walled off for repairs.

We also hear gunshots. The first time we heard them was a few months ago, at the Returnees Club, a swimming club for Iranians who studied abroad. Suddenly a series of popping sounds burst from the other side of the wall. Ali and I were playing cards by the pool and we froze in mid-game. So did the men playing soccer, the kids on the seesaw, and the women wading their babies through the children's pool. Ali and I knew from TV what gunshots sounded like, and we could tell these were close. The grown-ups stood there in their bathing suits and looked at each other. But no more shots came, and after a minute or so the kids on the seesaw started up again.

But now the shots are right outside our house. We hear them while we're watching *The Flintstones*, and we run into Mama and Baba's room to look out the window. It is just a basement window, so all we can see are feet, but we get there just in time. The dark shapes of legs run down the front alley. Then another set of legs. Then more shots.

"Really, Mom, there's nothing to worry about," Mama says on the phone as she waves us away from the window. Grandma has heard about the unrest and has called to see if we are all right. As if to torment her, one last shot rings out and Mama has to reassure her all over again. "It just sounds bad because we're near the university, where the protests are. But I promise, we're absolutely fine in here."

We are fine. The shots made us jumpy at first, but now we listen for them. Sometimes there are yells and hurried footsteps and sharp explosions that sound like cars backfiring. Sometimes it's just a single shot, like a slap. Our bodies stiffen, our hearts race, and then we relax. Only Sufi is still scared because Ali and I tell her the bullets will hop over the wall and chase her around the house. She runs in circles, whimpering, until Mama comes in and tells us to stop teasing.

So Ali and I go outside to play. We climb up the vines at the bottom of the garden, perch ourselves in our usual spot on the wall and wait for something to happen.

"There's probably stuff going on right up the street," I say, eyeing the row of garden walls. We sigh and keep looking down the alley.

"Eh-*Khoda*! Get down! Get down!" Soghra runs out of the house toward us, clutching her scarf. Sufi trots out behind her with a finger in her mouth. "Crazies! Come down before the bullets get you!" Soghra shakes the grapevine branches and holds out her arms. Ali jumps and she catches him. I want to stay up here, to give it just another minute for a fight to break out or a shot to be fired. But nothing happens, and after a few more seconds I turn away and slither down into Soghra's arms.

Inside the house, Mama is on the phone again.

"I used to wonder how people could keep living in Beirut when it was so dangerous," she says to her friend who lives in North Tehran. "This probably looks like Beirut from the outside, but it doesn't feel so strange. I mean, as long as the guns aren't pointed at you, your life doesn't really change. You just get home before curfew and you don't go to places where you know there's going to be *shoologhi*."

Shoologhi means messiness or disorder, and lately Tehran has had it almost every day, despite the new martial law. The protests make traffic worse than usual, especially at night when everyone is racing to get home before curfew and honking to get past the people setting fires and fighting with policemen. Bags of garbage lie all over the sidewalks because the garbagemen are on strike, and we sit for hours in long lines of cars outside the gas station because the gas workers are on strike. The lights in our house flicker on and off because of the electricity strike, and the American Top Forty keeps getting interrupted by the fuzzy yelling of policemen shouting instructions to each other across the city.

But once we get used to these things it's like Mama said—our lives don't really change. The school bus still picks us up every morning and drops us off in the evening. On weekends we trade stamps with the Dars and go to the park or the mountains with our parents. I keep up my scrapbook, adding a few of the biggest headlines, like "Hit-run battles in Khorramabad" and "Massive marches on, off campus in Tehran." Political prisoners go on hunger strikes to protest the shooting of demonstrators. High school students boycott school in support of their striking teachers. Baba says all these protests are a step in the right direction. He says people want more rights and more help for families like Soghra's so they won't have to live in *kharabehs* anymore. He says hopefully all this *shoologhi* will force the Shah to improve his government and make everyone's life better.

Upstairs at Aziz's, none of my relatives agree with each other.

"It's the Shah himself who is behind all this," one says. "He had them set the fire in Abadan so everyone would blame it on the religious people."

"Yes, it's true," says another. "The religious ones only burn cinemas that show foreign movies, and that was an Iranian film."

"Well, if it's the Shah who is behind all this, then why doesn't he put a stop to it?" someone else says.

"He will, you'll see. He's just trying to satisfy people by allowing the *shoolooghi* to go on a little longer than usual."

"*Naa-baba*, what are you talking about? It's the Americans, don't you get it? Iran has gotten too independent since the Shah drove up oil prices. America wants Iran to stay backward because it's easier to control that way."

"Independent? This Shah is just a servant to the Americans. Why do you think he released those political prisoners last week? Because Carter told him to. If he weren't so scared of Carter he'd shoot them all and get it over with."

"He *is* shooting them! Don't you look at the papers? If they're admitting to shooting that many people, it means the real number is much higher."

"No one listens to me." Agha Vakili's voice rumbles out from the corner chair. "The English planned this out a long time ago. They put Reza Shah in. And now they'll take his son out. There is nothing anyone can do to stop them."

"Well," his daughter Niki says, "*I* heard that someone in the Defense Ministry said it's not the Iranian Army doing the shooting. They've brought in soldiers from Israel to get the job done."

"Dirt on the heads of this Shah and all his family." This last remark is from Aziz, but she doesn't sound as angry as usual. Aziz loves the *shoolooghi*. "Do you know what I said to the butcher today?" she says, unable to suppress a smile. "I told him that the Shah should burn in hell for everything he's done to Iran. I told the butcher and everyone in his shop that I hope those protesters go right into the palace and kill him."

The color drains from Dadash's face. "Have you gone insane, Aziz-jan?" he hisses. "The police are probably on their way over here right now to arrest you!"

She tosses her head. "Relax. I am just an old woman. What do they care about me?"

At school there is a boy I like named Kurt. He is in my grade and he has straight brown hair and tan skin and sometimes last year we would talk to each other before class. At the end of the year I secretly got my fifth-grade teacher to give me Kurt's picture from the display where the teacher had put all our pictures up with captions to describe us. Kurt's was "nonchalant." Mine was "cool, calm, and collected." It was a perfect match. But I don't feel calm or collected when the phone rings and it is Kurt on the line. No boy ever calls me, let alone the one I like, and I clutch the phone tightly, my heart pounding hard.

"I just wanted to tell you we're going to America tomorrow," he says.

"Oh." My stomach shrinks into a ball. "For good?"

"No, we'll just be gone a few weeks. I'll be back by Christmas."

He doesn't say goodbye, but "see you," and, euphoric and heartbroken, I run into the closet and bury my face in clothes. See you, see you—he wants to see me. Only two months until Christmas.

Soon after this, school closes for a day, and then reopens. Mama starts calling ahead in the mornings to check. Usually they say everything is fine and our bus shows up as usual. But every day at school there are more empty desks besides Kurt's.

In the afternoon our bus driver smokes cigarettes in the schoolyard with the other drivers, waiting to take us home. Sometimes the *shoolooghi* forces us to stay late, and the drivers turn off the engines of the buses parked in the courtyard, and the kids do homework or play dodgeball or try to convince the gatekeeper to let us go to the corner store to buy *alballu-khoshke*—dried sour cherries—or *lavashak*—fruit rolls made of dried plums or apricots.

Community School is the only international school I know of in South Tehran, far from where most foreigners live. It has high brick walls around it, and only the gatekeeper can decide who goes in or out. On the days we stay late, he sits with one hand on the radio and the other clutching the telephone receiver, trying to find out which neighborhoods are safe to drive through. Our bus, passing through the Tehran University area, is usually the last to leave, and we who ride it feel distinguished as we watch the others depart, knowing that we would be in danger if we went home.

"Bus fifty-seven is leaving!" our driver finally yells in a piercing voice. Ali and I and the other kids climb back onto the bus to find the bags we put there two hours ago.

Outside the gate, nightfall blurs the neighborhood. Lately, because

of the *shoolooghi*, the ride home has taken an extra-long time. Two
hours is normal during the evening rush, so the extra hour it takes
now doesn't bother us much. Since it is too dark to read, someone
wads up a piece of paper and we play soccer in the aisle.

Our driver is a little bald man with a thick mustache. We call him
Limoony because after he told us he hated lemons, students started
boarding the bus in the morning holding out plump juicy ones, elic-
iting dignified refusals and warnings that the next person with a
lemon would be ejected. But we like Limoony too much to believe
him, and we know he likes us because he sometimes stops on the way
home and buys us big pink boxes of gooey pastries, which we pass
around as he maneuvers through the narrow streets to our houses.

But tonight, no matter how much we beg for pastries, he tips his
head up and clicks his tongue no.

Come on!

Please?

It's late, and we're hungry.

Just this once?

We'll never ask again.

"Not tonight," he says.

We pout quietly in our seats, hoping he will change his mind.

But he knows more than we do. The lights are off in the pastry
shop, and the metal grate is pulled down. We look at it and drive on.

A few blocks later, Limoony almost jumps out of his seat. "Close
the curtains!" he yells. "Get down!" Usually, if anything is ever going
on, we crowd up around his seat to see it. But tonight something in
his voice makes us obey. We pull the curtains closed and put our
heads down. The sounds of honking and yelling blare in from the
street. We crouch down, thrilled when we see the flicker of fire
through the red curtains. It glows brighter as the flames shoot up the
side of a building. We hear people running back and forth, and then
a smash—a storefront crashing into slivers, and I imagine the broken
shards catching the firelight as they fall slowly, tinkling into little
jewels on the pavement.

The ride home lasts four hours. Limoony drops each child off, not
at the end of the alley as usual, but in front of the doorstep.

Finally it is just me and Ali. Limoony turns around and gives us a
long, worried look.

"I can't take you to your house," he says. "It's right by the university."

"Okay," we say excitedly, eager to see what else will happen tonight. "Where are we going?"

"I'll take you to your cousins'." He turns the bus off its usual course and down a dark alleyway. Somehow he knows where our cousins live. He pulls up to their door and makes us ring their bell to make sure they are home. Baba's cousin Amir sticks his head out the window and calls out a cheery hello. "See you tomorrow," we say to Limoony, and he gives us a little smile and a wave as we run inside.

But the next day school is closed. It is closed the day after that and the day after that, for two whole weeks. Then it opens and we are happy to go back and see our friends and compare notes from the long holiday. More people are absent; but I don't count the empty desks anymore. Everyone says the *shoolooghi* should be over soon. In the meantime, my typing teacher has disappeared again. I get my free period back and, sitting under the trees in the courtyard, I run over the letters I've learned so I won't fall behind—*a-s-d-f-j-k-l* and the *e* we'd just gotten to when school closed. The other teachers give us backlog homework and I take home a tall stack of books for the weekend.

But the next week when we call they tell us not to come. And the next day they tell us not to come. And then, no matter how many times we call, no one answers.

We start our own school. I am the teacher, and I keep meticulous records of Ali's and Sufi's grades. We listen to "Carry On, Wayward Son" and "Slip-Slidin' Away" on the tapes from Mama's office, but we can't get any more tapes because Mama's office is closed too. Since Mama can't go to work, she starts writing a children's musical in Farsi. It is about two cats—a boy cat from a South Tehran family, with cat sisters and cat aunts sitting in chadors under the *korsi*; and a girl cat who lives in a big, modern North Tehran house with a swimming pool. Their families don't like each other, and the two cats have to meet in the bazaar or in the mountains to drink tea together and plan their wedding. Mama draws the white girl cat at her window in a frilly dress and the orange boy cat outside on the wall in a white undershirt and baggy pants. The two cats sing love songs together, with English letters spelling out the Farsi phonetically. Baba says Iran has no children's musicals like this, and that this one will probably be a big hit.

In the afternoons, Mama, Sufi, Ali, and I pull on our coats and boots, hold hands, and walk down the street toward Tehran University. There have been protests there almost every day, and the start of classes is still delayed. But where we are walking, just a block away, all we see are the dry leaves fluttering down around us.

Beige tanks sit at the boulevard intersections. Soldiers pop up from them like rabbits and train their large machine guns on us, turning to follow as we pass. *Don't look up, don't change pace, don't give them a reason to notice us or stop us*—we know these rules without saying them out loud. And yet deep down we don't really feel like targets. We are not the ones burning banks, spray-painting "Yankee Go Home" on walls, or throwing bottles at policemen. And we are not the Yankees, either.

We walk to the English Bookstore. It just opened recently, and it is much closer to our house than the other English-language bookstores. The aisles have a fresh-print smell, and the children's section is neatly stacked with Tintin and Enid Blyton books, just in from England.

The bookstore owner, a Lebanese man, has already told us how he closed his shop in Beirut when the war came there. Now, as we wander around his shop, he gazes at Mama with mournful eyes.

"Everyone said, 'Go to Tehran,'" he tells her. "They did a business study and said Iran was the most stable country in the Middle East. We moved our whole operation over."

"I'm sure things will get better," Mama says comfortingly.

"That is what they said in Beirut," he says, raising his eyes sadly toward the newly painted ceiling.

I get a book about dogs, which I choose over a book about two Swedish orphans that Mama says I can get next time. But when we go back a few days later, the metal shutters are down and the English Bookshop sign is gone.

Walking home, we stop to buy Sufi some tennis shoes. The salesman, a short, middle-aged man with a worn brown sweater, gets down on his knees to tie her laces. After doing one shoe, he looks up at Mama.

"Are you American?" he asks.

A few days ago, when a sharp-voiced man on the street asked her that, Mama tipped her head up and clicked her tongue no. "*Faransavi-am,*" she said, which means "I'm French," and the man walked away. But we have bought shoes from this man before, and I think he's asked before if Mama is American.

"Yes," she says, gripping my hand a little more tightly. "But my husband is Iranian."

"Aha," he says, not surprised. "But do you support the people? Do you like Khomeini?"

Something in his face—an openness, an interestedness—says he is not judging; he just seems to want to find out.

"Well, I'm staying here, aren't I?" Mama says.

The shopkeeper raises his eyebrows and nods, contemplating this. "But which is better," he asks excitedly, "Iran or America?"

Mama doesn't hesitate. "Iran," she says warmly.

He nods his head again and murmurs, "Iran is good."

On any day before this she would have said both were good. On any day before this he would have argued. He would have told her how long he had been waiting for a telephone, how badly his son needed books and how the school would not pay for them, how his children needed new coats and his family could not eat meat more than once a week. But now he just hands Mama a bag with Sufi's new shoes in it, and as she reaches for the bag, he throws in a pair of Minnie Mouse socks, for free.

Khomeini's face is in the moon. Everyone's talking about it. Taxicabs brake in the middle of traffic so people can jump out and look up at the sky, and neighbors gather in the alleys at sunset to point at the outlines of his eyes and his nose and his turban.

At my cousin Niki's house everyone huddles over tapes of Khomeini declaring in his country dialect that the Shah must go. The tapes come from Paris, where Khomeini has gone after living for many years in Iraq. We eat fruit and yogurt and tea, and my great-aunt Ammejun talks about the old days in the village when Khomeini was a divinity student and he and his brother used to come to Agha Jan's house for lunch. She also talks of the time years later, in Qom, when she was friends with Khomeini's wife and Khomeini was arrested for making a speech against the Shah. That, she says, was when people really started liking Khomeini.

"It was sixteen years ago," she says, not stopping to count the years on her fingers. "Ayatollah Borujerdi had just died. Thousands of people came to Qom every day, buses were lined up outside the city gates, everyone was wearing black and carrying black flags and hitting themselves with chains. The Shah had sent an old mullah from Tehran to replace Borujerdi, but the people wanted Khomeini to be the new Shiite leader. The Street of the Judge's Icebox, where Khomeini lived, was filled with people. On the day of Ashura, everyone set up tents at the religious school where the Shah's people had killed a student. Khomeini got on top of a tall chair and talked about how the Shah was stealing all the money from the oil and giving it to the Americans, and how the Shah's sister was importing and exporting heroin, and other things like that.

"At three in the morning Khanoum Khomeini called me. She was very upset, crying and saying they had come from Tehran and tied her Agha's hands and taken him away in an army truck. I told her I would come in the morning. But by daylight they had closed all the schools and universities and sent the Army out. My sons were in high school then, and they came home and said, 'Mama, they're taking all the boys our age and shooting them.' They were also shooting anyone who was wearing the *aba* and turban of a mullah. I locked my door and made my children stay inside the house for a week."

Ammejun tells us that when they let Khomeini out a few months later, crowds of people lined up outside his window to kiss his hand. But soon he made another speech against the Shah, and after that he was exiled.

That night, Leila-khanoum looks up at the moon, sees Khomeini and faints. Another night, Baba looks up and sees the face there too, beard and all, before he shakes his head and it goes away. Naneh still stands in her doorway, wrapped in a black chador, but she no longer complains about her sons beating her. "God is great," she says, her voice high and creaky and filled with delight. "Agha is in the sky."

Mama's producer calls in the middle of the night. "We hear they're evacuating Americans," he says. "You've got to get out of there!"

Mama laughs as she tells us this in the morning, standing over the stove, making apple fritters. The kitchen is warm and cinnamony, and the producer's nighttime phone call sounds funny and melodramatic as we eat our breakfast around the big gas heater.

After breakfast Baba tells us to put on our coats. We are going to a demonstration. Mama is going to wear a chador to make her fit in better; she digs it out of the closet and asks us if we're sure it covers the bottoms of her jeans. My cousin Niki, who usually wears miniskirts, shows up at our house in a chador too. Even Aziz, who stopped wearing chadors fifty years ago, puts one on. I don't have one, so I wear my red ski jacket.

It is Ashura, the national day of mourning for Emam Hossein, who died thirteen hundred years ago. Last year on Ashura Aziz told us that Hossein was attempting to overthrow an unjust government and establish a new one, and we all went to South Tehran to watch the men and boys stream down the street, moaning and hitting themselves. They swung wooden-handled flails with chains that forked into branches and fanned out over their backs. Their shirts were wet with sweat and blood, but they didn't mind. "Ya! Hossein!" they chanted as their arms arced up and the chains beat the rhythm.

Today the marchers are closer to our house, and there are many more of them. Baba lifts Sufi up onto his shoulders and Mama hoists me and Ali up onto the pedestal of a lamppost so we can see.

A river of people is flowing down the boulevard. Some are very religious, with the men separate from the women, and the women covered in chadors. Some are not. Two young men in jeans carry a large poster of Khomeini, with his black turban and black eyebrows standing out against the white background. A middle-aged woman with big dark glasses walks by, one fist in the air, the other holding a cigarette. A group of college students link arms and shout *"Marg bar Shah!"*—Death to the Shah!—and they have the same sort of glad expression that the shoe salesman had on the day he asked Mama if she was American. But these people also have another look—a kind of exhilarated astonishment, as if they can't believe no one is stopping them.

The crowd stretches down the street as far as we can see. Many people are carrying pictures of Khomeini; some also carry pictures of

Mossadegh, a bald-headed ex-Prime Minister who Baba says was once so popular that he was able to make the Shah leave the country for a few days.

There are also pictures of ordinary people, young ones, in black and white. They look like huge school photos, floating above the crowd in a ghostly processional.

"Who are those pictures of?" Ali asks.

"Those are people in jail and the marchers want the government to let them out," Baba says. "Or they think they're in jail but they don't have any information about them."

Suddenly I recognize Aziz in the crowd, holding out bottles of milk to the demonstrators. She dodges around them and comes back to get more bottles from her bag. "Young people need milk," she explains, her eyes shining. Then she pushes her way back into the crowd.

When all the *shoolooghi* started, Ali and I asked why everyone suddenly hated the Shah. Mama said that the people were mad because the Shah was too busy having parties to pay any attention to their problems. "What will happen if he leaves?" I ask now.

"Oh, people will be freer and be able to say what they think more and not worry about getting in trouble," she says. Baba tells us this is a historic moment, no matter how it turns out. "Just look at all these people out here together," he says.

> *Valiahd-et bemir-e!*
> *Shah-e jallad!*
> *Chera koshti*
> *Javanan-e vatan-ra?*

It starts as a low rumble from far down the boulevard; by the time it reaches us it is a roar.

"God, do you hear that?" Baba says, his eyes wide. "I can't believe they're saying it out loud." Mama shakes her head and raises her eyebrows, and Baba translates:

> *May your crown prince die!*
> *You butcher Shah!*

Why did you kill
The youth of the motherland?

Even though I'm not sure of all the Farsi words, the tune and rhythm of it get into my head. It is fun to be here, chanting silently along with the thousands of people streaming by. I even kind of wish the police would come and we could see fighting and *shoologhi* up close. Then I would really have a story to tell my friends—even better than Carla's story about the tanks in Afghanistan. And wouldn't Grandma and Mama's producer be amazed to hear that we were out here in the middle of all the excitement when they were worried about us just being at home.

But all that happens is a helicopter appears and hovers over our heads. A man looks up and shakes his fist. "It's the son-of-a-burnt-father Shah!" he cries. "He's come out to watch us." Other people look up and start yelling. "What's happened to your great Army?" a woman calls out. "They've all put flowers in their guns! They've left you and joined us and now we have become too many for you to shoot!"

"Marg bar Amreeka! Marg bar Shah!" Ali and Sufi and I run around the living room, chanting and protesting and waiting for the English-language TV station to sign on. Finally, at four o'clock, we turn on the TV and settle down on the couch.

"Are they showing him?" Mama yells from the kitchen as the national anthem starts up.

"Who?" Ali yells back.

"The Shah. Is he still on TV?"

"Yeah," Ali yells. "But he's lower."

Mama comes into the living room, her hands flecked with ground meat. "What do you mean, 'he's lower'?"

Ali is right. The Shah is there as always—his salt-and-pepper hair, his furrowed eyebrows, his lips curved up slightly on one side as if he is unsure whether or not to smile. But the image is an inch or so too low on the screen.

Mama laughs. "I wonder if they're doing it on purpose."

The next day when the anthem begins Ali and Sufi and I start laughing. "Mama, come look! He's even lower." The anthem plays through and the Shah stares out, his shoulders almost cut off by the bottom edge of the television. At one point he begins to flicker in and out, which makes us laugh more. Then, at the end, he is jerked back up a little, as if someone is trying to set him right.

Baba brings one of his partners home from the office to spend the night because he has stayed out too late to make it home before curfew. Bijan is a short, bearded man who is slightly younger than Baba; he shakes all our hands and sits down on the couch with a cup of tea. "Can you believe what is happening?" he says. "Sometimes I think we ourselves don't fully understand it. It's just like Mossadegh's time, when they nationalized the oil, remember?"

"I was in high school," Baba says. "Some soldiers came into my classroom and stood behind the teacher with machine guns. I remember demonstrations in the street . . . but there were lots of demonstrations in those days. I don't know if the ones I saw were for Mossadegh. But I do remember when the Shah left. The newspapers started saying that his sisters were prostitutes and in the drug business. And then I remember they arrested Mossadegh in his pajamas."

"Yes, that's right!" Bijan says. "I was out in the streets myself, twelve years old, when they announced the Shah had left. How happy everyone was—hugging and kissing and saying, 'Long live Mossadegh!' and 'Death to the Shah!' It was like a big party, with acrobats doing flips and jugglers juggling and strong men lifting weights in the middle of the street."

"So what happened?" I ask. "Why did the Shah come back?"

"Ah, I don't mean to be disrespectful, but it was your mother's country that brought back the Shah. He was hiding in Rome—destitute, he hadn't brought any money out! I was in the street with a group of boys; we had just pulled down a statue of the Shah's father. Some older boys had told us they'd give us money if we pulled it down, but afterward we didn't know what to do with it, so there we were, running up and down the streets, carrying this heavy statue like a coffin.

"All of a sudden on the far side of the intersection we heard 'Long live the Shah!' and 'Death to Mossadegh!' It was only a few people, but slowly it became louder, until half the voices were for the Shah and half were for Mossadegh. Everyone started yelling and punching and kicking each other. We put the statue down and climbed on top of it, and from where we stood we saw the army men putting up pictures of the Shah. Then we knew it was over." Bijan swats the air with the back of his hand. "You see, America was scared Mossadegh was a Communist. So the CIA paid some of those acrobats to start up the chants for the Shah. They knew that it would confuse everyone, that as soon as people thought the Shah was back they'd get scared and want to be on his side. That's the way people are."

Baba smiles and shakes his head. "I remember after that my uncle was so mad that he used to whisper every night in his baby daughter's ear that England and America were the enemies of humanity," he says.

"Well, what if the same thing happens again?" Mama says.

"Ah, Karen-khanoum, this time it's not so confused," Bijan says. "Can't you feel it? It's not just a few tough kids, it's not just a few political guys. The people in the streets now are happy just like last time, but now it is rich people, poor people, old people, students—everyone is fed up with this Shah. And the point is"—his voice drops—"*the Americans are letting it happen.* Where is the CIA? Where is Carter, who is supposed to be the Shah's friend—what is he doing about this? I'll tell you: nothing. I don't know why. It seems like this time America wants him out as much as we do."

"That's great, if it works out," Baba says. "But do you really think America wants Khomeini?"

Bijan frowns. "I don't know. But don't you see? That's not the point. It's not about what the Americans want. This time it's about what we want."

I don't care that the Shah is falling down the TV screen. Whether he stays or goes doesn't make any difference to me. A bunch of Americans got evacuated a few days ago; they're making such a big deal of the *shoolooghi.* But I like when Bijan makes a big deal of it—as if the *shoolooghi* is going to make everything different, as if next year we won't just be living in a new neighborhood but in a whole new country. And he is not the only one who feels this way. People in the streets look at each other and talk together with a new interest, as if they've all just discovered they're distant cousins. They even look at me differently—like I am a grown-up, or a part of something grown-up. If they aren't actually smiling, they have a look on their faces as if they are barely holding in smiles, and the very act of holding them in makes a warm energy pulsate into the chilly streets.

"*Allahu Akbar!*"

Late at night, they cry thinly from their rooftops, defying the curfew without leaving their houses.

"*Allahu Akbar!*"

God is great up there under the winter stars.

❖

Snow falls and the city becomes hushed. A soft white carpet pads the streets and silences the footsteps and hides the burn scars on the pavement.

Bijan dejectedly proclaims the movement dead. Iran, he points out, has the sixth-largest army in the world—now that the protests are winding down, there is no reason for the Shah to leave.

For a couple of weeks I don't find anything interesting to clip out of the newspaper. We go over to visit the Dars. We haven't seen them for two weeks because of all the *shoolooghi*, but Mama takes us over there now because Pamela and her family are leaving on a ten-day vacation to Rome, and we can't imagine letting a whole month go by without seeing each other. We play all afternoon, and their Indian maid makes puffy bread for us and Turkish coffee for Mama and the Dars' mother.

After the Dars leave there is not much to do. We don't even have a Christmas tree to decorate. Not one of the men who usually line pine trees up along the sidewalks and warm their hands over trashcan fires has shown up this year. So Baba cuts a branch off the big fir tree in our backyard—making sure not to cut the branch we use for looping up birthday piñatas—and we prop it up in the living room. It is shorter than I am, and it curves apologetically to one side, but we cut a roll of aluminum foil into strips and drape the thick, stunted tinsel over its boughs.

The electricity dies every night. In the middle of a movie the room goes dark and the TV picture compresses into a white dot that glows for a second and then fades out. Still half hoping the movie will start up again, we feel around for the antique glass oil lamps and light them with spluttering matches.

"This is how they used to do their homework in *Little House on the Prairie*," Mama says, gesturing at the dancing yellow flame.

"This is how *I* used to do my homework," Baba says, and I imagine him in the mud-walled village house, hunched over a notebook as the servants' silhouettes passed back and forth in the fitful light.

BBC radio has started to call it a revolution. Mama laughs. "As if these people running up and down the street were the Russian or the French Revolution," she says. How can it be a revolution when the *nafti* still clanks down the alley with his big greasy canisters, singing "*Naft!*" in his piercing voice? Baba goes out to him and comes back in with two large black containers of oil almost sloshing over, and now we have heat for the next few weeks.

But we are almost out of cooking gas, and the place where we usually get new canisters has been closed all month. Mama comes home with crackers and peanut butter and a stack of the blue triangular cans of Danish ham that doesn't need cooking. It's fun to eat from a tin, and Ali and I take turns winding the metal key around the triangle until it pops open to reveal our pink dinner, glistening in the light of the oil lamp.

Lists are posted in the mosques. My cousin Javad, who is a student at Tehran University, tells us that there are lists of Imperialists, lists of Westernized People, lists of Friends of Americans, and so on. One day, Javad says that a friend of his saw Baba's name, on a List of Freemasons.

"What's a Freemason?" Baba asks, baffled. Everyone looks at Mama because *feremesan* is a foreign word. She shrugs and looks at Dadash, who doesn't know either. Maybe one of Baba's students who got a bad grade in his class put his name on a list. Maybe the list makers have confused Baba with someone else. Or maybe his name is not really on that list at all.

We move upstairs to Dadash's house because it's easier to conserve oil if we all use one heater. We sit with Dadash, Leila-khanoum,

Javad, and Roya around their *korsi*, which has a glowing electric heater
underneath. It has such thick blankets that even during blackouts the
day's heat stays trapped under the table.

We drink tea all day. We play backgammon with Dadash and
rummy with Leila-khanoum, who flips the cards out, eleven each.
Hurry, hurry, she says when we take too long to put down a card,
and when her turn comes she pounces on the table like a tiger.

"I miss school," I say.

"Me too," says Ali. "I'm sick of cards."

"Well, your school will open again soon, *enshallah*," Leila-
khanoum says. "Then you'll miss these lazy days." She pulls us up
against her warm legs. "This is all we used to do when I was a girl,"
she says. "Talking and tea drinking and poem saying." To show us,
she half closes her eyes, raises her eyebrows, and rounds her lips into
the grand, vowely voice Iranians use for poems.

> *We would throw this world into flames.*
> *We would upset the wheel of the universe,*
>   *take the stable mind and throw it into anarchy.*
>
> *We've come undone, we cannot tell head from toe.*
> *We've lost control, running to and fro.*
> *We are the polo mallet, confused in the hands of the king,*
>   *letting thousands of balls roll under his feet.*
>
> *Now we are silent; but in silence lies the seed of madness*
> *And wisdom is a flame hidden in cotton wool.*

But we are not all silent, or hidden. Javad runs around in the streets
with his girlfriend until the last minute before curfew, and every night
a whirlwind of terror rises up inside Leila-khanoum. The later it gets,
the thinner her lips get and the stonier her eyes get until she looks
nothing like her usual self. She alternately stares out the window at
the black sky and rushes around the house, finding her coat and
gloves, saying a mother can't just sit still while her child is in danger.

But before she ever leaves we hear Javad's key jiggle in the lock,
and then Leila's coat is off and she is smiling and hugging him, and

no one ever mentions how she was just about to go searching for him.

Javad shakes the snow off his long black hair and slides his legs under the *korsi*. Leila-khanoum brings him a glass of toffee-colored tea that glints in the lamplight and he wraps his hands around it to thaw them. "They've started going after SAVAK now," he says one night as he sits down.

SAVAK is the Shah's secret police. People have always whispered nervously about who might be a SAVAK agent or informer; since no one knows, most people just keep their mouths closed and don't make jokes or unflattering comments about the Shah. Students in Iranian schools memorize poems about his greatness, and merchants and businessmen hang portraits of him over their doorways to fend off questions from the nosy SAVAK.

But now that everyone is speaking out against the Shah, no one is scared of SAVAK anymore. In fact, Javad says people are talking about tracking down the SAVAK agents and punishing them for putting so many people in jail.

"They're saying that anyone whose car has a license plate that ends in an even number is SAVAKi," Javad says.

"That's the most ridiculous thing I've ever heard," Baba says. But then he frowns. "Do we have even-numbered plates?"

We haven't driven our car for days. There's nowhere to go— stores, cinemas, and restaurants are closed. Still, we scramble out from under the *korsi* and strain to look through the window at the cars parked in the dark garden. But they are blanketed in snow.

A few nights later Javad comes home and says the new rumor is if your license plate ends in an odd number you're SAVAKi. This time no one goes to the window. Everyone is too busy talking about another rumor, heard from someone whose brother knows a top government official: the Americans and Russians have decided to divide Iran in half.

"It's all set," my uncle Jamsheed says. "They're going to draw a line right through the middle."

"Of course, it makes sense," Dadash says glumly. "The Americans will get the oil and Russia will get another Afghanistan."

"If it's true, then maybe we should move south," Mama says. "We don't want to end up on the Russian side."

Everyone nods. "But where will they draw the line?" Leila-khanoum asks. "Where will the new capital be? God forbid we move to Esfahan and then it turns out to be in Russia."

We would never let this make us leave Iran.

Mama tells this to everyone who calls from America—that most likely it will all blow over, but if it does turn out to be a revolution we will stay and live in the new country that follows. It's just for now that we have nothing to do all day, especially since we moved upstairs. I've read all my books and I've played hours of backgammon. I've tried calling the Dars, who were supposed to be back by now. But every time I call, their maid says they're not back yet. Then one day I call and the phone just bleats into dead air.

Most of my other friends aren't home either, and Mama says they might also have left the country. Sometimes when we're just sitting around we start talking about where we would go if we were leaving.

"England," Mama suggests, because she has always wanted to see it.

"But they hate foreigners in England," Baba says.

"We're not foreigners," Mama says.

"You're not," he says. "I am. How about Egypt?"

Egypt is where Carla's family went after getting kicked out of Afghanistan. Her mother writes that Cairo is a lot like Iran, with "a big international community and good schools for the kids." Ali's American friend Billy is moving there too, and Baba has heard Egypt has good job opportunities.

So Ali and Sufi and I arrange a trip to Egypt. We set up chairs in the living room to make an airplane, and we sit through long flights, serving meal after meal and never getting there. Mama laughs and tells us we don't have to sleep on the plane, because Egypt is not like America; it's only two hours away.

But then one day Baba comes home from the travel agency with four tickets to Los Angeles—one adult and three children. He is not coming. We are not moving to Egypt; we are not moving anywhere at all. We are just going to America for a few weeks to see Grandma and Grandpa and wait until school opens again. Schools do not shut down for good, and neither do countries.

Since we're not really leaving, I do not look carefully at everything in our house. I do not hide a special rock under the stairwell or go down to talk an extra amount to Aziz so that the sound of her voice will etch itself into my memory. I call Shahrzad, my best friend at school this year, and to my surprise she picks up the phone. She promises to write to me in America. Mama calls the airline and explains that we are bringing our dog and need a ticket for him too. We each pack a bag and say goodbye to everyone.

It is the middle of the night when we carry our bags downstairs. The garden is silent. No lights are on, but the snow, piled up to my thighs, is bright enough to guide us. We dig a path to the car, and as we dig, Baba glances up at the neighbors' windows. We don't want to wake them; we wouldn't want them to think there is anything strange going on when it is really just that we are leaving to catch an early morning flight. But their windows stay dark. Baba heaves the suitcases into the trunk, clicks it shut, and gets in to warm up the car.

And then we are the only thing moving, easing out of the driveway and down the snow-packed street to the airport.

We wait there three hours. Finally someone at the check-in counter says our flight has been canceled. We go home.

The next day we call first. We try several different airlines. All flights are snowed in, they say. Try again tomorrow.

The following morning they tell us to come, and we say goodbye again, uncertainly, because we might be returning home in a few hours.

The airport looks ready to burst. People are fighting to get to the counters, waving tickets and yelling that they arranged their reservations months ago. Behind them, old people and children sit on the floor, their luggage and coats piled around them like little forts.

We push past a woman in a fur coat with gold rings on all her fingers. We squeeze between two men in suits who are arguing with each other. I am not sure why the crowd moves aside for us so easily when everyone else has to yell and shove—maybe it is the oddity of seeing a little dog snout poking out from the plastic kennel's barred window. In any case, we eventually reach the front of the baggage check-in line. We put our bags on the scale. Sufi's is light; she has packed two stuffed animals almost as big as she is. Ali has packed his framed photo of the Iranian soccer team, our Farsi books, our stamp collections, and one of each kind of Iranian coin, which he got from Dadash. In my suitcase, between my Polaroid camera and my yellow sweat suit, are my favorite books, my lacquered box of beads and stones, and my school notebook with all the work I've done this year. I give my bag a lucky pat goodbye and watch it get thrown onto the conveyor belt.

We follow Baba toward the hallway that leads to passport control. But when we get there he stops short. Hundreds of people are camped out on the floor, stretching down the hall as far as we can see. We can't step over them, we can't tell them we have a flight to catch; they are all trying to fly out too. Not even the people at the front are moving, and it looks as if they never will.

We go back to the main lobby and stand there, unsure what to do. People are pushing and yelling all around us, and we can barely hear Mama telling us to stay close by. Then, all of a sudden, a man's voice cuts through the din.

"This way!" he yells in English. It is an Iranian man with shoulder-length black hair and a black goatee, steering a tall blond woman in front of him. He looks at Baba and points at the check-in counter. We run back over there. The attendants who checked us in have disappeared, and under the sallow fluorescent lights, nobody sees us slip behind the counter.

The conveyor belt is still moving. Baba jumps over it, and Mama hands Sufi to him. It looks fun to ride, and instead of jumping over, I put my foot down and feel it start to move me. But before I can stand all the way on it, Baba and the black-bearded man scoop me up and deposit me on the other side.

The black-bearded man leads us through a door in the wall, and we find ourselves in the wide hallway that leads to the departure gate. A few people scurry by with bags; otherwise it is empty. Baba and the man shake hands and the man looks at Baba and wishes him luck. Then he disappears with the blond woman.

We hurry over to a booth to get our passports stamped. Baba takes us to our gate, hands Mama the tickets, and kneels down to hug us goodbye.

I wasn't scared to leave Baba in Iran that day. He had decided to join us in the States for a week or two since nobody was going in to work at the office and he had nothing much to do in the meantime. He told us he'd have a ticket in a few days, and we had no reason to think he wouldn't.

It was not until much later, in junior high, that I got scared. That was when Mama told me that the real reason Baba's office had closed was because an anonymous caller had threatened to bomb them if they stayed open. And that was when I learned that the real reason we had moved up to Dadash's was so if anyone came to arrest Baba for having a foreign wife or for being on some list they would not find him home. For a year or two after finding these things out I would break into tears when I read stories about lost fathers; sometimes even when Baba was just going to work, I would get scared that he might not come home, that something might still happen to him while he was apart from us.

But on the day we left Iran I did not know that this would be the last week of things the way we knew them. I did not know that four days later, on the day after Baba left, the Shah himself would fly away, the airport would close, and thousands of people—pro-Shah, anti-Shah, and neutral—would be arrested and jailed and killed. And so that morning when Baba knelt down and hugged us and kissed us hard on our cheeks, I was not sad.

"I'll see you guys soon," he said. He pulled us each back again to kiss the tops of our heads. Then he turned around and walked away.

The passengers at the gate leaned back, relieved, even a little proud. We had made it. The whole hysterical, euphoric, bewildered nation no longer existed here. We waited for our flight to be called and then we filed out onto the tarmac, and I blinked, surprised at how light the sky had become. I climbed the movable stairway set up against the white Swissair plane, taking deep breaths of the jet fumes I loved to smell when we traveled. And then, as I waited at the top of the steps for the passengers ahead of me to go in, I turned around.

I didn't want to get on the plane.

I strained to look past the airport building at the gray swath of smog hanging below the charcoal sky—another day beginning over Tehran. This was my home. It was in trouble and I was leaving it. At that moment, Iran in all its shakiness became more precious to me than any safe country could ever be. I looked hard at the horizon, casting out for some building or mountain peak to keep with me while I was gone. There was nothing. So I forced myself to take in the nothingness, to memorize the hazy sky over Tehran, and I kept the picture burning into my mind's eye long after I walked down the aisle and took my seat.

The Landscape

❖

WHEN BABA ARRIVED IN L.A., THREE DAYS AFTER US, WE PICKED him up at the airport and drove him to Grandma and Grandpa's house just in time to watch the Shah and Queen Farah stepping off their private jet in Egypt. The Shah said he was taking a short vacation, but the newscaster repeated this in a voice that meant we all knew better. The Shah himself must also have known. He was said to be carrying a jar of Iranian soil, and as he stepped forward to receive a kiss from Anwar el-Sadat he looked drawn and shaken; he may even have been crying. (Years later, Mama told me that on that first night Baba had cried too, for all he had left behind. It was the only time except for when his father died that she ever saw him weep like that, heavily, his head dropped down in his arms. Afterward he did not cry again.)

Mama cried a few days later, when she saw that a single scoop at Baskin-Robbins had gone up to thirty-eight cents. She had just discovered we couldn't afford a down payment on a four-bedroom house in west Los Angeles, but when we walked into the ice-cream store and she saw the thirty-eight where the twenty-five had been, it hit her what kind of trouble we were in.

So we went north. The further we got from L.A., the cheaper things got. Perhaps by going far enough we could find a big house in a safe neighborhood with good schools for a price we could afford.

By the time we crossed over into Oregon we had been on the road almost two months. The Malibu had become a friend, a capsule just large enough for the five of us, and the more we drove, the less I wanted to stop and fit myself into a new place. We would wake up in the morning and start off into the green-gray mist, following logging trucks up the slow inclines, far from Iran or California or any life we had ever known. In the front seat, Mama made another round of sandwiches. Rain began to fall, pattering a rhythm on the windshield. The car rocked softly, pulled by a larger force than its engine, like a piece of wood drifting on waves.

We pick Portland partly because anything further north seems forsaken. If we don't stop driving, we will slide over into a third state and then right off the top of America. We also stop there because, leaving Iran two months ago, my uncle Jamsheed urged us to join him in Portland, where his wife's brother lives. Portland is exactly like California, Jamsheed said, but cheaper. And so, as the sky turns dark and the rain starts up again, we ease the car into a misty compound of wooden buildings and search for the E building to knock on Jamsheed's door.

Jamsheed should also have added that Portland is wetter than California. Between rains, the mud never dries. The trees smell mushroomy and their rotting bark shreds like beef jerky under our feet. Our unit, in building B of the Timber Creek Apartments, looks just like Jamsheed's. We have a living room, a bathroom, two bedrooms, and a kitchenette, all lined with pea-green yarn carpeting that smells like old cigarettes and hamburger grease.

Timber Creek doesn't allow pets, so Mama calls to tell Grandma not to send Yip up to us for now. When she gets off the phone she tells us that Grandma has some friends who live on a farm in Nevada and would like to adopt Yip. Mama says don't we think Yip would be much happier on a farm than cooped up in a little apartment.

"Can we go visit him there?" we ask, and she says we can. We are sad, but Mama tells us to think about how much Yip will enjoy running around herding sheep and making friends with the baby pigs. We don't really have a choice about Yip anyway, since Timber Creek is the only place we can afford. Mama doesn't like our apartment, but she says we shouldn't be spending all our money on rent when we can save it for a house of our own. We only brought a little money out of Iran, but Mama says as soon as she and Baba find jobs we will buy a house. So, since we have no furniture, we spread our sleeping bags out on the living-room floor and try to figure out things for them to do.

"I should have gone to medical school," Baba groans. "There's nothing here for architects."

"At least you have a skill," Mama tells him. "What kind of job am I going to get?"

"Why don't you make another album?" I ask.

"That's not a job you can count on," she says. "And anyway, I don't have a contract anymore."

Baba looks in the paper and circles everything listed under "Architect." There is not very much.

"Did we bring those pictures of Shahrak from Iran?" he asks. He pulls out a suitcase and sifts through it, then frowns and dumps it all out to go through again.

Those pictures are locked safely in my suitcase. When we were leaving Iran I peeled them all out of our photo album and slipped them into my school notebook. Now Baba wants to bring them around to architects' offices. But Baba has been losing things ever since we got to America. First his new camera was stolen in Los Angeles. Then an embroidered tent-runner disappeared from our motel in Corte Madera. Baba suspected the management, but no matter how much I told him to report the theft, he said it wouldn't do any good. I hated that he didn't even try.

I'm sure if I give Baba the pictures he'll lose them or forget them somewhere and then we won't have a trace of Shahrak. So I watch guiltily but don't say anything as he pulls another suitcase out of the closet and empties it onto the floor.

"Maybe we forgot to pack them," Mama says.

"But I was sure we brought them," Baba says. "How am I supposed to get a job if I don't have anything to show of what I've done?"

"Can't you show the blueprints from Shahrak?" I ask helpfully.

"I didn't bring them."

"Oh," I say. "Well, can't you have them call Iran and talk to people you worked with?"

"Call who? The office is closed. Anyway, they're not going to call Iran for me. They'll just hire someone else who has references here."

Guiltily, I go over to my suitcase.

"Baba?"

"What?"

"If I gave you those pictures of Shahrak, would you promise to take good care of them and give them back to me after you get a job?"

"Yes, of course. Why? Do you have them?"

"Baba, really. You have to promise."

"I promise, I promise."

I unzip my bag and slide the pictures out of my notebook. My stomach feels hollow, as if I am losing yet another piece of Iran.

New relatives arrive from Iran—my father's tall, laughing sister Massi, her big bald husband, Zia, and their daughters Shireen and Haideh (their son, Siamak, is in Ohio). They get an apartment in Timber Creek too, and in the evenings everyone comes over to our house to watch our little black-and-white television. The news no longer shows as much about Iran, but every night we still turn it on full blast so that if something does happen we will be ready.

Zia jerks his head forward as each new picture comes on the screen. "Iran?" he cries. "Is it Iran?"

"No," Mama says. "That's Afghanistan."

"Well, why are they showing it?" Zia says, agonized. "Afghanistan doesn't concern us. Where is Iran? They are not interested in it anymore!"

"They'll show it, *enshallah*." Massi's low, steady voice tempers her husband's loud one.

"Bah," he mutters. "They're killing us with these Afghanis, the sons of burnt fathers." Zia is a retired policeman who used to line us up in Aziz's hall and teach us to stand at attention as we giggled and squirmed. "Children! Listen to me! Son of a burnt father, this man is!" He waggles a meaty finger at Peter Jennings. "Do you know what that means?" We nod, and Zia's blue eyes bulge approvingly. "You're good kids . . . Oh, is that Iran?"

"No, those are Americans," Baba says.

"I heard them say Iran—no, you're right; those are American cars. But why are they lined up at the gas station like Iranians?"

"They're saying there are going to be gas shortages here because Iran's not sending oil."

"Shh!" Jamsheed says. "Iran, Iran!"

"Quiet, let me hear," Baba says. He is the best English speaker of all of them. Even though Jamsheed also went to Berkeley, Baba has had many more years of practice, with us. But now he doesn't say anything. The camera skitters like a silent movie, panning over a row of men lying on the floor of a room. The men's faces are frozen into skewed expressions, with dark spots where bullets have pierced their foreheads.

"*Akh*, what happened?" Zia cries. "What are they saying?"

Baba shushes him.

"They killed all the generals?" Zia asks.

"No, those couldn't have been generals," Jamsheed says. "Maybe it was an old clip of dead people."

"Shh . . ." Everyone listens carefully as Baba translates into Farsi: "International organizations tried to intervene on their behalf, but to no avail. General Nematollah Nassiri, former chief of SAVAK under the Shah, was executed by firing squad for crimes against the Iranian people."

Everyone is quiet for a moment.

"The Shah himself put him in jail, months ago," Zia says. "Remember? People thought it was just a trick, to make it look like the Shah was doing something against the SAVAK. I thought for sure they'd sneak him out of the country."

But a lot of generals and ministers were not sneaked out. They are quickly tried, one after the other, and for a few days every time we turn on the news one of them has been shot. We hear that the old Prime Minister even had a chance to escape from jail when the Shah left. Someone opened the prison doors for him but he refused to leave. "I haven't done anything wrong," he said. "I have nothing to be afraid of." But he ends up like Nassiri and the others, shot by the firing squad.

Zia tells us that kind of thing almost happened to old, retired Agha Vakili, Homa-khanoum's husband. Out in the village, the revolutionary guards arrested him for having been a "feudal"—a landowner—thirty years ago. "The *komiteh*—the new police—came and told him to go with them. Homa cried and begged him not to go, but Agha Vakili said, 'I haven't done anything.' He went into the house, shaved, combed his hair, put on his old military uniform, and climbed into the back of that police truck!" Zia pauses to let the suspense build. "They drove him to the next town, and as he was getting out of the truck a young man passing by said, 'Agha Colonel, what are you doing there?' It was a soldier who had been in Agha Vakili's military unit, years before! When Agha Vakili told him what had happened, the young man said, 'In that case they'll have to arrest me too.' The young man's friends offered to go along as well, and on the souls of my children I'm telling you, by the time they got to the police station there were fifty of them, all demanding to be arrested. The police finally had to let everyone go or there would have been another revolution right there." Zia lets out a hearty laugh and then becomes serious again. "Let me tell you," he says. "The good things in your life help you later. Those men who were at the police station—a few years before, Agha Vakili had managed to save a couple of them when they had been arrested by SAVAK; and God bless them, they never forgot it."

Others have not been so lucky. The sixteen-year-old granddaughter of one of Aziz's friends was accused of having connections with a dissident group. She was taken away in the night, and her mother, a talkative, flirtatious woman, has not spoken a word since. Massi and Zia say lots of people are in jail like that, taken away from their families in the middle of the night. They say it is a different Iran from the one we know, and that it can't last long.

Baba interviews at a few architects' offices and eventually finds a drafting job. He never does get the pictures of Shahrak back, although he keeps insisting they're around somewhere. Mama finds a job going to old people's houses to change their sheets and feed them. "You see," she says in a let-this-be-a-lesson voice, "I never really worked before, so this is what I have to do."

Mama takes me and Ali to the school down the road and explains for the second time in one month why we have no records. This school is not very different from the one in Corte Madera—a long yellow-beige building, rows of tetherballs hanging from tall poles, and monkey bars with black padding underneath. In class I race through all the work, and my teacher, Mr. Neff, takes me aside and tells me that after I settle in he will give me more advanced work so I won't get bored. I'm not exactly bored. School in America has always been easier than school in Iran; what really bothers me is being back in elementary school after having already been in middle school. And yet the kids here know things I don't know. One day Mr. Neff takes us all down to the library and the librarian tells us we have forty minutes to write an in-class essay on what we think of nuclear energy and Three Mile Island. I wait, expecting the librarian to explain what these things are. But the other kids start writing and the librarian leaves the room. "Nuclear energy is very useful," I write, guessing that if it is energy it can't be wrong to say it is good.

Every Friday Mr. Neff hands out slips of goldenrod paper for us to write Dr. Feelgood notes to each other. We're supposed to write down nice things we've seen each other do that week, and I am surprised at how seriously everyone in the class takes it. And yet the fact that they've been writing Dr. Feelgood notes all year seems to have made them extra-friendly. They surround me on my first day of class and go around in a circle, introducing themselves. At first I can't remember them all because all the girls wear exactly the same wide-leg jeans and have the same layered haircut. But soon I am able to tell my new friends apart. They know a lot about clothes and dating—one even has a boyfriend in the ninth grade—and I am careful about how I act around them because I don't want to do the wrong thing. In fifth grade, when we were in L.A. for Mama's second album, I was walking in the yard with my friend Carol when a sixth-grade girl stopped us and said we shouldn't hold hands. "People will think you're gay," she said. Neither I nor Carol knew what gay meant, but we let go of each other's hands because we knew it was bad.

"We skate on Friday nights," a girl named Jill tells me. The following Friday I ask Mama to drive me to the Beaverton Mall Skate Center but I forbid her to come in. She gives me three dollars and says to call when I'm ready to be picked up. Congratulating myself for having taken ice-skating lessons in Iran, I walk into the arena expecting to feel a blast of cool air and hear the steely sound of blades on ice. But the air is warm and sugary, and all I hear from the rink is the whirring of wheels and a heavy disco beat pounding from the loudspeakers. I lace on a pair of suede-booted roller skates and lurch over to the wall, wondering how I will ever work up the courage to join the people whizzing by on the rink.

"Hey, Tara, up here!" Some girls and boys from my class are crushed into a booth, sucking on straws from perspiring paper cups. I totter up the steps and squeeze in between them, relieved that I don't have to skate right away. "You made it," Jill says, smiling at me. Someone passes me a cup of Dr Pepper, and I am immediately glad that I came.

The P.A. announces couples skating. The lights dim. A boy named Kyle gets up to skate with a girl named Lori, and the rest of us watch as the spinning mirror ball makes glittery lights race around them. As Kyle glides smoothly backward with his arms around Lori's waist, Jill takes me over to the beginner's run and shows me how to skate up and down it. She leaves me there to practice, and by the end of the night I skate well enough to go out on the main rink with Jill holding my hand, which must be okay because she is the one who took my hand and she is a popular girl with a boyfriend.

One day at recess Jill asks what my school was like in Iran. I end up telling her about how they closed the school down because of the revolution, and by the end of my story a crowd of kids is standing around asking me to repeat the parts they missed. I tell it again, and from then on there is always someone asking me to tell my story because they haven't heard it yet.

Each time it is the same story, full of precise, disjointed details. "It was November 4," I start in a dramatic voice. "We went to the park with our parents and it was the first cold day of the year, when you can really feel the bite in the air. The next day at school my friend Fei-Fang gave me a white rat, and that was the day they kept us really late. The streets were full of rioting and people yelling and starting fires, and our bus driver made us close the curtains and get down. I held the rat in the sleeve of my jacket to keep it warm, and it crawled up my sleeve and all around inside my coat . . ." I describe how it took us four hours to get home, and how when I got home my mother said I couldn't keep the rat, but then school closed for two weeks and I got to keep it until it opened again. Everyone listens gravely, nodding at the right moments, reminding me when I leave something out. And then the next day they bring over another kid who hasn't heard it and say, "Tell him about the revolution," and I solemnly start from the beginning as if it were some holy legend.

It is. It scares me to think that I am the only one in my class to have seen these things, the only one to whom Iran is real. A whole country, a whole life of streets and shops and shopkeepers and bus routes that only I know. With my classmates gathered around, I search my mind for every shred of it that I can remember, like the old ladies in Iran who include in their stories facts like what plates Khanoum So-and-So served lunch on thirty years ago, or what color the walls of the women's quarter were in Haji So-and-So's house in the village. Now I see why the old ladies do this. Repeating each detail, no matter how small, is a way to keep alive something that only they remember, something that would disappear forever if they did not repeat it. And it works. "Don't forget the lettuce your aunt fed the rat," someone interrupts, and I nod and go back to that part, washed over with gratitude that I have found friends who care just as much about the rat's lettuce as I do. They ask for my story again and again, and I tell it gladly, desperate to save myself from forgetting.

Sitting in class, I notice that every single shoe has a long crest running down the side. "Yeah, they're Nikes," Jill says when I mention this coincidence. "You can get them at the Nike store at the Beaverton Mall."

"You'll have to think of a nickname and then get it ironed onto a baseball shirt at T-shirts Plus," Lori says. "Everyone has one."

"You can get these at the Gap," Julie says, fingering the heavy denim of her wide-leg jeans. "Ask for San Francisco Riding Gear."

"And you really should get your hair feathered," Lori adds. "It would look so good."

Mama takes me to the mall and buys me two pairs of San Francisco Riding Gear, a pair of brown Nikes, and a yellow baseball shirt with my new nickname, "Dandelion," ironed onto the front. When I tell Mama the part about my hair she asks me if I'm sure. "It took so long to grow out," she reminds me, and I stroke my long braids, remembering how happy I was the day they finally brushed the top of my jeans.

"Well, maybe just a little," I say, and I tell the hairdresser to just take a couple of inches off the bottom and sides. But at school I still look different from everyone else. "Go to Renee at Apropos," Julie instructs me, and the following week I come out of the hairdresser's with thick, fluffy layers, a new curling iron, and a metallic-blue spray can of AquaNet.

I skate out on the main rink now with everyone else, and I even stay on for girls' fast skate. Jill says she's never seen anyone learn to skate as quickly as I have, and I try not to smile too hard. With my new hair and my jeans with the thick creases down the front, I hardly stick out at all anymore.

Now I go to work on Ali.

"You really should get your hair feathered," I say, using my fingernail to carve a white part through the top of his hair. I walk him over to the bathroom mirror. "And why don't you get wide-leg jeans?" I add as he squints at himself.

"Because I don't want them," he says, and ducks out from under my hands.

Suddenly I feel silly. I look in the mirror at my own chopped-up hair. I don't regret cutting it, but I wonder what Ali thinks of me looking so different from when we left Iran. I hope he doesn't think I have changed. I haven't. I still play Primary School in Africa with him and we still play our space games where we fly out to visit each other on different planets. Ali must know I haven't changed; he never notices hair or clothes anyway. He just shakes his hair out and goes back to the letter he is writing to a center forward of the Iranian soccer team who he has discovered is living in Tulsa, Oklahoma. He tells the soccer player about how last year we got up in the middle of the night to watch Iran play in the World Cup. The soccer player writes back, thanking Ali for remembering him and writing at the end, "God willing, we will all be back in Iran soon and I'll send you and your family tickets to see us play."

Mama wants a house of our own, in a better neighborhood.

"Mom, this neighborhood is fine," I say, horrified at the thought of moving again. Julie and Jill and I are already making plans for seventh grade at Cedar Park Junior High—we've figured out what we're going to wear on the first day and what classes we'll take. We've heard the older girls in junior high can be mean, but we're going to stick together and not pay any attention.

"Don't tell me you want to stay in Timber Creek all your life," Mama says. "Don't you want a nice house, with a yard and a room of your own?"

"Sure, but why can't we get one here?"

"Because this is not the best school district," she says. "You said yourself it was too easy."

I don't care if it's easy. All my friends are here, and I couldn't bear to have them go on to junior high without me. Feeling the tears well up, I run into the bedroom and bury my head in my sleeping bag. After I stop crying I write out a prayer in secret code, using a lucky orange crayon I brought from Iran. I start making up rules for everything I do, as if scrunching up my toes whenever I pass a parked car or always placing my foot on the place where the carpet meets the linoleum will make us get a house in this school district.

But even though Mama insists on looking at other neighborhoods, I can't stay mad at her. She is the only adult in my family who knows anything. She knows I want to dress like the other kids in my class, and she doesn't pay any attention when Baba says those clothes are too expensive. She also knows things like what to do when we have a fifties dance at school. She sews a felt poodle onto one of her skirts and buys me bobby socks and a big ribbon for my ponytail, and as I stand in front of the mirror I realize how lucky I am. The Iranian mothers I know would never have known how to do this. But Mama expertly curls my bangs under and paints my liquid eyeliner on in the fifties style, telling me to keep my eyes closed while it dries.

"How do you know all this stuff?" I ask, squinting as she uncaps a cylinder of white lipstick.

"It's easy; I was your age when it was the fifties."

I close my eyes all the way and hold steady under her hand. She is magical, like a fairy godmother, to know America so well.

Nobody else does. I go with Baba and Massi to 7-Eleven, and Massi picks up two boxes of crackers and pushes them into Baba's hand. "Bargain it down," she hisses.

In Iran, shopkeepers would change their prices if you asked them to. In fact, they used to run after Baba with even better deals if he walked away. But now, to my relief, Baba says no.

"Go on," Massi whispers. "Tell him we're getting two and we want a discount. Your English is better."

"He won't do it," Baba says.

"Fine, give it to me."

I cast an agonized glance toward Baba, then hide down the aisle.

"Hello!" Massi's voice is loud, her accent painfully clear. I peer through a rack of potato chips and see her in her purple sweatpants and high heels, waving crackers over her head. "Fifty cents," she proclaims.

"That's one ninety-nine, ma'am."

"Yes," Massi says. "But we buy two. So make each one fifty cents."

I peek around the aisle and look at Baba, pleading with my eyes for him to make her stop, to leave her here and get the two of us safely home before anyone sees us acting like beggars. Baba frowns and walks over to the cash register, and I relax, grateful that he is going to put an end to this.

"Come on," he says, "can't you give us some kind of discount?"

I stand there, mute and miserable, sure one of my school friends will walk in.

❖

In the summer, we move into a periwinkle blue ranch house with a garden full of ripe strawberries, raspberries, plums, and rhubarb. We sew curtains, paint the moldings, and polish the hardwood floors.

Grandma and Grandpa send up a truckful of their old furniture, and like magic we have beds, clocks, couches, and lamps.

My prayers weren't answered. Our new house is in the West Hills, miles away from Timber Creek. My friends have promised to visit, but for now I play in the yard with Ali and Sufi as a stream of new neighbors walk up our driveway holding pies and cakes. A lady with brownies tells us she's lived on this street twenty-five years; before that she lived down near a place called Hayhurst. Mama tells her where we are from and she smiles and says, "How interesting." A lady with a blackberry pie tells me she has a daughter my age named Tanya, and the next day the daughter comes over and we go to the park with Hedwig, the new puppy we got when we moved.

When we first got to America, Mama said nothing was going to stop us from getting our own rooms. At first I didn't care that much; Ali and I had shared a room for years, and the idea of having our own rooms had never come up until Baba started the plans for Shahrak. But revolution or not, Mama said as we looked at houses, we were going to have a room for each child. So I started to get excited about mine. "See, isn't this much better than Timber Creek?" Mama says hopefully, and I have to admit it is. I have the master bedroom. I have the double bed and matching nightstands that Grandma sent from Los Angeles. Mama sews me flowered curtains and pillowcases and a dust ruffle, and I stay up late, listening to music on Grandma's old clock-radio.

Our new house actually has only three bedrooms, but we're going to turn the garage into a new master bedroom. In the meantime, Mama says, she and Baba don't need a room. They are going to sleep on a mattress on the living-room floor. I am used to Mama and Baba sleeping in strange places. In Iran they slept for a while in a bed-sized alcove next to the bathroom. Sometimes on hot nights they slept outside. So I do not think their bed in the living room is strange until I start going to the houses of other kids in the neighborhood. Theirs are exactly like ours—Mama calls them tract houses—and the only way to distinguish between the designs is that some have the three bedrooms to the left of the front door and some have them to the right. When I go to other people's houses it is easy to find my own room. It is the big one with the corner windows, and it is always the parents' room. "Where do your parents sleep?" the neighbor kids ask when they come over. Embarrassed, I make a vague gesture toward the living room and garage, hoping they will not ask me to show them.

Although we have no money, we don't know how to be poor. Mama drives me to a private school set inside a dark grove of trees, and I spend a day seeing how I like it. My hopes of its being like Community School dissolve as soon as I get there. It is just like all the other new schools. The girl assigned to me takes me to her locker and shows me her hockey stick and gym shorts. But I am tired of girls being picked out to be nice to me. I choose the public school near our house.

At my new school, no one gathers around to welcome me or ask me for stories. There are three seventh-grade classes instead of the one sixth-grade, and besides Tanya no one even talks to me. To them I'm just a new girl who can't play football, and, along with the girl from special ed, I am always the last to be picked for gym-class teams. I don't tell them that in Iran I played soccer but not American football. I'd feel silly asking for instructions on when to run or how to catch the pointy, uncatchable ball. It's been eight months since we came to America, and I feel like I should know this stuff by now.

I'm ahead in English class, though, so my teacher sends me out to the portables to tutor English as a second language. As the thin-wristed Vietnamese and Cambodian kids dig their pencils fiercely into their notebooks as they copy out English words, I think of my Tai-wanese friends at Community School. They all spoke English well and were never sent into rickety metal trailers to do their work sep-arately. I wonder where they are now. I never exchanged foreign addresses with them, or with most of my other friends. When we first got to Los Angeles I looked up at every passing airplane and wished Pamela Dar onto it, although there was no reason for her family to have come to America. Mama called the United Nations, where Pam-ela's father worked, but they did not have him listed. When we got to Portland I even checked the telephone directory, just in case. But after that there was nowhere to look.

I have only one address now, for my friend Shahrzad, who moved to Van Nuys, California, a few months ago. We exchange long letters about Community School, where, we both agree, everything was better and everyone was nicer. "Remember the time Ronnie dropped all his books—how much we laughed?" we write. "Remember the lunch kiosk and how fun fifth period was?" We send drawings and snapshots of our old friends back and forth, with notes that say, "Promise to send them back?"

Two months after school starts, Iran is in the news again.

"Listen to this," Baba says at breakfast, his face lighting up like it does anytime he finds a newspaper article about Iran. "Moslem students stormed the United States Embassy in Tehran today. They seized about ninety Americans and vowed to stay there until the deposed Shah was sent back from New York to face trial in Iran."

Mama puts down the Arts section. "Anyone we know?"

"It doesn't say. Was John still there?"

"I think so. His wife didn't want to leave her parents."

Mama says the Americans will probably be released by the end of today or tomorrow, but in the meantime we chain ourselves to the TV news again, turning it up high when Iran comes on. An American hostage is led into a courtyard, his face covered with white cloth, and we peer behind him to see if we can recognize that part of the embassy. We see a picture of the New York City hospital where the Shah is being treated. We see footage of the revolution—the same boulevard filled with the same black mass of people that we've seen on TV so many times now. But we could not be more riveted if they were showing us our own faces on the news.

Yellow ribbons dot the neighborhood. They pop up everywhere—tied around trees like in the song, but also laced through garden gates, wrapped around chimneys, and hung wreathlike on front doors in big bows that sag and droop after it rains.

At school a boy borrows the teacher's scissors to cut pieces off a spool of ribbon and hands them out to his friends and anyone else who asks for one. I curl down in my chair, betting no one will pass one to me. Last week the same boy gave out bar mitzvah invitations to almost the whole class except me. I wonder if the kids in my class even know I'm from Iran. There are no other Iranians. As far as I can tell, everyone is one hundred percent American, born and raised right here in Portland.

If they did pass me a ribbon I would feel flattered, but I would never tie it onto the loop of my jeans like the others. I would stuff it into my pocket and later I would rip it lengthwise into tiny threads. I hate the people on TV who wear yellow ribbons and shout for Iranians to get on their camels and go back to the desert. And even though I can't help thinking it's a clever idea, I hate the band that sings the Beach Boys' "Barbara Ann" with the lyrics changed to "Bomb Iran."

"Hah," Ali says, pulling at the sleeve of his sweater. "I told these guys at school that this hole was from a bullet in the revolution and they believed me."

"What?" Jamsheed says, biting his bottom lip. It is late at night but he and his wife have dropped by to tell us that they have bought a restaurant downtown. "You told them you're Iranian?"

"Yeah, so what?" Ali says.

"You shouldn't tell people," Jamsheed says. "They'll beat you up."

"Not in this neighborhood," Mama says confidently. She sets a tray of tea on the table. "They don't bother the kids about that stuff."

"You never know," Jamsheed says.

"My friends all know I'm from Iran," Ali says. "When I had on my Tehran Community School T-shirt, Mark Ahern and Jim Shulevitz told me I shouldn't wear it because it would make other people mad. But I told them I'd wear it anyway. It's my favorite shirt."

"Don't you watch the news?" Jamsheed says. "They beat up an Iranian student so badly he almost died."

"Where?" Mama asks.

"I don't know. Ohio? Omaha? One of those places."

"Well, they aren't doing that here," Mama says, looking at us to make sure we hear her.

"Have you heard anything else?" Jamsheed asks Baba. They ask each other this every few minutes.

"Just what I said. Carter's not attacking."

"Aah," Jamsheed makes a disgusted face. "All they need is two days to topple that government. What's he waiting for?"

"My brother says it won't last another month," Jamsheed's wife says. "America will do something."

"The U.S. didn't do a thing to help the Shah stay in Iran," Jamsheed says. "It's not going to put him back again. In fact, I've heard the Americans put Khomeini in there because it was better than letting Iran go to the Russians. Now they're waiting for the right moment to take him out and go in themselves."

During the World News we sit up, alert, ready for anything. The revolutionaries swarm in front of the embassy as they have every day since November 4, burning effigies of the Shah and shouting *Marg bar Amreeka*. Most of them frown, but one boy laughs and waves at the camera.

It is unbelievable that these students have held the American Embassy for two months now. I look around at my family, watching the TV with such serious, attentive expressions. Lately I've noticed something else on their faces, or maybe it's just that I feel it on mine. It is an almost invisible smile tugging at the corner of my mouth. I know it is bad to take over an embassy. But it is hard not to feel a twinge of pride, seeing what Iran can do. It can have a revolution that no one expected would succeed; it can bring down the Shahanshah, "King of Kings, Light of the Aryans"; and it can scare the Americans so badly that they flood into their own streets and shout slogans, just like the Iranians. The newscasters have even started saying the name of the country right—not "Eye-ran" like they used to.

Shahrzad writes from California. "I am going to a new school in Simi Valley. I've changed my name. I'm telling people I'm a Catholic Italian now." She signs the letter "Love, Sherri," with a bubble dot over the i.

Catholic.

Italian.

My eyes run back and forth over the two words. I might be embarrassed by my relatives. I might not tell people at school that I am Iranian. But this letter is like a slap in the face. Shahrzad—my partner in a fifth-grade oral report on Iran's Khorasan province, the only friend who understood how much I missed Community School—has

slipped from Iranian to Italian like the misreading of some alphabet-
ical list. Why Catholic? I want to ask. Why Italian? How can you say
you miss Iran if this is what you do? And who will remember it with
me, if not you?

It is one thing to keep silent; it is another thing to lie. I want to
fly down to California, find Shahrzad's school, tell everyone what she
is and show her that she can't just cut away her Iranianness. Instead
I tuck her letter into a drawer and stubbornly keep writing "Dear
Shahrzad" in response to the letters she signs "Sherri."

And then at school I get a shock. Snaking through the noisy hall
toward the cafeteria, I look up to see the freckled nose and dark hair
of a boy named Frank McClaskey. When he sees me his face wrinkles
into a scowl and he hisses, "Go home, Iranian."

I don't flinch. I don't let my eyes lock on to his for more than the
second it takes for me to hear what he says. The other kids sweep
me down the hall and I take my place in the lunch line, keeping my
face blank, as if by refusing to react I can erase those three words.
But inside I feel dizzy, as if suddenly, in the middle of a crowd, someone has punched me in the side.

Ali, who tells everyone about the revolution, would not have
walked away. Ali would have said something back, something so smart
that it would have left Frank McClaskey standing there with his
tongue too big for his mouth. But what should I have said? *I was born
here and I'm as American as you?* It's the truth; but it's not what Ali
would have said. I should have just coolly said, *Maybe you should go to
Iran yourself, Frank. Don't you have some hostages over there who need
rescuing?* But I wouldn't want to sound like a barbarian or a fanatic.
I can't figure out what Ali would have said, and I don't want to ask
him. It would be too embarrassing to admit that someone said "Go
home, Iranian" to me. It would be making a big deal out of it, which
is just what Frank expects me to do.

And yet I also feel strangely gratified. I hardly know Frank Mc-
Claskey, and I know that what he said is idiotic. But he is a popular
boy, and what he said means he has taken time to find out who I am.
I begin to keep a nervous lookout for him, the way I would with a
boy I had a crush on. No one says anything like that to me again,
but whenever I see Frank now I feel a welling of anger mixed with

an odd exhilaration over the fact that here, in a place where I am used to being ignored, someone with plenty of friends is aware of me. I am even a little proud to have been identified as an Iranian, to be sharing something with the worried-looking Americanized Iranians who were on the news earlier this month, sitting in the Washington, D.C., airport, their visas suddenly revoked.

❖

Baba has quit his job at the architect's office. Now he spends every morning at home, poring over the classified ads. I don't like it. I never know how he is going to act. Sometimes he is just like he was in Iran, taking us downtown to the Saturday market for crisp, sugary elephant ears or coming home with a little ceramic animal in his pocket for Sufi like he used to do for me and Ali in Iran. I am too old for those little presents now, but I used to love it when my handsome, smiling father would come home and reach into his coat for the rhinestone butterfly or opalescent string of worry beads he'd bought for me that day.

Now he mostly yells a lot. He yells if we play music too loudly or if we leave the back door open or if we turn the heat up too high. He yells at me the most, because I get mad and yell back, and our yelling explodes into huge fights, after which we don't speak to each other for days.

But sometimes Baba doesn't yell or bring home toys for Sufi. Sometimes he just sits there and looks tired, the way he did when we picked him up at the L.A. airport last January.

Out of nowhere he decides to become a carpenter. Every day he gets up at four in the morning and drives an hour and a half east to a town called Cascade Locks, where hundreds of workers are building a dam across the Columbia Gorge. "Bridge of the Gods" is the name of the place where they are working, but Baba does not look like a god when he comes home at night. His flannel shirt is steaming with sweat and rain, his woolen army pants are caked with mud, and the corners of his eyes are gummed up with white mucus from blinking back the cold. Mama says he quit his drafting job because he didn't like to work under a boss after running his own firm in Iran, but he gets mad when she says that. "I just want to learn carpentry," he says with a shrug, as if it is the most logical thing in the world.

To celebrate his new job, we go out for Mexican food.

"Can we get chips?" I ask as the waitress hands us our menus.

"No," Baba says quickly.

"Oh, everything comes with chips and hot sauce," the waitress says, and I flash Baba a triumphant look. When we order, he tells me I can't get shrimp because it's too expensive.

I haven't told anyone my father is a carpenter. All the fathers in my neighborhood wear suits and go to offices with telephones where their kids can call them during the day. They come home from work clean and dry. I still tell people Baba is an architect, but even though I have friends at school now, I rarely invite them over. If they saw Baba come home with his three-day beard and his matted hair, they would know I'd been lying. Instead, I sit at the dining-room window in the evenings and watch the men in suits step jauntily out of their cars holding briefcases. I wish one of them were my father.

"Hey," Baba says, suddenly looking around the Mexican restaurant. "What time did we get here?"

My chest tightens up and I look desperately at Mama.

"Not too long ago," she says cautiously.

"Eh, then where is our dinner?" As his voice rises, his accent gets thicker. "Waitress! Where is our food? We ordered two hours ago!"

"Baba, shut up!" I hiss. "We did not!"

"Don't call me shut up."

I want to run over to the startled waitress and tell her to ignore us. But she waves her pad from across the room and hurries over. "It should be coming up soon," she says, throwing a scared smile toward the back of Baba's head.

When the food comes I gaze appreciatively at my crisp bowl-shaped tortilla filled with iceberg lettuce, shredded beef, and grated cheese. I break off a piece and let the flaky shell melt on my tongue. Baba lifts a forkful of burrito to his mouth. He chews a few times. Then he frowns, opens his mouth like a dog when it's coughing up, and pushes his plate to the middle of the table. I look at Mama again, but she just stares down at her food.

Baba sees me looking. "Well, what's wrong?" he says. "I'm not paying for bad meat. Waitress? Could you come here? This meat is old. I want to send it back."

I stop eating. I can feel the stares of the families in other booths, normal people who can come to a restaurant, eat dinner, and go home without any incidents. If I weren't too embarrassed I would pick out one of those families right now and pretend to be sitting with them. Instead, I fantasize about my parents getting a divorce. Baba would disappear, Ali and Sufi and I would stay with Mama, and we could be a regular single-parent family. Maybe Mama would even marry an American, and then our lives would click into the easy way of those families at the other tables. As far as I can see, if we do not fit into this life, our Iranian father is the one to blame.

I do what I can to make the rest of us fit in. "Don't you want an Izod?" I ask Ali, fingering the embroidered alligator on my shirt, hoping to tempt him. But he raises his eyebrows and tells me he likes his old T-shirts from Iran. In fact, Ali, who used to beg every day to go to the toy shop near Tehran University, has stopped asking for anything at all. As I present arguments about why I need a certain kind of shoes or jeans, Ali quietly draws pictures or plays soldiers with his friends. The only thing he asks for all year is a machete from the Army Surplus store, which is a strange request but, it being all he wants, Baba buys it for him.

"I miss our piano," I say offhandedly one day. The following Monday when I come home from school there is an upright piano in our living room. When I said it, I was not even sure I meant it; after all, in Iran I had stopped going to lessons, and last week was the first time in months that I had even thought of playing the piano. But later that night I heard Mama talking to Baba on their living-room mattress, saying that I needed a piano and that they couldn't take everything away from me; and then, all of a sudden, I really wanted one.

Now I sit down and piece together a song I memorized just before I stopped my lessons. I play through it slowly, my fingers remembering more than my head does. I hadn't realized how much I missed playing the piano. The more I play, the more it comes back to me. When it's over I turn around and see Mama sitting on the couch. She tells me that hearing that song makes her want to cry.

I want to cry sometimes too, especially when I walk home from school, hoping against hope that I will see our red car in the driveway. That is the car Mama drives. Baba has bought a used yellow Datsun to drive to work, and I never expect to see his car in the daytime. But I hate walking down the hill and rounding the corner with all my fingers crossed only to come upon an empty driveway and a dark house. Sometimes I go over to Tanya's, whose mother is always home; other times Ali and I make pots of Top Ramen soup and watch *Three's Company* reruns while we wait for Mama to arrive with Sufi, who spends the day at day care. But the house never feels like home until Mama gets there.

None of us talk much about how our life used to be. We are no longer missing it together. Sufi has forgotten all the Farsi she once knew. She meets the pack of little blond girls on our block at the same time they meet each other, her friends call our father Baba because they think that is his name, and as they pick strawberries or build snowmen on the front lawns, she does not compare her life with the one she used to have. Ali and I have more to hang on to; he with his soccer-player letters and his second-grade Farsi book, and I with my photographs of the Dars and of our old cat and dog. But even though I know Ali misses Iran and he knows I do, there is not much to say beyond that. Ali joins the school soccer team and starts taking Spanish. I make new friends, and I love our dog Hedwig, who follows me to school and runs up to greet me when I get home. I look for things that approximate what I am missing, and slowly the new things start to replace the old.

I think Mama and Baba are too worried about money to miss Iran. Every night they lie awake trying to decide what to do with the little money they brought out. They have already used part of it for the down payment on our house. Another chunk has gone for food and clothes. When Mr. Tehrani, an Iranian we met at Timber Creek, calls to ask if we want to go fifty-fifty on a rental property, Baba cheers up. Tehrani is a real estate agent who's lived in Portland for years and knows what to buy. At the last minute Mama panics and doesn't want to sign the papers. Her voice gets high and tense and she reminds Baba about how Aziz always said not to trust people with black hair and blue eyes like Tehrani has. But she can't think of a better reason than that, so she signs her name and two apartments along the Beaverton-Hillsdale highway become half ours.

One day Mama comes home from the supermarket with a copy of *Working Woman*. "Job of the Month," says the cover: "Welder." The blond woman in the picture has a welding mask around her neck and a big smile on her face. "She supports the whole family with her welding," the caption says.

Mama quits her job changing people's sheets and enrolls in a welding class at Portland Community College. Her classmates are prison inmates in rehab. Her teacher has a Ph.D. in history. On the first day of class he stops in front of every desk to show the students his eyes—milky white in the middle—and warns that that is what will happen to people who forget to pull down their masks.

Mama doesn't paint or play the guitar anymore, although she still has the radio on all the time. When she's not at welding school I try to go with her on errands as often as I can. After school I wait, watching cars until I see the Chevy's square headlights coming down the street. I climb into the front seat beside Mama and the two of us drive around, singing along with Supertramp or REO Speedwagon, making stops at the supermarket or the drugstore or the bank. Driving with her, I don't feel alone, and if we're stuck in traffic with the rain soaking the front windshield and the heater air blowing on our faces as I tell her about my day, so much the better.

On weekends we go to D.J.'s Sound City at the Washington Square Mall. I go to the back of the store, where one wall is covered with forty-fives of the week's hit singles, and Mama goes to the large record bins to find the records of people she used to sing backup with in Los Angeles. But to me, none of these singers or bands can match Mama. I have both her albums on my shelf at home, and every time we go to D.J.'s I look her up in the big yellow catalogue of records in print. Her name is there, in block letters, with her two albums listed underneath, and it always reassures me to see it. I have something no one else has—a mother who is a singer—and even though she is in welding school right now, her name is printed right here in this yellow book of singers, to prove it.

❖

It rains and rains. All the girls at school have reversible raincoats with matching umbrellas. I get a set too and I don't mind the rain, but Baba says this weather makes him feel dead. I don't want to have to move again, so whenever the sun pokes through the clouds I hurry to point it out, as if it's been there all along. But one sunny day in May we walk out of a movie and the sky is filled with mysterious white flakes. Mount St. Helens has erupted, says the radio announcer, and it's raining ashes. Baba frowns and mutters something about lung cancer and drives us all to the drugstore for surgical masks.

At school we have a lecture about volcanoes. Afterward my teacher calls me up to her desk. "Afsaneh doesn't speak English," she says, pointing at a thin-faced girl with long hair who just arrived today. "She's from Iran. I had her put in our class so you two could talk. Maybe you could stay after school and give her a little extra help."

"Sure," I say, nodding so that Afsaneh will see that I am agreeing. She stares back with a blank, new-girl expression.

The next day I sit in the back of the classroom with her and explain how to spell "cat" and "rat" and "fat" in English. After each word she gives a tiny nod and then lowers her head, as if curling down far enough could make her disappear into some other world.

I don't ask her about that world. I don't ask her if she misses it as much as I did when I arrived here with my suitcase full of pictures and keepsakes. It's not that I don't still miss Iran, but I'm sure that what I miss is different from what she misses—I miss my life there and she misses hers. We didn't go to the same school and we didn't know the same people, and I don't know what exactly we would talk about if we did talk about Iran. Anyway, after what Frank McClaskey said I am not about to start speaking Farsi in front of everyone.

Go over and say hi, Baba used to say when we were traveling in Iran and he spotted a little girl selling corn by the side of the road or a foreign girl playing alone by the fountain at a hotel. *I'm sure she wants to play with you; go tell her your name.* I used to do what he said. Now, however, I stay far away from Afsaneh. It's not that I don't feel sorry for her being lonely—I do. And yet I know it's temporary. Sooner or later someone will teach her how to dress and cut her hair, just as my friends in Cedar Hills taught me. But that someone is not going to be me. It will be a girl who has lived here all her life, a girl so American that making friends with foreigners could never make her look foreign herself.

Baba can spot a fellow countryman in any disguise. "He's Iranian," he says, pointing at a stocky man standing in front of a hotel in a maroon uniform and cap. I roll my eyes—this could take ages—but I follow Baba across the street.

The man is about sixty, with wavy gray hair neatly combed away from his forehead. He is staring glumly at the cars going by, but when Baba says, "*Salaam, hale-shoma-chetoreh?*"—Hi, how are you?—his face lights up.

He shakes Baba's hand and starts asking him eager questions in Farsi. What is your name? When did you come? 1979. They both nod—that's the year everyone came—and they fall into a long conversation about someone the man knows who has almost the same last name as us.

Some women walk out of the hotel and the man hurries to open the door for them, stepping back with a click of his heels. He looks down at his uniform, then at Baba. "I was the Vice-Minister of Tourism under the Shah," he says, standing up a little straighter. "In Iran a car and driver came to my house for me every morning. Now I sleep on my daughter's couch, and I have gotten this little job to keep my head warm."

Baba shakes his head sympathetically. He points to Mama and Sufi, who are two blocks up looking at shopwindows. "We have to go," he says. "*Khasteh nabasheed.*" Don't be tired.

"God take care of you," the man answers.

We have come across other men like that—security guards and sandwich vendors in their fifties or sixties who hardly speak English and who always tell us what their positions were before the revolution. Mama asks Baba if it isn't dangerous for them to be telling everyone they were the directors of companies or government ministers under the Shah—what if some Iranian revolutionaries come to America looking for them? But Baba says they were probably not high up enough back then for anyone to go after them now. And who even knows if it is true? Any old Iranian guy could say he was a minister under the Shah—none of it matters much now that they are all warming their heads in the lobbies of fancy hotels.

Other Iranians we meet are full of gimmicks to get rich. Most of them, like Mama and Baba, have gotten a little money out of Iran and they can't rest until they do something with it. Everyone is sure they'll be millionaires if they just invest the right way. Coming up with plans, they have the feverish passion of gamblers with only one shot at the table.

Jamsheed's restaurant isn't doing very well, but he and his wife have lots of ideas for pulling in customers. They tell us excitedly about how they are going to put a well in the middle of the room so customers can draw their own drinking water. And a hook on the wall that says, "Tie your camel here." And signs on the seats that say, "Watch your ass." ("You get it?" his wife says. "It's an American expression.") But each new idea for the restaurant is replaced by another one before they have time to carry it out.

Massi buys a truck-stop diner from the real estate man, Mr. Tehrani. She and her daughters wake up at four in the morning to make eggs and sausages and pancakes from industrial-size boxes of batter mix. Massi looks pale and haggard, nothing like the glamorous aunt I knew in Iran. "See how well they speak with the customers," she whispers, pointing at her daughters, who are waiting tables, and it's true; they take the breakfast orders in impeccable diplomat's English with just a hint of foreignness, then repeat the order in Farsi. "Mommy!" twenty-two-year-old Shireen yells. "*Yek* Western omelet *o ye* side of bacon!" The truck driver sitting in front of her stares up as if some willowy, exotic creature has wandered in off the highway.

Baba and an Iranian man named Behnam come up with a plan to go around and paint people's addresses on their curbs in fluorescent paint so visitors looking for houses at night will find them more easily. Behnam, a talkative man with a bushy beard, goes from door to door, and after a couple of hours he has a list of housewives who have given him contracts to paint their curbs. "All we need to do now is buy the supplies," he tells Baba. But Baba points out that for once it is a beautiful day, and they decide to play a few sets of tennis first. By the end of their game it is dark and they never get around to painting.

Zia finds another scheme to get by in America. He parks outside our house and hammers on our door to tell us. "Free cheese!" he cries. "They're giving away free cheese! On the souls of my children, it's free to refugees, can you believe it? *We're* refugees!" He comes into our house and pats Baba on the back. "Free cheese!" he yells, in English this time, and I am scared his voice will seep through the walls and carry out into the neighborhood.

"Ready?" Zia says exuberantly, as if they're going to Las Vegas for the weekend.

"I'm not going," Baba says. "We don't need it."

"Nonsense," Zia says. "Of course you do." He has one foot wedged in the front door as if to keep it from shutting the free cheese out. "What's the matter with you?"

"I'll go," Mama says, pulling on her coat. She comes home with a foot-long block of Tillamook cheddar. Baba says he doesn't want any, but when she makes broccoli with cheese sauce he eats it along with the rest of us.

Mama says welding school is too depressing. She drops out and decides to write a book instead. Setting up a typewriter at the dining-room table, she writes a novel about an American woman married to an Iranian architect in the last days of the Shah. An agent in New York agrees to represent her if she will put in one sex scene per chapter. So the book becomes a circus of encounters—the wife cheats on the husband, the husband picks up prostitutes in revenge, the husband's niece is murdered by her brother after he discovers her secret lover. The husband and wife finally reconcile, but just as they are about to leave for America he is arrested by revolutionaries—an arbitrary arrest; they have confused him with someone else. While he is in jail the husband and wife make spiritual connections—she wills his release, and at that very moment his captors tell him they are going to release him. But they come back to his cell at midnight. He is executed in the dark courtyard; she wakes up screaming.

Mama's agent says a publisher is interested in the book. He wants to know if Mama will go on TV and say it's true. She tells him no.

These things did not happen to us and it feels like bad luck to say they did. So the manuscript sits around our house, with the title, "Paradise of Fools," typewritten across the front. I take it into my room and can't put it down. I hate Los Angeles, where the wife goes on vacation and meets her stupid American lover; I hate how she thinks that just by being in a different place she can wipe out her real life. I hate the mother and children for leaving Iran and flying back to America after the father dies. I hate them because I cannot separate them from us. The house they live in is our old house, the hotel where the husband takes the prostitutes is the hotel across the park from us. I know it has all been made up by Mama, with the juicy bits added by a neighbor from down the street who used to sit at the table giggling with her. But it is hard to tell where the truth stops, and late at night I cannot keep dark thoughts from creeping in. What if my parents had not always been so loyal to each other? What if our life had really fallen to pieces like that?

When I finish the last chapter at two in the morning, I am cold with fear. We could easily have gone to pick Baba up at Los Angeles International and learned he was not on the plane. "Flight snowed in," he might have wired. "Coming tomorrow." But there would not have been a flight the next day or the next week or the week after, because once the Shah left, the airport closed. Or maybe he wouldn't have wired us; maybe he wouldn't have had time before the revolutionary *komiteh* came looking for someone to arrest and ran into Baba and took him away because we were not there to warn him or hide him or save him.

I slip out of my bedroom and go down the hall to where my parents are sleeping. My room is not the master bedroom anymore. A few months ago, Baba woke up on the living-room floor and said, "This is ridiculous." He doubled Ali and Sufi up and gave me the smallest room. I felt relieved—it is much more normal to have parents in the big bedroom, and tonight, when I open its door, I am glad they are there.

The hall light spills onto their bed and I strain to see both their shapes under the covers.

"What's wrong?" Mama's sleepy voice cuts through the darkness. Suddenly my tears are flowing and I climb into the bed.

Baba strokes my hair. "Tara-*e* sweet." His hand is gentle, and I cry even harder when I hear the Farsi way he speaks English. No American father talks like this.

They don't ask me what is wrong and I don't tell them, but I stay in their bed, sobbing more each time I think of all my bad thoughts. I think of how I wanted the neighbor fathers as my own. I think of how last week when Baba and I were fighting, I asked Mama in front of him to get a divorce. His hand is resting on my head now and I wonder if he remembers that. He must have thought I hated him.

"It's okay," Mama says softly. But it is not okay. I don't want another father. I don't want Mama to have a new husband and I don't want Baba to go away. But I can't say these things because I am already embarrassed to be crying so much; so I stay quiet, and slowly my breathing falls in with my parents' and we drop off to sleep.

A week later, Baba and I are fighting again.

"Tomorrow is Shireen's wedding," he says at dinner.

"I told Lisa I'd spend the night," I say.

He frowns. "Why did you make plans on the day of Shireen's wedding?"

"Well, that's all right," Mama says. "If she'd rather go to Lisa's she can skip the wedding."

"No, she can't. This is my family and she is a part of it. What am I going to tell them—that she'd rather go to her friend's house?"

"Tell them I have homework."

"I am not going to tell them that."

"Why not? They don't care if I come anyway."

"Of course they care," Baba says. "*I* care. Why don't you want to see my family?"

"Because they're rude and obnoxious and they don't know how to act."

"*You're* the one who doesn't know how to act! *You're* rude. You just sit there when they're here and you don't talk. They think there's something wrong with you. When we went to the store with Massi the other day she asked me if you were sad. She wanted to buy you candy. What am I supposed to tell her? That you don't want to see her?"

I don't want candy. I want relatives who speak English. I want to be like other kids, whose parents and uncles and aunts know how to get by in this country.

The next day Mama buys me a powder-blue dress with tiny pearl buttons. When we get home I pull on a pair of her nylons and slip into my wedge-heel rope sandals and stand in front of the mirror with my hair pulled back, considering how grown-up I look.

In Massi's apartment, we drop our coats onto a pile of damp coats in the corner of the living room. We don't know most of the guests; they are the groom's family, and they are dressed in fancy suits and dresses that make the apartment look even smaller and shabbier than usual. My slim, spaniel-eyed cousin Shireen is dressed in a plain white cocktail dress with her long dark hair pinned up at the sides and hanging loose down her back. She is sitting cross-legged in front of the *sofreh*, the big cloth laden with flowers and candles that Iranian brides and grooms sit in front of to be married. When she sees us she jumps up. "I've been waiting for you!" she says, tilting her cheek so we can kiss her. "Look at my ring. Purest gold." She drops it into Mama's hand. "Feel how heavy."

"He's a doctor," Massi tells us in an awed voice, although she already told us this before. "Mr. Tehrani introduced us. He has his Ph.D. from the University of Texas, and now he's applying for a job at Berkeley or Stanford." Her hushed voice sounds like the voices of people in Iran when they would tell us that their son was going to boarding school in England or that their new chair was an exact replica of the chair the Shah's sister was sitting on in such and such picture, the chair itself a copy of something French.

Although we are not supposed to know this, Baba told us that after the revolution Massi and Zia went to see Shireen in Ohio, where she was going to college, and found out that she had a boyfriend there. They were not prepared for this. They had sent Shireen to college in the hopes that afterward she would return home and meet a rich Iranian from a good family who would buy her a fancy house in North Tehran near Massi and Zia's own new home. When they learned that their daughter had fallen for an American who worked at a local radio station, Massi cried for days. Zia cried too, and finally Shireen herself cried and agreed to go with them to Oregon.

Zia is not here now; he went back to Iran a couple of months ago to try to sell some of the property they left behind and bring some money back. Jamsheed is not here because he doesn't approve of the doctor. He said Zia is not going to approve either, when he gets back, but Massi shushed him and told him he didn't have to come if he was going to make trouble.

I'm not sure why Jamsheed doesn't approve of the doctor, but I know I wouldn't want to marry him. He is old—around forty—with bowed legs and tinted eyeglasses and a perpetual grin. I don't know his name; everyone just calls him "Doctor." That's an Iranian custom—calling people "Doctor" or "Professor" or "Colonel," as if the titles they've acquired have overridden the names they were born with. In Portland, where there are hardly any Iranians and nobody knows anyone else's family, the word "doctor" is at least something to grab on to. Shireen was destined to marry a doctor, and so we are standing in the Timber Creek Apartments to witness it, although the grand wedding she would have had in Iran has had to be scaled down in light of everything.

"For the time being they'll work at the restaurant," Massi explains. "It will be more of a family business than ever. I'll cook, Shireen will serve, and Doctor will run the cash register—until he gets his position at the university."

A mullah comes and reads verses in Arabic and asks Shireen three times if she wants to marry Doctor. The first two times she doesn't answer, because the bride is not supposed to be too eager. The third time, she says yes. Doctor, sitting straight-backed in his satin shirt, tight vest, and wide tie, answers yes right away. The women scream "*lulululululululu*" in high voices and everyone runs up to kiss Shireen, who is still staring down at the Qoran, her face silvery with eye shadow and rouge, her right hand twisting her gold ring around and around.

"*Bah, bah*, what a pretty girl!" A short lady I've never seen digs red fingernails into my cheek and draws my face toward her. "Soon it will be your turn to get married, *enshallah*, to such a husband."

"Yes, God willing," says another lady. "What is your name? Are you Shireen's sister? How old are you?"

"Thirteen."

"Oh, but you're not. You are not thirteen."

"Yes, I am."

"No, with those shoes, she looks older," the first lady says disapprovingly.

"A thirteen-year-old child does not paint her lips." I press my lip-glossed lips together as the second lady reaches an arm out and runs her hand down the front of my blue dress, over my new training bra. "She's probably the same age as Pooya."

I back away toward the edge of the room. I grab the bathroom doorknob but it is locked, so I stay back near the damp coats, letting the hum of Farsi swirl around my head. I haven't spoken Farsi for months, and talking to those ladies felt like I had rusty machinery in my mouth. I whisper the words to myself to be ready if they ask me again—*"Chera, hastam,"* "but yes, I am"—but the two ladies have returned to the crowd, where everyone is kissing the bride and groom. Doctor grins as a slight frown puckers his forehead. Shireen smiles hard as her eyes wander over the heads of the guests. She spots me and gives a little wave, but at that moment the bathroom door clicks open and a woman comes out. I slip inside, lock the door, and lean up to the mirror.

Soon it will be your turn to get married to such a husband. I watch my mouth form the words sarcastically in the mirror, my face scrunched up and wrinkled like the woman who said them. She is wrong. I would never get married to such a husband. I would just let my parents cry.

Baba comes home from work and says the guy sitting next to him fell off the dam.

"One minute he was sitting there beside me with his hammer; the next minute his rope broke and he was gone."

"How far up?" Ali asks.

"Pretty far," Baba says. "He died."

Mama turns pale. She already wants him to quit, ever since he told us about one of the carpenters having a bumper sticker on his car that says, "I don't brake for Iranians." Does he know you're Iranian? she asked, and Baba laughed and said that every day in the lunch hall a radio host talks about the hostages, keeping track of "Day 178" or "Day 293" or whatever day it is. If Baba walks in while that show is on, every single head turns to look at him. But he's got his friends, other apprentices whom he eats lunch with and who invite him to come smoke pot behind the woodpiles, although he says he would never risk losing his job like that.

After the carpenter dies Mama calls her book agent and says she will go on TV. It's worth lying a little, she says, if she can make enough money so that Baba can quit his job. But the agent never calls back. So she looks for a new job, and a few weeks later she is back at Portland Community College, teaching Vietnamese refugees how to say things like "refrigerator" and "dustpan" and "my mouth is on my face."

Baba doesn't quit, but he gets a week off at Christmas and we drive down to L.A. to visit our grandparents. When we get there, Ali and Sufi and I head straight for the kitchen, which is stocked with all the foods we can't afford, like pineapple-coconut juice, avocados, Campbell's Chunky soup, and Häagen-Dazs raspberry sorbet. We carry plates of it into Grandma and Grandpa's bedroom and watch cable TV in color, running outside every now and then to jump in the pool. Grandpa is at work all day, but Grandma plays us songs on the piano and tells us tragic stories about composers who died in shipwrecks. She drags out a big wooden game board and teaches us to play crokinole, which she used to play when she was little. She also sets aside a special day for each kid, and on my day we go out to lunch and to Bullock's department store. "Pick out anything you like, darling," she says, and I get the suede Cherokee sandals I've wanted for months.

Los Angeles is full of Iranians who came after the revolution. You can tell they brought a lot of money out of Iran, because they live in big houses in Beverly Hills and drive around in fancy cars. The year before the revolution, when we came for Mama's album, I did not see a single Iranian here. But now, each time we drive down to visit our grandparents there are more of them. The last time we came we were walking down Westwood Boulevard when we spotted a café with Farsi writing on the sign. We couldn't believe it; it was like a sliver of Iran from out of nowhere. The café is still here now and so are a new Iranian bookstore and a grocery store that sells expensive pistachios. In fact, Westwood is getting so full of Iranians that they've given it a nickname—"Tehrangeles." I don't like it. I don't like the clumps of Iranian girls dressed in Gloria Vanderbilt jeans, holding little black purses with gold-chain straps, and I don't like the café, which is overpriced and full of dressed-up Iranians with nothing better to do in the middle of the day than sit on wrought-iron chairs and drink tea. They all say hi to each other and not to us, and I wonder if they think we're just Americans wandering in off the street. I don't care if they do. I know that this is not like the real Iran. In the real Iran this would be a pastry shop, and a scruffy-faced man in a blue tunic would shovel fresh raisin cookies into a box and let Sufi put her finger on the knot of the string when he tied it. But even though it's not like that here, Baba loves Tehrangeles. He spends hours in the Farsi bookstore, talking to the men behind the counter and buying books in Farsi that he could never find in Portland.

We drive to Hollywood to show Baba the house we lived in when Mama made her second album. When we get there I recognize the long, flat doorbell ringer that I kissed goodbye on the day we left to go back to Iran. It is strange to think that that was only three years ago. Ali and I were so excited about America in those days. Everything fascinated us—the Sears catalogues, the machine that made wax zoo animals, the Chewy-Louies from the liquor store—silly things that we can find anywhere now. When I look back on how we spent three whole months on this boring little street when we could have been living our old life in Iran, it all seems like a thoughtless mistake.

❖

My friend Lisa's father is also foreign, but he is Danish, which seems to be the opposite of Iranian. Nils is tall and silver-haired, and he tells silly jokes that make me and Lisa roll our eyes. He has a foreign accent, but it is a wispy Scandinavian one, which is not embarrassing. His voice is never loud and he never gets mad about money.

"So," he says in his lilting voice when I am over there on a Friday night, "are you two gals coming to Mount Hood with me tomorrow?"

"No, thanks, Daddy," Lisa says.

"Why not?" I say quickly. "Don't you like skiing?"

"I'm sick of it."

I wonder how anyone can be sick of skiing. I have only been skiing once, on a trip with Community School. Fifty fifth graders were drawn from a hat to go on the trip, and we drove high up into the mountains and broke a trail through deep snow to get to an unheated cabin where we rolled out sleeping bags and sang "Tavern in the Town" and "Cider Through a Straw" to keep warm.

"Ah, you like to ski, Tara?" Nils's voice is as silvery as his hair. "Careful, Lisa, maybe I'll take your friend skiing if you don't want to go."

"Come on," I beg. "It'll be fun."

So, grumbling, Lisa pulls out two sets of scarves and gloves and ski pants and finds me a pair of her brother's old skis. Nils packs it all into his silver car and the next morning we are off.

On top of a ridge, in the middle of a snowstorm, I glide behind him. I rub my eyes, hardly able to see, but as soon as Nils looks back and bares his teeth I turn my skis straight downhill, ready to follow as fast as he goes. At the end of the run I stop, breathless and elated, and wait for Lisa to come down and ride the chair back up with me. "We shouldn't have come," she groans as we sway high over the rocks, the wind whipping sharp pinpricks of snow into our faces. But I am in love with this chair and this cable and these jagged rocks, and I wish Mama and Baba could see me and see what things I do when I am away from them.

It is not just skiing that I love. It is also the feeling that skiing gives me. It doesn't matter that I am not a great skier. Just being on the slope, with the lift ticket wired to my old fifth-grade jacket and my feet buckled into Lisa's brother's blue-and-red skis, I feel as if I belong to a world of silvery accents, as if there is no difference between me and the other skiers who glide smoothly by me down the mountain. Just being here is enough to make me belong.

In the spring, I drag Lisa to ballet classes, and our parents take turns driving us. I used to take ballet when I was little, and I like doing the same exercises I learned so long ago in Tehran from a teacher with wild black hair who had a Russian accent and an aura of having danced long ago on a now vanished stage. But Lisa doesn't like ballet as much as I do. She quits after a few months and then Baba has to drive me on his own.

"How was ballet?" he asks as I open the door of his yellow car.

"Good," I say. Tonight I have to ask him for a check for the next month of classes, which I hate doing.

"You know," he says, "I think it's great that you take ballet. You've always been a good exerciser. Remember when I used to take you to ballet class in Iran? With your teacher who was a Russian?"

I perk up, thinking this would be a good time to ask for the check. But Baba keeps talking.

"Do you remember when I would come pick you up in our Mercedes?"

I nod, suddenly remembering. We only had that car briefly, when I was seven; an elegant black 1951 sedan with wide running boards and a long, shiny hood. Baba bought it on a whim, a deviation from the more practical cars we owned before and afterward. The backseat was forest green, and Ali and I used to sit on it and stroke it like a large velvet animal.

"I should never have sold it," Baba says. "I should have shipped it here."

We should have shipped everything, I think. Other people I know, even those who moved a lot, still have their first shoes, their little wooden boxes of baby teeth, their cloth animals the same age as they are. Sometimes I try to remember what things we would have brought here if we had had more time and more room. My old stuffed rabbit. The books that Ali and Sufi and I illustrated and Mama sewed together with thread. And what else? By now there must be things I don't remember. But Baba does not usually talk about what we have lost, and it is strange to hear him bring up that old car.

"Baba?" I say as he pulls into our driveway.

"What?"

"I have to pay for ballet tomorrow."

He turns off the car. The wipers freeze in mid-sweep and the rain patters on the windshield. "How much?"

"A hundred and twelve dollars." I say it quickly, miserably, hoping he will not notice it is more than last month.

He doesn't say anything. He pulls the keys out of the ignition and ducks his head down as he runs into the house. I grab my bag and run in after him.

Mama is heating up spaghetti in the kitchen.

"Mom," I say, "I need to pay for ballet."

"Get a check from Baba."

"It's supposed to be eighty something," he says from the living room.

"Well, I have to go four times a week now. You have to take four classes to go on pointe."

"You're going on pointe?" Mama says, in an impressed voice. "How much more is it?"

"Too much," Baba's voice calls out.

"Mom?"

"Essie," she says, "it's important to her."

He comes into the kitchen. "Everything is important to her. Why does she have to do everything everyone else does?"

"I was like that too," Mama says. "When I was her age I wanted the things my friends had, and then when I got older I grew out of it."

"*Akh,*" Baba says, disgusted. "Where do you think all this money is coming from? You know, when Zia found out what I'm spending this money on he told me I'm crazy."

I know Zia and the other relatives think it's Mama's Americanness that makes us spend money on a house in the West Hills when Beaverton and Tigard are so much cheaper, or on my ballet classes—for what? Not to help me get a job or be marriageable.

"Zia's right, you know," Baba says. "To borrow money from my sister's son and then use it for this crap."

"Okay," Mama says. "Let's not—"

"What do those guys know anyway?" I yell, turning down the hallway to my room. "They married their daughter off to someone for money and they even screwed that up."

It's true. After four months of the Doctor working at their restaurant without finding a real job, Zia finally returned from Iran and called the University of Texas. The school's records showed he had dropped out in his first semester. There must be some mistake, the Doctor insisted, but Massi and Zia had heard enough. They kicked him out of the house and had to go to court to stop him from taking away half the wedding presents.

It never would have happened in Iran. There, they could not have met this man in a void; relatives and friends would have checked up on him, found out who his family was, and helped make the decision. Some friend of the family or enemy of the Doctor who knew he was not what he claimed to be would have come forward. But in America you can meet someone out of the blue and all you know is what he tells you.

I try to come up with a way to pay for the extra ballet class on my own. I can't get a job because I am still fourteen. Babysitting pays one dollar an hour, and the people on my block don't go out often enough to pay for the class every week. Mama and Baba have almost no money now that neither one of them is working. Mama has started law school—so she can finally, as she puts it, get a real job. Baba finally decided carpentry was too dangerous after one of his co-workers was smothered inside a form being filled with concrete. He is looking for an architecture job, but he says the timber industry is in a depression and nothing is being built. In the meantime, Grandpa is paying the mortgage on our house and we are on food stamps. I would die if any of my friends found out, but Mama is always careful to check that no one we know is in the supermarket before she takes them out of her purse. In fact, the only time anyone we know sees our food stamps is when Mama goes down to Social Services to pick them up and runs into her old Vietnamese and Cambodian students in line.

Since Baba doesn't have a job, he has been spending his time keeping up the repair work on the apartment we bought with Mr. Tehrani. That is, until the bank calls to say that Tehrani, who was supposed to be using the rent money to pay the mortgage, has not paid it for the last six months. He is nowhere to be found and the lender is threatening to foreclose. Mama and Baba show their contract to a lawyer and it turns out that since Tehrani is not here they cannot sell the apartment. The foreclosure is going to cost thousands of dollars, and the lawyers' fees to transfer the responsibility to Tehrani will cost thousands more.

If I ever see Mr. Tehrani again I will denounce him in front of everyone in Portland. In my perfect American accent I will describe how he stole our money, lied to Shireen about the Doctor, and sold Massi a failing restaurant that it turned out he had just repossessed from another newly arrived Iranian family. Someday I want to make enough money to pay off all of Mama and Baba's debts and buy them a house with a swimming pool, where Mama will paint and play her guitar and Baba will play tennis and read poetry, just like they were going to do in Shahrak. But until then I need Baba to pay for my ballet lessons. He reaches slowly for his checkbook, hesitating before he writes the amount on the line. I say thank you, and I hope he can tell from my small voice how much I mean it.

Eventually, Baba borrows money from me. Over the winter of ninth grade I get a rush of babysitting jobs and save up a hundred and fifteen dollars. He comes into my room one night, asks how much I have, and promises to pay me back as soon as he gets a job. But even giving him all my money does not insure me against moving again. When my parents start talking about going to California, I panic. I've just started high school and I've thrown myself passionately into it— choir, drama, dances, soccer matches—striving to capture the blissful stability of my friends whose families have always lived here and would never leave. My friends hate school, but I secretly love it. I even get up and go to class when I am sick, already foreseeing the time when I might be far away and yearning for these precious days.

In the meantime, I try to talk my parents into liking Portland.

"You should really go visit the neighbors," I say, hoping they will make friends and want to stay.

"Only three more years and I'll be done with school," I remind them, hoping to hold them off just long enough for me to graduate.

"Look," I say, passing a magazine around the breakfast table. "This article rates California as the second-worst school system in the United States."

I even make up statistics. "You know, psychologists say high school is the worst time to move a child." It sounds reasonable, and I think I see the deepening of a worry line in Mama's face when I say it.

"We'll do our best," she says. But her words do not soothe me; they are heavy with resignation and guilt over the fact that I'll soon be made sad.

I threaten to run away. I cry. I run for sophomore class secretary, although I have no interest in student politics; I figure that if I win I will have no choice but to stick around to fill the post. I convince Lisa's mother to let me live with them until the end of high school. I pray for the sunny days Baba loves, and I keep an eye out for nearby open houses in the wild hope that perhaps just changing houses can satisfy the moving requirement that the fates keep pressing on me.

But in the end it is not the rain or even the perpetual shroud of anxiety that finally makes us leave Portland. We leave because we have run out of money, and nothing I say can change that. "We have to give the piano back," Mama says. I can't argue; the piano men come and carry it out the door. When our neighbor Mrs. Shoemaker sees this she tells me I can come over and play hers whenever I like.

Early one morning Baba comes into my room to kiss me goodbye. I have been awake for a while, listening to him get ready, but when he walks in I pretend to be asleep. He is leaving and I should hug him, but we haven't hugged in so long that it would be embarrassing. So I stay still as he kisses my forehead and walks out. The front door opens and clicks shut and I push aside a corner of the curtain and watch his yellow car back slowly down the driveway.

Down in the street it pauses for a moment, suspended, as if it wants to boomerang back up to the house. Then it starts up the street and disappears behind Mrs. Shoemaker's trees. A knot of tears sticks in my throat.

I didn't know that day that Baba had only sixty dollars that he'd borrowed from Jamsheed to drive down to California. I didn't know that he didn't want to leave and that Mama actually had to push him into the car at the top of the driveway. But I knew that since we had left Iran something in him had become fragile. And I knew that people could be mean to him; I knew this because I had been mean myself. And I was afraid that that thing inside him would become even more fragile now that he was going out into America alone, without us to translate for him.

❖

On a hot day in August, the four of us pile into the Chevy and start driving down Highway 5, right behind Baba, who is driving the

U-Haul. Through the whole ride down I manage to keep out the thought that we are leaving Portland, but when we pull up to our new house in Palo Alto, I burst into tears.

"It's stucco," I sob. "You promised it wouldn't be."

"It's not stucco," Mama says in a pleading voice. "It's plaster."

"It's the same thing. You promised."

That was the concession Mama gave me during one of my fits of misery before we left. I said I was sure in California the school would have a fence around it and the houses would be made of stucco. I hate stucco, I told her. It's ugly, it's crummy, and no house in Oregon has it.

"It's just a rental," Mama says, her voice edged with exhaustion. "Come on, it's not so bad. Look at what a nice street this is, right by a park. Just like our house in Portland."

"It's *nothing* like our house," I say, aching for our tree-lined cul-de-sac, the blackberry patches down by the creek, and the lazy neighborhood dogs lying in the road.

"Who's that man?" Ali points at a shadow in the window of the stucco house.

"Oh God, it's Bob!" Mama says. "He was supposed to be gone by today." Mama has told us about Bob. When she came down last month to help Baba find a house, an old man was standing on the front porch beside an oversized American flag. He had a white bristly buzz cut and a long rifle in his hand.

"Nice gun," Baba said. Baba likes rifles because they remind him of his childhood hunting trips.

"Yeah," Bob said. "I'm taking it up to Idaho. Too many foreigners moving in around here. Mexicans, Japs, Chinks, Eye-ranians. It's time to move on."

Baba has been mistaken for a Mexican and a Chinese man before. But that day Bob mistook Baba for an American.

Today, though, Mama motions for Baba to stay in the U-Haul. She pulls the Chevy up beside him.

"Don't get out. The tenant's still here. What if he figured out you're Iranian?"

Baba tosses his head. "Come on, we've rented the place. Let's go inside."

"*No*, the landlords said not to go in there until he was out. That would just be the perfect ending—if he shot us just when we'd made it all the way down here." Her voice is verging on hysteria, and Baba throws us a grin to tell us we're not really going to be shot. But just to be sure, we drive to the landlords' house. Ali and I stay in the car and tell Sufi we've driven up to this house to give her away to the Jehovah's Witnesses and that Mama and Baba are inside arranging things. By the time they come out Sufi is wide-eyed with fear, but Mama is calm, although her eyes are red, and she tells us everything is going to be okay.

Mama floats around the stucco house with a look on her face like she's been released from Siberia. Baba carries a chair out to the back-yard and sits there with his shirt off, letting the sun seep back into him. He doesn't care that he has to drive forty-five minutes to work each day. We could have moved to San Jose, where his office is, but Mama says Palo Alto has the best schools around. Baba got a job in Oakland on the first day he got to California just by walking into an architect's office, but the pay wasn't enough to support us. At the end of the summer he applied for a position designing computer facilities and got one of IBM's last guaranteed-till-retirement jobs.

Mama isn't going to go to law school anymore. California is expensive and we need two incomes, she says. She becomes a paralegal and then a real estate agent, and Grandma sends up her old car, a two-year-old Oldsmobile with a sunroof and automatic windows, for Mama to drive her clients around in. We get new school clothes, new bicycles, and a Pong video game that attaches to our TV.

High school here is nothing like it was in Portland, where most people's parents had gone to our school and even had the same teachers we had. Here, almost everyone's parents are divorced, and most of my friends have moved here from somewhere else. I make friends with Pat and Toby, boys who wear leather jackets and eyeliner, and Leslie, a girl who wears black. The four of us roam around the quiet, leafy streets until late into the night, complaining about the smallness of the town. In Portland my friends and I could ride ten minutes on a bus and get off downtown, but Palo Alto is nothing but houses and lawns and a sleepy downtown that is abandoned at night. Walking from one end of town to the other, we reassure ourselves that *we are* not really from here, since all of us have parents who are from some other country or have at least lived abroad.

My parents don't impose many rules about me staying out late or having my friends tap on my bedroom window at all hours of the night. I let them in, and we sit on my bed, making plans to get out of Palo Alto.

"You and I could rent a warehouse in Italy and live in it together and get jobs as waitresses," Leslie says. "Then we could go visit Toby in Germany and Pat in France."

"That sounds great," I say. "But I want to go back to Iran too."

Pat looks up, alarmed. "Are you insane? You'd get killed."

Toby nods. "Pat's right. It's a totalitarian government. You can't go back there."

"It's not as bad as you think," I say. "I could just stay with my grandmother. It would be fine."

Pat gets up to go to the bathroom, and as he is coming back down the hall we see Baba open his bedroom door. "Oh, hi, Pat," he says, rubbing his eyes and slipping past him into the bathroom.

"When you said your dad was from Iran I thought he'd be more hard-core," Toby says. I shake my head. Baba is not like most Iranian fathers. Jamsheed swears he will never let his daughter out of his sight once she is old enough to date, although he is already encouraging his thirteen-year-old son to find a girlfriend. But even when I start going out with Toby, Baba doesn't mind. He says romance is good for everyone.

I'm not embarrassed about Baba being Iranian anymore; I like it. We still have fights about my messy room and my loud stereo, but my family is slowly starting to relax. On weekends we go hiking in the hills together, and Baba's cousins, who live in San Jose, invite us to their weddings and barbecues and Noruz parties. Some of the cousins are my age, and we play volleyball in the garden and eat dinners of *zereshk-polo* or *ghormeh-sabzi*, which I've lately discovered I like.

After a year we buy a small house across from the Children's Theater. We fix it up ourselves. Baba designs a second story and we use Ali's Army Surplus machete to hack through the seventy-year-old plaster. Baba teaches us how to nail up Sheetrock and strip the old paint off the front door. We paint the walls a creamy beige, which is then slashed over with thick pencil lines to mark where the light fixtures are going to go. Then we run out of money, and for a year the front door has no frame, just a rut of raw wood; and the pencil lines don't get painted over. Rain drips into the living room and we tack up shower curtains and push everything to the middle of the floor, and under the new French doors we stuff yellow cottony strips of insulation that lodge invisible glass in our fingers.

And then one day the house is done. Suddenly we can't have Hedwig inside and we can't leave coffee cups on the table or dishes in the sink. "Palo Alto is hot," say the excited real estate agents who drop in, and with the right touches someone might buy our fixed-up house for three times what we paid for it. Even that is not enough to pay off our debts, but it's a start. Mama frames photos of us young and old, in Iran and in America, and to someone walking down along our stairway wall, our life looks deceptively continuous. It is these pictures, Mama says guiltily, that make a doctor couple pay a lot of money for our house. The husband-doctor even asks if he can stroke the bed, and Mama lets him run his fingers over the jade Ralph Lauren comforter that she bought to make the house look good to buyers. Mama says the doctor and his wife have had marriage troubles, but they feel that in this house they will stay together, and that their yet to be born children will come home for the holidays and see their own pictures hanging along the staircase. They do not know that Mama just put our photographs up last week, and they cannot imagine how many pale, shocked, puffy-eyed pictures she had to sort through to find them.

❖

Just after I graduate from high school, Aziz visits. Baba does not trust the Heathrow Airport staff to help her find her gate, so he flies all the way to London to sit beside her for the ride to California. We are excited; seeing her again is like traveling back in time. She seems shorter than before, in her flowery old-lady dress and the thick glasses that turn her eyes into marbles. She hugs me tightly, and as soon as I smell her sweet cardamom scent and feel her warm, soft cheek I realize I have been waiting six and a half years for her kiss.

She has brought Baba the ties from his closet in Tehran. "I know you need these for work," she says. They are seventies ties, ridiculously wide, with bright diagonal stripes, and we hold them to Baba's neck and laugh. But as I stroke the corrugated surface of one of the ties I get a pang of longing, and I wish I could go back to that closet and see the other things we left in Iran. "Couldn't you have brought any of my old handwritten books?" Baba says. Aziz shakes her head; it is too risky to bring old Qorans out of the country, although she has managed to smuggle out a few scraps of her own shakily penned poems against the mullahs. At least the Shah let her keep her children around her, she says, but thanks to this bad-luck regime everyone in her family has run off to America and left her alone.

"You have to make sure she doesn't see Chip," Baba says. My new boyfriend Chip comes over a lot, which is fine with Baba as long as our Iranian relatives don't find out. When Grandma and Grandpa visit from L.A., Chip comes over for dinner and watches TV with us as always, but when Aziz is here I have to whisper to him on the phone, and even when I speak English, and as deaf as she is, I worry that she might catch some inflection and know that I am talking to a boy.

"I have to go to work now," I lie in Farsi.

Aziz reaches her hand out to find me. "You're a very good girl to work so hard," she says, embracing me with her soft arms. I hug her tightly, hating that she thinks I am good.

A little way down the street I climb onto the back of Chip's scooter and we ride off, leaving Ali to help Aziz with her insulin shot and listen to her stories and poetry. "*Mashallah,*" she will say, drawing Ali's head in to kiss him when he places a bowl of hot stew in front of her. He will sit down beside her to talk, his Farsi getting better each day, while I sit on a scooter behind this tall, sandy-haired boy, my arms wrapped around his waist. As the wind whips my hair, I feel a wave of anger. I want to jump off and run home, I want to go help Ali make Aziz's stew, but I don't know how to tell Chip this. Chip keeps saying that since we're going away to different colleges in the fall we have to spend as much time as possible together. I can't really tell him I want to be with my family, because he doesn't have a family;

his father has gone on to a new wife and his mother works late. So we go to his dark, silent house. Chip makes me an omelet and turns on the TV, but all I can think about is how around now Mama and Baba and Sufi will be getting home from work and day care, and how as evening falls they will all sit around the dining table with Aziz, cutting up vegetables for *torshi* and exchanging stories. I feel homesick only blocks from home.

At the end of the summer I start college at Berkeley. My family drives me there to help me move, and Aziz comes upstairs and starts wandering down the dorm hallway. I take a nervous look around, wondering what people will think of this old woman in a scarf, feeling along the wall with her fingers.

"This is a good place," she says when we find my room, a bright, airy one with a view of San Francisco Bay. She hugs me and tells me she is glad I am going to college. "God willing, you will meet a fine Iranian boy here to marry."

I smile, surprised. I don't know any Iranians who aren't my relatives, and anyway, it is far too early for me to think about marrying. But I am glad Aziz said it. It means she still sees me as one of her own, not lost to America. I put my arms around her, adjusting to how small she has become, and I say, "God willing."

The main library on campus has a few books about the Iranian revolution. I start reading, and am surprised to find out how early the *shoolooghi* started. People were protesting in Qom as far back as January 1978, months before we ever noticed a hint of trouble.

By the time we went, like parade spectators, to watch a demonstration, the danger of protesting was over. Many smaller, more timid marches had ended in tanks and soldiers surrounding the marchers and shooting so many people that more protests would take place forty days later, after the proscribed period of Islamic mourning, to commemorate them. That would bring on more soldiers and more shooting and, forty days later, more protests. Baba never took us to the demonstrations that turned into massacres, where schoolchildren soaked notebook paper in pools of blood and held them out as testimony to passersby. But now, reading about it, I learn that Community School was only blocks away from Jaleh Square, where the biggest slaughter took place. Unaware that martial law had been declared early that morning, thousands of people gathered for a peaceful demonstration. The Shah's army surrounded them, firing round after round at the unarmed marchers. That day became known to revolutionaries as Black Friday, and to historians as the turning point. Looking up the date, I am shocked at how early it was. Friday, September 8, 1978. The end of the Iranian weekend. We would have gone to school the next day, our buses still on time, our walled-in community still oblivious to the rest of South Tehran. Our music teacher would have arranged us on risers and passed around a lyric sheet, and there we would have stood, singing "Grease Is the Word" while a few ramshackle blocks away the blood was drying on the asphalt.

By the time we left Iran, ordinary citizens were being dragged from their homes in front of their families and taken before revolutionary committees. Anyone who didn't like someone could whisper that that person was on the side of the Shah or the Americans—a knock on the door would follow. There were no clear rules. They might decide to arrest anyone who had studied in America, or anyone who had married an American, or anyone who had ever played a few games of tennis at the American Embassy, if one of the ball boys decided to make a report. I did not know that, while we were still in Iran, our neighbor had been shot on her balcony while out hanging laundry. I did not know that my second cousin's husband, visiting from Germany, had stepped out of his parents' house just as curfew lifted and had been killed by an anonymous bullet.

Now we hear plenty of details—about what was happening in Iran then and what is happening now. Human rights groups report that young girls in prison are being raped before their executions so they won't die as virgins and go to heaven. They report that as many as 113,000 women were arrested in one year for letting hair stray from underneath their scarves. They report that the torture devices of SAVAK are now being used by the new regime, that people are being stoned to death for adultery; that little boys are being kidnapped off the streets and sent to the war front. Hands are cut off, eyes are gouged out; the lists go on and on.

Jamsheed visits from Portland and tells us that our relatives in Iran are in Dadash's village, hiding from Iraqi bombs. The Iran-Iraq war has been going on ever since the hostage crisis ended. Both sides claim to be winning, although Iranians proudly point out that Iraq has U.S. support while Iran is on its own.

"Don't you wish we were there?" Baba says wistfully, when Jamsheed tells him about the relatives in the village. "I bet it's just like the old days—everyone sitting under the *korsi*, eating pomegranates, telling stories."

"I know," Jamsheed says. "By God, why are we working ourselves to death here? I'd much rather milk cows in the village for the rest of my life."

Of course, neither Baba nor Jamsheed could really go back. Even men their age are being taken away in buses to fight in the war. It's mostly old people and women in the village. The young ones, especially the boys, have to go to more desperate extremes.

"Kamran just got to America," Baba whispers at a barbecue at the home of a distant cousin. He points at a black-haired teenager in a polo shirt and jeans. "They called him for his military service, so his parents got some Baluchis to dress him up in a sheepskin and let him creep over the border with their sheep."

"I heard those Baluchis didn't feed him for days," another guest says in a hushed tone. "His parents hadn't paid them enough. Or they didn't want anyone to see that he ate like a human. For nine days he had to eat grass. Then in Pakistan someone dressed him as a mullah and put him on a donkey, and when anyone stopped them he had to pretend he was deaf or they'd know from his accent that he was Iranian."

I want to ask Kamran about that, but looking at this casual, handsome guy drinking a beer by the swimming pool, I feel shy. I cannot think of what to say to a boy who crawled out of Iran in a fleece and rode out of Pakistan in a turban and a long, cloaklike *aba*.

Soon, though, such stories become common. My seventeen-year-old second cousin has just gotten married when her husband is drafted, so she stashes her wedding gold in the heels of her shoes and the two of them hide in potato sacks in the back of a truck that drops them off in Turkey. They buy fake German passports and convince the Turkish airport officials that they are German students returning to Heidelberg after a vacation. Their interrogators do not speak German; they wave them onto the plane.

Sometimes I try to imagine how I would have been different if there had been no revolution. We would have stayed in Iran. I would have spoken better Farsi and I would have been closer to my relatives. I would have spent my college summers in Iran, seeing old school friends; maybe I would have dated an Iranian. Baba would have liked that. He never says that he'd like me to go out with Iranians, but I suspect it's true, and whenever I bring a boyfriend home from college I am always nervous that the boy will seem too American. Mama and Baba like the guitar player from Argentina because he is like us—he even attended a Buenos Aires version of Community School. But Baba is suspicious of other boys, as if their Americanness is some failed gene that will prevent them from knowing how to treat a girl.

He doesn't like their clothes. Anything more complicated than T-shirts and jeans makes a guy look like he cares too much about himself. The boy with the white button-up shirt and black vest, the boy with the spiked hair and earrings, the boy with the bleached hair and surfer shorts—all get offered beer, and they whisper that they can't believe my dad is so cool. But they don't hear what gets said later.

"Why did he hug Mama the first day he met her?" Baba says, his eyebrows furrowing at the untrustworthy American who hugs you in the beginning but leaves you later.

"Baba doesn't like him because he wears girls' pants," Mama explains another time, half apologetically, but also as if there is some truth about this boy that I am missing.

"Pleated pants are in style," I answer. But after that I cringe each time he wears them.

Even if I wanted to date an Iranian, I never really meet any. The co-op I move into in my sophomore year is known as an anarchistic sixties holdover, and the Iranian parents I know would be appalled by the psychedelic murals and the marijuana-and-incense scent lingering in the hallways. I do see Iranian boys on campus; they tend to run in a pack. Hearing a flash of Farsi at the leafy outdoor terrace of Café Roma, I look up to see five or six of them—long-legged, dark-haired guys gathered around one table, sipping espressos and flirting with pretty freshmen, just as Baba and Jamsheed once did. I try to imagine bringing one home. Would Baba call his gelled hair and cologne *gigolo-ee* like he used to call the men in Iran who wore gold necklaces and shirts unbuttoned to their navels? Or, once the boy sat down and began speaking Farsi intelligently and not in the grunts and pauses Ali and I use with the relatives, would Baba overlook his fancy hair and clothes? The boy would, after all, be familiar to Baba. He would state his father's name, he would say where his father went to high school and what village their family originally came from, and Baba would hand him a beer and start talking about his own Berkeley days.

❖

For Thanksgiving of my senior year my parents and I drive up to Jamsheed's house in Portland. We spend the night in a motel just short of the Oregon border, and the following afternoon Highway 5 lets us out into the old familiar landscape of dark green hills. I went to see my Portland friends a few times in high school, and Baba has flown up for visits, but this is the first time since we moved that Mama has been back here.

"Thank God we got out," she says as soon as we pull off the freeway. She glares at a ridge of trees. "I'm having a flashback; I just got this feeling of terror."

I look up at the sky—varying shades of gray clouds overlying each other above the hills. I guess it could have seemed oppressive for someone who had spent thirty-three years in California and Iran. But when you're fifteen and going to your first high school toga dance the sky isn't the most important thing.

When we get to Jamsheed's he shows us a family picture from before the revolution. I am about ten, with an arm draped over the shoulder of Massi's daughter, Haideh. Jamsheed's son Fereidoon is reaching over to touch Sufi's head, and Ali's arm is linked through the arm of Parviz's daughter. I've never seen this picture before, and it surprises me to see how close we once were, growing together like vines around the family houses of Tehran.

Fereidoon is the cousin closest to my age. He is a dark, skinny boy with a goatee and a little mustache that hides his thin upper lip. "Let's talk about something interesting," he says at dinner. "Let's have a talk about happiness." But mostly we just sit in Jamsheed's living room. From morning to evening we drink tea with cardamom, and by nightfall the caffeine makes me crazy. I go upstairs to write a letter to my boyfriend, Brad, who is traveling in Nepal. Fereidoon follows me in.

"What are you doing?" he says, plopping down on the bed beside me. "Writing a letter? Can I read it?"

"No," I say, scooting away.

He peers over my shoulder and I fold the letter up quickly. *You don't want to end up like Shireen*, my parents always say whenever they remind me not to tell anyone in the family that I have a boyfriend. Shireen, long divorced from Doctor, still lives in Portland, but nobody except her own family ever sees her. "It's probably nothing," Mama says. "I'll bet she's just living with a boyfriend." It wouldn't make any difference to us if this were true, but her family won't say a word about it. If you tell something to one person in the family, everyone will know.

It rains every day. We eat and drink and play backgammon, and Baba and Jamsheed tell stories about their childhood. My cousin Haideh talks about Iran, where she has just been. Massi and Zia moved back to Iran a few years ago, but they still have a house in Portland, and Haideh is staying there now. The plain, overweight cousin I remember has been transformed into a stylish twenty-four-year-old with big black eyes, long hair, and a curvaceous figure. She tells us who has gotten married, who has moved, who is happy and who is not. She gossips dramatically: "I could not *believe* it when I found out; I was *dying*."

Later the two of us talk alone. "You wouldn't last two weeks in Iran," she says. "You'd be *so* bored. You can't do anything if you're a woman. But it is fun to just go visit. Everyone pays a lot of attention to you. When I was there they were trying to *khastegari* me—find me a husband. The boy comes to your house with his parents, or you and your parents go visit them. They tell your parents about their son. Your parents talk about you. You and the boy look at each other. If he's interested, he calls you the next morning and you set up a date to go out."

"A date? I thought you couldn't be caught on the streets with a man who wasn't related to you."

"Oh, well, if they stop you, you tell them what you're doing and they call your parents to make sure they know you're out together."

"So did boys come for you?" I ask.

"Yeah, lots." She fluffs out her hair. "It was nice. They send you presents afterward—flowers, jewelry. I liked that part. And they *always* called the next morning. But I wasn't interested. You see," she says, lowering her voice, "I had a boyfriend."

I lean in, startled and pleased that she is confiding in me. "I was in love with an Arab guy," she whispers. "I used to see him whenever I came to the States. But the last time we got in a fight and then he went back to the Emirates." She sighs, and her dark eyes expand with sorrow. "I'll never see him again," she says, looking down at her hands. Then she looks up at me. "You know, Tara, I think you can only fall in love, really in love, once in your life. After that it's never the same. You know what I mean?"

I don't answer. I am not supposed to know about falling in love. Neither is Haideh, but it is less risky for her. An unattainable suitor in the Emirates cannot ruin a reputation in the same way a real-life boyfriend in Berkeley can.

"So why don't you try to find this guy?" I say. "Why don't you write him a letter?"

"No. It's too late. It just didn't work out."

I want to argue, but I stop myself. She is bowing to fate, and it is not my place to interfere. Instead I ask, "Are you just never going to get married?"

"What? Oh no, I'll get married. In about a year, when I get my degree, I'll go back to Iran and marry one of those guys."

"But you said you could never fall in love again."

"Well, I can't, but that's not the important thing. In Iran lots of people marry people they don't even know. It works out. There aren't many divorces there, not like here. People there learn to love each other."

There is one other guest here from California—Minoo, a friend of Jamsheed's wife. She is in her late thirties, with thick auburn hair cut in straight bangs. She tells animated stories with crescendos and explosions that keep us laughing for hours. But alone in the kitchen, she gets serious with me.

"Taraneh-jan, my son has just started school at Berkeley. I can't tell you how worried I am. I'm so afraid of what kind of girls he will meet."

"Well, I'm sure they're the same kind of girls he'd meet anywhere."

"Yes, but all the things you hear about Berkeley! What if he becomes addicted to drugs? Or gets a disease?"

"Berkeley is very safe," I tell her. "I've lived there four years and I've never had a problem."

"But you must get lonely, living alone. Don't you go home every weekend to your parents? Don't you miss them?"

"Not really. I have a lot of things to do on the weekends."

"But, Taraneh, tell me something." Minoo's eyebrows are knitted together in concern. "How have you managed to survive at Berkeley without becoming a drug addict?"

I laugh. "It's pretty easy, actually. Most people do."

"I can't sleep at night because I am so afraid someone will offer my son a marijuana cigarette."

"Marijuana?" I say in a burst of daring. "But everyone tries that in college. It's not such a big deal."

"Really?" she says, and suddenly I am afraid I have gone too far. What if she asks me if I've tried it? Jamsheed looked shocked the other night when I had a glass of wine. What would he think if he heard me telling Minoo that marijuana was no big deal? *She's been ruined by living alone—she takes drugs and then shames her own father by talking about it.* But Minoo doesn't ask me anything else except for my phone number, in case her son needs advice.

After dinner we make Turkish coffee so Minoo can read our fortunes. I empty my cup and turn it upside down to let the grounds dry into scaly patterns. Jamsheed's cup says he is going to lose money. For the rest of the evening he moans and asks Minoo to read his fortune again, but she won't read anyone twice. My cousin Shapur's cup says he won't get married for ten more years, which devastates him because he is trying to find a wife and has told people in the family to be on the lookout for a pretty Iranian girl. Minoo reads mine and warns that once I get what I've been striving for it might not be what I really want but afterward I will find what I want. Then she looks at my cup again and says, "There is a thin boy with glasses who likes you very much." I stay silent, but Mama laughs, amazed because Minoo is right.

Everyone jumps on Mama. "Really? Is it true? Is there really a boy with glasses?" She doesn't answer, but for the rest of the evening Shapur keeps asking her if there really is a boy with glasses, as if she is the one in charge of my life.

Late that night, when I leave the living room to go to bed, Fereidoon follows me up the stairs. "At last we can talk," he says, shutting the bedroom door behind us. He stands close, looking hard at me, almost touching me. "I want your advice," he finally says.

"About what?"

"My girlfriend," he says. "What should I do about her? I mean, should I sleep with her?"

"Do you want to?" I say, taken aback.

"Yeah! I don't think she's ever slept with anyone before. I mean, I'm sure she hasn't."

He keeps his eyes trained on me and I try to think of something to say.

"Why do you want to sleep with her?" I ask.

"Because she's a virgin!" he says brightly.

"That's a horrible reason, Fereidoon. That shouldn't be the reason you want to sleep with someone."

"You don't understand," he says. "It's a guy thing. It's best for a man if he's the first one, because that way it's really important for the girl. She will always remember you. And physically too, you know, virgins are the best."

I don't answer. He presses on.

"So . . . how old were you when you had your first boy-friend?"

First boyfriend, I think to myself. That's okay. It doesn't mean I slept with him. "Seventeen," I say.

"Well, how did you feel when you first slept with him?"

Well then, he knows. Of course he knows. He's practically grown up in America. This is a new generation. Haideh has had a boyfriend; he probably knows that too. And Fereidoon seems to want to talk so badly.

"I don't know," I say.

"Well, how was it?"

"Okay, I guess."

"What was his name?"

At a loss for a lie, I uncomfortably say the name.

"What?"

I say it again.

Fereidoon starts to show me pictures from his high school yearbook, pointing out girls he once dated, but I can't concentrate.

"I've got to go to bed now," I say, getting up. My stomach churns as I realize what I've just done. I need to get away from Fereidoon, to shut the door against his questions. But he follows me out of the room.

"So who's the guy with glasses?"

I am too concerned to think of a lie. "He's in Nepal."

"Is that who you were writing to?"

Suddenly I feel sorry for Fereidoon's girlfriend. "You know, once you sleep with her she won't be a virgin anymore," I say. "Then what? Are you going to break up with her?"

"No. I'll still be the only one she's slept with. It's girls that sleep with other people that are slutty. I hate slutty girls."

I dash into the bathroom and lock the door.

Driving back to California, we gossip. I tell Mama and Baba about Haideh and her boyfriend. Mama talks about how Fereidoon is searching for someone to talk to.

"I'll say he needs someone," I say. "All weekend he was saying he wanted to talk to me, so last night we talked. He told me about his girlfriend."

"Oh, he has a girlfriend?" Mama says. "What did he say about her?"

I tell them.

"Did he talk about himself the whole time?" Baba asks. "I mean, did he ask you about yourself too?"

"Well, he asked me some things," I say slowly. Should I not tell them? But that is what Fereidoon probably expects me to do, to not tell anyone. So I describe, without much detail, what he asked me.

"What exactly?" Baba says, his voice suddenly serious. "What exactly did you say?" And then: "Why? Why did you tell him that? After all these years of being so careful! How could you forget?"

"It was so late. I was tired. And I don't know, I just figured we were both growing up in America, and that this generation . . ." I trail off, looking for a better explanation. "Well, Haideh told me all that stuff about her boyfriend."

"Haideh is a girl," Mama says. "She was telling you that stuff girl-to-girl. You know she won't tell anybody because she's in the same position."

"You think Fereidoon will tell people?"

"Of *course* he'll tell. He's a pipsqueak. He's got a hot piece of news that no one else knows. Next time he's trying to be cool with Shapur and the guys, he'll let it out."

How could I be so stupid? By tonight Fereidoon will already have told. My head is reeling and I lie back in my seat, grasping for a way to save myself.

"Did you tell him anything else?" Mama asks.

"Well, he asked me who the boy with glasses was, and I said he was in Nepal."

"So you told him everything," Baba says quietly.

"Now he can tell everyone you've been sleeping with men since you were seventeen," Mama says.

"But how could he?" I say. "He knows how bad it would be."

"Yeah," Mama says. "But the next time Jamsheed is getting down on him for something, saying, 'Why can't you be like Tara?' he'll say, 'Well, I know something about Tara,' and he'll tell them. You know, you've ruined it for Shadi," she continues. "Now Jamsheed has an excuse for never letting her do anything. He'll say, 'Look at what happened to Tara. They let her drive, they let her move out of the house and live alone.' Oh—and now they'll think the reason you live alone is so you can have your men over."

"But that's not true," I say weakly.

"It doesn't matter, it's what they'll think."

"Why did you have to answer him?" Baba says, agonized.

"I don't know. I felt bad lying. I mean, what's the use of talking to people if you're going to lie?"

"Well, you didn't have to say anything. You should have just said 'none of your business' and left the room. He has no right to ask you those things."

"I guess I didn't feel that insulted. I felt like it was a normal thing to talk about. I mean, he's been raised in America."

"Remember this," Baba says solemnly. "There are two things you should never talk to anybody about. Your finances and your sex life."

We drive on in silence. Signs whip by us. The sky is full of stars and I am wishing on them—wishing I could lobotomize Fereidoon before he has a chance to talk; wishing I could go back fifteen years to when we were all in Iran and none of this had started. I lie across the backseat, keeping my face hidden so Mama and Baba won't see me cry.

"But why Fereidoon?" Baba finally says, agitated as ever. "They're really going to wonder at your judgment. Telling Fereidoon, of all people."

"No one else would have asked," I say, controlling my voice so it won't shake. "If Fereidoon had been like them and lived in Iran longer, he wouldn't have asked either."

"If you had lived in Iran longer," Baba says, "you would have known not to answer."

They drop me off at my apartment in Berkeley and I step inside the hallway. With its bright red carpeting and tinted lights, it suddenly looks to me like a whorehouse. I hurry up to my apartment, which is beautiful, with large windows, hardwood floors, Iranian *kilims*, and a big white goose-down comforter that I can sink into with a book and no one to bother me. But tonight I don't want to be here. Tonight I feel lonely all by myself. Then where do I want to be instead?

When I was sitting in the back of the car, I had thought I just wanted to stay there, speeding down an endless, unlit road. But that's not it. The truth is, I want to be back in a houseful of Iranian relatives. If I were right there in front of them they wouldn't be able to tell stories about me. As long as I sat with them, drinking tea and playing backgammon, I would be protected—in full view of everyone, and safe from the world.

❖

Mama and Baba are finishing up another house in Palo Alto. They have pushed the roof up and added a family room and hardwood floors and skylights. Ali has also started at Berkeley now, and Sufi groans on the phone and tells us how lucky we are to have escaped the remodeling this time. Mama and Baba are tired and overworked —which must be why when I am talking to Mama on the phone she only mentions offhandedly, in the middle of a list of reasons why she is so busy, that Aziz is dying.

"Wait, what do you mean, 'Aziz is dying'?"

"They found out she has cancer all over her body. Stomach, liver, I don't know."

"What? I can't believe this. Did you call her? Did Baba talk to her?"

"It's too late," Mama says. "No one can talk to her. She doesn't recognize anyone."

"But she was fine just a little while ago." I slide down the wall and onto the floor, cradling the phone with both hands. I just talked to Aziz three months ago, when we visited Jamsheed in Portland. Everyone gathered around the phone, and when my turn came I made my Farsi as smooth and clear as I could. Despite her deafness she didn't ask me to repeat anything, but I did anyway. I said, "My heart has become tight for you," two or three times, like a parrot, simply because I knew how to say it.

"Write me a letter," she said in her soft, achingly familiar voice. "You know how to write in Farsi. I've seen you."

"Yes, yes, I do," I said, pleased that she remembered me doing my homework in Iran.

I meant to do it right away. But I was in Berkeley, and Baba, whose help I would need, was in Palo Alto. And although Aziz had been diabetic for years there was no indication that anything else had ever been wrong with her.

"Can't we send her a letter now?" I say, desperate for it not to be too late. I want to keep my promise. "What about FedEx? Do they go overnight to Iran?"

"Baba already asked about that," Mama says gently. "It came on really fast. She started feeling sick about twenty days ago."

"Twenty days! Why didn't we hear about it then? We could have at least called her up to say goodbye."

"That's exactly what I said," Mama says, exasperated. "But you know how Baba's family is. They didn't call anyone here because they didn't want to make us sad."

I hang up the phone and stand up, my shock sharpening into anger. I hate this about Baba's family. No one tells anyone anything. Or, if they ever do, it is with whispers and secrecy and warnings not to repeat it. And so when one cousin gets engaged we are sworn not to let on that we know, and when another cousin buys a house near us we have to pretend we haven't heard. When Jamsheed's mother-in-law dies, the news trickles out slowly until everyone knows about it but her only son, Mehrdad.

"By the way," Jamsheed says when he arrives at the airport to pick up Mehrdad, who has come to visit, "we hear your mother is a little sick."

"Oh? I hadn't heard. I should call her."

Jamsheed mentions it a couple more times during the drive home.

"Your mother is quite sick, actually," he finally says. "She's been sick for a while."

"Really? What's wrong with her?"

"It's not clear," Jamsheed says. "However, I think she might be in a coma."

They arrive at Jamsheed's house. Mehrdad's sister opens the door wearing a black dress. Mehrdad finally gets the full message, at which point the shock sends him running into the bedroom, where he beats his head and wails inconsolably for the rest of the weekend.

Mama says it would have been better to tell him when his mother first got sick, and I agree, but that is not how Baba's relatives work. Partly it is a real desire to protect each other from pain and to hold back good news until it can no longer be jinxed. But in some of them I sense a hoarding instinct that infuriates me. When big news is kept quiet an exclusive group forms around it. The people in the know get to be the important ones, the ones who decide who can handle the news and when they should hear it. Aziz is in the hospital, they tell us. But I don't believe them. They've waited so long that by the time we hear it she has probably been dead for days.

Baba tells us there will be no memorial service. He says he would rather mourn privately than put together a big funeral for a bunch of relatives who weren't that close to Aziz anyway.

"All the people who live around here are the people she hated. She and the Jalilis used to fight all the time, remember? If she had known they were going to come to her funeral she would have spit on their heads."

The phone rings. It's Baba's cousin, Amir Jalili, calling to say that he will make the *halvah*, a special flour-and-saffron dish served at funerals, even though when Aziz came to California she never visited him once. "Ha, ha," he says now. "Wouldn't she be mad if she heard that I was the one making the *halvah*?"

"Did you tell him not to bother?" Mama says after Baba hangs up.

He sighs. "It would look bad if we didn't do anything. They're coming on Sunday afternoon."

We rent chairs and buy stacks of little dishes and spoons and knives. We get three pictures of Aziz enlarged and framed—young, middle-aged, and old. They are passport photos, and blowing them up makes them look washed out, like three ghosts presiding over our living room. Baba buys bouquets of tall flowers, and then he goes out and buys more. He arranges them around the house and steps back and frowns, as if they are failing to live up to some Iranian ideal of funeral flowers.

"I know we can't serve anything sweet except for the *halvah*," he says. "It's not proper."

"So what do we serve?" Mama asks. She gets nervous enough when Baba's relatives come over for regular visits. She usually spends the whole day in the kitchen, making *khoreshts* and *tadeegs*, rolling the final handful of rice in saffron water and sprinkling the dyed grains over the white rice mounds so they look like orange jewels on snow. But for a funeral there is no feast, and Mama doesn't know what to do.

"I don't know," Baba says. "Fruit, I guess. Fruit is all right. I can't remember anything else." Baba comes home with so many bags of fruit that Mama sends me back to Safeway to buy more little knives to cut it with. This is how we are with being Iranian—we don't worry about it for years and then something happens and we suddenly try to look as if we know what we're doing, as if we've been doing it all along.

People flow into our house all afternoon. The women wear black dresses and black panty hose and carry black handbags, and the men wear black ties over black shirts and pants. "They must lie there waiting for funerals," Sufi whispers, and we laugh at the thought of them sitting like this at home, waiting for the phone to ring. Now they huddle in our living room like a huge inkblot, and despite the high ceilings and skylights, when I look out the window I am surprised by the brightness of the day.

"Tara!" Baba whispers. "Go serve fruit."

"I did," I whisper back. "I put it out on all the tables."

"They won't take it. You have to offer it. Bring out plates and put the fruit on the plates for them." He follows me into the kitchen, where a group of women stand murmuring together. I take out a stack of small dishes and turn toward the living room. "Serve the old ones first," Baba hisses, as if it is a trick he's just remembered.

The old people have settled deep into the soft white couches and armchairs. Not one of them has touched the fruit bowl. I approach it apprehensively. Mama once told me that when Iranians are sizing you up for marriage they come over and watch how well you serve fruit and tea. But she never explained how to do it. I know that part of it has to do with who gets served before whom, but looking across the waxy white heads and the three-piece suits and the saggy black dresses, I'm not sure which one to start with. The old people themselves know very well who was higher up in the village; they remember whose mother bettered herself by marrying a rich man, whose father used to receive visits from Qajar princes, and who is just a hanger-on from a low family. It has little to do with how much money they have now. "Our family is better than the Jalilis," Aziz used to growl under her breath, although the Jalilis became rich after our family became poor; in any case, the two sides have had so many marriages back and forth that sometimes it was her own grandchildren she was muttering against.

For later generations, all this is hard to keep straight. A few weeks ago at a dinner my great-aunt Ammejun, the mother of the Jalili cousins, stood up in greeting and Mama kissed another old lady before kissing her. Ammejun did not speak to her for the rest of the night, and glared straight ahead whenever Mama tried to catch her eye. Mama used to get more slack for being an American, but by now she is expected to know these things.

Serving fruit, I see I don't know anything. The old men sitting back with their teacups smile benignly as I enter the room. But my eyes stop on a gnomelike old woman with dyed-black hair, a round nose, and a protruding lower jaw that moves in one piece when she talks and otherwise stays clamped shut in an indignant grimace. It is Ammejun, and her raisin eyes are trained on me. Remembering Mama's mistake, I decide to serve her first.

I pick the biggest thing, a bunch of purple grapes, put them on a plate, and hold it out to her.

"No, thank you," she says.

"*Bokhor,*" I say, imitating the no-nonsense tone of an Iranian hostess. "Take some."

"No, no, I'm fine."

"Please," I say, knowing that the guest is supposed to decline two or three times before accepting. "Just a little bit," I plead.

"May your hand not hurt," she mumbles, taking the dish from me. But something is wrong.

"Uh, would you like anything else?" I say.

"Oh, no, thank you," she says. So I turn back to the fruit bowl, hoping the next person likes apples. And then something taps on my back. I turn around. Ammejun pulls me down and whispers, "For each person, you must put an apple, an orange, a banana, and some grapes."

"Oh," I say awkwardly. "I didn't know." I bend again, fill the plate and straighten back up, conscious of every position of my body, each movement that risks exposing me as graceless, uncivilized, American.

I hold the plate out to the next person.

Again, the tapping.

"And a cucumber," she hisses. "Put a cucumber too."

Other women at the funeral kiss my hair and pinch my cheeks. "Congratulations, you're almost done with college," they say. "What did you study? What are you going to do now?" Their own children are doctors, lawyers, and engineers, and they chirp proudly about *Haarvaard*, *Estanfoord*, and *Medeecaal School* as they ask me about my plans.

A few months ago I got into trouble when an Iranian woman at a dinner party told us her daughter was planning to study dentistry. I told her I was planning to visit Prague, where some of my friends were living. She stared at me, confused. "What is *Per*-ague?" she asked, and when I told her she said, "Ah, so you're going to study there?" No, I just want to hang out, I started to say, but Baba interrupted and said that yes, I was interested in studying the history of the Czech language. Later he got mad at me. "Why don't you become a dentist?" he said. I reminded him that he himself had told me to do what I found interesting. "Well, dentistry is very interesting," he retorted.

"I studied English literature," I tell the ladies at the funeral.

"Ah, so you'll be a professor?"

No, I want to say; *I don't know what I'm going to do with my life and neither do any of my friends.* But I smile and say that maybe I'll be a professor later; for now, though, I'm going to stay in Berkeley and find a job.

"Ah, teaching English literature?"

"Yes." Lying is easier.

"But aren't you scared to live alone, a young girl all by yourself?"

I pause. I no longer live alone—I've just moved in with Brad—but nobody is going to trick me into saying so. For weeks, whenever I thought about Fereidoon and Portland a wave of nausea would roll through me, but since then I've seen Shapur and Jamsheed and the others and they have greeted me as warmly as ever.

I start to tell the ladies that I like living alone, but they interrupt me. "You *can't* like it!" they insist. "You must get lonely. And scared."

"Nah, she's not scared of anything." A familiar voice cuts through the chatter. "She's a free spirit."

I turn around gratefully. It is Reza, Homa-khanoum's tall, sweetly handsome youngest son who used to go hiking with us when we first moved to California. Reza is something of a free spirit himself. He is only a couple of years older than I am but he has been living apart from his parents since the revolution, when they sent him out of Iran to his brothers in San Jose. Not speaking a word of English, he picked up a book of American history, sat down with a dictionary, and memorized a thousand words in four days. Then he walked over to the local high school and signed himself up. After high school he started taking classes at a community college but dropped out when he got a job dealing cards at the casino where his brother worked. He stopped hiking. He started chain-smoking. And now, no matter how often we call, he rarely comes over because his job goes until 4 a.m. and he needs to sleep in.

Reza rescues me from the women and leads me into the kitchen, where Baba and Ali are hiding out. "Ah, Reza," Baba says. "How are you doing? How's work, how's life?"

"Life is great," Reza says, cracking a smile. "Haven't I told you? I'm going to Iran."

He says this so casually that we think he is kidding.

"What about your military service?" we ask. The war is over now, but every man over eighteen is still required to serve for two years before he can leave the country.

"Paid it off. Ten thousand dollars buys you three years."

"And your passport?"

"Just got it in the mail."

"And you're not on any list?"

"No, why should I be? For God's sake, I left when I was a kid."

He has quit his job. He has sold his car, his TV, and his stereo. He has bought a one-way ticket back to Iran.

"All I want out of life is to wake up in my father's village," he says. "I want to go outside and see the snow on the mountains, hear the rooster crowing, toss sticks into the river."

I throw him a skeptical look. Whenever my relatives talk about Iran they reminisce about a life of horses and rivers and mountains, a life in which it was never necessary to get up and go to work in the morning. Baba really did have that kind of childhood, but I remember Reza living in a cramped apartment just down the street from ours in Tehran. It seems, though, that that is not what he plans to go back to.

"Uncle Essie, I swear I'm going to get a horse and travel around," Reza says. "You know how Iran is—anywhere you go in the countryside people will take you into their homes, give you dinner and conversation and a place to tie up your horse, and roll out mattresses by the heater for you to sleep on. What else can you ask for?"

"*Bah, bah*, that's all I want to do too," Baba says, beaming. He throws an arm around Reza, forgetting for a minute that he's supposed to look glum for the guests sitting beside Aziz's portraits.

A couple of weeks later, when I am visiting my parents, I receive an invitation. "Ammejun has asked us over to Mehdi's house for dinner," Baba tells me. "She inquired a few times about you. She really wants you to come."

"Is this a *khastegari*?" I giggle.

"No, it is not," he says, annoyed. "We're just having dinner."

But when we arrive, Ammejun's son Mehdi answers the door in a dress shirt, pleated wool pants and a pair of narrow, pointy loafers. He smiles and shakes Baba's hand, and Mama's, and then he squeezes my hand and locks his green eyes meaningfully with mine. Baba gives me a quick look to say that maybe he was wrong.

White flowers are set out in vases around the living room. A fire crackles in the grate. Ammejun sits on the couch watching a football game. When we come in she stands up, a sturdy four-foot-six-inch woman in a black dress. No one knows exactly how old she is, but she has eight children between thirty-three and sixty. She embraces me with arms that are delicate but strong, and she grins and chuckles as I mumble my greetings. Sitting in armchairs, we switch between Farsi and English, and during the English parts Ammejun turns, still smiling, back to the American sportscasters.

It wasn't until we moved to America that I began to like Iranian food. Now I take every opportunity I can to eat it. Ammejun has cooked *ash* (bean and herb noodle soup), *kashk-e-bademjoon* (eggplant stew with an *x* of whey dribbled across the top), *ghormeh-sabzi* (the herb and lamb stew I used to hate), *fessenjoon* (chicken in pomegranate and walnut sauce), green salad, pickled vegetables, yogurt-cucumber salad, soft rice, *tadeeg* (crunchy rice), and rice with a saffron-flavored yogurt-egg crust. It is enough for several families, but Mama and Baba and I are the only guests here.

"The *ash* is great," I say, blowing on a spoonful of the thick, tangy broth. "Can you give me the recipe?"

Ammejun beams. "It doesn't have a recipe. These things are taught by mothers to daughters. I will teach it to you."

I look back down at my soup.

"*Voh*, what a beautiful baby Mehdi was!" Ammejun suddenly says, licking her lips and looking around the table. "Do you know, when he was next to the other babies everyone always said, 'What a beautiful child! What lovely eyes! What smooth skin!' Other babies were red and scaly, but not Mehdi. He was whiter than flour! Take some more *tadeeg*, you haven't eaten anything." She glances at my stomach and piles more rice onto my plate. "It was embarrassing. I used to tell the other women their babies were pretty too, but everyone ignored the other babies; they just looked at Mehdi."

Mehdi is close to forty now, almost twice my age. I suppose the doctor-mothers would consider him a good catch—better than Homa-khanoum's rangy, handsome sons who work in casinos. Mehdi has a computer company and a three-bedroom house and a bronze Porsche with a tinted sunroof. He knows all the latest pop music, he follows American football, and he has even had American girlfriends, one of whom I met while Ammejun was still back in Iran. It seems out of character that after all this Mehdi would want to be set up with his own cousin's daughter.

"So, Mehdi, tell me," Baba says. "How is your company doing?"

"Great, really great. We're looking to hire another person."

"You should hire Tara, she's almost done with school." I look at Baba as if he's crazy. "It's a rising field," he says lamely.

"She wants to learn how to make *ash*," Ammejun says, putting a protective arm around my shoulder. "I'm going to teach her."

"That would be great," I say, grateful for the change of subject. "What about *bademjoon*?" she asks. "Do you want to learn how to make that?"

"Sure."

"I will teach you." She nods decisively to herself, and I glance at Mama, who has a smile pasted on.

Ammejun looks at me sharply. "What about chadors?" she says. "Do you know how to wear a chador?"

"I haven't worn one since I was little."

"Really? Do you want to learn how?" She jumps excitedly up from the table and leads me down the hall to the bedroom. Mehdi and my parents follow.

Ammejun pulls out a large blue cloth. "You hold it like this, here." In the mirror's reflection my jeans and sweater vanish under the soft folds of cloth and my eyes look darker, my lips redder, my face more Iranian. Ammejun nods and strokes my head, and I have a sudden desire to make her happy, to thank her for making such a nice dinner, to agree to marry her son and give her grandchildren. Mama, watching from the doorway, says, "Be careful, it's not as easy as it looks" —and for a second I think she is talking about something else besides the chador. But then I see what she means; I pull the cloth forward and it slips back. I laugh and ask Ammejun how to hold it and she smiles, adjusts it on my head, and nods approvingly.

I wouldn't really consider marrying Mehdi or any other cousin. It's not just that I'm not in love with them or that they're related to me; it's also that to them it doesn't seem to matter whether we are in love or not. Still, I want to be part of their families. When Ammejun puts a chador over my head and offers to teach me how to cook, I feel like I am discovering a lost side of myself, a side that, in moving away from our relatives at Timber Creek all those years ago, my family chose to put aside.

Now we are used to our separate life. Mama and Baba put so much energy into their work and their supplementary job fixing up houses that they don't have the time or the desire to go visiting at the end of the day. Baba rarely even calls the cousins who live twenty minutes away. But after Aziz visited I began to feel I was missing something —a connection to the cousins who might have been like extra brothers and sisters to me, and the aunts and uncles who might have taken me beyond what Baba taught me of Iran.

"Why don't you get married?" the women in Baba's family ask me now that we have started to see more of them. "There are so many excellent Iranian men without wives."

I shrug. It's not that I have anything against Iranian men; I like their looks, I like their voices, I like the way they joke around with each other, one arm draped un-Americanly over another one's shoulder. I like how affectionate they are with children and how un-ashamed they are to show their emotions. But often when a woman is present that ease disappears—they become self-conscious, and every look and gesture becomes fraught with meaning. Sometimes I sense that they subtly disapprove of me, even as they assure me that it's great that I am so different from other Iranian girls.

Back in Berkeley, my phone rings early in the morning. Brad reaches over to the nightstand, but even though I am half asleep, something tells me to grab the phone first.

"Hello, Taraneh?" A man's voice. An accent.

"Mehdi?"

"Yes, how did you know?"

"I don't know, I just recognized you. How are you?" I blink my eyes, trying to sound awake, my heart pounding at the near-slip.

"I was calling to see if you want to have dinner sometime," he says.

"Dinner?" I motion to Brad to keep quiet. "You mean go out for dinner? Well, sure, I guess. But I don't know when I'm going to be in Palo Alto again. It might not be for a few weeks. I'm really busy here."

"That's okay," Mehdi says. He sounds relaxed and confident, as if he is laughing at my nervousness. "I'll come up to Berkeley."

"Oh no, that's way too far. It's silly for you to drive all the way up to Berkeley when I can just go to Palo Alto and meet you there. I'll call you next time I'm down there. It's really much closer for you."

I hang up and stand under the hot shower, letting the water stream over my face. He sees through me; he is laughing at me. Maybe I should have just let Brad answer, an easy mistake that would have changed everything. I think of Shireen, who recently moved to a small town on the Oregon coast, far from anyone in the family. I wonder if the rumors are true about her living with a man.

The following morning the phone rings again.

"Mehdi?"

But this time it is Masood, another second cousin from the funeral. He is up in Richmond on business. He wants to stop by and visit. Brad leaves for work, and I hide all his shoes. I hide his toothbrush and razor. I show Masood around the apartment that seems too big for one person, with the double bed and the desk covered with papers on which, if he looked, he would see two kinds of handwriting.

Masood calls back that very night. "You know, Taraneh, I have something to tell you," he says. "I love you."

"Well, I love you too," I say.

"As more than a cousin."

I tell him I love him as a cousin and get off the phone as quickly as I can.

"Who was that?" Brad asks.

"Another cousin."

"Well, why are they all suddenly calling you now?"

I don't know. They have never called before. Is it because I am about to graduate from college? Have I unknowingly been put on some list of eligible Iranian girls? Was the funeral at my parents' house an inadvertent coming-out party, a green light for the cousins to start calling?

For a few weeks I hold my breath every time Brad answers the phone. But neither of them calls back. The next time I go down to Palo Alto, Baba says they must have gotten the message, because they haven't called him either. Only Massi has called lately, to pass on a startling piece of news. Reza, whom we last saw a month ago when Baba drove him to the San Francisco airport, is getting married in Iran.

"But that's not why he was going there," I say.

"I know," Baba says. "But Massi says they had all these girls lined up to meet him." He frowns. "I don't know why they're doing this."

"They" are Reza's mother and older sister. For years they have been begging him and his brothers to marry. "If you won't find wives yourselves, let us find them for you," Homa-khanoum says whenever she visits. But until now they had not listened.

"It's ridiculous," I say. "He never said a thing about wanting to get married." His brother Shapur has talked about it; he has sent messages to the relatives in Iran to look out for a young, pretty girl from a good family—and everyone has tried to think of who has a daughter the right age. But Reza has never once showed an interest in this kind of matchmaking.

"Baba, call and convince him not to do it," I say. "I thought he was going to ride a horse through the mountains."

"Yeah," Mama says. "If Ali went to Iran and decided to get married out of the blue, wouldn't you call him?"

"Come on," I say. "He'll listen to you. They're probably just pushing him into it and there's no one around to tell him to think it over."

But Baba shakes his head. "It's none of my business. Remember the last time Jamsheed tried to interfere, when they were marrying Shireen? Massi just got mad and it didn't change anything."

"Well, he was right," I say.

Baba throws his hands up in the air.

❖

My last semester at Berkeley I sign up for a Farsi class. I get the idea partly from Baba, who is always announcing new regimes.

"A new regime," he says. "From now on we're only speaking Farsi."

"Okay," Ali and I say, eager to see how far we can go before we hit a word we don't know.

"That's not fair," Sufi says quickly.

"You'll learn by listening," Baba says.

But she purses her lips. She does not want to be reminded of what she does not remember. At three years old Sufi used to come home from nursery school singing songs in Farsi. While we taught her English words, Soghra taught her their Farsi equivalents, and had we stayed in Iran she would have been the most fluent, the most Iranian of all of us. But in America her Farsi faded as easily as it had come.

And so did a world of memories. Ali and I still have them; Ali can turn to me as we're walking down Telegraph Avenue and ask, "What were the three kinds of popsicles at Ramezan's?" and I will see the colors in my head before I can get out the words, "Orange, lime, and cherry."

"Oh yeah," he says. "And remember those candies called Negroes? Brown on the outside and marshmallow inside? Can you believe they were called that?"

And suddenly I am back in the dark store, standing a little taller than my round-headed brother, watching him rip open the plastic package and bite into the chocolate shell. As we have gotten older we have become complementary pieces of a puzzle; we keep the details alive by reminding each other of their colors and flavors. But even with our parallel recollections there is a world of memories we have lost. To unearth them would require twenty more siblings.

Sufi senses she has missed out. "Why aren't there any pictures of me when I was little?" she asks as she sorts through a box of family photographs.

"That's not true," I say, picking out her school pictures, her soccer team photos, the snapshots I took with my high school Instamatic— but these are all different from our Iran pictures. Sufi was born eight years after me, five years after Ali, and only three and a half years before the revolution. In the childhood she remembers, Baba yelled at waitresses and Mama cried in the supermarket because she could not afford to fill her shopping cart. In my childhood Baba always had his Nikkormat around his neck, and the pictures of me and Ali at six and three are fine, sharp, close-up images that showed how intensely he was focused on us. "Oh, look," we say, pulling out a picture of us all eating breakfast at a table in a garden. "That's the house we rented on the Caspian." All Sufi knows of that house is what she sees in the picture—her smiling two-year-old self, frozen between me and Ali. But I can smell the damp sea air, I can see the hazy light filtering through the tall trees on the adjoining street and feel the bumpy dirt path under my bicycle wheels.

Sometimes I worry that Sufi doesn't remember what made Mama cry in the supermarket in Portland. "Don't you see how hard Mama and Baba are working?" I say to her when she is in junior high and starts asking for the things her friends have. "Don't you realize how much those clothes cost?" Mama and Baba have steady jobs now, but when we moved to California I suddenly became reluctant to spend money, as if in belated response to our Portland days. Having discovered thrift shops, I couldn't imagine spending hundreds of dollars on clothes like some girls at school did. Even at lunch, as my friends bought lasagna and corned beef sandwiches from the gourmet market across the street, I ate sixty-nine-cent burritos from the school cafeteria. Anything more would have been extravagant.

By comparison, Sufi seems indifferent, not guilty enough. "You're *so* Palo Alto," I say to her one day when she is fourteen and trying to get Mama to buy her a pair of seventy-dollar boots.

Her eyes fill with tears, startling me. "Just because I didn't grow up in Iran doesn't make me any more spoiled than you!" She runs to her room and slams the door.

Mama gives me a reproachful look. "You asked for many things like that when you were her age. And we had less money then."

I don't answer. I want to undo what I said—not just because Mama is right, but because of what my words must mean to Sufi. This town has been her home since she was seven; she has nothing to strike back with when I accuse her of being "Palo Alto." She doesn't have an alternate reality like I do—although, now that I think of it, in the fifth grade she did write an essay about how other foreign-born students in the class didn't say the Pledge of Allegiance, and therefore she, born in Iran, shouldn't have to either (her worried teacher called Baba, who had no idea what the Pledge of Allegiance was. "The pleasure of what?" he said, and when the teacher explained, Baba gave his permission for Sufi to be excused from it).

I never realized how hard it must be for Sufi to grow in the midst of our sacred Iranian memories; I never thought about how well she has memorized a family lore that barely includes her, and how faithfully she has safekept her own shadowy memories of Iran: "I remember running with you and Ali and some other kids to go get popsicles and you stopped and waited for me; I remember being with you and Ali in a big open place, collecting pretty rocks in the sleeve of my coat; I remember playing hide-and-seek with you and Ali on some grass near a big building that we weren't supposed to go into because a man with a beard was going to get mad."

The next time Baba announces a new regime, I don't try to convince Sufi that she'll pick Farsi up by listening. I can understand her not wanting to be left out of yet another picture.

But Berkeley offers Farsi classes. I already know the alphabet, so I join the intermediate class, full of Iranian students who are in it for an easy A. I spend hours at night with Baba's heavy Persian-English dictionary; my classmates, who have grown up with Farsi-speaking parents, can read by guessing, knowing by instinct how a written word should sound.

Once I join their class I begin to see them all over campus, as if some kind of Iranian invisible ink has been revealed to me. Walking home one foggy night I run into Kourosh, a tall, wavy-haired boy from my class.

"Hey, I'm on my way to watch soccer," he says. "Want to come?"

I sit beside him on the edge of the spotlighted Astroturf, his coat pulled around my shoulders. Two teams of Iranians run back and forth in the mist, calling out to each other, hugging jubilantly after a goal—a nocturnal society of compatriots I never knew about.

"Oh, but we've always played here," Kourosh says. "I'm just not playing tonight because I hurt my leg. See, that's Sassan, my roommate, and there's my other roommate."

"Are all your friends Iranian?" I ask.

"Yeah, mostly," he says. "But my girlfriends aren't."

"Why not?"

"Well," he says a little sheepishly. "I like to go out with blondes."

"You mean Americans?"

"Yeah," he says. "Or Europeans are all right too."

"But not Iranians?"

He gives me a guilty smile. "I have a lot of friends who are girls and who are Iranian. But you know how it is."

"Iranian girls aren't as fun to date?"

"Yeah," he says. "You know how they are, always talking about marriage, always wanting you to be a doctor or an engineer."

"Yeah, I know," I say. "So what do you want to be?"

"I don't know. I guess I'll major in engineering or something." He kicks his heel against the concrete. "But you get sick of them asking, and their mothers too—'What's he studying, what does his father do, where is his family from?'—like they're already planning the wedding."

"Not all Iranian girls are like that."

"All of them," he says with a decisive nod. "You're half-and-half, you're different. But full-Iranian girls are all like that. And, you know, they don't like to have as much fun."

"What do you mean?"

He shakes his head, grinning, and flicks his wrist out toward the soccer game. "All these guys, even the older ones, when they were young they went out with blondes. Then they married their wives." He pauses and looks at me. "Don't get me wrong; I'm definitely going to marry an Iranian girl. But you know the saying—blondes have more fun."

"Oh, you mean they'll sleep with you and Iranian girls won't."

His face reddens and he grins harder. "God, you don't have to be so direct."

One weekend in March the Farsi class arranges a ski trip. We spend two days at Lake Tahoe in someone's parents' enormous house with mirrored walls. To my annoyance, we only ski a little; we spend most of the time playing board games and watching horror movies on a huge television built into the wall.

"*Akh*, my legs hurt," says a plump black-haired girl, rubbing her thigh.

"We're getting old," says another girl, wincing in sympathy.

"Remember Shemshak?" the first girl says. "Which was better, Dizin or Shemshak?"

The second girl pushes back the long black ringlets that fall forward over her face. "Dizin had better slopes."

"You always say that," the first girl says. "But *to-ke batcheh boodi.* How old were you when you left?"

"Nine," the second girl says.

"*Khob deegeh,*" the first girl says. "You were too young to remember."

"*To cheh meedooni?* I skied all the time. *Akheir,* Dizin was bigger."

I pick the sausage off my pizza, listening to the seamlessness of the

Farsi running into English. *"Rast meegeh,"* I say. "I was almost twelve when I left, and *man yadam hast,* Dizin was bigger." It is fun to speak like this, to lazily pick the best words from each side and form a fused language you'd have to be one of us to understand.

The second girl smiles. *"Deedee goftam?* You think I don't remember Iran?"

But when I ask if she ever wants to move back, she says, "No way. I like my life here, thank you very much."

"Well, what about just to visit?" I say. "Aren't you curious to just see it again?"

"With the way they treat women over there?" she says. "Not a chance, baby!"

"I would go," says the first girl, who is carefully painting her fingernails under a lamp. "I want to visit all my cousins. But I'd wait for wintertime."

"Why?" says a chubby, assertive boy who wears a gold pinkie ring. "The summer there is beautiful."

"Yes, but if I'm going to go around covered in black from head to foot, I'm not going when it's a hundred degrees out. Can you imagine not being able to wear short sleeves?"

"You're right," I say. "I'd go in the winter too."

"I can't believe you guys are worried about that," the boy says. "You're blowing it out of proportion. Iranian women have been wearing chadors for centuries. I'm sure you could handle not wearing shorts and T-shirts for a little while."

"And what about when I went to the beach?" the girl says. "Could I swim, or what?"

"Of course, women can go to the beach just like anyone," he says.

"Really?" I say. "In bathing suits?"

"Well, no," he says. "I actually haven't been back to see it. I guess they just go in the water with their chadors. It's no big deal." I smile, imagining a group of women running toward the water, their black chadors streaming behind them.

"I've heard they have separate men's and women's beaches," another boy says. "They put curtains up to divide them."

Lying in bed that night, I picture a curtain rod extended precariously over the slate-colored Caspian, the tall curtains swaying with the waves. I wonder how far they go out. As a child, I used to ask what lay on the other side of the Caspian. The Russian border, Baba would say, and I imagined a crooked iron fence jutting out from the water just past the horizon, with lonely men stranded in watchtowers, keeping guard. But there couldn't really have been a fence like that. There can't really be curtains in the water. What lies in Iran now is a world I have no idea how to imagine.

❖

On a visit to Los Angeles, I look up my old friend Shahrzad. We have not spoken for years, but when I call information I learn that her family is still in Simi Valley, in the same house she moved to in the seventh grade.

She arrives in a red Toyota and whizzes me up the freeway. She is a bigger version of her childhood self, with a curly bob, bright red lipstick and, around her neck, a gold pendant in the reclining-cat shape of Iran. In a steady, uninterrupted stream, she tells me she says "Persian" instead of "Iranian" because "it sounds less terroristic, and anyway, it was the original name of our people." She tells me she is engaged to a Persian man, and that she is still a virgin "although none of my friends are, even though they claim to be." She tells me Persian girls are all getting hymen-reconstruction surgery before their weddings. I think back to what Kourosh told me about Iranian girls being no fun—maybe they, like their future husbands, have simply been using this time to date Americans.

The first thing I see in Shahrzad's house is a color print of the Shah. Framed in gold, hanging alone in the front hall, it reminds me of Tehran public buildings before the revolution. We walk through the house and Shahrzad's mother smiles at us from the kitchen table, where she is spooning out rice for three cropped-haired children. For a moment I am taken aback; it seems strange that Shahrzad's parents kept on having babies after they came here. Mama and Baba had planned to have one more, but coming to America changed their plan; sometimes I used to imagine the brother who would have been four or five years younger than Sufi, an invisible little boy drifting around America with us. But Shahrzad has acquired two new sisters, little girls who have never seen Iran but who babble together in rapid Farsi as we pass by them.

Shahrzad's bedroom wall is covered by a huge Iranian flag—not the current one that says "Allah" in the middle, but the old lion-and-sun one. She pulls her fifth-grade yearbook off a shelf—the one I lost somewhere between Portland and Palo Alto—and I flip through it eagerly, picking out myself and Shahrzad and a few other friends. She touches the faces gently. "Remember how mad we used to get at Chantay? Remember how nice Kambiz was? You know," she says, lowering her voice, "I miss them so much, I still cry at night."

We go into the den and she slips in a video of a famous singer from the old days belting out prerevolution favorites. As it plays she pulls another video off the shelf. "This one is really good. The store just got it in."

It is a stroll along the streets of Tehran just before the revolution. The camera follows two foreign-looking women in summer dresses and high heels as they walk up Pahlavi Avenue, past cars and trees and a modern-looking restaurant. "*Akh*," Shahrzad says. "Remember Chattanooga?"

I shake my head.

"Chattanooga," she says urgently. "The chic-est restaurant in Tehran. I think they had dancing there."

"But we were eleven," I say. "Did you ever go?"

"No. I wish I had."

"Well, you're definitely different now from when you changed your name to Sherri and said you were Italian," I say.

"What are you talking about?" she says, stiffening. "I never did that. You must be thinking of someone else. You know, so many Persians still change their names, it's not even funny. They say they're from Mexico so they'll fit in better. Jesus Christ, by now there are so many of us around here you'd think they'd get over it."

She closes the yearbook and slides it carefully back onto the shelf. "It'll never be like Iran here," she sighs. "In Iran people really care about you. They want to know about you, they ask what you're doing, they make sure you aren't lonely. Here you could die on the sidewalk and everyone would just walk right by."

"Oh, I'm sure they'd stop to see if you were okay."

"Even if they stopped, they wouldn't really care. In Iran, if you just go out and buy a cup of carrot juice people know about it. You can see that the guy selling the juice is interested in you. Even if he's never seen you before, you're more than just a customer."

"So why don't you go back on your next vacation?"

"*Akheir*, you don't know how much I want to. But I can't. I'd want to go for more than a couple of weeks, and then I'd lose my job at the bank."

"So you could get a new job."

She sighs again and her gaze stops on the red, white, and green flag with the yellow lion staring balefully out. "I had a friend who went back," she says. "She was so excited. But she said Iran was so different she didn't even recognize it. All her memories were shattered." Her hand goes up to the flat gold pendant at her throat. "Don't you see? I can't risk having my memories shattered too."

After we went to America, Aziz used to remind us that our places were empty. "I have your things that you left me to take care of," she would say, her soft, mournful voice crackling over the long-distance wire.

"*Enshallah* we'll be back soon to get them," Baba always answered.

I loved the ties she brought over for Baba when she came. I wanted them. But I didn't ask for them; they were what Aziz had chosen to bring out of Iran for Baba. For me she had brought one of the gold bangles that Iranian girls wear, with modern-looking gashes along the edge. She had guessed too large; it slipped right off my hand and I put it away in a box.

In Iran your place becomes empty when you leave and stays empty as long as you are away. But what if the one who leaves forgets about his empty place? What if, by living so long in America or England or France, he starts to become part of those countries and no longer remembers his original home? After college, I visited my uncle Parviz and got the feeling that something like this had happened to him.

I had not seen him since the revolution. He and his family were living on a quiet street of lush trees in a suburb of Washington, D.C. Compared with most of my close Iranian relatives, they were an American success story. Parviz was a professor and his wife was a scientist. Their children had gone off to college leaving behind bedroom shelves stacked with prom pictures and sports trophies. There were bagels for breakfast and a pet dog in the living room, and, except for a few Shirazi picture frames, their house did not feel Iranian.

"I'll never go back there after what Iran did to me," Parviz's wife declared. "It separated me from my mother—when she got sick I couldn't go back because of this damn regime. She died without ever seeing me again."

"We're American now," Parviz said, his slow Southern drawl only slightly tinged with foreignness. "This is the best country in the world."

I tried to ask him about his teenage years. In California Baba had recently met a friend of Parviz's from high school who remembered Parviz as a brave, headstrong boy who had belonged to a political street gang back before the Shah had banned opposition groups. Baba too remembers a rebellious teenage Parviz who fought so much with his parents that he moved out and got his own apartment. At age ten, Baba used to bring over food baskets secretly prepared by Aziz, and on one of these visits he remembers Parviz pulling rolls of beautiful carpets out from under his bed and unfurling them to reveal a cache of guns.

But when I asked Parviz if he'd ever moved into his own apartment in Tehran, he shook his head. "You must be thinking of someone else," he said mildly.

"My father said he remembers it very clearly," I said.

"Well, I'm afraid your daddy is mistaken."

In Farsi there is a word for a person who lets Westernness take over his Iranianness. It is a derogatory term, coined thirty years ago to describe Iranians who replaced their own cultural traditions with Western ones. The word is *gharb-zadeh*—"West-struck"—as if it is literally a Westernizing blow that strikes a person in the head and makes him forget who he is.

Maybe, with my half-American genes and my U.S. birth certificate, I was always too Western to ever be called West-struck. Even in Iran I was never really on the road to becoming an Iranian woman. Baba's relatives might judge women by the way their rice came out and the way they handed tea to guests; to Baba it was more important that I learn to dive and play tennis. And yet, for all of his embracing of romance and freedom, Baba's dervishness is not complete. Once in a while another side of him surfaces, straight from the *khastegari* tradition.

"She's not at all feminine," he complains when I am home for a weekend.

"That's not true," Mama says. "You just don't like her boots."

"Well, why does she wear these things like she's in the Army? Who will want to marry her like that? I guess she just doesn't like herself and she doesn't want boys to like her."

"He's right," I say sarcastically. "All the girls I know wear Doc Martens to stop the boys from liking them."

Once in a while he decides that these American impulses are Mama's fault. "If you had liked Iran more, the kids would be more Iranian," he tells her.

I rush to her support. "How can you say she didn't like Iran? She *loved* it."

"Not all the time," he says.

"Yes, she did," I say. "Anyway, who do you want us to be like? Those Iranian kids who spend half their time studying to become doctors and the other half looking for doctors to marry?"

"Well, at least they don't have to worry about making a living."

"I'm not worried about making a living."

"You know I liked Iran," Mama interrupts. "I didn't want to leave any more than you did. You think I wanted to come here and sell real estate instead of living in Shahrak and doing my painting?"

"Well, you never spoke Farsi to them," he mumbles.

"Well, neither did *you*," we say in unison.

Still, as much as Mama might have liked Iran, lately she worries that I am Iran-struck. Maybe it's true. At the San Francisco magazine where I started interning after graduation, I recently opened an envelope containing an unsolicited article about daily life in Iran, written by an American woman living there. My editor rejected it, but I kept the woman's crooked snapshots of the bleak Tehran streets in winter. The mountains in the background and the trees growing out of the *joob* brought back a jolt of recognition like a kick in the chest.

However, I don't know what to say when Shahrzad tells me she still cries at night. She and I came to America at the same age, missing the same things, and I was just as excited to see her yearbook as she was to show it to me. But I don't cry at night. Maybe my American side has dulled my pain. Maybe I am too much like Mama, who has no patience for people caught up in the past. "How can they stay fixated on that stuff?" she says of my forty-year-old cousins who still live together and talk about returning to Iran to find jobs and wives. "It's not healthy. They're smart, they're good-looking, they could do anything they wanted here if they would just stop this Iranian back-beating and take an interest in what's around them."

I agree; if they are going to live in America they should try to adapt. But sometimes I worry that Mama's healthiness goes too far. When I look for our tape of the songs from Mama's cat musical or ask about the ties Aziz brought for Baba from Iran, Mama tells me she taped over the songs and gave the ties to Goodwill. She doesn't understand why I get upset. "They were just ties," she says. "They were out of style."

Maybe it is the Iranian in me that would have taken special care of those ties, just as it is the Iranian in me that perks up when I spot a group of Iranians walking down the street. I follow behind them, eavesdropping, wanting on some level to be acknowledged for the simple fact that I am Iranian too. But they don't recognize me. As much as Americans might call my eyes dark and my hair black, in a group of full-blooded Iranians my color gets washed away. My hair is too light, my eyelashes are not thick enough, and my skin looks greenish next to their Middle Eastern apricot glow.

Still, Americans look for the exotic in me. "How did it feel to grow up in purdah?" well-meaning friends ask. "What was it like for your mother to have to wear the veil for so long?" Even people I know well seem to miss a part of my Iranian side. "I'd love to see Iran," says my boyfriend, who has already traveled through Turkey and India. I think he envisions us with backpacks, taking trains and buses over misty mountains to Zoroastrian fire temples and Safavid palaces. He would be polite and friendly, eager to learn everything about the culture. It is hard to put a finger on the problem of his Americanness. Is it that he would smile too much? Or take too many pictures of village children? Or maybe, coming from America, he wouldn't understand something that a person knows who comes from a country that has been weak and small and defeated somewhere in its history. No matter what Iranians feel about Iran's government, they empathize with the country as with a sentient being; and with all those centuries of military and religious and cultural invasions, the passion rises easily. Baba's high school teacher kept a map on the wall—not of modern Iran but of the Persian empire at its peak, when the red-colored section spanned from Europe to Africa to China. *Ah, what Iran once was!* the map proclaimed. *Ah, what it would be today, if not for the Greeks, the Arabs, the British, the Americans.* For those with such far-reaching nostalgia, the borders we see today do not encompass the real Iran. And yet hardly any of us in America have gone back to see what the real Iran might be.

These days only my oldest relatives go back and forth regularly. These people who started their lives in tiny hillside villages are spending their final years jetting out to Europe and America, visiting their children and stocking up on Nescafé and ecotrin-coated aspirin. Thousands of young Iranians are denied entry to the United States, but the old ones slip in and out of the visa offices like spirits, floating above war and politics. They sit in suburban houses, unable to speak English, unconnected to America except by their children, who go out into it in the morning and come back at night.

We see them at Noruz parties and weddings, gripping their canes, chuckling over their grandchildren, nibbling on fruit and tea served to them by their aging daughters-in-law. And then they disappear. "Aziz's brother is going back to Iran," Baba announces, and we pile into the car to go to a goodbye dinner. We arrive to find four generations sitting around the pool, drinking beer and Cokes and mixing English and Farsi. The toothless old man who, sixty years ago, was Khomeini's roommate in theology school sits in a white plastic chair, his soft, bald head nodding above his dark suit, a teacup and saucer delicately balanced in his hand. His teenage great-grandniece, born in America, comes up and massages his back and the cup begins to shake. A wave of tea splashes over its edge. The old man turns slowly and takes in the bright yellow of his great-grandniece's leggings, her shiny high heels, her red fingernails; then he frowns and looks forward again, his bespectacled eyes focused on something the rest of us cannot see.

It is hard to picture him boarding a plane on his own, shoving his bag into an overhead compartment, navigating the terminals of London or Frankfurt or Amsterdam with a note pinned to his bony chest. "I am from Iran. I speak no English. Please take me to Lufthansa flight 600, leaving at 4:55 p.m. Thank you." The sheer physicality of flight—the popping of the ears, the drying-out of the skin, the tightening of the seat belt across the lap—seems too jarring for this old man who was born a century ago into a fragrant, unmechanized world.

But he makes it back, and months pass before we hear he has died. The funeral hosted by his daughter in San Jose is a representation. People in Iran have already hired a mullah and wailed aloud and poured rose water onto his marble gravestone, so we in America simply put up his pictures and eat fruit and *halvah*. In fact, we are more interested in the funeral of Khomeini, which takes place at almost the same time. For the first few years after the revolution, Iranians used to say that if only Khomeini would die we could all go back. People were always predicting his imminent demise—after all, he was already seventy-nine, as old as the century, when he took over. But he persisted for so long afterward that he started to seem immortal. After all, as Iranians liked to point out, sourly or exuberantly, Khomeini's older brother was over one hundred and ten and he still felt fine.

And so it is a shock, whether one likes him or not, to hear that Khomeini is gone. We sit around the TV and watch the camera pan over a black mass of people crying and beating their heads to a sorrowful rhythm. "The biggest funeral in the history of the world," the newscaster announces, and as the camera backs up to show the immensity of the crowd we look hungrily at the sidelines; trying to recognize the streets of Tehran. But the camera zooms in again and our eyes are drawn back to the oblong blip floating on the sea of heads. We see agitation, a struggle; the people around the coffin wrench it open and tear at swatches of shroud—and then a white limb is hanging over the side. "*Ey*, Emam Khomeini, come back to us," the people cry, pushing to get closer. The same frenzied crowd that met Khomeini at the airport ten years ago when that arm was sheathed and waving cannot bear to let him go.

For a few weeks afterward, people say that Iran will probably become more liberal now. Baba says we should all take a trip there. Jamsheed says he's sick of America and wants to move back. But after a while the subject is dropped. None of us has the right passport anyway. I can't get a visa on my American passport; as the daughter of an Iranian, I am considered Iranian. And the Iranian passport I share with Mama, Ali and Sufi has not only expired; it is imprinted with a petulant-looking lion standing against a sun. A crown floats above him and *"Empire de l'Iran"* is inscribed below. It could never get me into the Islamic Republic of Iran.

Baba talks about mailing all our passports to the Iranian Interests Section in Washington for renewal; like other Iranians, we would cross our fingers and hope our name is not on a list. These lists loom in a mysterious, threatening cloud. No one knows where they are, but every Iranian in exile has heard of them—there might be a list of people who would be arrested on arrival, or people who would be allowed in but would then be forbidden to leave, or people who might be kept at the airport and interrogated about some long-forgotten detail of the revolution.

"By now the lists are probably entered into computer databases," Mama says.

"Oh?" says Baba. "You think they've got computers?"

"Of course," I say. "You think nothing new has gotten in there in the last decade?"

"You never know," he says. "Ah well, someday we'll all take a year off and go there. We'll go to Yazd—do you remember how beautiful it is? And we'll get horses and travel into the mountains where I used to hunt when I was a boy."

"Great," I say. "When?"

"In two more years, when I get my retirement." But Baba's length of tenure at IBM is never clear. He will eventually get his pension, but until then he cannot visit Iran, where departure dates are not always reliable, where a bad omen can suspend a voyage, where airlines can cancel flights with no warning. "What if I got held up there and lost my job?" he says. If he did not show up the day after his vacation ended, he could be fired and left with nothing.

Ali can't go back either. He would not be allowed to leave Iran until he fulfilled his military requirement or paid the money to get out of it.

"Maybe I should just do it," he says when we are home from Berkeley at Thanksgiving. "Think of how fluent my Farsi would become."

Mama's hand stops mashing the potatoes.

"Yeah," Baba says. "They'd make you an officer because you speak English."

"They wouldn't make him an officer!" Mama snaps. "They'd see he doesn't speak Farsi and they'd send him to the front line to explode the mines."

"The war's over," I remind her. "And anyway, *I* wouldn't have to join the Army. Maybe I should go."

Mama whips the potatoes ferociously. "Why would you want to?"

"I don't know. Just to see it."

"There's nothing to see."

"Let her go if she wants," Baba says mildly, as if it's a trip to Los Angeles.

"How can you say that?" Mama's face is white with anger. "Now she's going to listen to you and go buy a ticket." She turns to me, trying to be calm, but there is a bitterness in her voice that I have never heard before. "What are you looking for? Your childhood? You can't get that back."

I don't say anything more. But later that week I call the Iranian Interests Section in the Algerian Embassy in Washington, swallowing my fear that when I give my name I will be investigated and found to be on a list. The following week a packet arrives in the mail. I must send twelve photographs of myself with a scarf on my head. I must send my old passport and national ID card. And I must send nine hundred and eighty-seven dollars, the charge for separating my childhood passport from my mother's and issuing me a new, Islamic one.

I get my picture taken. I ask Baba to read carefully through the Farsi sections to make sure there are no loopholes in the fee structure or injunctions against people with foreign mothers. But in the end I don't do it. Nine hundred and eighty-seven dollars is a lot of money for a trip I'm not sure I will take.

Perhaps Mama's bitterness at the suggestion of me going back to Iran can be explained by something she said many years after we came to America, something that until then she had only vaguely hinted at. "There were times when I was miserable and lonely in Iran. Sometimes I really resented it."

I was surprised, but I shouldn't have been. For a girl poised on the brink of the sixties—a smart, pretty, artistic girl whose professors had urged her to go on with her studies and whose friends in the music industry had pushed her to go on with her singing, Iran, with its sleepy afternoons and vast stretches of desert, must have been a terrible mismatch. However, having declared one night in Oakland that of course she could live there, she couldn't admit that sometimes she didn't like it. Not even to herself. Other American wives complained, other American wives got fed up and went home; but not Mama. Mama loved Baba so much that she loved Iran too, simply because it was his.

Or so I believed. All through my childhood, "Isn't this fun?" was Mama's credo. She did not dwell on what her life would have been if she had stayed in Los Angeles to promote her music, or if she had gone on to graduate school in New York. Not until twenty years later, when she found herself reluctantly selling real estate for a living, did she admit to herself that in those early years Iran had not been as fun for her as America might have been. And yet, by the time of the revolution, she had switched her focus from singing in Hollywood to painting in Shahrak. Returning to America eliminated both those options.

Later, Mama told me that when we first moved to Iran she felt bad that Ali and I were being deprived of an American childhood. The creative birthday parties, the extra attention, the combination of a tight Iranian family and a free American life were Mama's attempt to give us a childhood that took the best from both cultures and missed out on nothing.

When she told me that she had felt guilty, I found it strange. I had always thought of my childhood in Iran as idyllic; it had never occurred to me that living there was depriving me of something. If Iran had negative aspects, Mama and Baba shielded me from them. I did not feel held back there, as I might have in a more conservative Iranian family. I did not feel estranged there, as I might have in a more Westernized American family. But now I began to wonder how much of my perception of Iran was shaded by Mama and Baba's presentation of it—both before the revolution and afterward, when Iran continued to be filtered to me through the eyes of adults. On one side, Baba's fond memories colored my vision. "Sure, we've found a place that sells pomegranates," he and Jamsheed would say with a sigh. "But no American pomegranate will ever taste as good as an Iranian one." On the other side, Mama was finally revealing the misgivings she had always been so careful to hide.

I listened to them both. And yet neither one could give me a full picture. People might tell me stories about what Iran was really like, but they were not talking about "my" Iran. We had left at the end of my childhood, and like childhood it had frozen in my mind into a mythical land. Once we landed in America, I lost the power to separate Iran from my memories of what it had been. The only way to do that would be to go back and see it for myself.

The Garden Again

❖

WHEN WE FIRST MOVED TO AMERICA I PROMISED MYSELF I would never live there longer than I had lived in Iran. I'd been in Iran for nine years, and, counting Brooklyn, I'd been in America for three. When we arrived in Portland I had six more to go. In the meantime, I began to feel I was missing something that could only be found outside the United States. So I went on a high school exchange program to Italy. I spent a college year in France. I traveled as much as I could, always attuned to what was different from America and what, when I got lucky, was like Iran. Italian boys riding double on scooters, Polish villagers walking with donkeys, the middle-aged Spanish businessman who picked up me and my Berkeley friend on the side of the Barcelona-Zaragoza highway and proudly treated us in his favorite restaurant—all brought on pricks of recognition. ("We can't let him pay for us," whispered my worried friend, but I knew that we couldn't not let him pay.) In Istanbul I fell joyfully into the bazaar. I wanted to hug the old coin sellers who sat cross-legged on the ground. I filled my pockets with spices simply because I remembered their scent. Ignoring the glistening Mediterranean, I took an overnight bus to the farthest edge of Turkey and stared out to the east, unwilling to believe that I couldn't keep going.

I think that on some level, I moved to New York because it reminded me of Tehran. I liked the man who held the subway door open so a stranger could race down the stairs and make it onto the train. I liked the officious woman behind me in the deli checkout line who told me that everyone was using olive oil now at the table instead of butter. New Yorkers were different from Californians, who don't take trains and who have so much room in supermarket aisles that no one needs to talk to anyone else. New Yorkers pried into each other's affairs and looked out for each other in the same way Iranians did.

In New York I met a woman who had attended Community School a few years ahead of me. Persheng graduated in the spring of 1977 and headed off to America. She went to college, worked in cinematography, and married and divorced an American; eventually her parents and sister joined her in the States. At some point during those years, Persheng made a promise to herself so familiar to me that when I heard it I wondered if many others hadn't also made the same one. Having left Iran when she was seventeen, she vowed to return before seventeen years had passed in America. Meeting her made me think back to my own arbitrary promise, which of course I hadn't kept. Six years had passed, and then six more, and I was still in America. After attending journalism school in New York I got an internship at an American newspaper in Brussels, and it was there, sitting in my office, that I got the call to go to Iran.

"Haideh's getting married in Tehran," Baba tells me over the phone. Immediately I think back to Portland, and to my cousin's fervent declaration that she would never fall in love again. She has done exactly what she said she would—returned to Iran to get married. "You're halfway there," Baba says. "You should go to the wedding. Massi and Zia are going to be there and you could stay with them."

A hundred excuses race through my mind—I still don't have a valid Iranian passport; I would want to go to Iran for at least a few months and I would feel bad imposing on Massi and Zia for that long, although I am closer to them now that they have been going back and forth to Iran, stopping in California each time. Somewhere along the way, Massi discovered garage-sale shopping, and she would get me up early in the morning and teach me how to bargain. My adolescent embarrassment long past, I loved the way she shamelessly called out amounts that were a fraction of the original prices. Through sheer enthusiasm she usually got what she asked for, making off with a pair of crystal goblets for two dollars or a silver necklace for fifty cents, and laughing about it for the rest of the day.

The next time I talk to Mama and Baba about going to Iran they pick up both phone extensions and cancel each other out.

"What if you get trapped and have to sneak out?" Mama says. "Are you prepared to spend a few years in Iran?"

"Oh, people go back and forth all the time," Baba says. "And anyway, what's so bad about being in Iran for a few years? I think it would be fascinating."

I call my boyfriend in New York. "It means I won't see you for an extra few months," I say.

"You've always wanted to go," he says. "I'll be here when you get back. I'll miss you, but you really should go."

"It'll be different there. You can't visit me. You'll have to censor your letters. I think they read what comes in from America."

"Don't worry, I'll be cool."

"I mean it, you've really got to be careful. You've got to make sure you don't say anything romantic; in fact you should sign your letters with a woman's name." I stop, unable to think of enough precautions to impose.

Over the next couple of weeks I run through the worst extremes of what I've heard—women whipped for wearing sunglasses, women raped in jail and then stoned for their resulting loss of virginity. People imprisoned for years, unable even to write letters to let their families know where they are. I wake up early in the morning and sprint through the wet forest near my house, imagining what it would be like not to be able to do this anymore.

Everyone at work asks if I am afraid. They have correspondents in Bosnia and Somalia and Georgia—but when I mention Iran they all ask if I am sure it's safe. Their questions invade my sleep; I dream of interrogation rooms and unconfirmed tickets; I wake up nauseous, my hands and feet like ice. "Have you seen *Not Without My Daughter*?" a woman at work asks. Yes, I have seen Sally Field weep on the reproduction of a Tehran street corner as dark, unconcerned strangers pass by. It is a one-sided view of Iran, a skittish foreigner's view. Iranians hate that movie. But it still haunts me, like an obvious warning I am not heeding.

And then one day I realize that I have dwelt so much on going to Iran that I can't not go. Perhaps by envisioning every horror, I have moved beyond the fear that was holding me back. I call the Iranian Interests Section in Washington. The price of a passport has not gone down. It costs about three hundred dollars to convert my passport from "Empire" to "Republic," plus an additional seven hundred to separate me from my mother.

"But that's so much," I say, trying to bargain like an Iranian.

"That is what it costs," the man on the line answers in a bland, American voice.

"But I don't have that kind of money. Isn't there anything else I can do?"

"I'm sorry." Then his voice softens and I am rewarded. "Of course, if you wanted to, you could always get your passport in Iran. That costs about fifty dollars. And it only takes a week." He tells me that right here at the Iranian Embassy in Brussels I can pick up travel documents that will allow me into Iran. He reminds me to dress Islamically when I go to get them. And so, one sunny morning, I put on a raincoat and scarf and take a tram across town to a tree-lined residential street.

In a stately house nestled behind a high iron gate, I enter a waiting room full of Iranians dressed in somber colors. I pull my scarf forward, hoping I look Islamic enough, but the man at the counter hardly glances up as I hand him my application. Back outside I keep my scarf on until I have boarded the tram, just in case anyone is watching.

Three days later the same man hands me a sheaf of documents with photographs and signatures and seals. My face is stapled through the forehead, but the papers look weighty and official, and no one seems to have noticed that in those black-and-white photos I have pinned a blue pillowcase around my head.

Baba calls with a to-do list. "Make sure you visit Khal-khanoum and Mohsen and tell each of them that I especially told you to say hi from me and give them a big kiss. Make sure you go to Esfahan and Qom. Eat *sohan* in Qom. Get me whatever new poetry books are popular now. And get me a map of Iran with all the little towns on it. And a map of Tehran. And posters. And a silver ring with turquoise in it. And go see Agha Shoja in Tehran and ask him what is going on with the Vanak land. I bought it in your name when you were born, so you are the only one who can sign papers on it. Don't sign any. In fact, forget it. Don't even ask about it. Just find my Samsonite briefcase. The deed to the land is inside it. Take it out and bring it back to me."

"Baba, I'm sure that briefcase is gone. Did you ask someone to keep it for you?"

"Someone will have it," he says. "The deed is like a little book, with stamps and brown pages and your name inside it. I'll need it if I ever want to do anything with that land."

As I pack my suitcase a systemic guilt tingles in my spine. Baba is the one who recently ordered and paid for his passport, tucking it safely into a bedroom closet, counting the months until he retires. Baba is the one who is really from Iran. By buying a ticket and going there alone I feel I am usurping a right that belongs to him.

Flying over the Alps, I check my carry-on bag. My Iran outfit is all here: the raincoat reaches below my knees, the jeans are long and baggy, the thick socks hide the shape of my ankles. When I called my cousin Shireen, who just got back to Portland from a visit to Iran, she listed all the body parts I needed to cover, leaving out only the face and hands. I have followed her instructions. I have scrubbed off all makeup residue; I am wearing no perfume; my bag is purged of fashion magazines, political literature, and pictures of myself with any male who isn't a relative. But now, in a panic, I notice that the meter and a half square of black cloth that I bought in Brussels has little strings hanging off it where the clerk cut the fabric.

If I land in Tehran with this cloth on my head—obviously not a real scarf—the authorities might pounce on me: "An impostor!" they would shout. "She clearly does not cover her head in her daily life. And now she wants to enter the Islamic Republic with little strings hanging off her *hejab*! She probably eats pork! She probably doesn't fast! And just ask her if she knows how to pray!"

I tear through my bag, angry at myself for having been so neglectful. I find a needle and a spool of black thread. Still jittery about what else I might have forgotten, I pull out the cloth and begin to put in tiny stitches, transforming the raw fabric into a legitimate article of clothing.

Turkish Airlines. Tehran. 20:40

I stare hard at the Atatürk Airport departures board. I don't know if I trust it. Tehran disappeared from my internal travel map long ago. Foreign exchange rates in the newspaper skipped from Indonesia to Ireland; and when, on a whim, I asked a Berkeley travel agent about fares to Tehran, she looked at me as if I were inquiring about the moon. I never saw Tehran listed as a destination; I never saw an advertised fare. And now here it is, on this sign above my head. For a second I feel like those of us in America have been duped. Iran has been here all the time, with biweekly flights ferrying people back and forth; it was we who failed to see it.

I float toward the boarding ramp, feeling as if I am watching a movie of someone else's life. The idea that when I step off this plane it will be onto Iranian ground is too strange to think about; and so I try to forget it, instead looking around the cabin to see who is traveling with me.

They are all Iranian. As soon as we are in the air they leave their seats and roam the aisles, leaning over the backs of chairs, comparing notes like guests at a reunion that is long overdue.

"When did you leave?"

"Have you been back at all?"

"I went back in '87 and '91. It's much better now."

"Your name is Esfahani? From Mashhad? I think I know your father."

Releasing my seat belt, I think of Shireen's advice. *Once you get on the plane, don't let anyone touch you. Don't answer anyone's questions. Don't*

*look into people's eyes, but don't look away or you'll seem timid. Pretend you
don't know Farsi. Don't give anything to anyone or accept anything from
anyone. They might be carrying drugs.*

"Where are you from?" asks the middle-aged man next to me. His
hair is short and curly and he is wearing a tan suit. His voice, like all
the other voices, has the friendliness of strangers thrown together by
a storm or a flood—just being here removes the formalities.

"New York," I say quietly.

"Oh, my brother lives in New York," he says. "Me, I've just been
in Istanbul for business. I import things—televisions, VCRs. Is this
your first time back?"

"Yes."

"You've been away a long time, haven't you?"

"Yeah," I say, taken aback, because I have only said two words.
"You can tell by my Farsi?"

"Yes. But it'll get better once you're there."

He asks me a few more questions and then calls to a group of men
across the aisle. "It's her first trip back. She's traveling alone. Her
cousin is getting married tomorrow."

"Ah. What is her family name?"

I tell him.

"Oh, from Kerman?" I shake my head, not wanting to say where
exactly my family is from.

"How long are you staying?" asks a thin man with wire-rim glasses.

"Just a month. I've got to get back to school," I add quickly, as if
saying one month instead of three will throw them off the scent.

"Good for you," he says. "Everyone who is living abroad should
come back to Iran, even if it's just for a month. Maybe when you're
done with your studies you can move back for good."

"What are you, crazy?" laughs a younger man sitting next to him.
"If they were smart enough to get out of the country they'd better
be smart enough to stay there. If I didn't have a wife and kids in Iran
do you think I'd be on this plane?"

"Why?" I ask. "What's so bad about it?"

"Nothing." The man with the glasses smiles reassuringly. "He
doesn't know what he's talking about."

"What do you mean?" the younger man says. "Admit it, you can't

even earn enough to stay there all year round. He goes to the Emirates to work whenever he needs money."

"Yes, but I always come back," says the first man. "You know," he
says, leaning in toward me with the charged excitement Iranians in
America get whenever they find some link between Iran and the
West, "Iran was the original spot where Paradise was supposed to be,
where Adam and Eve started out. It says so in the Bible. The scholars
have figured out that it was in northern Iran, in the Alborz Mountains, to be exact."

"It's true," says the man next to me, with the same animation.
"Paradise is an Iranian word. Even the English is directly related to
the Farsi. *Pardis*—Paradise, see?"

"In fact," says the man with glasses. "You know the mountain
where the devil first landed on earth? That was Mount Damavand."

The younger man snorts from down the row. "It's funny how often
the devil picks Iran to come to."

"Don't listen to him," the man next to me says. "Many people in
my family live abroad and come back to visit. They all say the first
time back is the best; everything is wonderful. The second time it's
still interesting, but you're not so enchanted. It's not until the third
time that you can't wait to get out."

The stewardess holds out two sets of forms—large ones for foreigners
and small ones for Iranians. I almost take a large form. But about a
half hour ago we crossed an invisible border and I stopped being an
American. So I take the Iranian form, fill in Name and Nationality,
and then stop.

"You need help?" my neighbor asks immediately, as if he has been
waiting for this. He translates the questions into English and, careful
as a child, I write my answers in the curvy script I learned years ago.

Occupation: student.

Place of residence: America.

Date of last departure from Iran—I frown. The American date was
January 12, 1979. In Iran now, the year is 1372, with the zero point
set to the revelation of the Prophet Mohammad. The Iranian year,
unlike the roving Arabic year, always begins at the same time—the
first day of spring. It is now September, or Shahrivar, the sixth month
of the Iranian year; which means that the winter day on which I left

Iran would have been in the tenth month. But the tenth month of what year? In 1976 the Shah decided that rather than springing from the birth of Islam, Iranian time should reflect the dawn of the Persian empire. Like magic, the entire country skipped ahead twelve centuries; all clocks and calendars and newspapers instantly reflected the change. At the end of his regime, trying to save himself, the Shah apologized for this arrogant move and reversed the edict. But it was too late; according to my old passport, my last departure from Iran took place in 2537.

"Skip that question," my neighbor advises.

But at the next line I stop again. "Passport Number." All I have is my travel documents. I don't even have a copy of my old Iranian passport, and my American one is hidden deep in the money belt under my jeans. "Whatever you do," Baba warned me on the phone, "don't show them your American passport. In fact, don't even bring it."

"But I have to bring it," I said. "How else will I get through all the other countries?"

"Okay, bring it, but don't let them find it. Can you sew it into your clothes?"

"Baba, you can't sew a passport into your clothes. They check your clothes. I'll put it in my money belt. But what if they ask if I have an American passport?"

"Lie."

"And if they search me?"

"That's true." He paused. "Then don't lie. But don't let them see it. If they ask how you were able to live in America, just say your mother is American and leave it at that."

"Skip that question too," my neighbor says when I explain all this. "Just tell me if they give you any trouble." I smile, grateful and frightened, like a runaway who arrives in the city and latches on to the first man who is kind to her.

The plane dips toward the ground. My heart pounds as I peer out the window. We are flying low over a sea of yellow pinpricks—tiny bulbs too weak to diminish the blackness around them. From above, Tehran looks ancient, as if lit by a thousand candles.

We graze the runway. My neighbor turns to me, alarmed.

"Do you know you're supposed to have something to cover your head and body?"

"Oh, yes," I say proudly. "I have it right here." I pull out my raincoat and the black square of fabric that I finished hemming in Istanbul. I drape it over my head. The bulky material barely knots at my neck, and it hangs way down below my shoulders like a nun's habit. Using the window as a mirror I center it, carefully tucking in every single hair, when suddenly I hear a burst of delighted laughter.

"You don't need such a big one," the man next to me says. "Look, it's her first time back. Look at what a big scarf she has brought." The men across the aisle laugh too.

None of the other women in the cabin are wearing scarves like mine. Theirs are sheer and colorful; a few are fringed with gold. A middle-aged woman in front of me ties on a leopard-spotted scarf. Her eyes are coated with thick mascara, and a pair of Christian Dior sunglasses pokes defiantly out of her raincoat pocket. She fluffs her bronze bangs out from under her scarf, then turns and gives me a quick nod, as if to say I look okay.

Outside the plane, they'll have a bus waiting, Shireen told me. *You'll have to run and fight to get on it. Keep a sharp eye on your bags.* I imagined a Brueghelesque scene: a crush of bodies crawling over each other, catfights between veiled women, tiny hands deftly unzipping my duffel bag and rifling through my pockets as the bus pulled off without me. Instead, we file calmly onto a sleek shuttle bus. "Let me help you with that," says my neighbor from the plane, taking my bag onto his shoulder. "In Iran," he explains, "we are chivalrous."

The bus pulls up in front of a low building. We step off it onto the pavement, and in my first whiff of the soft, balmy air, a dam of memory breaks and a long-ago night floods in—a string of lights dangling over an ice-cream stand, twangy sitar music playing on a transistor radio, a crowd of families milling about, enjoying the relief of summer midnight. The sweet, dark taste of Iran.

In the front room of the building, two men in pistachio-green shirts sit inside two booths. Everyone lines up behind the one on the left. "But this line is for passport holders," my neighbor says. He hands me my bag and gently points me toward the other booth.

A man with a mustache sits behind a thick glass window. I put my mouth to the hole in the glass and say in my clearest, strongest Farsi, "I am Iranian. I have come with travel documents."

"What are these?"

"*Laissez-passer* forms?" I say, trying the term from the Brussels embassy.

"Never heard of them."

I begin to explain, but he waves his hand at me and says, "Where is your passport?" In the greenish fluorescent lighting, his mustache looks blacker than hair—alive, almost. "Why don't you have a passport?" he says again.

The line of passport holders has emptied out. My neighbor from the plane looks back at me from the other side of the booths and raises his eyebrows in a question. I shake my head and he comes back to explain everything I have just explained.

"Why is her Farsi so bad?" the man in the booth asks suspiciously. He hands me another form that my neighbor fills out in an impossible scribble.

Another bus rolls up and my neighbor and I step aside as a planeload of new passengers line up. The man in the booth motions a group of them over and begins to process their forms.

"What about her?" my neighbor asks.

"They are checking on it."

I feel guilty for keeping him here so late. It is almost two in the morning, and there are probably people waiting to meet him. "You can go," I say. "I'll really be fine. My uncle should be here any minute."

He glances at his watch, and then at me. "Are you sure?" He looks relieved. "Here is my phone number. Call me if you have any problems." He slips between the booths and I am alone.

The man with the mustache points toward a small waiting area. I sit in a chair and cross my legs, but my raincoat slips off my knee, so I uncross them. The room is hot and airless, and soon I am soaked in sweat. But I keep my raincoat pulled tightly around me as I watch for Massi and Zia to appear at the top of the exit area staircase. In the meantime, two armed men in green uniforms pace back and forth in front of me.

Finally I stand up.

"Sit down," one of them says.

I sit.

They pace. The hand on my watch inches down to two-thirty, and then up to three.

"So what should I do?" I finally ask one of the men passing by. He looks at me as if for the first time, then walks over to the booth and flips through my papers. "What was the date of your last departure from Iran?" he asks.

"I don't know."

"Why did you come without a passport?"

Other guards gather around. With their green shirts and guns and unshaven faces they look like jungle guerrillas. But they are not hostile; they act more like I am a stray cat that has wandered into their hideout and won't leave.

"But how did you travel to Belgium without a passport?" another guard with a mustache asks.

"Well, my mother is American, you see, so it's okay," I say, cringing at how weak this sounds.

And then, as if he doesn't want to ask but has run out of questions, the first guard asks if I have an American passport.

Later, I run through that night again and again, trying to redo it.

Had my Farsi been better I could have insisted that they accept my travel documents and they might have just waved me through. Had I immediately asked them to page Zia, he could have come down and talked them into letting me go. Had I lied when they asked me if I had an American passport, they would not have asked to see it and then they could not have given it to their superior officer, who disappeared with it to some other part of the airport.

As it is, when I finally think of paging Zia and Massi they appear immediately. Zia looks tired—it is almost four in the morning, but it is not just that. For the first time in my life he does not seem like a giant. His hair is almost completely white, and the fleshy neck and big bald head that used to tower solidly over me look slightly deflated now. But Massi looks the same as ever—a middle-aged beauty with dark shaggy hair, finely drawn eyebrows, and an expressive face that right now is wavering between excitement and anxiety. She hurries over and gives me a big hug, but when I try to hug Zia he jumps three feet back.

"*Never* do that!" he hisses.

Confused, I back away. "They have my American passport," I whisper. His blue eyes bulge in horror. Without another word he hurries over to the airport men, who usher him into an office.

Massi and I wait in the hall.

"Can he get it back?" I ask her.

"I don't know."

"Is it a big problem?"

"I don't know." She has the numb look of someone in a hospital waiting room.

We hear muffled voices. Then a bang like a hand against a desk. Then quieter voices.

After fifteen minutes, Zia storms out of the office and slams the door.

"Let's go!" he barks.

We trot behind him, out a set of glass doors and into the warm night. He opens the door of a dented white Renault hatchback.

"Get in," he says.

I eye his pants pocket. "Did you get it?" I ask.

"Get in the car."

"Did you get it?" Massi asks.

"Did I get it?" he says. We are inside the car now with the doors closed. "Did I get it? We're lucky we got out with her!" He turns to me and speaks in slow, heavily accented English, to make sure I understand. "They . . . wanted . . . to . . . send . . . you . . . to . . . jail."

"Why?"

"Why?" He slips back into Farsi. "She asks why! They said that since you had no record of having left the country, you must have escaped illegally. Anyone who arrives without a passport goes to jail. I had to promise to take full responsibility for the fact that they were letting you go. Otherwise—" He pauses and pulls at his loose jowls and widens his eyes, finishing in English: "Jail!"

We speed down the road. Suddenly Zia swings around from the steering wheel and grabs my head. The car swerves. He pulls me up to his face and kisses my forehead with wet, trembly lips. "*Now* I can kiss you. Never try to kiss me in a public place. Why the hell did you show them your American passport?"

"They asked if I had one. What was I supposed to do?"

"Lie!"

"But my father told me to tell them the truth. Shireen did too. That if they asked—"

"Truth!!?" he explodes. "What truth? In Iran, you must learn one thing. Never tell the truth!"

"Well," Massi says, "what's done is done. There's no use arguing over it now."

But what about my passport? There is no American Embassy here. Even the Swiss Embassy, which takes care of American interests in emergencies, will not help me. I am the daughter of an Iranian. I am Iranian.

We are on the freeway now. To our left is the white Shahyad Monument, a tall, truncated wave of concrete swelling up against the night sky. Years ago, I visited it and rode an underground movable walkway through pitch-black halls as slides of the Shah and his family flashed on either side. Passing it now, I should feel some flash of nostalgia. But I am too busy remembering to breathe.

"Hey," Massi says, "do you know what that tower is?"

"Yes." My voice sounds far away. "Shahyad."

"Eh, she remembers the name," she says, too cheerfully. "Only now it is called Freedom Square."

"But what about my passport?" I say.

"What will you do," Zia says slowly, "if you never get it back?"

"What do you mean?"

"Forget the passport," he says. "It's gone."

❖

"*Salmani! Salmani!*"

I jerk in my bed.

"*Salmani!*"

A blurry Zia fills the doorway. "It's nine-thirty!" he barks. "You'd better get up if you want to go to the *salmani!*"

I have no idea what he is saying.

"Don't you want to get your hair done? Hurry up! Massi has made appointments."

Ah, *salmani* is the hairdresser. I shake my head and sink back into my pillow. I only fell asleep an hour or two ago, after three hours of tossing under the hot sheets and fretting about my passport. All I want now is to stay asleep for as long as I can.

But Massi's soft voice joins in with Zia's, cajoling me. "Your breakfast is on the table. Come drink some tea."

Already dressed in her long coat and scarf, Massi leads me to a table set with little plates of feta cheese and sour cherry preserves and flat bread. She looks serene; all her tension from last night has dissipated, and she smiles and places a glass of hot black tea into my hands. I can barely eat—I am still too tense and exhausted—but I swallow the tea down and start to tie on my own scarf. Massi stops me.

"You can't wear that, it's too hot. Here, put this on." She hands me a flimsy black scarf with a gold fringe. It feels weightless. "It won't mat your hair down," she explains, adding, "You might want to put on a little lipstick too."

"I thought it was illegal."

"Hah." Massi's mischievous grin reminds me of Baba's. "Look at me." Her high cheekbones are coated with foundation, her almond eyes are lengthened with black lines, and her lips are painted hot pink.

"But I do have to wear socks, right?" I've crammed thick socks into my black flats, to hide the shape of my ankles.

"No, no, don't worry. We're just going to the hairdresser." The socks come off, leaving me with cool feet and misgivings.

Outside, a wave of heat hits me. I hurry to roll down the car window. Summer lasts longer here than in New York or California; I remember wearing shorts well into the start of the school year, and the weather would stay clear and mild until one day in early November we would awaken to snow-covered mountains and a cold snap that had arrived in the night.

That day feels far off now as I shift in my seat, trying to let air circulate around my raincoat. The car rattles down leafy residential streets, mostly empty except for a few women whose scarves are tied back to reveal quarter crowns of dark hair. We are close up against the beige wall of mountains, but even without this landmark I know we are in North Tehran, the less crowded, more affluent side of town.

We pull up outside a blue metal gate and Massi gets out and raps on it with her fingernails.

"Who is it?" a female voice whispers.

"It's us."

The gate swings open. A middle-aged woman with short yellow hair, a white tank top, and denim culottes leads us through a shady courtyard and down to a basement where a mirrored wall reflects a counter strewn with hairpins, rollers, and fashion magazines.

"This is my brother's daughter," Massi announces, settling into a chair in front of the mirror. "She's a *do-rageh*, from America."

The blond *salmani* looks me up and down and instructs her teen-aged assistant to finish the other customer, a woman whose half-bleached hair sticks up in spikes through clear plastic wrap. Sucking on a Marlboro, the *salmani* pulls Massi's hair tightly around rollers as she fires off questions. "Who are the caterers? Who's doing the videotape? Which store is the dress from?"

I keep quiet, shy about my Farsi.

The *salmani* turns to me. "Would you like a cut or a brushing?"

"A brushing."

She wets my hair, takes out an industrial-looking silver blow-dryer, and starts brushing. Every few minutes she turns to pull on her cigarette, leaving the dryer fixed on my scalp until, just before the smell of singed hair would have signaled her, she yanks it away and blows smoky breath onto the injured spot. Finally she holds up an aerosol can and sprays until my hair is a hard sheet. Even putting my scarf back on doesn't disturb it, but Massi forbids me to tie the scarf and tells me to walk carefully as she sweeps me out to the car.

"Do you think these will be okay?" I nervously hold up my white bustier, black jacket and black miniskirt. After the tentlike coats we wore out in the street, these clothes look blasphemous.

"Of course, they're beautiful," Massi says, beckoning me into her bedroom. But I can tell my outfit is too plain for her taste. Across her bed lie two taffeta floor-length dresses: sea green for the afternoon and sun yellow for the night. I lay my clothes down next to hers and leave her at her dressing table as I wander through the sprawling six-bedroom apartment. Four years ago, Massi and Zia bought a house in Portland, and since then they have been switching homes slowly, transporting their possessions in large suitcases each time they fly to America. I walk barefoot from room to room, pausing to cool my feet on spots of floor tile left exposed when the carpets were carted away.

A man walks in the front door, staggering under huge bouquets of white flowers. Another man carries in a stack of metal rental chairs. Zia's voice bellows from a back room, telling the men where to go. I am tired and slightly nauseous, still unable to believe that I have no passport. I want to ask Zia if he meant what he said last night, but he is too busy. I consider taking a nap, but I don't want to risk messing up my blow-dried helmet of hair. So I go into a bedroom to look at the *sofreh*—a satin cloth spread out on the floor and decorated with tall white candles, gold-painted eggs, wild rue, flowers, and jasmine sweets. In a few hours, Haideh and her groom will sit here and read together from the Qoran as the wedding guests grind pillars of sugar over them for sweetness in their marriage.

"How do I look?" Massi asks nervously, standing in the doorway. She has put on the sea-green dress, and her hair is piled high, bringing out her sharp cheekbones and the long lashes of her laughing, almond-shaped eyes.

"You look like Iran's Sophia Loren," I say truthfully, and she flashes me a pleased smile.

"Put all your things in our bedroom," she says conspiratorially. "We're locking all our valuables in there during the wedding." She cocks her head in the mirror again. "We were going to rent a big garden to have the wedding, but since it was commercial property, and outdoors, there would have been more chance of the *komiteh* coming. It's safer at home."

Shireen and I had a long phone conversation about the *komiteh*, the morals police who arrest you if your coat is too short or your shoes too revealing. She told me Baba's cousin Afagh and her daughter were arrested a couple of years ago for wearing scarves with red flowers in the pattern. Red flowers were un-Islamic, said the *komiteh*.

"They threw them into a room with thirty other women and no furniture," Shireen said. "No beds, just a dirty carpet. They wouldn't let them make one phone call, not even to tell her husband where they were. They fed them scraps, the same scraps they give to criminals. Then in the morning, the ones who had money were allowed to have their husbands come. Afagh's husband had to bring the deed to their house to get them out."

Afagh and her daughter had to return to *komiteh* headquarters for sentencing. They joined one of three lines of women who were in for similar crimes. A different mullah would decide the punishment for each group. After several hours, the first mullah walked to the head of his line. "Eighty lashes each," he proclaimed. ("The whip leaves scars if they do it hard," Shireen explained. "And eighty lashes . . .")

The second mullah, standing next to the first, shrugged and yelled, "Eighty lashes each!" At this point, a woman in the third line, where Afagh and her daughter were standing, began to scream. The group around her hissed furiously. "Shut up! Or he'll give us more!"

The third mullah frowned at the commotion. He turned to face the women and spoke as if addressing a roomful of naughty children. "This time I am sending you home with a warning," he said. "But I never, ever want to see any of you in here again."

By five o'clock the house is crammed full of people. A three-man band plays Iranian-style techno-pop in the living room. A buffet is spread out in the garden.

"I'll tell you a secret," Haideh says. She hikes up her tight white gown and sits down with me under a hot photographer's lamp. "My parents think I met Mansour through friends." Her dark eyes sparkle beneath the gauzy white veil flipped back over her head. "But really we saw each other on the street. We looked at each other and then he turned around and I gave him my phone number."

"Isn't that dangerous?" I say.

"Yes, if the *komiteh* had seen it we would have been arrested. But what else could we do? Did my parents really expect me to sit here and turn thirty while I waited for them to come back from the States and find me a husband?"

I look at Massi, who is sailing from guest to guest, elated. This is the first of her children to marry since Shireen's wedding to Doctor, fifteen years ago. If someone were to whisper to her right now that Haideh had met her husband on the street, I doubt the news would upset her.

The men here wear suits and ties, although the government frowns on such Western apparel. Most of the women have on tight sequined dresses and teased-up hair, although a few old women have on simple pink-flowered chadors.

"*Mashallah*, Taraneh," they say, hugging me tightly. "What a lady you've become! You look exactly like Karen. Do you remember me? You were this small when I last saw you. How are your parents? Their places are very empty tonight."

I don't remember them all, but they remember me as if I had been gone only a few months. I kiss them and say how happy I am to see them; they fold me into their arms and I feel a rush of gladness to feel so connected. "My parents are well," I say. "They say hello." It is true; my very presence here is a way of my parents saying hello.

Homa-khanoum and Agha Vakili have just flown in from America, and Dadash and Leila-khanoum are here too. They look amazingly unchanged—Leila's hair is just as black and her skin is just as smooth as when we left. And, except for a few wrinkles around the eyes, Dadash is still the slender, immaculately groomed uncle I remember. They embrace me and tell me they have driven up from the village for the wedding; they are staying with their daughter Roya, who lives in Tehran with her husband and children. Their son Javad emigrated to Canada years ago. Like all the other relatives I see tonight, they make me promise to come stay with them soon.

"That's my father-in-law," Haideh says, pointing a red fingernail at a square-jawed man with white hair. "Doesn't he look Swedish? Not Iranian-looking at all—see, he has blue eyes. And you know, my father has blue eyes. So I am hoping"—she gives my arm a squeeze—"that one of our kids will have blue eyes too."

A young woman in a magenta dress sashays up. "Is that the mode in America?" she says, pointing at the slight platform on my shoes. I nod. "How cute," she says unsmilingly, and flits away. And then I notice other women doing it, glancing at my miniskirt, my jacket, my long, blunt-cut hair—taking note of how someone from America looks.

I walk up to the glittering banquet table and a group of women open up their circle to include me. They are talking about a girl recently caught on the street by the *komiteh*. Her hair was showing under her scarf, and instead of pulling the scarf forward when they confronted her she argued back. The *komiteh* man shot her in the head. "It happened right here in Tajrish," one woman says as she loads her plate with eggplant stew and saffron rice. No one is safe, the women's shaking heads say. I must look alarmed, because one of them adds, "Don't worry, you just have to know how to talk to them." She smiles reassuringly. I nod back, fill my plate with food, and sink into one of the chairs lined up against the wall.

"One donkey inside another donkey," says a familiar voice. I turn to see my cousin Reza. He is wearing glasses now, and his closely cropped hair is flecked with gray. But his sweet, cigarette-seared voice is unchanged, and it floods me with homesickness for California. "It's an Iranian expression," he says. He sits down beside me and his brown tie slides forward over his white shirt. "No matter how deep you go, they're all donkeys. Coming here is like going to Africa and living with the cannibals."

"What do you mean?"

He shrugs. I've already heard, secondhand, that Reza and his wife split up a few months after their wedding. No one knows why, and his family won't talk about it. One rumor says the girl was bad-tempered; another says she lied about her age and her high marks in school; a third says it was she who left Reza. The latest news is that the girl's uncles and brothers have been going around looking for Reza, and that it's lucky his parents live so far on the outskirts of town and don't have a phone. Even so, people say Reza has been sleeping at a different relative's house each night because the men in his wife's family are after him to return the dowry money. They haven't gotten the money back, but they have managed to make Reza *mamnou-ol-khorooj*, which means "forbidden to exit." The words are stamped right in the front of his passport, meaning he won't be al-lowed out of Iran until he pays the dowry.

"That stuff that happened with your passport last night," Reza says. "You think that's rare here? Everything you do in Iran is like that." His words drift off as a young woman in black walks by holding a camera. "She's beautiful," he says. "You know, every video crew has to have one. That way if the *komiteh* raids the studio and asks who took all the pictures of women they can say it was her."

"I guess it creates jobs for women," I say.

He rolls his eyes.

"I thought you liked it here."

"You like it at first," he says. "Everyone pays attention to you, they visit you, you visit them, they cook meals for you. But then you start to see how it is. You can't get anything done. It takes the whole day just to buy meat. My parents have been waiting over a year to get a phone connected."

"But I thought you were going to travel around the countryside on horseback—"

"Shh," he says, jumping up from his chair.

The music has stopped. Without looking around, Reza points me toward the bedrooms. And suddenly I see all the women are flying back in that direction as the men surge up toward the front door.

"*Komiteh!*" Reza's sister Niki hisses. She grabs my arm and pulls me into a side room. Thirty women are burrowing through a mound of clothes, deftly wrapping coats and scarves around their party dresses and fancy hairdos. "Where is your scarf?" a woman says, looking mistrustfully at my black-stockinged thighs. I shake my head, wide-eyed. All my belongings are in Massi's room and the door is locked. I look for her but I see only a sea of heads, hands adjusting cloth, nobody recognizable.

My cousin Niki, draped in black now, pushes me into the next room and shuts me in. The room is empty; there is no bed to hide under, no chair to crouch behind when the *komiteh* come in. As my mind races with stories of prison rapes and girls getting shot in the head, I pull open the closet door. It is packed to the top with suitcases, but in one corner is a rolled-up carpet waiting to be shipped to America. Just this morning I helped Massi weigh it and drag it in here. Now I consider hiding in it.

I reach out.

The doorknob turns.

Niki's uncovered head peeks into the room.

"They're gone."

"What do you mean, 'they're gone'?" My arm is still stretched out, ready to unroll the carpet.

"The men paid them something," she says. "They won't come back. It's how the *komiteh* make their money."

I follow her down the hall, indignant to see everyone acting as if nothing had happened. Massi's door is hanging open and I slip inside, find my scarf, and carry it into the living room. The women are back, in their sparkly dresses, dancing furiously as the band plays with abandon.

I perch myself on a chair on the edge of the dance floor and find myself sitting a few seats down from Ammejun, my great-aunt who made the *khastegari* dinner for me and her son. About two years after that dinner, Homa-khanoum told Baba that she had heard that Mehdi had inspected me and passed me over. "That's a lie!" Baba said. "He called her back that very week! The Jalilis are spreading this story to protect his *aberu*, to save his face." He picked up the phone and dialed Massi, to tell her to pass the word around that it was all made up, but Massi wasn't home. I hope he forgot about it after that. I didn't see Ammejun again because she left for Iran shortly afterward, and I don't want her to be mad at me.

But when she sees me her protruding lower lip softens into a wide smile. "Good, good, you sit here," she says, patting the chair next to her without looking away from the dancers, whom she glares at threateningly whenever they come too close. I sit down beside her.

"Were you afraid when the *komiteh* came?" she says. "You shouldn't be. Everyone is always scared when they first arrive here. My own sons won't come because they're afraid. And look at you, a girl coming all by yourself. Hmph! I could tell them some things! This is not the only time they've come after people. Wear a chador, don't wear a chador." She chuckles. "When I was the same age as you, Reza Shah forbade chadors."

I've heard this story before—how as soon as Ammejun and Aziz heard the news they put on European hats and coats and strutted through town. They parked themselves in a public garden and set out a picnic, giggling at everyone who stared. But tonight Ammejun takes the story farther.

"Everyone celebrated Reza Shah's new law. They had to, whether they liked it or not. The government kept track of who showed loyalty. The day the law was passed a landowner in Khomein had a big party. You know Khomein—the town of Emam Khomeini." As she talks, the wrinkles on her face almost disappear; just telling the story transforms her to the time when she was twenty-one. "The landowner laid out carpets in front of his fort—*akh*, what a fort, with plaster fruit decorating every corner. An Esfahani artisan had been brought in to carve those walls and now that house has become a museum. We will go there together." She puts her soft old hand over mine and squeezes it tightly. "Where was I? Ah, that day we went to his fort and he served everyone tea and sweets. We were so excited. It was the first time we had ever drunk tea with the men of the town."

"What did your husbands think?"

"Oh, they didn't mind. It was the peasants who were cursing. Their women didn't change clothes—they just kept going out into the fields like before. So Reza Shah's police went out and ripped the chadors off their heads, and if the women still wore their hair in the old way, with twelve or thirteen long braids, they took their knives and sliced off the braids.

"All night people were dancing in the streets. Musicians were banging on drums. Men and women who wanted to get drunk had gone to a certain house that had alcohol. But we wanted to go to bed. As we walked away, a friend of Agha Jan's nodded and stepped aside to let us pass. 'Sisters, please go ahead,' he said. 'With this bully on the throne now, things are going to come down on all our heads.'"

"He was right," I venture.

"Everyone is right. They say that about everyone, and they're all right. This *komiteh* is not doing anything new. They just don't know how to do it. Bah! You give them money and they go away. In the old times even the greatest ayatollahs had to lower their heads down to the boots of Reza Shah." Her mouth droops and the oldness returns to her face. "Rub my back, here, where the pain is," she says. I press the heel of my hand into her birdlike shoulder. "Ah, you are a good girl," she says. "You shouldn't worry about these things—you dress one way one time and another way another time. Whatever they tell you to do, you do. And then you come home and do what you have always done."

❖

"At least they're not sending her passport to the Swiss Embassy," Zia says a few days later. He is explaining my situation to his cousin Agha Billou, a gaunt older man with a gray goatee and a cane who has come to pay a call. "Then we'd never get it back. Fortunately I got the airport chief to promise to give it back if we get her an Iranian passport."

The way Zia describes it, I showed up at the airport waving my American passport in the guards' faces. "I went in and tried to fix the damage," he says. "But they said the only way they would give her back her passport was if she immediately got back on a plane and flew out of Iran."

Should I have done that? Would I now, if I had the chance? It feels like a cop-out, to finally come here after so long and then to be scared away as soon as I arrived. I want it both ways—to enter Iran as easily as an Iranian and to leave it as easily as an American.

Agha Billou sips his tea and clucks disapprovingly. "It could take five or six months to get her an Iranian passport," he says slowly, drawing a pipe out of his breast pocket and cradling it in his hands. He is perched carefully on a straight-backed chair with his legs crossed. His mother, Khanoum Qodsi, sits sunken into the living-room couch, wrapped tightly in a black chador, slowly lifting a teacup to her lips.

"But the embassy people said it would take only a few days," I say, annoyed at the whining-little-girl petulance of my Farsi voice.

"Yes, but now that this problem has come up with your American passport, it's different," Agha Billou says. He was once the Iranian Ambassador to some small country, and he knows these things, not like the women at the wedding who hugged me and said, "Don't worry, Taraneh-jan, everything will work out fine, *enshallah*." It is that "*enshallah*," that "God willing" tacked on at the end, that bothers me. It is hard to pin things down when everything depends on the will of God.

Once, when Homa-khanoum was visiting America, I asked her how long she was going to be staying. "What do I know?" she said, her Mongol face as impenetrable as if she were standing in a sandstorm in some desert over which no plane had ever flown. "Whenever God wants it."

"Well, what does your return ticket say?"

"It's unknown," she said, shrugging.

"But how can your ticket not be clear?" I insisted.

"Soon, *enshallah*," she answered. "Then you can come visit us."

And then one day she was gone, but by the time I heard about it her plane had landed. No one had known her travel date so no one could choose that day to wish her harm. It infuriated me, that unwillingness to give out information, that constant assumption of ill fortune. But now I wonder if I should have been more cautious somehow.

"It doesn't matter," Zia says, pulling me over to his side and planting a big kiss on my forehead. "You can live with us. Do you know what a good girl this is?" He laughs and pats me on the back. "She is my very own daughter now."

Agha Billou's mother, Khanoum Qodsi, turns to me, her eyes huge behind Coke-bottle glasses. "Taraneh-khanoum," she yells deafly, holding her chador over her mouth like a screen, a habit some old ladies have from when women muffled their voices to avoid arousing men. The result is a shrill, pebbly sound. "How are you getting back to America?"

"I don't know," I say drily. "They took my passport."

"No, no," Khanoum Qodsi yells, brushing away my words with the back of her hand. "I mean, when you go to America what will you use to get back?"

"I'm taking Turkish Airlines."

"Ah," she says, "an airplane, then." She nods vigorously, chattering to herself.

"She should have just said no when they asked her about the American passport," Agha Billou says.

"But then what if they had searched me?" I say.

"Yeah, what if they had searched her?" Zia says.

"Oh, everyone knows they don't search people anymore," Agha Billou says, raising his eyebrows up into the wrinkles of his bald head.

"Taraneh-khanoum!" Khanoum Qodsi cries.

I turn, trying not to look annoyed. "Yes?"

"I see you haven't heard about the InterFrance boat."

"The what?"

"The InterFrance boat."

"No, I haven't."

"Ah, my dear, you must go to America that way. All the millionaires take the InterFrance boat. You will sail across the ocean with the rich people. Can you imagine? A boatful of millionaires—some without wives! On the soul of my mother, I am telling you this because it is the best way for you to go."

Where would such a boat leave from? Where would it go? Most likely the InterFrance boat is something Khanoum Qodsi heard of seventy years ago, something that had stopped running long before I was born.

"What would I do here for six months?" I ask no one in particular.

"Oh, anything you want," Agha Billou says. "You know, with your English skills you could get an excellent job. I'm sure you could teach English. Or you could be a secretary."

I think back to Brussels, where just last week I was writing editorials on international politics. I must look disappointed, because Agha Billou adds, "As a secretary you could make a hundred dollars a month."

I force a smile and say that surely my Farsi isn't proficient enough for that.

Khanoum Qodsi yells from the couch. "So? Taraneh-khanoum? Will you take the InterFrance boat?"

"Yes!" I yell back. "I will!"

She sits back and nods, apparently satisfied. But a few seconds later she looks up again. "Massi-khanoum!" she cries. Massi hurries out from the kitchen. "Why doesn't Siamak come back to Iran? He's been in America a very long time. You should bring him back here to get married. God forbid he should marry an American girl; that would be *very* bad . . ."

In Iran it is no longer just political dissidents who lead double lives. Defying the rules has become a national pastime. When our car approaches an intersection where the *komiteh* have set up one of their ubiquitous roadblocks, Massi nibbles at her pink nail polish like a guilty schoolgirl. When we walk down a street and a small woman in black barks out, "Clean off that lipstick!" Leila-khanoum wipes the back of her hand across her mouth. But as soon as we pass the woman, Leila cups her lipstick in her hand and swiftly reapplies it. Stuck in traffic, I hear rock-and-roll music blasting from the open window of a car; the man in the driver's seat smiles at my shocked face. At the apartment of some family friends, crystal glasses of homemade wine are passed around like a rare delicacy; the conservative, middle-aged guests exchange mischievous glances as they reach out for it. Still spooked from the wedding raid, I refuse to take one, and they laugh and drain their glasses to show me it is safe. Even a religious old woman whom Massi and I visit smiles wickedly and opens a cupboard to show us her tiny bottles of Jack Daniel's and Stolichnaya. "From the airplane, when I visited my son in Europe," she says with a twinkle. "Gifts for my grandchildren."

But the fear is also there. I've heard three different times now about the girl with the scarf who got shot, and every now and then she appears in my dreams, along with green-shirted passport controllers who grab me as I try to leave the country. In public I constantly reach up to feel my scarf, and I cringe when I see police cars, especially after seeing one go by with a young couple in the back, the boy pale-faced, the girl crying.

I can't stop worrying about my passport. Baba cheerfully tells me over the phone to enjoy myself. That is his Iranian voice. Once he is off the phone and Mama asks him how I am going to get out, he will surely be more sober.

Meanwhile, every morning Zia and I get in the car and thread through traffic, past the flashy strip of gold sellers, past the mosque, past the huge mural of Khomeini looming over a mass of heads with one arm raised up four stories. We find a parking space on a crowded block that houses a central bank, a photography studio specializing in passport photos, and four or five young men who have set up crates on the sidewalk and are offering their writing services to applicants who cannot read or see well enough to fill out their forms.

Zia and I pass through separate entrances to the passport compound. A couple of women in black chadors look inside my bag and pat me down; I meet Zia in an inner courtyard bustling with passport seekers and civil servants, and he leads me into a far building where he spends two or three hours with the green-shirted men behind the counter. They never notice me, but they've started hugging Zia when he arrives, bringing him tea and calling him Zia-jan. They apologize to him for how long it is taking for my papers to arrive from the airport. Zia shakes their hands and pats their backs like a politician, and I watch, remembering how I once found his Iranian familiarity embarrassing—it seemed so excessive when I was thirteen. But now it is exactly what is called for. From across the room I can read his body—he purses his lips, alternating between the top and bottom ones, when he is worried; he raises his head and holds his arms straight to his sides when he is hopeful. He never shows that he remembers me sitting on the other side of the counter. But when he's done for the day he strides out of the room with a jerk of his head and I jump up and trot out behind him, hoping for a breakthrough.

"Tomorrow, *enshallah*," he says. "You know the one with the reddish hair? He's a good boy, he wants to help us. But the thin one with glasses—how many stars does he have on his shoulder, did you see? Three. Our boy has only two. That means he can't do anything until the other one says so, and that one won't do anything until the documents arrive from the airport. And on the soul of your father, if they've written on them that you arrived with an American passport . . ." Zia's eyes protrude in mock horror as he snakes the car through traffic.

When we get home Massi sets out plates of chicken and french fries. "Don't be upset about the passport," she tells me. "Have some cold watermelon juice." Then she and Zia go to their room to nap.

I walk through the cool, dark house, peering through the blinds. There are no people out in the midday heat, just a "Pink Floyd" someone has sprayed in English onto the brick wall across the street.

I crane my neck to look up above the buildings, where the speck of an airplane is moving, far too high to be stopping in Iran. I think of my boyfriend in New York, waiting patiently for me to return. I have filled every inch of a blue airmail foldout, but then I decide not to worry him with my long, tearful account of my arrival. And I don't want to write about how all I do here is drink tea and go to the passport office. What I really want to do right now is to get out of the house. But Zia has forbidden me to go out alone. "Anywhere you want to go," he says, "I or another relative will take you." So I flip through the Lonely Planet book Mama sent me in Brussels—the only English-language travel guide to come out on Iran since the revolution. I read the section on Shiraz. I read the section on the Caspian Sea. My plans to travel around Iran alone seem ridiculous now.

Finally, one day when Zia goes to sleep after lunch, I pull on my coat and scarf.

"I'm going for a walk," I whisper to Massi.

"Wait," she says. "I'll get my scarf and go with you."

But I tell her that I need to be alone. I promise to be back in forty-five minutes, and to my surprise, she nervously lets me go.

I start off down a quiet street lined with modern apartment buildings. A few grand old trees remain from when this area was all gardens. For centuries, Tehran was known mainly as a village of highway robbers who lived in underground caves. They would attack caravans traveling in and out of the ancient town of Rey, whose crumbling foundations can still be seen a few kilometers south of the main Tehran bus terminal. Nestled below a ring of white-peaked mountains, Tehran later became popular as a royal hunting grounds, but it was not until 1788 that the Qajar kings made it their capital. The city grew slowly until the late 1800s, when Nasreddin Shah, hoping to hurry its progress, had the existing municipal walls torn down and new ones built far out in the desert. The town expanded from five to eleven miles around and received European-style ramparts, a moat, and twelve elaborate glazed-tile archways that, seen from afar, promised grandeur within. But the traveler entering through one of those gates met with disappointment—behind the wall lay a rocky wasteland that had not yet caught up with the king's aspirations.

Nasreddin Shah should have built his walls further out. The places where his tiled gates once stood are now buried deep in the heart of the old city. All but one of the gates are gone. Reza Shah had them demolished in the 1930s, in his quest to bring Tehran into the modern world. Now, beyond the old Qajar borders, concrete suburbs stretch on for miles, having long ago swallowed up the nearby villages and the kings' old hunting grounds.

Walking alone in Tehran for the first time in fifteen years, I feel as if I've been given the key to a locked garden. I want to talk to people, but hardly anyone else is out at midday. The one woman I do see is loaded down with groceries and barely looks up as I pass. I walk cautiously, keeping an eye out for anyone who might tell me to pull my scarf forward or put on some socks. I wait an unreasonably long time at curbs, letting all the cars whiz by before I venture out. But the drivers are no more reckless than they were when I was a child, and after going a few blocks I start to remember the rhythm of Tehran traffic and the art of not getting hit.

I dash across a street and duck into a little general store, and its odor of sour cheese and stale candy immediately takes me back to Ramezan, my own old corner store. In fact, the merchandise here is so familiar that I don't even need to look at it carefully—I know the unbleached paper notebooks whose stapled binding falls apart after a day, I know the rooster-brand chiclets that have to be worked in the mouth before they become soft enough to chew; I smile when I see the little red-and-orange bags of Pofak cheese curls hanging along the wall like old friends. Back in the street, it feels perfectly natural to walk along the trickling *joob* underneath the dusty plane trees, and yet I get a rush each time I turn another corner.

I return home exactly forty-five minutes after I left. Zia is sitting up in bed, waiting.

"On the souls of all of my children, my brother, and my departed sister, this is the first and last time you will take a walk alone!" His eyes bulge ferociously. "I don't know why Massi let you go, but it won't happen again!"

"Why? It was fine, see—"

"I don't care! Anywhere you want to go, I'll take you."

"No, really," I say. "You don't have to go out every time I do."

"Yes, I do. I told your father I would be responsible for you here and so I am."

"But my father knows I'm used to going places by myself."

"Not in Iran. In Iran a girl does not go out alone."

"But Haideh goes out alone."

"Well, she's married," he says, exasperated. "And she shouldn't go out either. Are you listening?"

I look to Massi for help.

"She's American," Massi says quietly. "She needs to be alone sometimes."

Suddenly, as if a switch has been pulled, Zia's bluster evaporates. He gives me an odd look—recognition, perhaps, or incomprehension. Is it that I am American, not of his kind? Or am I doing something he understands, something he himself might have done in my position? Whatever it is, after that day he doesn't say anything more about my going out, and although Massi still begs me to be careful each time, she gives me my own set of keys. Zia even begins to proudly tell visitors how I insisted on taking a walk alone.

"She's a very smart girl," he says. "I've told her she's not Essie's daughter anymore; she's mine. She goes out all by herself and takes taxis all over the city, with no help from anyone."

"Really?" the visitors say, turning to look at me. "Telephone taxis or street taxis?"

"Telephone taxis," I say, not wanting to sound too wild, although after a week I stopped calling the two-dollar private cabs that picked me up at home. After a few days in Tehran, two dollars seemed like a lot compared to the ten-cent ride I could get in a shared cab. So, first tentatively and then aggressively, I began shouting into the windows of the orange cabs shooting down the street with four or five passengers packed inside. "Freedom Square!" "Worker's Avenue!" I yell for streets that were once named for kings and princes, and the taxis swing over to let me squeeze in.

In shared cabs, strangers complain to each other about everything from the price of meat to the heavy traffic; sometimes they openly agree that everything is "much worse now than in the time of the Shah." Their gripes always center on economics and never on politics, although the two are difficult to separate. No one seems afraid, though, and as they grumble and shake their heads without looking over their shoulders I wonder if after all the years of SAVAK surveillance they are simply tired of being careful. Or perhaps some of the boldness of the revolution has stuck and people are no longer as afraid of their neighbors as they once were.

In discussions I overhear, some say the new regime is doing more for the people than the Shah did. The villages have electricity now, and the literacy rate is up. With its new parks and freeways, Tehran is greener and less congested than before the revolution. Others argue that those villages were all set to get electricity under the Shah, and that the new regime just plugged them in; still others point out that at least in education, the mullahs deserve applause, since religious people who would never have sent their daughters to school during the Shah's time are sending them now that they are assured of Islamic curricula and sex segregation.

Not only have the schools been reorganized, but recently when I flipped through a copy of Roya's daughter's third-grade reader I noticed that the books have been altered as well. The primer's main nuclear family has remained intact since the days when I used the book, but all the furniture has disappeared from their house. The girl, Sara, the boy, Dara, and their parents now sit on the floor in traditional Iranian style. Their father has gotten rid of his old suits and ties and sports a new Islamic five o'clock shadow; their mother has substituted scarves and cloaks for the perky dresses she used to wear.

But even people who miss the Shah's time don't seem to miss the Shah himself. Political repression and corruption aside, the Shah could be embarrassingly childish in his drive to imitate the West. He disregarded the sensibilities of his people, sometimes overtly offending them. In 1971 when he decided to celebrate 2,500 years of Iranian civilization, he invited world leaders and dignitaries to a multimillion-dollar party at Persepolis, the ancient seat of Iranian kings. But almost none of the millions were spent in Iran. The food, the liquor, the tents, the furniture, and even some of the carpeting came from France. Iranian merchants and craftsmen were not considered.

The present regime is more respectful of working-class Iranians, but it too has its skeptics among them.

"These mullahs are clever," says a taxi driver who picks me up in South Tehran. "The Shah built all those palaces and bought all those cars and jewels, and when he left, he left them all here. But these guys are sweeping up all the money and sending it to bank accounts abroad. If anything ever happens, they'll be ready. They'll just drop their *abas* and turbans on the floor and get on a plane with one bag."

Outside the cabs, people are just as bold. "Three hundred toumans a kilo?" a shriveled grandmother mutters angrily as she scrutinizes the sweet lemons in the grocer's bin. "God give these mullahs their deaths—before they finish the ruination of this country." I look nervously around the busy shop. "Ah, don't worry," she says. "I say these things all the time. At my age, what does it matter?"

And yet I never hear anyone criticize Khomeini. Even people who complain about the money being spent to plate his huge tomb with gold do not extend blame to "the Emam" himself. Maybe they are scared. But I also sense a lingering reverence for the man who pulled Iran out from under the Shah. Leila-khanoum and Roya, who sleep in lacy negligees, watch illegal American videos, and go to women-only fashion shows, also drive around with a tape of Khomeini's speeches in their cassette player. His voice is rich and mellow, and although his sentences are hard for me to understand, his tone is both soothing and provocative. Even without hearing Roya's simplified summary—that people who spend their lives running after material things don't realize that what they're really seeking is God—I can begin to understand how this voice could rouse a nation.

A cabdriver with an empty cab can be bargained with to go all the way to a particular destination. I flag one down and lean in toward the driver, a thin, grizzled man whose dashboard is decorated with a fringe of red and yellow yarn baubles and a row of laminated American pennies.

"Will you go to Revolution Square for two hundred toumans?"

"Sure," he says affably, and I immediately worry that I have offered too much. I get in anyway and he weaves through traffic, slowing in front of other pedestrians to see if they are going our way. As he drives, his eyes dart to the rearview mirror to size me up.

"You've been away a long time?" he finally says.

"Yes, I've been in America fifteen years."

"Ah, how interesting. I could tell by your accent. So tell me. Which is better, Iran or America?"

"They're both good."

"Yes"—he brushes off my answer—"but life is harder here."

I crane my neck to look at a long American flag painted down the side of a building. It has skulls instead of stars, falling bombs instead of stripes, and "Down with the U.S.A." stenciled in English across the bottom. "Life is hard there too," I say, trying to read the Farsi caption under the picture—something about even one second of co-operation with America not being tolerated—but the light changes and we speed away.

"True," the driver says. "I've heard in America you work all day with no break. Still, I'd like to see it. But after what Khanoum Mah-moody wrote, they probably don't like Iranians there anymore."

I tell him I cannot recall a change in Americans' attitudes toward Iran after *Not Without My Daughter* came out. "It was only bad during the embassy takeover," I say. "No one bothers Iranians now."

"Oh, but I hear that, much more than the embassy business, Kha-noum Mahmoody's book destroyed Iran's honor. It was the worst piece of anti-Iranian propaganda in all of our history. She said we did not wash. But Americans should know that Iranians are the cleanest of all races."

"Do you think it's not true," I ask, "what she wrote about being kept here by her husband?"

"How do I know?" He swerves to avoid a moped carrying a family of five down the wrong side of the street, then turns back to the rearview mirror. "Maybe there was one bad Iranian man who did this thing. But the wife should have known her husband well enough to know he might do it. People don't go crazy just because they come to Iran."

Every day at the passport office, the men say, "Tomorrow, *enshallah*." They have said this for nine days in a row, and each time I am less surprised. I also feel less nervous. It is as if my body is adjusting to a new, slower clock. Everything in Iran takes an indefinite amount of time, but everyone is patient. I even start to think about what I would do if I didn't get my passport and I had to stay a couple of years. Would it be so bad? Wouldn't it be interesting?

On the tenth day my papers arrive from the airport. Together with the travel documents and the landing forms and the passport appli-cation, my file is thick and daunting. "Here," Zia's friends behind the passport counter say. "Take this to the Colonel upstairs. And good luck."

The Colonel flips through the papers and frowns. "Why did she come here without a passport?"

Zia launches into a convoluted, emotional explanation.

The Colonel frowns again and looks at me. "I don't understand," he says, interrupting Zia. "How were you able to get from America to Belgium without a passport?"

Both men stare at me. Whatever I say will be wrong. We will go home and for years Zia will tell everyone how I ruined things for myself just as I was about to get what I wanted. *She told him, just like that, that she'd given them her American passport! What else could he do but refuse her?*

So, down on the floor where the Colonel cannot see, I dig my heel hard into Zia's foot.

He jerks his head back toward the Colonel. "Well, you see," he says, "her mother is American, so she was able to do that."

The Colonel nods slowly and squints at the papers, holding each one up until I see the one with the scribbles on the back that read, "Arrived with American passport." I grip my seat, praying he won't flip that piece of paper over, praying he won't notice that my forehead is slick with sweat and that my whole body is trembling. He turns to the last page, and then I hear the thuds—one, two, three stamps. He signs the bottom. "Here you go," he says, handing the papers to Zia. Still shaking, I follow Zia out the door.

To celebrate, Massi and Zia take me out for kabob.

"On the souls of my children, you should have seen this big-mustached colonel who finally approved her for an Iranian passport," Zia says, jubilantly poking a butter pat into his rice. "He spent so much time looking at those papers, I was sure he would find a prob-lem. When he asked Taraneh how she flew to Belgium without a passport, I thought it was all over." He turns to me. "You did a smart thing, to let me talk. Oh, and then when we went back to the airport, the airport chief who had said he'd give back her American passport was gone for the day. No matter what I said, they wouldn't give it back without his consent. And then can you guess what happened? What a stroke of luck, eh, Taraneh-jan! The phone rang, and it was that very same chief, just happening to call in from outside. 'Let me speak to him!' I said, and as soon as he heard my voice he told those men to give me the passport. The man who gave it to me said that never in all his time at the airport had he ever given an American passport back." Zia grins broadly and I think back to the man who took my passport out of a wall safe and handed it to me with the cover full of staples and pinpricks, as if it had been released from a voodoo spell.

"You're still my daughter," Zia reminds me. "Remember to tell Essie that." His face melts into smiles and his voice breaks. "*Akheir*, Massi-khanoum, I really love this girl; she's a very good girl."

I grin back, happy to be here with them, glad that we can all relax now.

"Well, keep your passport hidden now that you have it," Massi says, trying to make her laughing eyes serious for a second.

"Yes," says Zia. "Absolutely don't show it to anyone or tell anyone you got it back. A lot of people want to go to America and they might get jealous and do something to hurt you."

❖

One day I hail a cab and ask the driver to take me up Worker's Avenue and let me out on a small alleyway off of Tehran University. For years, in dreams, I have walked down this alley, pushed open a creaky white wooden door, and descended a bank of stairwells where panes of colored glass twisted the sunlight down onto faded tiles. The very last stairway had no light and no windows. It had dark, bumpy walls, like the passageway into a cave. Entering the cave, I would find old food in the refrigerator, dusty toys on the shelves, and, in the larger bedroom, a Russian piano, unplayed since 1979. *I am not dreaming this time*, I would always tell myself, and I would take in deep gulps of air to prove it was real—only to open my eyes to American sheets and a bright American morning.

I used to think that when I went back to our old house in Iran, I would know everything that had changed and everything that was the same. But as soon as I turn down our alleyway, the facts I have always known blend into and become replaced by what I see in front of me. Was that door across the street always blue, or was it green back then? Was it this tree that shaded our window, or has a different one grown in its place? Now that I am here I cannot remember, although a day ago I could have said for sure.

I ring the third doorbell, which used to be Dadash's. Our family still owns the building, and a distant cousin named Ali Reza now rents Dadash's apartment. I have never met him, but I called ahead, and he and his wife are waiting for me to eat lunch with them. Massi instructed me to bring them ice cream. "Stop at the corner of Amirabad," she said, still using the old name of Worker's Avenue. "Ask the fat man for the ice cream in the three-colored box." She always gives me shopping directions like this—go only to a certain store, talk only to a certain shopkeeper—buy two kilos of hard but ripe green pears, or a chicken that has not yet been plucked. "Alive or dead?" Alive, but with the feet tied.

Up on the third floor, the heavy curtains that once enclosed Dadash and Leila-khanoum's bedroom are gone. I eat chicken and rice and herbs with Ali Reza and his family at a sun-drenched table where the bed used to be. Afterward, Ali Reza's wife brings out tea and cold melon slices, and Ali Reza shyly offers to show me his photo album from the Iran-Iraq war.

I leaf through snapshots of young boys in fatigues, the boys my brother might have joined if we had stayed a few years longer. They smile inside a tent, holding up cans of food; they pose beside a sheep they have just killed for the New Year; they swim in a river on their furlough. They stand, arms draped over each other's shoulders, handkerchiefs at their mouths, behind a bloated, black-skinned Iraqi pilot whose dead arms are frozen in defense. "We had fun," Ali Reza says, touching the faces of the boys. "But he was martyred, he was martyred, and he was martyred."

From the university down the street, the moaning of Friday prayers wafts over, the mullah's voice amplified to reach the multitudes.

Down on the second floor, I knock on the mottled glass window in a wooden door. For a moment I am small again, rapping on the door that connects Aziz's life and ours. I used to press my nose against it and see hazily through to the flowers on her table, the pictures on her wall, the warm yellow ceiling lamp that the glass cut into golden diamonds. And then I would see Aziz herself, moving toward the door, opening it wide, and pulling me in for a sugar-scented kiss.

The door slowly falls open.

"They took it all away." A wizened old lady in a black chador stands in the center of the empty room. It is Banu-Aqa, Agha Jan's niece, whom I have never met and who has recently moved into Aziz's apartment. She gestures at the stained ceiling and motions for me to be quiet, then leads me down the hall and into the bathroom, where she points at a raw hole at the top of the wall. "They took my shower," she says. She shows me the kitchen, where the ceiling plaster has fallen in clumps onto the floor. "They took my gas too."

"Well, you should get a gas canister," I say, looking under a stove that doesn't seem to have been used for years.

"No, Ali Reza and the rest will just take it away again. You are the granddaughter of my dear uncle, God forgive his soul. You won't tell them what I've said. What can I do? I have become old. God give me my death." She throws up her hands and disappears behind a curtain.

I am left in the center of the room. In the corner is a locked closet, which Homa-khanoum has told me contains all that is left of my family's possessions. She gave me an old brass skeleton key that used to belong to Aziz. "It probably won't work," she said glumly, but after I slide the key in and twist it a few times, the lock turns over and the door falls open with a groan. A smell like dry flowers envelops me. I pull on a cord, and, miraculously, the bulb hanging above me lights up, casting a wan glow over the high-ceilinged little room. A set of antique carved wooden doors stands along one wall, and I suddenly remember the day Baba excitedly brought them home from the bazaar, for Shahrak. Next to the doors are an old saddle, a stack of canvases, and two large trunks that I remember from our closet, downstairs.

Using my heel to kick the spindly padlock off the first trunk, I begin to lift things out. Five carved wooden water-pipe stems. A charcoal drawing that I have never seen of a handsome young man who looks so much like Baba and his brothers that he must be the dead brother, Khosrow. Broken ceramic dishes, wrapped in newspaper. Metal first-aid boxes full of thousands of slides, with Baba's precise writing identifying each one. A pile of handwritten books, the black and red calligraphy still fine on shiny, fragile paper; the paper itself laced with the erratic hieroglyphics of bookworms that have respectfully spared the ink. In a manila envelope of Aziz's insurance documents I find a letter from my cousin Fereidoon in Oregon, scrawled out in painful, uneasy Farsi, dated the year before she died. I feel ashamed for not having written.

"They took your stuff too."

I look up to see Banu-Aqa by my side again. "*Akh*, what things!" she says.

"Like what?" I ask.

"Things you would not believe, they were so beautiful. I said, 'Those belong to my uncle's son, where are you going with them?' But they took them and I couldn't stop them, God give me my death."

Wondering what beautiful things I have missed, I pick up an envelope. It is full of Aziz's passport photos: as a young wife, as a middle-aged mother, as a white-haired grandmother. I find a blurred snapshot taken in the village—the family members standing straight and dignified beside a rushing stream, a reluctant old servant skulking at the edge, perhaps afraid, as many people were in those days, that the camera would capture his soul. Standing between her husband and oldest son, Aziz looks stern and uncomfortable. Maybe she was. When she was fourteen her parents had married her to a man who already had a wife, although she cried and begged and even told them about the young soldier she loved, who used to walk by each day as she sat by the creek braiding her hair. But Aziz's parents said the soldier's family was not rich enough. The husband they had found for her was thirty years old and already so important that he rode into town with fifteen horsemen behind him.

Aziz could have tried to do what her cousin had done when her family found her a rich husband she didn't want—she took a horse and galloped away. Her father's servants found her days later, near a village where the people had seen a girl sleeping under a bridge. They brought her home, dropped the subject, and eventually let her choose her own husband. But Aziz did not rebel. She married Agha Jan, not for love, but for the things that impressed her family. She would have her own house and her own servants, separate from the first wife. She would have money and clothes and a position as the wife of a great landowning khan. She asked for only one condition in her marriage contract—the right to choose where the family would live. The landowner agreed, the dowry was set, and Aziz put on a red velvet coat and married him.

Agha Jan had a condition of his own. His three sons were dead and his first wife was barren; he needed children to inherit his empire. Aziz bore him eight children, but she was never able to take the place of his first wife, the white-chadored villager woman with whom he continued to spend several hours each day. Aziz considered herself higher-class than Wife-of-Agha Jan, who was merely the daughter of a Qajar servant, whereas she, Aziz, was not only the mother of all the children but also the daughter of a respected mullah. As far as Aziz was concerned, Wife-of-Agha Jan was a relic of her husband's youth. But everyone could see he still cared for her very deeply, and Baba and his sisters and brothers all loved the sweet-tempered woman who stayed home when Aziz went out, and who was always there when they needed someone to talk to. When Aziz called Agha Jan's first wife "low" and "villagey," even her own children would come to their stepmother's defense, and Aziz would bristle with resentment.

And then came the land reforms, which took away everything Aziz had sacrificed for. Her younger sons were fine with their university degrees, and Dadash still had enough landholdings to live off; but Aziz had nothing left but her children. She threw her energy into them—first into their education and then into their courtships. One by one they married and found apartments near her, and on any given day any combination of her twenty grandchildren might come by to visit. And then came the revolution. The Shah fell, and Aziz's sons flew back to the States in the same order in which she had sent them twenty years before. Her daughters followed soon afterward. Even Dadash moved to the village.

I hold up a picture of Aziz glaring at the camera from under a scarf, and again I am a child, slipping into her bedroom when she isn't there, wrapping my fingers around the smooth, worn prayer

stone on her dresser. If I picked it up I had to put it back in its spot
by the time she came in to pray again. But that was before the revolution. I heard that after we left, Aziz stopped praying. Her children
were gone. Bombs were falling on Tehran. She slipped off a curb and
broke her tooth, and then a car ran over her foot. At some point she
threw up her hands. "It's just me and this wall here," she said to Baba
over the phone. She had stopped believing in a God who kept letting
bad things happen.

I struggle with the lock on the second trunk, picking at it with a piece
of wire. Finally it slips open and a mound of dusty books and papers
spills out.

"See how dirty?" Banu-Aqa shrieks. "They left them out in the
yard for months in the sun and the rain. I kept telling them, 'Those
belong to my uncle's son. Take them inside!' They got mad, but they
finally did. Otherwise all those books would be ruined."

"Thank you," I say. I sort hungrily through our old books. *The
Brothers Karamazov. Tintin in Tibet. Space, Time and Architecture.* Mama's childhood edition of *The Thirteen Clocks.* Ali's diary from the
third grade. School textbooks with my writing in the margins. An
illustrated magazine for teenage dogs that I made, dated January 8,
1979, with advice columns and fashion tips and a comic strip adver-
tisement about "How Skinny Yip Became Superdog." I smooth out
the pen marks with my thumb, trying to picture myself making them,
and my chest tightens.

"Here, eat dates," Banu-Aqa says, holding out a plate that she
seems to have pulled out of the air.

"No, thanks." I hold up my black, dusty hands.

"It doesn't matter," she says. "I'll put them in your mouth."

"Uh, thanks, I'm really not hungry."

"Eat! See, I peeled all the skin off this date and took the seed out.
Eat!"

I shake my head, wishing she would leave. I don't want an audience, especially not one to whom these scribbles mean nothing. But
Banu-Aqa doesn't say anything more, and soon I forget all about her.

"Mama's Phone Book Do Not Take." My heart races as I open it.
Names and numbers, people spilled out into the world; even these

old street names no longer exist. None of this can be dialed: American Embassy, American Hospital, American Wives Club. Tara's ballet. Community School. Frigidaire repair. The German Club, the Hilton Hotel, the Iran-America Society. Louise the Piano Teacher. Snow White Nursery School. Soghra's husband Amoo Hossein. Sanjar the vet, Mr. Mostafa the Violin Teacher, Zaven the Cellist. And Dr. Zangeneh, who correctly predicted I'd be as tall as Mama.

Here is a letter. To Mama from her future producer at Elektra Asylum Nonesuch records, with its logo of the cellblock door and the butterfly. November 15, 1974. "Dear Karen, The time is right for you to get your ass over here and make your assault on the consciousness of the musically deprived masses. We are as well situated as we are likely ever to be—at least in the foreseeable future—to perform the much-needed crankings and stokings of this giant star-making machine." Eight scrawled-out pages, the writing rushed and amped, with promises of money and fame, and promises to "make it possible for your family to sustain itself here without the necessity of Essie's working at something which is less than that to which he aspires."

Baba, planning his own office in Tehran, must have scoffed at this assumption of him as the inept foreigner. But four years later, when he and Mama found themselves jobless in L.A., why didn't they seek these people out? Why didn't Mama call the studio? Why couldn't they have gone on with the lives they knew rather than trying to remake themselves in a place they had no connection to?

Telex. January 20, 1978. "Karen, we need an answer regarding an album title immediately or the release will be delayed." Mama's red pen bleeds titles into the thin paper—"Voyager," "Lifeline"—and "Please Don't Forget Thanks to Tara, Ali and Sufi."

A handwritten résumé of Baba's experience. A draft of a brochure about his new office. His new business cards, with the logo designed by his partner who died in a car accident a year after the revolution. I cradle one of the cards in my hand. The last time anyone held it was when the office was still open. I hold the card up to my face, trying to inhale something from that time, but all I smell is dust. My throat catches. I want to run out and show someone this card, to flash this piece of solid proof that our old life really was the way I remember it. But even Banu-Aqa has retreated behind her curtain.

1979. Mama's scribbles: "Istanbul? Or Rome. Jan 12 Rome to London."

"Any bank will transfer money to— Rate? 70 rials."

My own round handwriting: "Swissair from Tehran 7:30 am Jan 10 #373. From Geneva #110. TWA #13 21:00-23:50 in L.A. 52,700 rials per person. 50% for children. Yip half kids' price."

Baba's neat architect lettering: "Saturday list—Bank Melli, pay for passports, other banks, photocopy passports, collect money from all banks. Sufi's school. Yip's papers." Yip, the scrawny dachshund we pushed through the airport the day we left Iran, made it all the way to L.A. We left him at Grandma and Grandpa's and within a month he was sent to live on a farm in Nevada. Fifteen years later, Mama and Baba admitted that there never was a farm, that after getting exit papers and airplane tickets for Yip and carrying him all the way across the world, we ended by abandoning him to the pound. "But then why did we go to all the trouble of bringing him out?" I asked when I found out; and Mama's answer had an odd, sweet logic: "We didn't want you guys to think that when things got tough we might abandon *you*."

Mama's cursive: "3pm Tehran-Zurich. 6am 2 to JFK—American."

My careful writing, in green ink: "1. Lock—Turn to right 2 times to 34. Turn to left 1 time to 8. Turn straight to 14 (put lock in pocket). 2. Books—Take out every thing that belongs to me. Also take out the DETAIL folder. 3. Location of locker—Ask for B-20. Upstairs from B-20 are some lockers. The third one (top, next to the wall) is mine. 4. Yearbook—Take the receipt. Go to Mr. Magana, Mr. Pajares, or Mr. Burt. Get yearbook. If there is no yearbook ask for a print of all the school pictures. If they don't give them to you, say that you paid 1000 rials and show them the receipt."

Fleeing the country, I still expected Baba to drive across the ravaged city to Community School. And I expected Mr. Magana, Mr. Pajares, and Mr. Burt to be there, a triumvirate of leaders in an empty garden, waiting for the fathers to come and collect the yearbooks.

Mama again: "Flight snowed in will not be arriving Jan 10 will call from NY." Later these lines too were scratched off.

In all the analyses I read after the revolution, one refrain surfaced. *We should have seen it coming.* The Shah, the Americans, and everyone else should have had their eyes open. The signs were there. They are now clearly outlined in books—the Americans ignored the opposition groups, the Shah ignored his subjects' deep religiosity and dissatisfaction. Everyone was so dazzled with what they wanted Iran to be that they missed seeing what it was.

And so did we. The revolution could not have come at a worse time in terms of how my parents were likely to react to it. Mama, having satisfied her desire to be a singer in L.A., had begun to like her life in Iran. Baba, having traveled the country for ten years, had opened a firm where he could finally start making real money. They were going to have a house of their own where they could actually invite people over—as Mama put it, they were going to "start being grown-ups and not hippies living on the floor." They were excited about entering this new, adult stage, and they were not about to let the Shah's downfall interfere with it.

So they resisted the revolution. They refused to feel implicated by the bullets, or to worry when our schoolbus dropped us off later and later every day. One afternoon, when the *shoolooghi* had reached new heights of chaos, Javad pulled in through the garden gate and caught one of our kittens under the wheel of his Range Rover. Mama put the mangled kitten in a box, covered it with a sweater, and placed it in the car. "Don't go out there," Javad said, but Mama drove off and spent three hours winding downtown past riots and burning buildings to get to the veterinarian.

The kitten died anyway. But going to the vet was something Mama had to do. In the middle of the smoldering city, she found a roomful of people sitting calmly with their pets, waiting for their appointments. Bringing the kitten there was a gesture of defiance, an affirmation that amid the killing and destruction there were still people engaged in the civilized act of healing their pets. To Mama, that meant the center must still be holding.

Once we got to America, Mama and Baba decided that the life we had been living had been wrong. They never said this, but they believed it. Until the revolution they had always done exactly what they liked; afterward they figured that this approach must have been flawed. So Portland became their punishment. Other Iranians flew to Southern California, bought houses that tripled in value, and opened

up shops on the block of Westwood Boulevard where just a year
earlier Mama's album had been selling at Tower Records. But Mama
and Baba drove to a sunless place and took up professions so different
from their old ones that it was as if they were in disguise.

Sometimes they ran their minds backward, asking themselves what
they could have done differently. Maybe we should have been more
political. Maybe we should have opposed the Shah more. Maybe we
should have supported him more. Maybe, all those times when they
showed the Shah's picture and played the national anthem before a
movie, we should have refused to stand up. Or, when Baba got the
anonymous call threatening to bomb his office if he didn't close
down, maybe he should have gone to work anyway. When the embassy started evacuating Americans, Mama laughed and said it had
nothing to do with us, although at that point we still might have sold
our house and gotten some money out.

Or maybe we should have stayed longer. I used to think that we
had stayed as long as we could—weeks longer than my friends who,
one by one, had stopped answering their telephones. But years later
I met an Iranian who showed me his cousin's Community School
yearbook from 1979, the yearbook I had wanted so badly for Baba to
pick up before leaving Iran. It came out the following June, a slim
volume empty of the usual "Sports" and "Activities" and "Trip to
Persepolis." It had class pictures, but only a few for each class—those
who had remained to finish out the school year after the Shah left
and before the new regime closed down the international schools. I
found my friends Shih-Fang and Fei-Fang, and I saw the handful of
teachers who had stayed behind to teach them. I saw sad poems about
absent friends, and quotes about "all we've been through in this special year." I looked for the picture I remembered sitting for early that
fall, with my neat long braids and my bubble gum lip gloss, and as
I looked, a wave of loss rolled over me. It had been building up for
years, and for a few moments seeing this yearbook made me suddenly
want to sink down to the floor and weep. In the pit of my stomach
I remembered, as sorrowfully as if I were still eleven, how proud I
had been to finally be old enough for that yearbook, to be entering
an age in which people would know who I was when they saw me on
campus.

Instead, I left. My name was crossed off the roster. Despite how important those last months at Community School had been to me, and despite how long I'd waited for it to reopen, I had not made the final cut. I did not find a trace of myself on those pages.

Packing up the trunk, I set aside Mama's phone book, Ali's diary, some of Baba's slides, and the envelope full of loose papers. I cannot fit anything more in my backpack. I lock up the closet, and after I thank Banu-Aqa and promise to come back soon for lunch, she closes the door behind me.

The next apartment down is ours. Strangers are renting it now, but Ali Reza has told them I am coming. I stop at the landing, surprised at how small the staircase is—it looks as if it was built to a child's scale, and it is darker than I remember. I start walking down and a cool, earthy smell rises around me. If this were fifteen years ago I would rap on the door, Mama would open it and I would sit down in a houseful of familiar objects, all safe and in their rightful places, not crammed into a dusty trunk. Soghra would be watching TV with Sufi and Ali; Mama would be preparing dinner; Yip would be chewing up a wooden backgammon chip on the carpet. I pause, wondering if I want to destroy that image. I have no idea how many people have lived here since then, or if the ones here now will mind me coming in.

I rap on the textured glass. A shadow moves behind it. The door opens and a dark-eyed young woman smiles shyly, pulls her white chador forward and backs through the apartment, beckoning me in.

What little furniture there is I have never seen before. The walls where Mama's paintings once hung are blank. The shelf that held Baba's collection of antique blue bottles is empty. In the spot where Ali and I used to stack up foam couch cushions and sway gleefully between column and wall, a single framed picture of Khomeini stares sternly down. Even the little kitchen is gone, expanded into a larger room that juts out into the yard; in the yard itself the pinata tree is missing and the grape vines that Ali and I used to climb have been cleared away.

And yet I am dizzy to be here. I return to each room, drinking in its shape, confirming that what I remembered was real. The bathroom is the most familiar room. Its floor is still brick-red, and the three tiles with painted-blue fish that Baba installed when we first moved to Iran are still set above the sink. I can even see, on the caulking between the white wall tiles, the remnants of lines where at age three I drew a collage of princesses and elephants.

A tightness wells up in my throat—a sadness shot through with elation. Almost nothing of ours remains, and yet I am wildly happy, simply for the fact that this house is still here and I am standing inside it.

"Would you like to take pictures?" the girl asks, gesturing at the camera slung around my arm. "Would you like me to take one of you?" I stand beside the arched window through which I used to spy on Mama teaching English to Soghra's children. The girl clicks the shutter. Then she steps back to let me wander, and I have a sudden urge to hug her—for opening the door, for taking my picture, for allowing me to walk through the bedroom, the bathroom, the living room—the world of my empty places.

That night the phone rings.

"Taraneh! It's from America."

"Hey, pups." The voice of my boyfriend in New York is both comforting and jarring. We exchange formal, self-conscious greetings as I try to assess whether Massi and Zia can hear me from the other room.

"Why haven't you written?" he says. "I check the mailbox every day."

"I have been writing," I whisper. "I just haven't sent the letters. They were all about the passport stuff."

"Well, send them," he says. "I miss you."

I stay silent, wondering who Massi and Zia think I'm talking to.

Sure enough, Zia appears in the doorway. "Who is it?" he bellows jovially. "Your professor from America? Say hi for me."

"I can't really talk now," I say.

"I love you," my boyfriend says.

I pause, then lightly say, "Me too," nodding my head as if I'm agreeing with him on some academic point.

"I really miss you," he says.

"I know," I say nervously. "But I've got to go now. I'll send that stuff soon." I hang up, guilty but relieved. The first time he called, a few days after I arrived, I was alone in the house and frantic about my passport; hearing his voice made me collapse into tears. He calmed me down, told me to try to have fun and promised we'd see each other soon. But now, just a week later, it is strange to speak English and even stranger to hear his voice. It feels as if he is calling from another world.

❖

All my relatives do *deed-o-baz-deed*, seeing and seeing again. Sometimes they drive for an hour across the city to drop in on relatives they have just seen the day before, without even checking first to see if they are home. If they are not, the visitors turn around and go home; otherwise, they are ushered in and the women pull off their coats and scarves and everyone sits down in a row on the couch as the hostess fires up the samovar for tea. "Are you well?" they ask each other. "Is your husband well, and your children, are they well?" "Yes, yes, thank God," they all say, but the questions go on. "Is everyone well on your side?" "Yes, yes, but what about you? Is everyone well with you?" The point is not to learn new information so much as to confirm the old information, and the same pleasantries are exchanged every day.

In a musk-scented bedroom where the women are sleeping off their lamb and eggplant lunch, I nestle myself under a lone ray of sunlight piercing through the window blinds. I take out Edward Browne's meticulously remembered journey through Iran a hundred years ago. Shiraz, Esfahan, Yazd—he spent weeks riding on horseback to each of those cities, and once he arrived, the town dignitaries would vie for the privilege of housing him. By the time my family rolled into those same cities in our sea-green Jeep, no one looked twice at strangers. The hotels had taken over for the dignitaries, and there were restaurants and museums and large blue swimming pools in which we could bathe our car-cramped limbs and forget the desert outside.

I wonder how these places look now. The swimming pools must be closed, but perhaps not much else has changed. Not like Tehran, laced with new freeways, encircled by new neighborhoods, three times as populous as it was when I left. Some of the newcomers are refugees from Afghanistan and Iraq; some were born during the Iran-Iraq war when birth control was frowned upon and women were exhorted to produce fighters for Islam. But the majority are provincials, lured to Tehran by the hope of making their fortunes. Each day they arrive by the busload into a split city—a cosmopolitan northern half whose residents walk in a state of low-level disobedience (the women sockless and lipsticked; the men in jeans) and a crumbling southern half which houses the humbler and more pious citizens. The capital is schizophrenic, but I imagine that the provincial cities might retain more of their old selves.

At the very least, in other cities I would be able to get out on my own. The longer I am in Tehran, the more I understand Mama's anxiety about my getting stuck here. She sat in these very living rooms all through her twenties, smiling and making small talk and counting the hours until she could get out and do something else; now, despite all my relatives' hospitality, I have the same urge to break free.

However, although the country has comprehensive transportation networks and cheap hotels, I cannot devise a travel plan. "Who would you stay with?" Zia says when naptime is over and I mention that I want to go to Yazd.

"I'd stay in a hotel," I say.

"But who would you go with?"

"Myself. I traveled here alone, didn't I?"

"Ah." He laughs, relieved to be able to clear up the misunderstanding. "Hotels won't give rooms to women alone. It's against the law." My vision of a five-dollar-a-night room dissolves, along with my hopes of being on my own.

"Taraneh, I'll go to Mashhad to make the pilgrimage and you can come," says one of my father's cousins. But when I try to set a date she looks surprised. "Well, I can't go this month because the kids are in school. Next month, if the weather is nice and my leg doesn't hurt and Mohammad's brother doesn't visit, then we'll go."

"Why don't you just come with us when we go back to the village?" Dadash says.

"Yes, just come in the car with us when we go back," Leila-khanoum says, laying her hand affectionately over mine. "What do you want to stay in this dirty city for?"

I promise them that I will come to the village soon. But first I want to see more of Iran—more than these walls, these hourglass-shaped teacups, these dainty knives for peeling fruit; these things that I see every day.

When I mention that I want to go to the bazaar, Zia curls his lip. "A girl should not be alone in there. You'll only get lost." But later that week, when a woman beside me in a cab asks the driver if he will take her down to the bazaar, I decide to go along for the ride.

The bazaar is like a little covered town, with mini-neighborhoods for each specialty. Every merchant can be reasonably sure that all the shops around him are selling almost exactly the same goods at around the same price. A customer might have a favorite shop, but there does not seem to be an intense competition among merchants. If one goes off for lunch or for a visit to the mosque, his neighbor will watch his store, and often a shop is empty because its owner is next door, sipping tea with his competitor.

In the cloth section, colorful scarves and sweaters hang lengthwise down the center of the vaulted ceiling. Women finger bolts of fabric, arguing down the prices, while shopkeepers bring out an unending supply of selections from the backs of the stores. In the gold section, rows of chains and medallions sparkle in the lamp-heated windows as women crowd around outside to stare. Gold has a very specific value in Iran. Eighteen-carat jewelry and coins are sold by weight and given as gifts at weddings and births, with the security of being resellable throughout the owner's life. In this way, wedding gifts function like a dowry.

Beyond the cloth and the gold, a dark hall opens out into a court-yard. Old men sit around the perimeter, drinking tea and fingering through trays of silver rings, loose polished stones, and amber and carnelian worry beads. Across the courtyard, a long passageway of domed ceilings leads deeper into the bazaar. From the tops of the domes, dusty shafts of sunlight fall onto the ground, and I walk below them, taking random turns past mosques and balconies and tiny courtyards I could never find again. The farther I go, the darker and emptier it gets. The air becomes cool and chalky, and as I pass through a tunnel of shoemakers' shops I have the sense that this particular spot would have felt the same at any time in the last few centuries—the same archways, the same hay-and-earth scent, the same muffled, rhythmic tapping of a hammer driving a nail into a shoe.

"Make way! Make way!" A man coaxes a pack donkey past a pile of copper pots. I flatten myself against the wall, and both the animal and its owner glare as they squeeze by me.

"Hello! Hello!" A young man skits left and right behind me, smiling hard, trying to enter my field of vision. "Hello!" he says in belabored English. "Where is your country?" I am in the carpet section, where years ago tourists must have come to shop. But why has this man picked me out? Is it my flowered scarf, so different from the black chadors of South Tehran? Or the aimlessness of my walk? Or is it my very presence, the strangeness of a girl alone, that says I must not belong?

"Sorry," I say, careful to make my Farsi perfect. "I'm Iranian." He turns away, and I feel a stab of loneliness. *Where is your country?* I run over the young man's question, and my answer. Here I am, back in Iran, proclaiming myself Iranian. But what does that mean, when the life I once had here is gone? I don't want to be a traveler anymore. What I really want is to go back to my old backyard off Amirabad Avenue and share a sweet white melon with Mama and Baba as the cool evening awakens the garden. Instead, I wander through the dim maze of the bazaar, trying to find my way out as the brick archways close in over my head. I circle back up toward where I think I remember the fabric sellers to be, but I am back at the shoes. Turning a corner, I almost run into two women, who quickly pull their chadors closed and disappear into a crevice in the wall. But they don't need to worry—I am a ghost now. A Farsi word for out of whack and unnatural is *avazi*. The word also means changed, reversed, switched. I am switched. Or Iran is switched. Once we fit together; now I am always either straining to burst out or drowning in its largeness.

Homa-khanoum mutters as she stoops to light a candle. The electricity has died in her neighborhood for the third night in a row, and she moves like an old woman, bending down slowly, turning her head to catch my eye. "A man needs someone to cook for him," she says.

"I guess so," I say. "If he can't cook for himself."

"Why don't my sons get married? They're getting old in America. Heh?" She nudges Agha Vakili, who is lying on the floor with a sweater over his face. He does not budge. The candlelight flickers on his ribbed white undershirt that stretches with each sleeping breath. "You should tell them to come here so we can find them wives," Homa-khanoum says. She pulls out a worn wooden backgammon board and lays out the pieces. "At their age people are supposed to get married and have children, not stay out until four in the morning and sleep all day." She hands me the dice. "It's good that you travel. Do all your traveling before you marry. Once you have a husband, you won't be able to do anything." She shakes her head again, her gold-rimmed teeth catching the candle's flame.

Homa-khanoum once looked like a girl in a Qajar-era painting, with wavy auburn hair and a dark mole above her upper lip. Baba told me that as a girl she used to ride out to the highway and race against the first trucks in Iran, urging her horse until she passed them and then tearing off into the hills. When she was thirteen she had the highest marks in her class and she begged to go on to high school. But a marriage had been arranged, and no amount of crying or refusing saved her from becoming the bride of a tall, square-jawed soldier with shiny black boots. She did, however, manage to put off going to his house for three years after the wedding.

"I never went to my husband while my brother Khosrow was alive," she says proudly. "My sister and brothers all attended school and went about their lives, but I didn't leave his side." She shakes the dice and scatters them on the board, but instead of taking her turn she stares at the open hand in front of her as if it is not hers. "We were one year apart. All through our childhood we were so close that people said it was strange. We did everything together . . ."

Her words draw a picture—Homa at six, Khosrow at seven, Baba not yet born to be toted around on his older sister's hip. The Homa-khanoum I know now has a lovely smile that sometimes strikes from nowhere—a shock of beauty before she subsides again into sadness. When she was six and playing with her brother she must have smiled all the time. And then, only ten years later, time had run out for both of them.

"Doctors came from all over," Homa tells me. "They said he had a fever in his heart. While they talked with each other, I sat alone with him and held his head in my hands, for hours." She cradles an invisible head in her lap. "His heart hurt so much he couldn't sleep, so he would sit up and we would talk all night. Sometimes his head would get so dizzy that the room would spin, and I would hold him until it stopped. It was just the two of us, alone in that room."

I can imagine the doomed frenzy in the rest of the house—Aziz drawing symbols on raw eggs, Baba yelled at for playing in the inauspicious mud, Parviz forced to get rid of his pet pigeons. The only image I cannot call up is that of a living Khosrow. "He looked like a mix between Jamsheed and your father," Homa-khanoum says, "but with an extra look of his own." He wrote articles that got published in a magazine that everyone in Tehran read. He argued with Aziz when she called Wife-of-Agha Jan lower-class. He was the best brother of them all, Homa tells me, and if they'd been in America his sickness would have been easy to cure.

"But he died, just like that, alone with me, his head in my arms." Homa-khanoum closes her eyes. "Afterward, I did not say a word for many days. 'Homa has gone crazy,' everyone said. 'Her poor husband,' they said—her poor *husband!*" She squeezes her eyes shut. "No one could imagine me living apart from Khosrow. Eventually, I talked again. But when I did, I found that my entire childhood was lost. I could not remember one thing that had happened before he died. Later, after I was living with my husband, my old school friends would visit and say 'remember this' or 'remember that.' But my mind was always empty."

Agha Vakili lets out a loud snore and shifts to one side. The sweater slips off his face, exposing the short gray hair sticking up on one side of his head and the silver bristle on his jowls that drowns out his square mustache. Homa-khanoum looks at him sideways and shakes her head.

And yet, despite her resentment about having been married off, Homa is the one who arranged Reza's ill-fated marriage. The way I heard it, right after Reza came to Iran he fell into a fever that lasted a month. When he recovered, his mother, Homa-khanoum, and his sister, Niki, had come up with a list of seven eligible girls. They scheduled meetings with the girls' parents and made up signals for

Reza to use in a girl's presence to tell them if he was interested. In the old days a man would drop a lump of sugar in his tea if he liked the girl, but too many people knew this trick now, so it was decided that after dinner Homa-khanoum would ask if a certain road near Reza's house in California had been asphalted. If Reza said yes, it would mean he liked the girl and they would try to set up another meeting then and there. But when Homa asked the question at the first girl's house, Reza ignored her. She asked over and over again until it became ridiculous, but he never answered. When they went out to the car, he said the girl was fine. That was it. He didn't even go to see the other six.

I still can't believe Reza let himself be married like that. I want to ask him why, but no one in this house will discuss his wife or the divorce he is trying to get. There are no pictures of the wedding, and when I try to bring it up, Reza simply says, "If you tell me about your personal life, I'll tell you about mine." I'm not about to make that mistake. So we sit on the back porch, eating dates and walnuts and fried eggs with Homa and Niki and talking of other things.

"Mmm, these dates are great," I say.

"Iranian food is the best," Homa-khanoum says, smoothing her hair into a small auburn ponytail at the nape of her neck. She puckers her cheeks and makes a sour face. "*Akh*, I've never in my life seen anything like what your father eats in America. What was its name? Some disgusting 'mofu'—he eats it every day."

"Maman, it's called tofu," Reza says, laughing.

"Yes, that's it, tofu. How much Essie loves that!" She shakes her head reproachfully. "He made it for us when we went there and I knew at once that it had pig meat in it. I could tell by the smell. But as much as I said this to Essie, he just laughed and told me it was made of beans." She lowers her voice and looks at me with a grave expression. "I even took a bite, but I spit it out when he wasn't looking. Now tell me the truth, Taraneh. Did I put pig in my mouth?"

I assure her she didn't, and remind her of the time before we left Iran when Baba invited his whole family to eat dinner at a Chinese restaurant near the German Club. Aziz and Homa-khanoum had never eaten Chinese food before, and they dressed up for the occasion. We all sat at a long table in the garden and Baba ordered beef chop suey and chicken chow mein, the least strange things on the menu. But when the food came, Aziz and Homa-khanoum clamped their mouths shut and refused to eat a bite.

"Aziz, God bless her, she did a good thing to tell me not to eat that night," Homa grumbles, spooning more eggs onto my plate. "What makes your father want to eat those Chinese things? He should know that Iranian food is better than this tofu-mofu he throws into his pot."

Avoid the unknown and stay out of trouble. It seems to be Homa-khanoum's strategy for everything. A few nights ago, we were all packed into the car, driving home from a day in the countryside. The freeway traffic was heavy and we rolled down the windows to take in some air.

Suddenly everyone gasped.

"What is it?" I said, leaning toward the front to look up at the black road.

"A man!"

"Smashed flat."

Other cars slowed to the side of the highway; none of them stopped. Reza turned from the steering wheel to look back. "He could be alive," he said.

"Drive on!" Homa-khanoum hissed. "Why are you slowing down? They'll think we did it."

"But maybe we should stop and help him," Reza said, and I nodded, trying to see through the rear windshield. A skewed pair of headlights from the next car shone back at me.

"Look." Niki pointed at the car beside us. "They must have done it; see how they're slowing down?"

"Get their license number!" Agha Vakili cried.

"Are you crazy?" said Homa-khanoum. "Keep driving. Look, they're writing down *our* number to give to the police."

Further on, a truck was parked on the side of the road.

"Aha!" said Niki. "He did it! He's stopped here to check and make sure there's no blood on the grill."

"Write down his number," said Agha Vakili.

"Shouldn't we tell someone?" I asked.

"He was smashed," said Niki. "What can we do? If it was a man, he was dead."

"God make it just have been a pile of clothes," Homa-khanoum murmured.

Reza slowed the car down.

"Eh?" Niki said. "Why are you stopping again? Speed up."

"It's a tollbooth," Reza said drily. "I don't know about here, but in America we stop at tollbooths."

"Yes, yes, we have to stop," Homa-khanoum said. "If we don't, they will really think we did it."

The booth was full of policemen. "Should we report it?" Reza asked.

"Have you gone crazy?" everyone hissed. "Absolutely not! Nobody say a word."

And nobody did.

"So, Taraneh," Reza says, passing me the dates. "Have you gotten your passport back yet?"

I nod, although I promised Zia I wouldn't tell anyone. "Zia got it. He was great; he made friends with all the officials and sent them flowers afterward."

"That's wonderful," Reza and Homa say.

"Hmph, it's nothing big." Niki sniffs as she goes inside for more tea. "Anyone could have done it."

"Don't listen to her," Homa-khanoum says. "Niki is *ghar* with Zia. She hasn't spoken to him for years."

"Why not?"

Homa pauses to remember. "A few years ago when Haideh returned from America, Niki invited her over and told her to take a taxi. Zia said Niki should drive over herself and pick her up. They both got offended and became *ghar*, and now that's the way it is. He doesn't talk to her and she doesn't talk to him."

Ghar usually stems from something minor—a misunderstanding, a hurt feeling, the glimmer of an insult—but it can go on forever. When Aziz visited us in America her brother was staying in a house twenty minutes away, but she did not ask about him once. Baba pointed this out, and then I realized that I had never in my life seen them in the same room together. No, Baba said; they had been *ghar* for thirty years. It had been so long that he suspected even Aziz herself could not remember why. Baba ended it—he arranged things so that one day the two siblings ended up visiting the same house at the same time. They sat on chairs next to each other, both with identical thick glasses and caved-in mouths. For a long time they said nothing, but finally they began a shy conversation and by the end of the evening they were talking and laughing, yelling into each other's deaf ears. Soon afterward, they both returned to Iran, where they continued to be friends until they died within months of each other.

This kind of story is not uncommon here. The Iranian sun moves slowly. People wait hours in lines for meat, for milk, for new telephones, for visas to leave the country. "Come back tomorrow," the clerk says at the end of the day, and they are there again at sunrise; perhaps they have even stayed all night. It irritated me at first, when Massi and I had to wait twenty minutes at the bread shop for the bakers to take a tea break before resuming their work. But I am getting used to it.

The lack of haste also extends to people who are *ghar*. I knew an eighty-five-year-old mother and her cancer-stricken son in California who, in the middle of his radiation treatments, became *ghar*. It didn't matter that either of them might die any day. *Ghar* is not sentimental. Niki and Zia have not sat in the same living room for years, but thankfully their cold war does not carry over to other family members. Homa-khanoum and Reza still visit Massi and Zia; Zia and Massi visit when Niki is not home; they all sit together and drink tea and leave Niki out of their conversations.

"Taraneh, for God's sake do what I tell you," Niki says, coming over to my side of the table and placing the teapot in front of me. "Now that you can return to America, go back and get Shapur and bring him here and marry him." I must look unconvinced about marrying her brother in Portland, because she adds, "That stuff about how cousins shouldn't marry each other is all nonsense. Genetically, intermarriage is actually better. If you marry within your own family you're not risking bringing in strange diseases from the outside."

Homa-khanoum nods solemnly.

"But none of our parents intermarried and we turned out fine," I say.

"We got lucky," Niki says. "Someone could have brought in something from the outside and we would have been walking around with one leg shorter than the other and our front lips cut up the middle like horses. If you marry Shapur you will know exactly what you're getting."

The instinctive fear of the unknown crops up even where there is no apparent danger. When I announce one sunny day that I'm going for a walk in the foothills, Homa-khanoum and Niki look stricken. With the same urgency they had on the highway, they warn me of flash floods, leopards, birds of prey, and Afghans. They are so serious that as I argue with them I start to wonder if perhaps one of these dangers is really lying in wait for me.

But at the same time Reza tells me not to worry about the *komiteh*, a far more real threat. He takes me to an underground restaurant where we drink tea and smoke water pipes alongside young couples who are married or pretending to be. We catch a shared cab to the hiking trails and he pulls me into the front seat and puts his arm around me. "Don't worry," he says loudly, in English. "How do they know you're not my sister? Or my wife?"

At the hillside village where the trails begin I recognize my first school, the Parthian. Its tall brick building is somewhat dilapidated, and the first floor, formerly the reception area, has been transformed into a holding cell for young men arrested on the trails for looking too Western. Reza and I start up the mountain, quickly bypassing the lower trails where groups of young people stroll. We hike high up to a teahouse on the edge of a cliff and order lentil soup for lunch.

"So what happened to riding around the country on a horse?" I say.

"I got married," he replies glumly.

"And your wife didn't want to ride horses?" I say carefully, not wanting to seem like I'm prying.

"You can't do that sort of thing when you're married."

"My parents went all over the country together."

"Your dad married a foreigner."

In the old days, Iranians would smash tea glasses after unbelievers had used them; even Aziz, who was so impressed by foreign educations and foreign fashions, once told Baba to bring his American friend Brian over for lunch and then carefully served him on different plates from the rest of the family. She didn't do this to Mama, but Mama had converted to Islam, and she was a woman. Perhaps a woman is a safer kind of stranger.

Sometimes I feel endangered by so much safeness. I try to explain this to Homa-khanoum and Niki. If you never go out on your own, you might not be prepared for the world when it crashes in on you. But they just shake their heads.

Mama once told me that one night a few years ago she and Baba lay in bed fighting about the way they had raised us. "They should have gone to Iranian schools," Baba said; "they would have known how to speak real Farsi, and they would have become doctors instead of sitting around writing and drawing pictures all day."

"But you yourself didn't want them to go to Iranian schools," Mama reminded him. "You said you wanted them to learn to ask questions, not to do all the memorization and regurgitation you did in school."

"Well, I was wrong," Baba said unconvincingly. He sighed. "We've done everything we can. They've gone to good schools, they know what it's like to have no money; what else can we do?"

The thing is, Baba only became worried once we grew up and it became clear we were following no plan in either world (after all, plenty of Americans' children were becoming doctors, too). Maybe he forgets his own role in making us this way. Soon after I was born, he and Mama read an Indian allegory about a small child by the edge of a river. The child walks along stepping-stones toward the middle, where the water flows faster, and the storyteller has an urge to run over and pluck him away from the danger. But he doesn't. He reasons that the only way the child will learn about the world is to venture into it alone; the adult must restrain his own fears. "I want my children to walk along the river," Baba said after reading the story. It was an uncommon sentiment for an Iranian parent, but it stuck. He stood by as I, age eight, strapped metal spikes onto my feet and climbed a sheet of ice in the mountains; he did not interfere as I, age nine, rode my new bike down the steep slope of one of Shahrak's unpaved roads. Still unused to riding a bicycle, I slammed on the brakes at the bottom of the hill and ended up with a bloody mouth and knees. Baba picked me up and cleaned my cuts. But he never told me to stop.

In the courtyard of a newly built mall, Massi, Zia, and I sit at an outdoor pizza restaurant. Across the road, behind a line of scraggly plane trees, stands a row of large new houses.

"See, those are all doctors' houses," Massi says, pointing at the Western-style peaked roofs jutting above the wall.

"She knows that," Zia says. "This is Shahrak-e-Gharb, where your father was building your house, remember?" He tells me the name of the neighborhood has been changed to Shahrak-e-Ghods—Little City of Saintliness "—but everyone still calls it Shahrak-e-Gharb."

I look at the houses again, startled. Shahrak is no longer empty lots. Where I once skidded my bike over raw desert, thousands of people now live in big houses and drive down paved streets and come shopping at this mall. "By God," Zia says, "that house of yours is worth a million dollars now. Your father sold it back then for nothing."

If we had not sold our Shahrak house when we did, we might have lost it anyway. After the revolution, the mullahs were said to be occupying empty houses (except for Khomeini, famous for eating fruit and yogurt on his own humble floor). When I heard this I imagined them coming in like Prussian soldiers, jumping on tables and wiping their beards on the handmade lace. But perhaps they had spared our house, since it wasn't finished yet. Perhaps they wouldn't have wanted to plaster the walls and screw in the light-switch plates. Maybe no one was living in our house. Even though someone else bought it, maybe they just left it alone. We could never go see, and that made everything possible.

"Taraneh, why don't you come stay with us in Shahrak for a week?" my cousin Roya asks. Her own house is being remodeled and she and her husband and kids are going to stay at the house of my uncle Parviz, who moved to Washington, D.C., during the revolution, leaving his just finished Shahrak house empty. We load up the car over a weekend, and as we drive west along the freeway I feel exhilarated, as if I am finally consummating something I started long ago.

Shahrak still has an unfinished look. The spindly trees let in more sun than the trees do on other Tehran streets. Some houses are under construction, and the sidewalks are strewn with bricks, tiles, and broken pipes. But even if everything were complete, these wide suburban streets would feel strange. Traditional Iranian neighborhoods developed organically around mosques and bazaars, their little streets following the paths of streams or the perimeters of gardens, even looping out around a big old tree that no one had the heart to cut down. Each narrow street has a convenience store, selling everything from soap to paper to ice cream. But Shahrak is a planned-out grid, a car neighborhood. Even for a carton of milk from the local grocery, Roya must get in her white Peugeot and drive five minutes down the road.

Roya says Parviz's house was saved by its ugliness. She says a mullah was brought here to be given the house but he turned down the squat, dark structure with the windows that look out onto brick walls and the stairways that lead nowhere. Bad design aside, after so many years the house is suffering. The ceilings are streaked with black soot, and frayed wires stick out of the wall. The cement floors are bare because the man who laid down the moquette before the revolution took it all up again when he saw that Parviz had left. But as ugly as it is, it has the distinction of having been one of the first finished houses in Shahrak. Parviz even got around to putting in the toilets and sinks, in deep orange, blue, and purple seventies chic. "Made in France" says the label still glued to the ceramic base of a rust-stained toilet. Beside it, a huge cockroach has lain upside down for so long that it crumbles when I sweep it away.

The only person who has ever actually lived in Parviz's house is Asghar, the servant Dadash installed about ten years ago to make sure no one else tried to take it over. The last time I saw Asghar he was a shorn-headed, red-cheeked boy a few years older than I who worked upstairs in Leila-khanoum's kitchen. Now he is a red-cheeked electrician with a thick mustache, living with his wife and two children in the basement apartment of Parviz's house. We grin shyly and tell each other what we remember.

"Your brother threw a book at you and made your nose bleed," he says, bobbing his head, speaking in his slow, affable village accent. "Oh, how much blood there was!"

"You picked up my camera and started taking pictures of nothing," I say, laughing. "I'm embarrassed to say I got so mad I threw a battery at your head." He laughs too and pats a cushion for me to sit beside him and look at the photographs from his wedding.

Asghar and his family live in the village way, on large carpets with bedrolls and hard pillows leaned up against the walls. The only modern touches are a black-and-white TV and the six-year-old son's racecar posters. It is funny to see rooms like this in a neighborhood full of posh houses and swimming pools, like the realization of a utopian revolutionary dream where villagers' families live next door to doctors' families and their children grow up side by side.

But mostly Shahrak is a haven for rich, Westernized Iranians, just as it was designed to be. The Golestan Mall, where Massi and Zia took me for pizza, is the neighborhood's Western-style shopping complex. Its outer walls host the most concentrated graffiti I have seen in Tehran. Much of it is in English—"Iron Maiden," "Slayer," "Ugly Kid Joe," and the ubiquitous "RAP," a rap music allusion that appears on walls all around North Tehran. Scrawled over all these is a derisive rhyme in Farsi: "Shahrak-e-Gharb = Western Clowns."

"How long have you been away?" asks a taxi driver who picks me up in front of the mall. He is not like people in the southern part of the city, who sometimes ask, "Where are you a child of?" as if my accent recalls an Azerbaijani or Turkoman or Loristan childhood far away from Tehran's cosmopolitan patter. Cabdrivers in Shahrak see enough returnees from abroad to know that my odd lilt does not betray a provincial background, but rather a gap in my Iranian life.

"Ah, then you left in the time of the Shah," the taxi driver says, sighing. "Back then, I was a young taxi driver. Women would come into the cab and sit right next to me. Sometimes they would agree to go have coffee with me or go to the movies. I was quite a good-looking young man." He raises his eyebrows in the rearview mirror and his forehead becomes crisscrossed with wrinkles. "Now, of course, boys and girls have their own program. You know what I'm talking about? They wait until the house is empty, then they call each other up to come over and watch dirty films. I never did things like that. It used to be only one or two theaters that showed dirty films, and you would never take a girl to them."

"It's pretty risky to watch those movies, even at home," I say.

"Oh, you mean the government?" he says. "They know all about these videos. As long as they can point to how the women in the street are wearing scarves on their heads they don't care about what's happening inside."

Roya, too, points out that young people, forced indoors by the Islamic regulations, are doing things their parents' generation never dreamed of. The attempt to eradicate Western culture seems to have produced a virulent resistant strain. Young people who want to be "Western" hook up illegal satellite dishes and watch American shows like *Beverly Hills 90210*, *Dallas*, and *Baywatch*. Since many of those watching have no other picture of what America is like, they assume from watching the TV shows that all Americans have a lot of sex with people they barely know. Striving to be like Americans, they do their best to follow suit.

I am dialing a pay phone at a busy intersection in Shahrak when I notice a teenage boy with longish gelled-back hair, sunglasses, and a striped T-shirt, standing beside me.

"Excuse me," he says in a low, urgent voice. "Can we talk?"

I halt, mid-dial. "About what?"

He pauses. "About anything, just talk. Will you come into that side street when you're done with your phone call?"

I tell him no, make my phone call, and walk away in the other direction.

A few days later, while sitting in the back of Zia and Massi's car, I look up to see a thin young man sitting on the curb. He catches my eye and winks. I look to see if Zia and Massi have noticed, but they are turned the other way. The boy dials an invisible telephone, his index finger going around and around, the other hand holding a receiver. I could easily hold up fingers, signal my number. But what would he do with it? Would he dial it? Whom would he ask for when Zia or Massi picked up the phone? "May I please speak with the girl in the back of the car?"

In America I would have just ignored this boy. But here, when he burns his eyes into mine, I don't look away. Partly it is defiance—the enforced covering makes me want to rebel, to demonstrate that this clothing code has not cowed me. But partly it is the fact that the draped cloth makes me feel safe, and oddly alluring. Government-issue graffiti all over the city proclaim that "the chador is a woman's freedom," and in a strange way it is. The scarf and raincoat are like a disguise, a protective shield that can make women feel bolder than they otherwise might. I can stare right into this boy's eyes without worrying about a catcall or a hand on my arm; the burden of fending him off has fallen to the state. In any case, it is hardly me he is looking at. Like every woman on the street, I am just a disembodied face to which he can assign hair, breasts, shoulders, and legs. Under this raincoat and scarf, I could be anything he imagines.

Maybe these boys are no different from Baba, whose teenage ardor gave him the courage to ask out the girl who ended up reporting him to her brothers. In Baba's youth it was a moral offense to ask a girl out to the movies; in the 1970s it was just starting to become acceptable. Now it is illegal. But while the law may have gone back to a more innocent time, the morals have not. I doubt that that boy at the pay phone just wanted to talk, and I wonder if girls here really do follow boys into alleyways. It seems so extreme—such random coupling amid so much protectiveness. One time when I get into a shared cab the men respectfully get out of the backseat and squeeze up front with the driver; another time the man beside me slowly slides his hand up my thigh until I give him a sharp elbow jab. This duality even crops up on the government-run television station, where Western music is banned, but where an electric guitar twangs "I Am a Woman in Love" during a TV game show, and a news program announces a book fair to a pulsating version of Michael Jackson's "Thriller."

Much of the media, however, is overtly anti-Western. On a radio broadcast of the weekly Friday prayer at Tehran University, a speaker belts out a scathing condemnation of *Sheitan-e Bozorg*, "the Great Satan."

"Nowhere in the world is there as much wife-beating as in the Great Satan! Nowhere else are children so unsafe from sexual danger! American children twelve years of age walk down the streets with cigarettes in one hand and alcohol in the other!"

The speech bellows out from the radio as I sit at lunch with Dadash, Leila-khanoum, Roya, and Roya's husband. I tell them I want to write an article about a local readjustment school for Iranian children who have been living out of the country. Roya's husband tells me I should go see the headmaster, tell him who I am, and see if he can help me. But Dadash makes a sour face.

"If I were you," he says, "I would absolutely not set foot in that school or give anyone your name. Nothing good can come of it."

Later, as I sit in the headmaster's office at the boys' school, waiting while he goes into a back room to call the school superintendent, I wonder if Dadash was right. In Iran, giving your name seems to be almost as bad as flashing an American passport—each time you divulge your identity, you risk having it written down and passed on to someone who might make trouble for you.

The headmaster returns to his office. My request has been approved. I spend the afternoon at the boys' school, where the students unbutton their regulation navy blazers to reveal "Nike," "Gap," and "The Big Easy" emblazoned on their T-shirts. They play basketball in the courtyard, yelling in English and German and French, flipping back the long bangs that are tolerated only at this school. The next day, behind the walls of the girls' school, I find a similarly relaxed atmosphere. Middle-school girls run down the hall, shouting in English. High school girls let their head scarves fall slack around their shoulders. In fact, the only girls in proper *hejab* are a class of first graders gathered in a foyer for a lesson on praying. In their flowered prayer chadors, they turn to face Mecca, bending down and rising up as their teacher recites the prayers.

"We know they're not used to it," says a young, friendly teacher in a black chador. "So we go slowly. We let them have their scarves off, but we make sure they understand it wouldn't be allowed in a regular school, where they'll be going after two years."

I sit in on a high school English class in which many of the students speak better English than the teacher. Afterward, the girls gather around me. Most of the ones in this class have moved back from America, and they are hungry for news. "What music are people listening to?" they ask. "Is there a new Chris Isaak album out?"

Yasi, a slim girl with long dark hair and striking almond-shaped eyes, tells me she used to surf in Marin County. Sima, whose hair is cut in a pert black bob, played high school volleyball in Texas. Soosan, a red-haired, blue-eyed girl who looks more American than Iranian, just arrived here after living all her life in Atlanta. Both her parents are Iranian, but they raised her speaking English, and she barely knows Farsi. She is twenty-one, a few years older than the others, and she has come to Iran for a year to learn Farsi; the school has taken her in as a special case.

After school Sima invites me to her house, and Yasi and Soosan accompany us. As soon as we step inside Sima's high-rise Shahrak apartment, the girls throw off their long coats to reveal tight T-shirts and baggy jeans. We sit together on Sima's bed and she pulls out a photo album from America. "That's my school," she says in a Texan drawl. "That's my friend Kelly and that's me and Melissa and Jackie in our volleyball uniforms." Yasi and Soosan nod as if the girls in the pictures are their friends too. "I miss them so much," Sima says. "I couldn't believe it when my parents said we were leaving Texas. I mean, there I was in tenth grade, living there since I was six, and suddenly my dad tells me we're going back to Iran. I didn't even remember Iran."

"Ooh, you should have seen me and Sima last year," Yasi says. "We just cried all night long and all day at school. That's how we became friends."

"Yeah, all I did was beg my parents to take me back to America," Sima says. "But they were scared that me and my brother were becoming too American. They said if we didn't come back to Iran now we never would."

"It was awful," Yasi says. "The first week I was here it was the anniversary of the hostage takeover. They took us out of class and told us to chant '*Marg bar Amreeka.*' Sima and I both cried and said we weren't going to say 'Death' to our country, and they finally told us we didn't have to. But we still had to march with the other students. I hated it."

Marg bar Amreeka. Ali and Sufi and I once ran around the house chanting those very words, unconcerned with their meaning beyond that the phrase was racy and rebellious. It did not upset Mama—at that point she did not really feel that patriotic toward the country everyone suddenly hated. America was not precious to us. We could go there any time we wanted.

On a Thursday night, the start of the Iranian weekend, the Golestan Mall is buzzing with activity. Brightly lit, ultra-modern shop windows display imported jeans, hiking shoes, perfumes, and snowboards. A jewelry shop glitters with Italian bracelets and Swiss watches; a stationery store offers Hemingway paperbacks in English. As we window shop, Sima points at the parade of young people strolling back and forth, grazing each other's shoulders. "Sit and watch for a half hour and you'll notice things," she says. "See that group of boys pretending to talk to each other? Well, they're really talking to that group of girls behind them."

We find Sima's girlfriends eating dinner at the outdoor pizza restaurant. The boys in their group, most of whom I interviewed at the boys' school, sit at a far table and make faces at us. *Come sit with us*, they mime, knowing we can't. They are kidding but not kidding. It must feel strange to be part of this Islamic society but to have also lived outside it. At school these kids are told that unsupervised women are liable to lose control of themselves in public, or that if a boy looks at a girl's hair he'll go to hell. The mirthfulness with which they repeat these warnings makes it clear how little they are affected by them; they stare across the café at each other in mute agreement over how absurd it all is.

All of a sudden the boys leap up, leaving their pizzas on the table. "Sima! *komiteh!*" one of them hisses as they file out the back exit.

Five or six armed young men in olive fatigues tromp through the bank of tables, glaring at the empty chairs and guilty faces. We sit motionless, pretending to be invisible—except for Sima, who, during an instant when the *komiteh* are not looking, ducks down to wipe off her lipstick.

As soon as they leave, we stand up. Our hands shaking, our appetites gone, we pick up our bags and escape into the warm night. Near a flatbed truck which the *komiteh* are loading up with young men, a taxi pulls over and we gratefully pile in. "Why are they being arrested?" we ask the driver innocently, bold now that we are speeding safely away.

"Rap hair," he says disgustedly. "Rap clothes. Anything the for-eigners do, they want to do too. They're just like monkeys."

We zip up toward a friend's house, past the big dark houses of Shahrak, and my fear melts into elation. This is exactly where I would have ended up if there had been no revolution. At age fifteen I would have been cruising around this very neighborhood with my friends, and sitting now in this carload of gum-chewing, shampoo-fresh teenagers, I get a whiff of those phantom Iranian teenage years.

We slip out of the taxi and tiptoe up to a dark house, keeping an eye on the road. A neighbor steps out of his front door to see what car has stopped here and driven off. Perhaps he is *komiteh*. Perhaps he has just come out to water his plants. We shrink into the bushes, our hearts pounding, and I remember Sima telling me how a few of the boys have been caught before—one had his long hair shaved off; two others were arrested in a general sweep while they were carrying snapshots from a party. They were held in jail overnight, and by the time they were interviewed in the morning they had managed to go through the photos, rip out all the girls' faces, and swallow them.

The neighbor goes back inside. We ring the buzzer.

"Who is it?" asks a deep, forbidding voice.

"Open up," Sima says impatiently. The door clicks open and we hurry in.

Once inside, we relax. A techno drumbeat pounds the basement floor where Yasi's boyfriend and his sister live; their parents are asleep in the upstairs part of the house. The kids tease each other's shoes off, joking around in English and German and broken Farsi, so there is always a sheen of confusion, never a moment when everyone un-derstands. They laugh and jostle each other and shimmy to the music without even drinking much of the vodka the host has slipped out of his father's desk drawer.

Passing around a Marlboro, they introduce me.

"She's from America," Sima says in Farsi. "She wants to hear *ko-miteh* stories."

"*Akh*, she should hear Jila's story," someone says. "Jila, tell her what happened."

Jila has bleached, spiky hair, a tight satin T-shirt, and a string of blue worry beads transformed into a choker. But despite her hard-edged glamour she seems fragile; her slightly Asian eyes look shadowy, as if she hasn't slept enough.

"A few weeks ago I was at a party and the *komiteh* came," she says. "My boyfriend said, 'Let's run,' so we jumped out a second-story window. They ended up letting everyone at the party just call taxis and go home, but they were so surprised to see a girl jump out a window that they came after us. We ran, and got split up. I hid in a broken-down building until three in the morning, shaking, too scared to come out. When I finally got home my boyfriend was asleep in my bed and my mother was crying. They'd beaten him so hard that he couldn't feel anything from the waist down. He was really screwed up for a few weeks. Now, I hardly ever go to parties."

But things don't usually go that far. "They just want money," says Bahman, a tall boy with movie-star good looks. "They stop you for something, they look at your clothes or what kind of car you're driving, and they name a price. If they see you're driving a shiny foreign car or you live in a nice house, they say, 'I won't let you go for less than such and such.'"

"It's not all their fault," says a beefy nineteen-year-old named Hassan. "My father says the *komiteh* don't get paid enough themselves. They come from poor families, and they see us driving around Shahrak in Hondas and Mitsubishis. All they have to do is say they're going to arrest us and our fathers give them three times the money they'd make in a week."

"They're still bastards," Bahman says. "They're totally uneducated. This friend of mine was stopped for having a leather cover on the front of his sports car—the guy wanted to know why his car was wearing clothes! My friend offered to take the car's clothes off, but the *komiteh* guy said, 'Even if you take them off, I'm taking you in. You have a rap car.'"

"They have no idea what rap even means," Jila says scornfully. "To them it's just anything Western or anything they don't like."

These kids flout the rules flagrantly. Couples on dates borrow babies to make them look married. High school girls cut their hair short, put on baggy shirts, and go bike riding, passing as boys. One boy who lived for a few years in the States boasts that despite his long hair he's never gotten arrested. "I've got this New Jersey library card," he explains. "Whenever they ask me for ID, I show it to them and they let me go. I think they're scared it might be some sort of diplomatic pass."

The opening synthesizer tones of an Ace of Base song cut through the chatter and everyone jumps up to dance. The whole group moves together in a half slam dance, half belly dance, loose with abandon. Jila grabs my hand and pulls me in. The gyrating bodies fall against me, and as I am sucked in they feel warm and familiar, as if I am dancing alongside my own teenage self.

In the morning I tie on my scarf and take a walk through Shahrak. I walk past the sun-bleached basketball court and the "Metallica"-emblazoned playground, right up to the street where our own Shahrak house stands.

I remember the address. I remember the shape, although someone has plastered the brick walls over with gray stucco. Under that thin veneer of cement lie the yellow handmade bricks that Baba picked out in Qom. Up on the left is a mezzanine—my mezzanine, in my bedroom, with my swimming pool outside. The windows stare down like lidded eyes, remembering me; and I look back in silent communion.

The front door opens.

Two girls walk out; one with a scarf on, the other bareheaded, seeing her friend out to her car. The car drives away and the remaining girl turns to go inside.

Before I know what I am doing, I step forward.

"My father designed this house."

I immediately scold myself. What am I doing? Why should she talk to me? This, after all, is not Aziz's house, where the people from upstairs are relatives and will introduce me to the downstairs neighbors. Here, I am a prying stranger.

The girl stops and looks at me. "Really?" she says.

"Yes. Before the revolution. We used to come out and look at it every day while it was being built." And then suddenly I am worried she will think I want the house back. "I live in America now," I add.

"How interesting," she says. "Please, come inside."

Too taken aback to *ta'arof*, I follow her in the door.

"Mama, Baba, this is the girl whose father built our house."

A plump, middle-aged woman steps out of the kitchen; a man with thinning gray hair looks up from his work at the breakfast nook and peers at me over his reading glasses.

"Really? What is your name?"

I tell him my name and my father's name. His eyes widen and then he starts to laugh.

"Do you know we looked for you for ten years? We never could find out what happened to you. You see, when we bought this house your father had already paid for the telephone service but they wouldn't give it to us without a receipt. We tried and tried to find your address, but finally we gave up and paid the money again. And now here you are, walking in the front door."

"We were in America," I say in a small voice, like a child who has come in late from the playground.

"Yes, we figured you had gone away."

I sit down and accept a cup of tea in the kitchen I once clomped through in rubber boots.

"But you must be dying to see the house." The girl stands up and I follow her through the dining room, into the living room, and up to the landing that opens onto the backyard and the bright blue swimming pool I never swam in. It all looks familiar, even though I don't recognize anything specific.

"Who plays the piano?" I ask.

"I do," the girl says shyly. "But not very well; I just started. Would you like to hear me play?"

I pick one of the overstuffed chairs in the living room, relieved that I don't have to talk for a few minutes. The girl seats herself at the piano and, after a self-conscious backward glance, she smooths out the sheet music and begins to play. Her back is turned, her long brown ponytail hangs down her back, her fingers hesitantly pick out the notes. She looks like me, right where I once sketched myself onto Baba's blueprints.

After she finishes playing, I thank her and she shows me the rest of the house, including my room, where the curtains are drawn and the mezzanine is being used as a storage space. We chat a little more with her parents and then I turn to go.

"We've always loved this house," the mother says.

"It's so nice to have finally met you," the father says. "Don't forget to ask your father if he still has the receipt for the phone."

"Come back another time and we'll go swimming," the girl says.

I tell her I will. But as I walk away, I realize that I don't need to come back here. This house, with its dim, curtained rooms and its hospitable Iranian family, is not mine any more than the high school kids at the party last night were me. And yet I am glad the house is still here, a solid testament to our old life.

❖

My cousin Haideh and her husband are applying for Canadian visas. "We need a certain amount of points to get accepted," she explains. "You get one point for speaking English, one point for having relatives already living in Canada, three points for your interview, and so on."

Haideh plans to sell off her wedding presents garage-sale style, only a few months after her wedding. She is placing an ad in the paper, and she says people will come to the house and pay hundreds of dollars for her crystal bowls and silver-plated trays. "It's the inflation," she says matter-of-factly. "People know these kitchen things are soon going to be worth more than the money they're spending, so I'll get the original prices back. This is what's going to buy us a refrigerator and stove in Canada."

"But won't you miss Iran?" I ask. "Canada's cold. You'll have to start all over again, and Mansour doesn't speak English."

"Bah, that's exactly what your father said on the phone. He told me not to burn my bridges. I said, 'What bridges?' " She purses her lips. "You guys have no idea what life is like here."

"But you and Mansour have good jobs. You have a nice house, and all your friends are here."

"Tara, Iran is depressing. Everyone who can is getting out. I mean, there are a few people making it big on pizza restaurants, but the rest of the country is getting poorer. Even if we could save a little money—which we can't—there's no way to enjoy it. Can you believe it—all those times we said this regime couldn't last two more years —and now it's been almost twenty! Are we supposed to spend the

rest of our lives drinking coffee at the Hilton for our fun? At least in
Canada if we work hard we can make a little money and do something
with it."

"Speak English to her," Haideh hisses to me when her neighbor Delbar comes upstairs to visit. "She has to practice for her interview so
she can get her Canadian visa too."

"Hello," I say in English. "Why do you want to go to Canada?"

Delbar begins self-consciously. "I want to go to Canada," she
enunciates carefully, "because I can't get a visa to America."

I smile. "Okay, but why do you want to go to America?"

She giggles. "*You* know why. It's better!"

"Why is it better?"

"You have more fun."

"What makes you think that?"

Delbar is silent for a minute and then she laughs and pushes away
an invisible load. "Too hard," she says in Farsi, winding a strand of
long hair around her finger. "Haideh, where is the new dance tape I
brought over? Do you have it?" She goes into the adjoining room
and starts rooting through the tapes.

While Delbar is out of the room, Haideh quickly whispers her
story to me. Slim, energetic Delbar teaches traditional Iranian dancing at the women's gym nearby. She was the girl in pink at the wedding who asked me about my shoes. Haideh tells me that last year
Delbar almost got married herself. "He was an engineer who lived
in Paris, so she studied French. Then at the last minute he changed
his mind. I thought she was going to kill herself."

I shake my head in sympathy. Haideh goes on. "Well, I'm sure
she'll meet someone else soon. She looks so good now. Did you notice her nose? She's just had it done."

"Why?" I ask, thinking of the long, dignified noses of Delbar's
brother and father, whom she lives with downstairs.

"*Akh*, it was so big before," Haideh says, sniffing with her own
small, round nose. "This nose is much cuter."

Delbar returns, waving her tape triumphantly. She sits down beside
me on the couch. "Taraneh," she says, "I've been wanting to ask you
something. Why don't you wear more makeup?"

"I don't know. I just don't."

"You would look so much better if you would just style your hair and wear some eyeliner," she says.

I shrug and look across the room at the mirror. Next to curly-haired, made-up Delbar I look washed out. My hair is limp and flat after having been matted down under the scarf all day, and my face looks pale. A few weeks ago, visiting some people I had never met, I was introduced as an American. "Of course, it's clear," said the hostess, not unkindly. "If she were Iranian she'd have on a lot of makeup and her hair would be done up, not in this simple, unadorned style." In fact, most people I meet here assume I am still in high school, not just because I wear so little makeup, but also because of the way I falter when I am grasping for a Farsi word. It's as if since I've gotten to Iran I have become a child again. I am dependent on my uncles and aunts; I cannot fully participate in adult conversations; I have no job, no home, no place in the Iranian adult world.

But I don't say this to Delbar. Instead, I say, "What's the point of doing my hair? I have to cover my head all the time, and they can arrest you for wearing makeup."

"Oh, but they don't," she says. "Not anymore—or only once in a while, on religious holidays. But even at the wedding, your hair was just straight. Don't you ever curl it?"

"No, not really." She stares at me, frowning.

I see this frown at other times too, whenever I do something that Delbar considers "villagey." When I return from a hike and leave my muddy shoes outside Haideh's front door Delbar picks them up with her fingertips and drops them into a far corner of a closet. When I talk about going to stay on Dadash's farm she rolls her eyes and asks why on earth I would want to. And when she looks at me I can see the question in her eyes: Are Americans really like this? Is this what she will have to become if she goes there? I think my faded T-shirts and loose ponytail make her nervous because she is not sure whether or not she has the right to despise them.

Haideh and Mansour and I pile into Delbar's car and she drives us through the streets of North Tehran, where in the waning light I can just make out the Farsi graffiti spray-painted on apartment building walls. "Death to America!" "Death to uncovered, anti-Islamic women!"

Up in these foothills that were once country gardens, high-rise buildings threaten to choke each other out. A city ordinance limits the number of stories that can go up in this wealthy neighborhood, but the rule has been trampled time after time by bribes. New apartment complexes sprout up every month, and as we drive past high cranes and half-constructed buildings, I see only one low wall that still preserves a few old trees and a crumbling country house waiting for its owner to die and the land to be sold off.

We park by a long wall right up against the mountains and Mansour rings a buzzer at the gate. The door swings open and the silhouette of a man ushers us into a garden, cursing us for not arriving earlier when everyone was swimming. He leads us out to a seven-sided pool that glints green under seven fountains, ringed by a jungle of enormous roses. Frogs scream out their night concert as stars shoot overhead.

Inside the house, the guests are gathered around a piano, swaying arm in arm, singing a wordless accompaniment to the tune of "Love Story." The men wear dress shirts and blazers; the women wear elaborate jewelry and makeup, and everything from jeans and silk blouses to stupendous ensembles of chiffon and taffeta.

The song ends and everyone begs to hear it again, but the piano player shakes his head and leaves the bench, cracking his knuckles. He nods to Mansour, who brings him a muddy cocktail of apple juice and sweet Jordanian whiskey.

"Good playing, Cyrus," Mansour says. "Have you met Taraneh? You two should speak English together." He steers me over to the piano player. "Cyrus's English is excellent."

Cyrus smiles modestly and slides into the seat next to mine. He is thirtyish, with wire-rimmed glasses, a small mustache, and straight light brown hair combed back from his high forehead.

"You are from America," he says in impeccable Oxford English. "You tell me. I've taught myself completely from language tapes. Never set foot out of Iran. How is my English?"

"It's very good. And so is your piano playing."

"Thank you. I must tell you, though, I don't like playing those songs." He looks sourly at the stereo, where someone has put on a techno-pop CD. A tall woman in a floor-length white gown rises languidly to dance with a dapper young man in a black tuxedo jacket and a silk ascot. "I try to play something that's good but they don't understand it," Cyrus says. "Then when I play that 'Love Story' nonsense they all gather round."

"What do you like to play?" I ask.

"Bach. Beethoven. Chopin."

The floor is filling with party guests who seem hard pressed to dance to the jarring, repetitive drumbeat. Iranian dancing is soft and organic; it works much better with the sinewy melodies of the old days. The dancers do their best, keeping one hand at the back of the head and the other on one hip as the electronic keyboard starts up. And then, all at once, they fan out around a single dancer—a fifteen-year-old servant boy who has leapt into the middle of the floor.

Impervious to the music, he moves fluidly, his limbs loose and detached. His eyes are half closed and his white shirt and black pants billow out from his body; he moves as if possessed by a graceful, shadowy demon. Mama once told me about a traditional village wedding she attended on her first trip to Iran, where the bride wore bangles and sequins and the groom threw a bloody handkerchief out the bedroom window. Male and female guests were kept separate, and in the women's quarters, the entertainment was provided by a pubescent boy dressed like a woman, with his lips painted red, his eyes lined with black kohl, and a beauty mark penciled in above an upper lip that was just beginning to darken. The following year that boy would be barred from the women's quarters, relegated for the rest of his life to stealing glances down hallways and through gaps in curtains. But on that night he was still a child, and whatever he saw of the bride and the festive, raucous unveiled women did not matter yet.

That tradition ended with the advent of white wedding gowns and synthesized music. Men and women began to mix; no one needed to see a young boy dressed as a woman anymore. And yet when this servant boy dances, everyone gathers to watch. His mother, wearing a colorful dress from her southern Qashqai tribe, puts down the whiskey glass she has been drying and shyly watches as her son whirls from side to side among the crowd of women who lean in, almost touching him as he passes.

The boy finishes his dance. The guests clap enthusiastically and spill forward to fill the empty space. Cyrus brings me a slice of chocolate cake.

"If I ask you a question," he says in his clipped English accent, "will you promise not to tell anyone?"

Biting on a forkful of cake, I nod.

"Ever since we met a little while ago, I've been thinking that you are the type of person I could get along with. I was wondering what you would think of us getting married."

I make an effort to swallow. "Well, I'm very flattered . . ."

"What?" he says, perturbed. "It's not flattery. I really mean it."

"No, that's not what I meant," I say quickly, looking around to see if anyone can hear us. "It's just that to marry someone I'd have to be in love with him."

"Well," he says, brightening up, "what should I do to make you fall in love with me?"

"I don't know. I don't even know you."

I turn to watch the dancers, my face burning. I almost want to laugh, but Cyrus is perfectly serious. It seems strange that he should be so picky about music and so rash about marriage. Is it because I have lived in America? Or because I said I like Chopin? I cannot think of anything else we have talked about.

He leans in to make sure I am looking at him.

"Maybe if I describe myself you will get to know me," he says. "I am [counting on his fingers]: Affectionate. Sensitive. Tolerable. Sometimes impossible. Hardworking."

He looks at me expectantly.

"And why do you think I would be a good match for you?" I ask.

"Oh, I can tell. You see, I am looking for a woman with the same interests I have—someone who does not like to go out [brushing his hand toward the dance floor], who would rather stay inside and have quiet conversation about music and books. I can see you are that kind of person. Also, you are young, but not too young, and educated, and you seem to be a reasonable person."

"Well, thank you. But, you see, I go out a lot," I say, hoping to invoke a wild American life full of endless parties. "In fact, I go out all the time. I could never marry someone who didn't want me to go out."

"Well, of course I didn't mean you couldn't go out," he says, leaning in close enough for me to see the slight film of moisture on his upper lip. "My meaning is that I don't want a woman who has friends."

"But I have friends," I say indignantly. "I wouldn't stop having friends just because I was married."

"Ah, but you wouldn't have special friends." He leans in even closer. "Male friends." I back away but he follows. "*I* would be your special friend."

"Well, you know, I'm going back to the States soon," I say, reaching for my drink. "So I don't know how it would work for us to get married."

"You don't have to go back, do you?" he says. "Wouldn't your father agree to let you stay here and marry? I am from a good family, I speak English, and I have a steady income from teaching piano."

"I'm not sure I want to get married," I say.

"Nonsense. Everybody wants to get married. Perhaps you think that I don't make enough money. But we would not need money. We would have each other, and that would be enough."

We are interrupted by the Qashqai maid, who walks in with a tray of tea. Haideh steps forward and coyly motions to a thin young man with glasses. "Here, Agha Doctor, you take one first."

The young man reddens. "Just call me Ramin."

"No, no," says Haideh. "That won't do. What would your patients think?"

"Well, my patients are in Germany," he says, laughing. "And over there my friends call me by my name. They don't call me Herr Doktor."

"This is not Germany, Agha Doctor," Haideh reminds him. I nod to myself. This is Iran, where fifteen years after the revolution, people cling more tightly than ever to titles like "Doctor" and "Engineer" —the new forms of the "Haji" and "Khan" that demarcated status in the old days. "Did you get enough to eat?" Haideh asks. Ramin nods. "Delbar," she says, "go get him some more cake."

The other guests pull up chairs around me and Cyrus.

"So," one of Ramin's friends says, "how does it feel to be back?"

"Good, good," he says, grinning. "Wonderful."

"Are you going to come back and stay, then?" says another friend. "We miss you."

"Me too," Ramin says. "But you know how it is. I have my practice in Germany."

"You could easily find work here, and then you would be close to your friends and family," Haideh says, winking at Delbar.

"No, he's right," Delbar cuts in. "Why should he come back here? It's we who should go there." She flashes Ramin a smile. "What do you think? Is it good there? Should we come?"

"It's hard to say," Ramin says. "It's true it's not the same when your friends and family are not there. And at first it's hard to learn German and meet people."

"Well, we have you to teach us German and introduce us," Delbar says with a flutter of her eyelashes. But Ramin is looking at the TV that someone has just turned on, a talk show in English.

"Where's your satellite dish?" Ramin asks the host, Payam.

"Out there, on the porch." Payam points out the window at an object swathed in sheets. "That's why it's fuzzy; the cloth obstructs the waves."

"But you get everything?"

"Most things. CNN; MTV; *90210.*"

"Hah," Ramin says. "That's more than I have in Germany."

"Taraneh-jan, who is that man?" Delbar calls out sweetly as an ad flashes out pictures of famous people.

"Hugh Grant."

"Yes, that's right, Hugh Grant. I've seen him in movies."

People in North Tehran watch a lot of American movies. Recently I saw *Sleepless in Seattle* and *Indecent Proposal* on videotapes that came via secret door-to-door vendors. One man carries them in the inside pockets of his coat; another dresses as a baker and places the video inside a hollowed-out cake, carrying it in a pink box to the door. And satellite TV broadcasts a constant stream of movies and soap operas from all over the world.

Ramin turns back to the TV. "Our show isn't on anymore?"

"That show?" Payam says. "No way, they canceled it ages ago."

Ramin turns to me with a broad grin. "It was this mullah who had a show where he would bring up questions, daily problems that might come up in your life, and then he would spend half an hour analyzing the problem and explaining how to deal with it Islamically. We used to have parties where we would watch it, because some of the questions were so funny. Like if a man is sleeping on the second floor and his aunt is sleeping downstairs and there is an earthquake. He falls through the floor and lands on his aunt, and through this action she conceives a baby. Is the child legitimate?"

"I think he said it was," Payam says.

"Or remember the one where a man jumps out a window to commit suicide and as he's falling someone sticks a knife out of a lower window and it goes into him. Is that murder?"

"It wasn't just this mullah," Payam says. "Religious scholars have been debating these issues for centuries. Sometimes they just go overboard."

From across the room we hear the tinkling of Cyrus on the piano.

"*Akh*, Bach," Ramin says appreciatively. We take seats around the piano, me on Cyrus's far right.

"Have you thought about what I said?" he mutters in English without stopping. "Promise me you'll think about it. In the meantime, we can get to know each other through letters."

"Hey, you've got Queen!" someone across the room cries, slipping a video into the VCR. A long-haired guitar player appears on the small screen, hammering out a frenzied solo.

"We'll have a letter relationship, then?" Cyrus whispers, finishing his piece with a flourish.

"Well, sure," I whisper back. "But, you know, I have letter relationships with lots of people."

"Yes," Cyrus says. "But this will be a special letter relationship. See, we have decided to have it for the purpose of getting to know each other for the possibility of marriage."

I go out into the balcony and stand beside the shrouded satellite receiver. Helicopters circle here in the daytime, looking for these dishes, which sell briskly on the black market. Payam pointed out earlier that the balcony across the street has had the same laundry hanging on the line for a year, and I wonder if the authorities will ever fly over it and realize that that shirt, that tablecloth, and that towel must be dry by now.

The city flickers on for miles, all the way down to the south end, where strings of light outline Khomeini's giant shrine and form a bright castle in the darkness. Closer in are freeways, high-rises, and, on a hill toward the right, the green light of the Hilton—now Independence—Hotel. Beyond it is a dark patch with no lights, and I wonder if it could be the park where my cousin Javad used to go walking with his girlfriend at night before the revolution.

Suddenly the glass door slides behind me and an agitated Delbar rushes out onto the balcony, with Haideh right behind her.

"Shh, drink this milk," Haideh says, holding a glass in front of Delbar. "Then we'll go home and you can get some sleep."

Delbar pushes the glass away and breaks into sobs. Haideh puts her arm around her and looks over at me. "She just found out Ramin is engaged to a girl in Germany," Haideh says solemnly. I shake my head.

Delbar cries for a few minutes and then takes a sip of milk, sniffling while Haideh pats her on the back. No one says anything. We stay out there for a long time, gazing at the city as the distant lights glitter and the opening chords of a Beethoven sonata drift out from the house.

❖

Before leaving New York I stopped by to see my friend Persheng. Her seventeen years in America had almost expired; she had recently visited Iran and was planning another trip later in the year.

She arrives in Tehran, and we go for a walk along shady, tree-lined Vali-e-Asr Street.

"You know what that is, don't you?" Persheng points at an unremarkable modern-looking building across the street. "That was Chattanooga. Remember?"

I smile and shake my head. All I remember is Shahrzad's impassioned wish to have gone there. "I never went," I say. "Did you?"

"Yeah, I went a few times in high school. My friends and I would go there at night, or to the Hilton, or to the Hotel Darband near the mountains."

Back in New York, Persheng, who is a documentary filmmaker, had shown me some archival footage from late-Pahlavi North Tehran. It looked outrageously decadent compared to footage from the rest of the country. While village girls in chadors wove carpets and herded sheep, Tehran girls in miniskirts and platform shoes thrust their bodies against long-haired boys in skintight T-shirts under the flashing lights of a discotheque. These were the kind of images the new regime used to decry West-struck Iran.

Persheng sheepishly tells me that back then she used to get chauffeured to school in her father's company car. "My friends and I did go to a lot of parties, but we weren't completely wild," she says. "There were plenty of people who were wilder. And even then I had a sense sometimes that it was all too much. Like there was this sixteen-year-old girl at school who threw an all-night birthday party in her own private garden outside the city. When I saw her in that garden, walking around with one guy on each arm, I don't know, it just seemed like there was something unnatural about all of it. Once in a while I would get a sense of how our lives looked to other people. When I was fifteen I was at a bakery with my mother near our house and some man yelled, 'Khanoum, cover up your daughter!' I had a button-up shirt on with the top couple of buttons open at the neck —nothing compared to what a lot of girls wore. My mom yelled back at the man to mind his own business. But at that moment I felt like maybe something about the way we were acting was wrong."

Persheng has come to Tehran now to work on a personal documentary about her return to Iran. She has been interviewing family members and she plans to film her old houses and schools, including an ancestral home in the mountains of Kurdistan. She says she has also come back this time to see if she could live here again.

"I know I can work and live in America," she says. "But as soon as I get to Iran, I close my eyes and hear all the voices and laughter and something clicks for me and I know I'm home. You know, I really think I want to stay. This is right for me. As soon as I got here, I felt this weight being taken off me, like I could finally be myself."

"But could you really live here without feeling restricted, after being in New York?"

"Oh, sure. I stayed there long enough so I won't be yearning to go to nightclubs and concerts. The things I've missed here are more important to me now—the warmth of the people, the way you feel like you really have a place here."

"Well, what would you do? Would you work?"

"Yes, that's the question. I would want to find work in film, like I did in the States. I have a friend who has gotten me in touch with some Iranian filmmakers, so I am going to go meet them tonight and see what they say. There's a lot happening with film here—Iranians are starting to win prizes at international festivals, and lately they're getting into issues like feminism and antiwar themes. A lot of them are much more interesting than movies in America."

A few days later Persheng invites me to meet one of the filmmakers. We take a taxi to a small, modern apartment building. Kambiz, a slight man with longish gray hair, a thick mustache, and friendly brown eyes, opens the door. Right in the street he shakes our hands, breaking the law against mixed-sex touching. Then he ushers us in.

I am immediately struck by what is missing from the apartment. No Louis Quatorze furniture. No ornate crystal ashtrays or china figurines. No heavy curtains blocking the sun. The rooms are bright and airy, the shelves are filled with books and videos; a few film awards sit by the phone beside family snapshots. The walls are hung with Iranian tribal art—colorful woven horse blankets, musical instruments, brass pipes—making the house look less like a North Tehran apartment than like the home of anthropologists who have lived in Iran.

We sit down on a pair of comfortable couches. Kambiz's wife, Fereshteh, a petite woman with a mass of dark curly hair, brings out a tray of tea and cakes and sits down with us. We talk about films— he is a director and she is an actress I recognize from an Iranian film I saw in the States. I can't remember seeing any of his films, though.

"I think mine haven't gone to America," Kambiz explains. "Germany, yes, and France, Australia, Italy, India, and Turkey. But so far not America. Although I hear that in the last few years there is starting to be more interest in Iranian film there."

Persheng and I mention a few movies we have seen, mostly by one or two big directors, and Kambiz looks pleased. He tells us about his own recent films, most of which take place in the provinces of Iran. "I go to a village and talk to the people there, and slowly the film develops in my head. I can usually take the main characters from among the villagers. They play themselves so naturally." I mention that many of the Iranian movies I have seen lately have had children as main characters, and Kambiz nods. "Ten years ago we were all making films about the revolution and the war. Slowly we got beyond that. Now the directors like to look at more complex issues, like relationships between people. If we use children the censors don't mind so much—they're not so worried about a boy and girl being in a film together if the actors are only nine. And you can have just as good a story with nine-year-olds."

Still, he says, some films end up banned by the Ministry of Culture, and Iranian directors find themselves doing a lot of self-censoring to avoid this. To supplement their government funding, some also work in conjunction with foreign directors. Kambiz has been invited to festivals across Europe and Asia, but he has never been to the United States.

"Why not?" I ask. "Are you not allowed to go there?"

He shrugs. "I could go if I wanted."

"You know, you're the first Iranian I've met here who doesn't say he wants to go to America."

"I've seen America on TV," he says. "The only reason I'd want to go would be to see what kinds of films people like over there. But if I'm going to spend my money on travel, what I'd really like to do is drive across China and talk to people in the villages."

A few days later Kambiz and Fereshteh invite me and Persheng out to dinner with them and their two sons. In a crowded restaurant near the South Tehran railway station we wait for a table to open up. Even though we have reservations it is not easy to find a seat in this brick-walled chamber where the patrons' animated conversations compete with the insistent drumbeat pounding from the carpet-covered stage. Next to the drummer, a sweating middle-aged man performs *mil-andazy*, traditional Iranian gymnastics using heavy clubs. Beside him, another man recites, in the melodic vibrato of poem-tellers, the tale of Rostam and Sohrab from the poet Ferdowsi's epic, the *Shahnameh*.

"You know the story?" Kambiz asks, and I nod. Baba told it to me and Ali when we were small, and Ali always liked Rostam, so much that in Portland he named his guinea pig after him. (Both Rostams came to similarly grotesque ends—one in a pit of swords, the other under the careless foot of one of Ali's friends.) The original Rostam is perhaps the most famous warrior in Persian mythology, a paragon of strength who leaves his pregnant wife in a foreign land, giving her an onyx charm with the instructions that "if the star of fate should send a son, then bind this father's token to his arm." The son, Sohrab, grows up to be as formidable a warrior as his father and he yearns to find him and join forces. They meet on the battlefield, and Sohrab, suspecting that such a brave, strong opponent must be none other than Rostam, begs him to identify himself "and I will speak to you of love." But Rostam refuses to reveal his name. The two fight; Sohrab almost wins but then releases his father; Rostam strikes the fatal blow, noticing too late the onyx fastened around his dying son's arm.

As the poet reaches the climax of the battle scene, we find a table in the back of the restaurant. Next to us an old man with a long white beard is telling fortunes using a handful of brass dice. Kambiz and Fereshteh's younger son begs to have his fortune told, but the old man shakes his head. Instead, he beckons me and Persheng and Fereshteh over and tells us vague fortunes that for me and Persheng involve getting married and for Fereshteh involve having more children.

"He says Taraneh will get married in seventeen months," Persheng says when we return to the table.

"I'll let you know," I say.

"Tell me, Taraneh," Fereshteh says. "Do you think you'll marry an Iranian or an American?"

"Whoever I meet and like."

She smiles. "I thought you'd say that. But don't you have a preference at all? Don't you feel more comfortable with one side or another?"

"I used to think it didn't matter either way," Persheng says. "I married an American thinking that all that was important was that we loved each other. When my grandmother was told that I was marrying an American, she cried, and I thought she was just being old-fashioned. But now I think these things do matter. There are certain parts of me that my husband never understood because he wasn't Iranian."

"Like what?" Kambiz asks.

"Like how I felt about Iran, or why I needed to be with other Iranians when we were in the States. He felt left out by my Iranianness."

"Sometimes I think the perfect person for me would be half Iranian and half American," I say. "Or at least someone who grew up half his life here and half his life there."

"Taraneh, can I ask you a question?" Kambiz says. "Over there, in America, do you have boyfriends?"

I freeze for a fraction of a second. And then I say yes.

He nods. "That makes sense," he says, and Fereshteh nods too. I relax. For the first time I don't feel like I need to lie.

"How did you two get together?" Persheng asks them.

Fereshteh smiles. "I had just gotten my high school diploma and was about to start at the university, but it was right after the revolution and they had closed all the universities down. They didn't open again until a couple of years later, after they had weeded out all the un-Islamic books and professors. In the meantime, the classrooms were still open, so a group of students put together a salon where we performed plays. I was rehearsing a Brecht play and Kambiz came in to help direct it."

"The government was letting boys and girls put on plays together?" I ask.

"It was only a year after the revolution. They hadn't completely consolidated power, and they hadn't yet made the rule about the *hejab*. That didn't start until a year or so later. First they just said we had to wear scarves. Everyone said if that's all it was, it wouldn't be so bad, so we all put on scarves but still went around in short sleeves and short skirts. Next they said no short sleeves. And so on until they got us to the way we dress now.

"So anyway, Kambiz and I met at the play and we liked each other.

But our families were against it. There was no work for him and no school for me and they kept asking us how we were going to make a living. But after they saw that we were going to get married no matter what, they had to accept it. They realized I would never have put up with *khastegari* and all those men coming to see me."

"But what if they hadn't accepted it?" I ask.

"Oh, I still would have married him. I mean, who do I see more in my life now—my parents or my husband? Why should I let someone else decide who that will be?"

"Don't you see your parents much?" I ask, thinking of Haideh and Roya and other married women I know here who, if their parents or in-laws are in town, see them every day.

She and Kambiz exchange guilty glances. "We don't have that much time for *deed-o-baz-deed*," he says. "I mean, if we were going over there and having them over for tea all the time, when would we get any work done?"

"Not that we never see them," she adds. "We bring the kids to visit sometimes on weekends. It's just that back-and-forth thing every day. Now that I'm used to not doing it, I think it would drive me mad."

"They're used to it too," Kambiz says. "At first my parents were hurt because I didn't come home all the time after I got married. Now if I started going over there too much they'd worry something was wrong between me and Fereshteh."

The waiter brings *ab-goosht*—the only food the restaurant serves. It is an aromatic stew of lamb, chickpeas, tomatoes, and potatoes. We each get an individual mortar and pestle, and we mash our food into a paste and then wet it down with steaming broth and bits of the rich sac of fat that hangs below the tails of Persian lambs. We mop it up with flat bread and chase it down with handfuls of fresh green herbs.

I wonder if Haideh and Delbar would like this restaurant. Some of the patrons look like them—women in stylish silk scarves with frosted bangs showing in front, sitting on the floor and mashing their *ab-goosht* with their pestles alongside the earthier South Tehranis. If this kind of synthesis is what the revolution set out to accomplish, in this room it has succeeded.

Roya has told me she loves restaurants like this, but I have the feeling that Haideh would still prefer a pizza restaurant or the Chinese restaurant near the former German Club (now a government compound with "the *hejab* is a responsibility, not a restriction" painted on the wall). The land reforms left Baba's family in a strange limbo that reaches all the way down to Haideh, even though she was not yet born when they went into effect. Having lost their privileged position to more Westernized, "*Shahi*" Iranians, and scrambling to reclaim a place at the top, they felt they could not afford to mingle with those they considered "low" or "villagey." Haideh and Shireen are still so concerned with who makes the most money and who wears the fanciest clothes that I'm not sure a visit to the *ab-goosht* restaurant down by the railway station would appeal to them.

I have sometimes thought that the biggest factor keeping me from living in Iran was the alienation I feel when I hear my relatives fervently discussing dresses and dishware; it is the same isolation Mama used to feel, sitting through Tehran tea parties, waiting to get back home to the books and records that connected her to a world that felt like her own. And yet the way that Haideh remembers how when we were little Ali and I were always naked when she came over, the way Reza remembers playing school with us on Aziz's stairs, the way Zia claims me as his own daughter—these move me in deeper ways than our different tastes and lifestyles.

In Kambiz and Fereshteh, however, I feel as if I've discovered a new side of Iran. They are what I would want to be like if I lived here. They take me and Persheng to traditional coffeehouses, to galleries that feature local artists, and to old mosques and shrines in South Tehran, without worrying about seeming backward or low class. They seem to embody a new direction some Iranians have taken since the revolution. During the Shah's time it seemed that no one but foreigners collected Iranian antiques, and no one stopped them from carrying bags full of them out of the country. Nor did anyone protest when traditional old houses, with their mirrored arches and overgrown gardens and tiled courtyards, were demolished to make way for new apartment buildings. Now, though, there seems to be a new regard for the old Iran. Airport officials check suitcases to stop antiques from leaving the country. The government has begun to put money into restoring old houses before they crumble away. There has been a recent proliferation of traditional coffeehouses, restaurants, and plays, and often they have a line out the door. When I mention that I want to buy some old embroidered tapestries like the ones my parents bought in Kerman, Kambiz laughs. "Good luck," he says. "Everyone wants those now. Everyone from Shahrak has already gone down to Kerman on vacation and raided the bazaars."

This reminds me of something else Kambiz told me, about his work. After the revolution, filmmakers had to abandon the sex-and-violence film themes of the Shah era. They took up current Iranian issues, like postwar readjustment and the ideology gap between aging revolutionaries and their children. And the new films were well received. The banning of Western influences, for all its extreme consequences, forced many middle-class, Westernized Iranians to turn to Iranian influences, and often they discovered that they liked them.

"Are you wearing black socks?" Kambiz asks when he picks me and Persheng up one warm afternoon. We show him our feet and he nods. We are on our way to a *ta'azieh*—a passion play honoring the martyrs of Shiism—and we have to look Islamic from head to toe.

Parking on a tree-lined street, we walk along the metal fence of a park. A light breeze rustles the treetops and the scent of blossoms wafts down over us. I recognize this park. Baba and Mama used to take us here on weekends, and Ali and I would sit on our Black Knight skateboards, tuck our legs up, curl our fingers around the sides, and go flying down the sloped concrete walkways. Now the park's main path is crowded with people dressed in black. We follow them toward a makeshift amphitheater draped in huge black banners with a hooks-and-daggers-style of Arabic calligraphy emblazoned on them. A crowd of mostly women and children are packed together on carpets and perched on ledges and walls.

"They have a different *ta'azieh* every night for the last four days before Ashura," Kambiz explains. "One for each martyr who died establishing Shiite Islam—Abbas one night, then Ali-Asghar, then Ali-Akbar, and finally Hossein. But they're all pretty much the same story, so it doesn't matter which day we go."

We find a concrete ledge where we can see the stage. The women scoot over to make room for us. A man with a microphone begins to

read the story of Ali-Akbar's fight with Shemr, the captain of the
enemy army, as the players, wearing chain-mail helmets decorated
with fluffy green and red plumes, act out the story.

When Ali-Akbar puts on a white shroud, a few mournful cries rise
up from the crowd. A drum starts to beat and Ali-Akbar and Shemr
begin a gyrating sword dance like the bucking of Chinese dragons.
The drumbeat gets louder; the fight intensifies as the swishing blades
slice the air. As the sun slips below the tree line, the women in the
audience begin to sway and moan.

Kambiz shifts on the ledge and stretches his legs. "I'm going to
walk around," he whispers. "I've already seen all this." As he stands
up to go, the women around us rise to their feet and begin to cry
and beat their chests.

"*Ey*, Ali-Akbar!"

"Run away, before it's too late!"

Shemr charges, drawing gasps and cries from the onlookers; then
turns away, giving them only a second in which to take a breath.
When he finally drives his sword into Ali-Akbar's belly, a collective
gasp of horror rises up. The martyr falls, a red stain blooms over his
white shroud, and a deafening burst of wails rings out.

An old woman on the ledge above me begins to cry uncontrollably,
her eyes trained on the stage as Ali-Akbar convulses there. A young
woman beside her rocks and sways, weeping freely, holding a sleeping
child in her arms. On all sides of me the women have broken into
such loud, racking sobs that they can hardly catch their breath. And
yet the prevailing mood is much more than just sadness. It is as if for
these few moments the women are all of one heart, sharing the burden of each other's pain, and it is that ability to empathize so closely
with each other that allows them to move beyond sorrow, toward
something that is more like ecstasy.

Ali-Akbar stops shaking. A strong wind gusts through the crowd,
lifting the chadors and billowing them up around the women's legs
before letting them float softly down. Then the air is still. The
women stop crying. The men bear the martyr slowly away. A few
children throw money onto the bloodied platform. I watch the
women gather up their blankets and walk away, and I feel left out, as
if a great release has taken place all around me but passed me over,

leaving me empty of sorrow and devoid of the catharsis that is the reward for giving oneself over to a common story.

❖

Once it became clear that my father's cousin was not really going to Mashhad, Roya took pity on me and called her mother-in-law, who lives in Esfahan. I am taking the bus down to stay with her for a week, and from there I'll go northwest, up to Dadash's farm.

Iran's intercity buses operate from seventeen "cooperatives," all more or less identical, all hotly competitive. They paint their buses in bright colors and decorate them with fringed curtains and mirrored decals. The window opposite the driver's seat always has a special message spelled out in colorful, bubble-lettered English, and as we pass by other buses I make a game of spotting them: BUTIFULL BUS . . . MY FERAND GOODBAY . . . WE GO TO GOOD BAY . . . LIKE A FIRE . . . MY GOD . . . MY GIRLL MABUBEH . . . BUSE BEAUTIFUL . . . COME INTO MY TENDER HANDS . . . LOCK TO YOU . . . BETRAVEL WITH US.

The men on our bus are squeezed three to a seat and crushed into the aisle, but I have two seats to myself, since men are not supposed to sit next to women they don't know. I stretch my legs forward and stare intently out the window, eager to see what lies beyond the smoggy south side of Tehran.

For an hour we speed down a four-lane highway, with rocky hills on either side. At the Qom turnpike exit, where a portrait of a different mullah is mounted above each tollbooth, a third of the passengers get up, thank the driver, and disappear behind a yellow billboard that shows the silhouette of a skeleton holding a machine gun above the words ISRAEL MUST BE DESTROYED. Beyond this, the desert is flat and colorless, heavy with the kind of heat that should break into lightning but doesn't. Far away, a wide lip of water glistens deceptively, the road mirage multiplied onto an entire horizon. We pass an arch that leads nowhere; a crumbling brick fort with a missing tower; the top of a hut sticking out of the ground—a hundred pasts broken down by the wind and the sun.

In a small town, three people board the bus. A woman sits down beside me. Vaguely annoyed, I scoot over and let her push a sack of rice and a vat of yogurt into the space under my feet. I cannot tell how old she is—forty or sixty, with black button eyes and faded blue spots under her skin—the tattoos that some village women put on their hands and foreheads. She offers me sunflower seeds, and then, cracking them between her teeth and spitting them into her hand, she begins talking in a fast dialect of which I only understand "niece," "nephew," "daughter," and enough inflections to answer, "Really?" "Tsk-tsk," and "Poor thing," each time she pauses.

"What could he have done about it?" she finishes. "Could he have done anything?"

"No."

"Of course not. These things are in God's hands, are they not?"

"Yes."

"Of course they are. We are only His servants." She begins a new story, which as far as I can tell is about two teenage brothers who get killed in a bus accident on New Year's Day, just as they are finally going to see their mother again.

"It doesn't do to count on anything," she says.

"No, you're right, it doesn't."

"Because in the end we are powerless."

She noisily cracks ten or twelve sunflower seeds in a row, then turns to me.

"Are you a student?" I nod. "Are you married? Do you have brothers and sisters? How old are they? Are they married?" She weighs each of my answers, adds it to the stockpile in her head, and finally synthesizes them into an invitation.

"Look," she says, her face lighting up. "Why don't you marry Abol-Ghassem?"

I smile to show I am honored, although I cannot remember from her story who Abol-Ghassem is.

"Ha, ha, this is a wonderful idea." She waggles her head up and down, looking at my hair, my face, and my lap, her excitement mounting. "He's a student and you're a student. It's perfect!"

To be polite, I ask what he is studying, and to my horror she reaches up the aisle and tugs on the sleeve of a burly young man in a turquoise shirt.

"Arts," she says triumphantly. "You can marry him, okay? And we'll tell everyone how we met on the bus and got to know each other. We must have sat here on this bus together because God wanted it to happen. It will be a great family story."

She starts to poke at me, her fingers darting out from her chador, stroking my face, pinching my breasts.

I try to think of excuses. "He is too young for me," I whisper. "He is only around twenty-two and I am twenty-six."

"It doesn't matter," she says, giving me a rapturous hug. "You can't tell from your face. And *I* won't tell."

"But my studies are in America and his are here."

"Then he can go to America."

"It's not so easy. You can't get permission to go to America just by marrying someone."

"Oh no? Well, then, you can finish your studies here, in Kish. Or in Qom." For a minute I push aside the fact that I've already finished my studies, and I try to imagine myself transferring credits from the Columbia School of Journalism to one of the theological schools in Qom.

"You want me to just leave my university and come here?"

She nods gleefully.

"I don't think they'll accept that," I say. "It's English there and Farsi here."

Her face falls. "Really?"

"Yes," I say, trying to sound genuinely sorry. "I'm afraid my Farsi wouldn't be good enough."

"Oh." For the rest of the trip she turns to me every few minutes and says, "What a pity your courses are in English," and each time I nod morosely at this unfortunate quirk of American universities.

She gets off the bus in a small town, covering me with kisses and invitations and promises to pray for me.

I almost believe she did want me to get off the bus with her. Maybe this was a mini-*khastegari*; maybe in these little towns such a thing does work. Everyone might have such similar experiences that people could almost become interchangeable. A particular girl may have her eccentricities, but nearly every girl will cook and clean and bear children. That woman beside me could not imagine what it might mean to be a single woman in America; she envisioned a parallel world to

Iran, in which I was twenty-six and still not married, and that, more than anything else, became my defining characteristic. So why should I not carry on my life here, where there is a man who needs a wife?

We pass a rest stop with three buses in the parking lot.

WE GO TO TRIP.

COME TRIP WITH US.

BAY BAY.

In Esfahan, Roya's mother-in-law shuffles into the room with a tray of tall glasses. "Watch," she says, her blue eyes wide as she squeezes a few drops of lemon into each glass. The purple-black liquid fires up into a cloud of magenta.

"Cow-tongue flower," she says, handing me a warm glass. "I made it because Majid has a headache. It makes stress go out the door."

"You'd better not have plans tomorrow," her son Majid says, his finely drawn eyes already half closed, his protruding Adam's apple bobbing up and down as he swallows the last drops. "After you drink this you will sleep for twenty hours."

But the next morning I am out again, ducking into one of the thirty-three arches along Esfahan's main bridge, breathing in the crisp air over the Zayandeh River. It is an American way to behave, leaving the house every morning to roam, returning only for meals. "She goes all over the city by herself," the family tells each other, and I can't tell if they are disapproving or impressed. But Esfahan, as the famous saying goes and as my hosts keep reminding me, is "half the world," and I am only here for a week.

It is a city of ghosts. Four hundred years ago, Shah Abbas I built the blue-tiled mosques and the ornately decorated pleasure palaces that later came to dominate the coffee-table books about Iran. Much later, merchants set up shops along the main square to woo the tourists, and their scratched-up welcome signs are still painted in English, German, French, and Italian beside each silent doorway. This is the same square where we once took Grandma on a horse-and-carriage ride, and I remember it being crowded with foreigners. Now it is almost deserted.

At the south end of the square, I pass below the imposing twin minarets of the Emam Mosque. A group of elderly Italian tourists—

men in khakis, holding camcorders, women in bright cloaks and silk scarves tied in glamorous, illegal side knots—are being ushered out as I walk into a vast, empty courtyard where the sun spills onto blue tiles. Blue, the color of water and sky, is soothing to eyes exposed too long to the bleak desert. It is everywhere in Esfahan—the clear, cloudless sky reflected in the wide river, the painted arches, and the intricately tiled mosques.

Most Iranian mosques are full of people, strolling around, washing their hands and feet, reading books or taking naps or praying. But the Emam Mosque is lonely and ornate, like a king too exalted for everyday contact. I pass from its first courtyard into an even grander one. From the other side, two blond men begin to cut across toward me. Suddenly awash in homesickness, I hurry over to ask where they are from, and when they answer in English I break into a grateful smile. They are from Australia and Holland, and they came into Iran on a bus from Turkey two days ago. Their original visas only gave them time to cross straight over into Pakistan, but they have taken their chances and stopped in Esfahan.

"We've given our passports to the foreign affairs office to see if they'll extend them another week," says the Australian. "Then we're off to India."

"And Tibet," the Dutchman says. "If we can get in."

We wander around the mosque, joined by an old man who waddles out from a shady arch and gruffly offers to be our guide. We cannot go up into the minarets, he says, but he leads us to a magic spot in the center of the furthermost chamber.

"Listen," the old man says, and positioning himself directly on the spot beneath the dome, he breaks into a long, nasal wail. The vaulted ceiling picks up his voice and echoes it back seven times, flooding the courtyard with sound. Two people walking in the sun stop, standing reverently until the old man has finished.

"Before electricity," he says proudly, pointing at the blond guys and nodding at me to translate. "Better than microphones."

We tip him and leave to get lunch.

"We've just got to pick up our passports first," the Australian says. "Our visa extensions are supposed to be ready by noon."

In a small, gray-walled bungalow, an officer with a big black mustache and a pale green uniform tells them in heavily accented English that the visa extensions will cost fifteen hundred rials each.

"We paid you that this morning," the Australian says.

"No, you pay now."

"*No*, we paid this *mor*ning, remember?"

The man shrugs. "You give fifteen hundred rials, visa is ready now."

For a moment they stand in silence. Then an officer behind another desk leans forward and says in Farsi, "They're right, they did pay it this morning."

A third officer shakes his head. "No, they didn't."

"Yes, they did," says the second one. "Foreigners don't lie."

"May I use the phone?" I ask in English. The first officer smiles charmingly and steps away from his desk. Leaving them to haggle, I dial Roya's mother-in-law and tell her I won't be home for lunch.

"Eh," she says, "why not?"

I feel American and ungrateful. "There's a museum I want to see," I say lamely, embarrassed to say I am eating somewhere else.

"I made *ghormeh-sabzi*. You said you liked it."

"Oh, I do! Can I have it tonight? Or should I just come home now?"

"No, no, if you want to see a museum, go."

"No, that's okay, I'll just come home." I think guiltily of her standing alone at the hall phone in her housedress, wooden spoon in hand, the pot of green stew simmering on the stove. But it feels so good to speak English, and it also feels good to be the only Farsi speaker, the expert for once.

"I'll come home," I say again, tentatively.

"No, go, go. You can have *ghormeh-sabzi* tonight."

I hang up. The boys are joking around with the officers, who finally open their passports, stamp them, and hand them across the table. But the officer who let me use his phone is staring at me strangely.

"Uh, thanks," I say in English. I move away from the desk.

"You speak Farsi?" he asks, looking at the phone and then at me.

"Yes," I say, prepared for a compliment.

"Are you Iranian?"

"My father is."

"Are you?"

"Uh, yeah."

"And are you a Moslem?"

"Yes."

Suddenly everyone is moving. Chairs are scraped aside, the Australian and the Dutchman are pushed to one side of the room and I am pushed into a chair. All three officers yell at once, "Why are you with them? What is your name? Who are you? Who are they?"

"You!" the head officer barks at the blonds in English. "Go!"

They remain rooted to the floor.

"Go! Now!"

"Uh, will you be all right?" the Australian asks.

"I don't know—no." I don't want them to leave—fellow travelers should stick together, even if they have only just met. And indeed my companion steps forward, moving his tall frame up between me and the officer.

"We're not leaving until she does," he says in an Australian tough-guy voice.

The head officer's face turns red. "Eh? Out! Go! Now!" In Farsi he tells the other officers to push them out the door.

"We'll wait outside until you get out," the Australian says.

"No wait!" yells the head officer in English. "No wait!" And to a younger officer, in Farsi: "Follow them and make sure they go down the street!" The glass door shuts with a bang and the two of us are alone.

"Why were you going here and there with foreigners?" His mustache is twisted, sneering.

"We were talking."

"Did you come here with them? How long have you known each other? Where were you going?" I answer quietly, hoping it will calm him down. But the calmer I act, the redder his face gets.

"What did you talk about?"

"Art."

"No, you didn't. What did you really talk about? What did they ask you?"

"Nothing."

"What did you tell them?"

"Nothing." I try to make my Farsi bad.

The other two officers come back, and I wonder how far down the street they chased my friends. I wonder whether they will go back to the mosque to wait for me.

"What right do you have to talk to foreigners?" the red-faced officer demands.

"I'm half American," I say. "I've lived in America fifteen years."

"You're an Iranian girl!" he says. "And you're Moslem. A Moslem woman cannot go around with foreign men. Who gave you the right to talk to them?"

"But I *live* in America. I talk to foreigners all the time."

"Oho! Why do you like foreigners so much? Why don't you spend time with Iranians?"

"I'm sorry," I say demurely. "I won't go around with them anymore. Can I go home?"

"Hah!" says the thin-faced officer who let me use his telephone. "Just because we tell you not to do it does not mean you will change your ways."

"Yes, I will," I say fervently.

He looks up to the ceiling and sighs. "My talking to you is not going to change you."

Twenty minutes pass. No one says anything. I stand up.

"I've got to go now," I say, looking at my watch.

The men leap out of their chairs and put their hands on their guns. "Sit down!"

I sit.

"What are we waiting for?" I ask a few minutes later.

"The commanding officer."

A scrawny policeman with acne scars leans forward. "You should keep quiet," he advises. "The more you talk, the worse it will be for you."

I begin to kick myself. A real Iranian woman would not have admitted she spoke Farsi. A real Iranian woman wouldn't have walked right into a police station or even talked to those boys in the first place. I should have understood this a few days ago when I saw a foreigner walk across the main bridge of Esfahan. The dark-clothed Iranians parted around a tall man with waist-length platinum-blond hair, a leather vest and a purple backpack. We stopped, turned, and stared with open mouths until he was swallowed up by the crowd.

What right do you have to talk to foreigners? Why don't you spend time with Iranians? Why should I have felt I could run after these exotic beings, talk to them and take them to lunch when no other Iranian was doing this? Have I insulted Iranians by choosing to talk to foreigners? The truth is, foreigners are the only strangers I would talk to. Had I casually approached two Iranian men in a mosque they would have thought I was a madwoman or a prostitute. Or, once they heard I was from America, they would probably have asked me if I could get them visas.

The office is filling up. A thick-necked policeman with three stars on his shoulder gives my handbag to a young soldier with a shaved head who looks as if he has been handed a basket of snakes.

"A book," he says, gingerly lifting it out of the bag. Another officer writes "One book" on a piece of paper.

"A notebook."

"A roll of film. An address book. Money." Something in the young soldier's voice begins to sound sarcastic, and I want to smile at him but I am too scared.

"Give me the number where you're staying," the thick-necked man says.

I shake my head. I don't want to worry Roya's mother-in-law. Even more, I don't want her to know that I lied about what I was up to. But the man will not let me go until I give him the number. He dials, and when she picks up he explains that I have been detained for talking to foreigners and asks her if I am who I say I am. Then he hands me the phone.

"What were you doing with foreigners?" she asks, her voice surprisingly strong, a voice for reassuring angry policemen.

"We were just talking."

"Well, tell them that!"

"I *did*."

"Then what's the problem?"

The officer grabs the receiver and starts barking until his hairy neck begins to bulge over his collar. "*Never* let her go out by herself! I don't want to ever see her in the street again! When she's staying with you I want you to keep her in control!" He listens for a moment and then his voice lowers. "You know, the strange thing is that when we caught her, she was surprised that we were angry. That is what I found very odd." He hangs up the phone and sits down in front of me.

"Bring tea," he says to the young soldier. "Give her her bag." He wrings his sweaty hands. "My dear sister," he says in a fatherly tone, "you are a Moslem Iranian." He looks up at the fluorescent ceiling light and then back down at me. "You can't be with foreigners here. This is not the West." Two cups of tea arrive and he gestures for me to take one. I do, trying not to let him see my hand shake.

"If you talk to foreigners," he says, pausing for emphasis, "they will *get* you."

"What?"

"Yes," he says in the slow, scary voice of Kobra when she used to talk about jinns. "They will get you and grab you! And then they will take you to their hotel!"

"But I wouldn't have gone to their hotel," I say in my most re-sponsible voice.

"Ah, but they're sneaky; they know how to make you go. They say, 'Come, we have a pretty picture,' or 'Come, we have a nice book to show you,' and they take you up there"—he pauses again—"and then they hit you!" He makes a quick pouncing motion.

"Oh, but I wouldn't have fallen for that trick," I say.

"Well, then they would have forced you," he says. "You must re-member to be careful of foreigners." He looks around at the other officers, who all nod their heads. "Go home now. Go home, be in your house, and don't talk to foreigners anymore."

"Okay," I say, and then, without intending to, I thank him.

"What they thought was that you were one of those Iranian girls who go to foreign men for money," Majid's older brother Amin tells me that evening. "They go up to the mountains together."

"Or some even go for no money," says the third son, Farshad, who is my age. "They like that look. The light-haired look."

"Well, I told them I live in America," I say. "They should realize there are plenty of blond men there if I wanted one."

"They were just trying to protect you," Amin says. "Really, they were on your side."

Roya's mother-in-law comes in with another tray of the purple glasses.

"Does Majid have stress again?" I ask.

"No," she says with a little smile. "This is for you." I watch her squeeze lemon juice into it, the pink liquid clouding up and then becoming clearer than before. I look up at her face, wanting to catch her eye. I did not come home to eat the lunch she prepared; I preferred to walk around with strangers, showing off my Farsi, talking about mosques and kings, about Shah Abbas's wine and dancing girls—stories I read in books, while nowhere have I ever read about this drink Roya's mother-in-law has prepared. What else would I have learned, staying home for a day with a woman who knows how to make stress fly away? I want her to look at me, I want her to know that I was not trying to go to the mountains with blond boys. But she turns away and holds the tray serenely out to her sons.

After he finishes his tea, Majid floats from room to room. He sings a traditional old song, his sweet tenor vibrating through the interconnected rooms of the house as the last rays of sunlight fade from the windows. His tall, thin frame seems to touch nothing as he picks up a wooden flute or an old-fashioned *tar*, playing a few measures in a minor key before putting it down again. I sip the sweet, smoky cowtongue infusion, holding the glass close against my body, feeling my shoulder blades sink away from my spine, and thinking that maybe tomorrow I won't go out at all.

❖

BELOW A RIDGE OF SNOWY MOUNTAINS, IN A SMALL VALLEY
dotted with cypress and poplar trees and green fields, lies Dadash's
apple farm. It is surrounded by layers of protection. One adobe wall
encircles the house and garden. A second wall encloses the barn and
apple orchards. The village itself is a third wall, a barrier of tiny mud
houses with a trickle of water as a moat and the villagers themselves
as sentries. From far off, they can recognize a strange car turning off
the main road and heading down toward them. Any car besides Dadash's and the taxi driver's is strange, and the village children run up
to Dadash's house to announce it.

"Khanoum! Khanoum! People are coming!" The little Kurdish girl
in the sparkly red sheath can hardly get the words out, racing through
the garden on bare feet, her shepherd's stick in her hand.

"Who is it? What kind of car?" Leila-khanoum jumps up from the
korsi where she has been transferring face cream from one pot to
another. Ammejun frowns. She lies down, pulls the *korsi* quilt over
her head, and snuggles up against a pillow as if she is asleep.

"A big orange car with ten people inside," the girl says importantly, kicking off her plastic sandals as she comes into the house.

"Are there women?" Leila asks sharply. If there were no women it might be just a business call and then Dadash would sit in the living room alone with the men. But just in case, Leila already has her dressing gown off and is fastening her wide bra to the tightest notches and pulling nylons up her legs. She wriggles into a black wool dress with leopard-spot trim. As she is fastening her hair back and running a lipstick across her mouth the knock comes on the door.

"Are there women?" the little girl asks her sister, who runs over and peers through the colored glass at the distorted figures waiting on the porch. But she cannot tell.

"Well, open the door, what are you waiting for?" Leila says, clipping on gold earrings and stepping into a pair of high-heeled pumps. She gives her hair one last dignified pat. All of this has taken under a minute. The older girl hurries over to start the samovar and the younger girl brings out a bowl of fruit.

Dadash and Leila-khanoum live in a house with no phones or mailboxes, but they are always ready to convey the impression that the guests have been expected. This was once the essence of village life, this magnified version of *deed-o-baz-deed*. The visitors, on horseback, would appear on the horizon, and for a few days they would fill all the corners of the house, the excited children packing into one room, the women going off to talk and sleep in another room, the servants pulling out endless bedrolls.

Now they come by car, without servants, and unless they are relatives they do not stay long. But some of the ceremony remains. We sit in the front room and drink tea with these guests who are passing through on their way to the next town—two women in stylish black dresses and a man in an orange gabardine suit that matches his car. Dadash joins us, other children having run out to the fields to alert him; his oxford shirt and khaki pants are spotless despite the fact that five minutes ago he was standing in silty mud under the quince trees. Agreen, the older girl, carries our tea in. Her eyes are laughing at the way Leila and I are sitting straight-backed, holding our teacups with two fingers, when just now we were all lying around the bedroom playing pick-up-sticks and backgammon as the shortwave radio rasped big-band music in from abroad.

Even Dadash himself acts like a master of the house only if he has guests or if he's dressed in his suit to go to the next town. Then he yells at the little girls to find his pocketbook and shine his shoes, and he ceremoniously drives his car out the gate, slowing down for the villagers who bow as we pass. But more often the formalities break down. At night we play hide-and-seek, and the same Leila-khanoum who is now regally holding out a silver tray of baklava to her guests will hide behind the woodpile and make a break through the bushes, shrieking and pushing the children aside to get to home base. If guests were to appear then, they would find us with frazzled hair, our skirts hiked up over our bare legs, chasing each other around the house. We would not have a meal ready, since at night we just eat bread and yogurt and fruit. On a really bad night they might even find us with our toes wrapped in plastic, hobbling around on our heels so the henna we've smeared on our toenails won't leak onto the carpets.

But today's guests arrived at eleven in the morning, and after a round of tea and sweets and blood oranges they stand up to go. Leila-khanoum presses them to stay for lunch and acts huffy when they decline, and we all go out to see them off and wave as their car backs down the driveway. Then we breathe a sigh of relief.

Not that Dadash and Leila are not good hosts. If the guests had stayed, Ami, the Kurdish woman, would have come over from the back house and helped Leila make a grand meal, and Leila would have begged them to stay all afternoon and even all night. We would have milked the cows, made new yogurt, and killed a lamb for to-morrow's lunch. Or such are the stories I hear. In the old days, no one was allowed to leave without drinking a tea, eating a meal, telling a story of the world outside.

Since the guests did not stay, we have enough food for the Kurdish girls to eat lunch with us, even after Leila-khanoum scoops up a large plate of stew and rice and herbs for the shepherds who come to the door. "The Qajar princes used to come to see Agha Jan," Ammejun reminds us over our lamb stewed with desert flower bulbs. "Ooh, what days we had." She adjusts the pillow on her seat to make her taller. "We had no warning, but all of a sudden we would see them coming over the hill—fifty or sixty men on horses, setting up tents in front of our house. We cooked them such meals as you have never seen."

"Why were the Qajar princes visiting Agha Jan?" I ask.

She looks at me sympathetically, as if I am a child who cannot keep track of the most basic things. "My brother was a khan," she reminds me. "All those men came to his house as a sign of respect. They would all go hunting together in the mountains while the servants prepared their meals."

After the Qajars fell, Agha Jan's dynasty continued for forty more years. Even when Aziz moved the family to Tehran, Agha Jan kept the old ways going, commuting faithfully between Aziz and the children in the city and white-chadored Wife-of-Agha Jan and his land in the village. After the land reforms, when Baba returned to Iran to find only two servants in the Tehran basement and Aziz heaping curses on the Shah, Agha Jan was not angry. He was old; his sons were educated and his daughters married. He had been a great man in an era of great men, but now that era was over. Maybe he remembered how when he was young Reza Shah had demanded the best gardens and houses of the Qajar families. Those who complained had been arrested and many had mysteriously died in jail. Or perhaps it was simply not in Agha Jan's nature to mourn. "Don't look for promises from this weak-cored world," he used to tell Baba, taking him onto his lap when he was small, "for this witch is the bride of a thousand grooms."

Many years later, Baba would drive us through the countryside and point to crumbling fortresses on hilltops and villages nestled into mountains. "All of this was Agha Jan's," he would say, moving his arm in a sweeping gesture, unafraid to claim the whole horizon. He smiled as he said this, and perhaps because of his smile I never took his ownership seriously.

Dadash, however, takes it very seriously. He does not sweep his hand, but points to specific boundaries. "This portion started precisely here, crossed the river, and spread up the mountain. This fort was built by Agha Jan, and so was that pigeon tower and that mud-brick barn." Everywhere the land is crossed with invisible lines of property, the exact points at which Dadash's lands began and ended. "This whole side here was Leila's dowry," he says as the old Volvo rattles over the dirt road. "I planted peach trees there and they gave them to a villager. See how he let them die." The twisted trees loom like corpses against the gray sky and vanish behind us.

At home, Dadash keeps mementos in his closet. "Here," he says gruffly. "This was your father's." One night it is a bag of old coins, heavy with dirt, engraved in stylized Arabic. The next night it is a green coat, bought when Baba first got to America. I stretch my hands through the elastic cuffs and bury my face in the fur collar, trying to find the faded scent of him.

"This is yours," Leila-khanoum says, producing a cassette tape. "It was in your house when you left." I slip it into the tape player and I am suddenly back in our old apartment, two years before the revolution. The wail of Mama's cello rises up; Ali's sharp little voice sings a song about Frankenstein. One-year-old Sufi asks, "Wassat?" "It's a button," Mama says. "Button, button," Sufi repeats, playing with the new word.

What else did they find? What other tapes? What clothes and records and carpets and musical instruments once filled our house, and who reduced it all down to a trunkful of sooty books and water-pipe fragments? Why this tape and not other ones? Why this bag of coins, this coat, as if after the revolution there had been some roulette wheel of our lives and every hundredth object had been saved? But it is too late to ask these questions, so I ask about Baba's briefcase with the deed inside it, because that is something that still might be found.

"That thing is long gone," Dadash says, annoyed. "What does he want with that land anyway, in the middle of the city and the smog? Come with me." He pushes his stockinged feet into a pair of plastic sandals.

Outside, the dust on the trail is as fine as turmeric. It seeps into my skin and coats my mouth as we walk toward the purple sunset. The poplars wave against the sharp-edged mountains as the crescent moon rises, clean and white as the chalky dust.

"These are peaches, these are nectarines, these are quinces," Dadash says, pointing at rows of trees. "These are all apples. Red apples, yellow apples, green apples." We get to a large mound of earth where no trees are growing, about a hundred yards from the house. "Tell Essie he doesn't need that property. He can build a house right here and have these mountains on one side and the river on the other. Wouldn't he like that?"

There is nothing Baba likes as much as land. When he and Mama are shopping for houses in California, he always heads straight for the yard. In one little house with a big field and a creek in the back he takes his shirt off and lies down in the grass, and that is the house they buy. But I wonder if Baba, who sometimes talks of building a house in his childhood village, can really imagine himself living out the rest of his life here. "Could I go to aerobics in Iran?" he asked when Haideh visited. "Do they have tofu there?" In a way, he would fit in even less well than Mama, who, despite her fears about my going, has started to think it might be interesting to visit Iran again herself. The very things Baba misses about Iran might make it impossible for him to live here—the way that when he strolled down the street everyone in his hometown would nod and say hello, the way everybody would know he was the youngest son of Haji-khan. When he realized he couldn't walk out of his house in a T-shirt and shorts anymore, that social intimacy might start to annoy him. Even if it didn't, I have a feeling that Baba wouldn't build a house here despite the vegetable garden and the birds singing all around. Baba wants his own land, separate from the family that loops around and around itself, never letting anyone be alone. Maybe, in that way, he is a bit of an American.

Ami, the mother of the Kurdish girls, walks through the house in a glittering tribal dress and baggy silver pants, clutching at her kidney. She has been like this for days, wincing with each step. Out in her mud-walled house, she shows me her medicine—a foil sheet of nameless tablets.

"Where did you get these?" I ask.

"From the doctor in town," she says weakly. "Agha took me." Dadash drove her there, paid the doctor and bought the medicine, just as Agha Jan used to do.

"They're probably antibiotics," I say. "What did the doctor tell you?"

"To take them for ten days. But they didn't work, so I got new ones." She pulls out a plastic pill container.

"Do those work better?"

"No, these didn't work either. Maybe I should take them to-gether?" She looks at me, fully confident in my answer.

"How long did you take the other ones?" I ask.

"Three days."

"But you were supposed to take them for ten."

"But they didn't work."

I tell her she won't feel better until she takes them all, but later that day I find her with her children in a mud hut at the end of the garden, her rosy face brighter than ever. She sits on her haunches with her knees up next to her shoulders and her cotton skirts hanging over her pajama pants. A shaft of sun slants in through a hole in the roof and illuminates her hands as she rolls dough into a ball, slaps it against a hard sack of flour, and tosses it into a hole in the ground.

"*Salaam*, Taraneh-khanoum!" She pats the earth for me to come sit beside her. "You were right; I took the old pill and I feel better." The ball of dough sticks to the underground wall and bubbles up. Ami's hand glows orange as she plucks out the hot discs of bread, and we stuff it into our mouths, our tongues burning on the pockets of steam.

"Taraneh-khanoum, I have a question," she says, punching the middle of a ball of dough. "How do people get married in America?"

"They buy wives!" guesses her son Mohammad, a tall boy with curly black hair like his mother's.

"No," I say. "They just choose each other."

"That's a good way," Ami says, nodding. She slams the dough against the flour sack and flattens it in one shot. "How funny it is that we are almost the same age, no?"

"Yes," I say, pointing at the dough. "Look at how many things you know how to do that I don't."

"Me?" she says, giggling. "But look at how old I have become and how young you have stayed."

"No, no," I say. "You look just like the children." She does. They all have the same white skin and red cheeks and delicate features. Even the littlest ones have spiderwebs of tiny lines around their eyes and mouths, from being outside so much.

"Bah, these hands, this face," Ami says. "Six children have turned my hairs white—see the hairs that are red? That's just henna."

Ami doesn't know how old she is, but Mohammad is almost fifteen and so she guesses she is around thirty. I can picture her at fifteen, just after she married—her clear skin, her small waist, and her tinkling laugh hardly different from now.

Her husband, Abu-bakr, appears in the doorway. "Let's have a piece of that bread." He sinks down into a cross-legged position, his baggy Kurdish pants making a pouch in front. "I've been waiting for Ami to come milk the cows," he says, chewing on the bread. He reminds me of a Romanian Gypsy or an Argentine gaucho, with his handsome, weathered face and piercing gaze. His youngest daughter toddles by; he swoops over and grabs her like a monster and she screams with delight.

In his lilting accent, Abu-bakr tells me how he was born in Iranian Kurdistan but grew up in Iraqi Kurdistan, serving in the Iraqi Army until he stabbed another soldier in an argument over a woman and had to flee across the border. "I wandered for ten years on horseback, working here and there. Every year I rode back over the mountains to visit my family and every year they told me the Iraqi police were still coming for me. My brother told them I was dead, but they didn't believe him and they said, 'We will be back for him.' But they are fools." With a one-handed flick of a matchbook he lights a cigarette and holds it out to me. I shake my head and he takes a deep drag and continues talking as I watch in vain for the smoke to emerge from his mouth. "After America beat Saddam, the police stopped going to my family's house. I could go back now. But now I have a wife and all these children." He winks at the child on his lap. "They're here, so I stay."

"I'm finished," Ami says, brushing the linty dough off her hands. She tells the children to bring the bread into the house and gestures for me to follow her out to the barnyard.

The sun is almost touching the mountains, and the breeze feels as cool as water. Ami crouches beside a cow and starts milking, quickly filling the first bucket. Tonight a vat of it will boil on the stove. In the morning, along with Ami's crisp bread and Leila's homemade apple, quince, pear, and plum jams, we will have café au lait, fresh yogurt, cheese, clotted cream, and butter, all deliciously tinged with a musky cow underflavor.

Stooping beside Ami, I push a bucket under a cow and gently

squeeze its rough, oblong nipple. I squeeze harder. Nothing comes out.

"No, no, like this." Ami puts her warm, wet hand over mine. We pull and twist and I feel the hot liquid rush between my fingers and splatter the bottom of the metal pail. "That's it," she says, turning back to her cow. I manage to get a few squirts out, but then my wrist cramps up, and Ami steps in to finish. As I stand watching her in the fading light, a calf wanders up and nuzzles me.

"He wants milk," Abu-bakr says. He is standing in the gap in the mud wall with his little daughter on his shoulders, staring at me intensely, as if trying to answer a question.

"I don't have any." I watch Ami's hands milking away, and remember how, on the first day I arrived here, the women in the village surrounded me, patting my cheeks and hair as if I were a doll. When I told them how old I was and that I was not married they looked confused. "But everyone wants to be part of a twosome," one of the women said to me.

A scarred, scrawny dog limps up behind the cows. Most Iranians hate dogs; the dogs here are tolerated only because they guard the house at night. But as this one approaches, no one kicks at it or yells at it to go away. Abu-bakr tosses a scrap of fresh bread onto the ground. "We must be nice to this dog," he says. "She is a mother." He gives a low whistle and the dog sidles up cautiously, grabs the bread in its mouth, and runs off. An Iranian proverb states that "heaven is under the foot of a mother," and Mama once told me she never got harassed by men in Iran when she was with her children. Even during the revolution, when it was clear that she was foreign, she sometimes thought that she deflected hostility when she took us out with her; more important than her Americanness was her motherness.

Abu-bakr lifts the little girl off his shoulders and hands her to Ami, who tugs down her shirt and begins to nurse. I bring my milking hand up to my face and inhale the thin-haired smell of an animal's belly, the pungent scent of living beings that is both repellent and intoxicating.

"I had wanted to take a shower," Abu-bakr sighs.

"Go in and take one," I say. "It's not late."

He clicks his tongue and raises his eyebrows no. "I'm waiting for Ami so we can take one together." He winks and makes the motion of scrubbing someone else's back. "That's what life is, after all."

Ami smiles and milks faster.

Back in the house, the children want to see my photographs.

"Who's that?" asks Omid, the younger Kurdish boy.

"My brother."

"What's that in his hand?" asks Arezou, the oldest daughter.

"A tennis racket."

"What's it for?"

"It's what they use to hit the ball in tennis."

"What's tennis?"

I try to explain but suddenly all the kids start laughing and waving a picture of my mother sitting next to Liesl, our German shepherd.

"There's a dog in your house."

"Yeah, that's our dog."

"But it's in the house."

"In America people let their dogs in the house. They let them sit on chairs too. Sometimes they even sleep in bed with people."

They choke with laughter. Each time it starts to die down someone says, "A dog in a bed!" and it explodes again.

"Doesn't it get the bed dirty?" Arezou asks.

"Well, no; they give the dog baths. They shampoo it and dry it with a towel. And when it's cold out, some people dress their dogs in clothes."

"In their own clothes?"

"No, in special clothes for dogs."

This is more than they can take, and soon we are all in hysterics.

"Do they really have clothes for dogs?" asks nine-year-old Agreen.

"And baths?" asks six-year-old Azadeh.

"No, silly," says Mohammad. "She was kidding."

"No, I'm not," I say. So they bring paper and a pencil and I draw a picture of a poodle in a coat. They snatch the paper from each other and for the rest of the day I keep seeing one or another of them running around with it and laughing.

That night, after dinner, I slip on my shoes.

"Where are you going?" Dadash asks me.

"To the Kurds'."

"You can't go there right now."

"Why not?"

"When I say something there is no 'why.'"

"What do you mean?"

"In any case, someone your age shouldn't be going out alone."

"What do you mean? I go out alone all the time. How old do you think I am anyway?"

Dadash pauses. "I don't know. Seventeen? Eighteen?"

"Seventeen!? We left Iran fifteen years ago and I was already this tall, don't you remember?"

He frowns. "Has it really been that long? Well, it doesn't matter, even if you were forty I wouldn't let you go to the Kurds' tonight."

"But Nasser the cowherd is singing Kurdish songs tonight."

"Ho!" says Dadash, as if all his suspicions have been confirmed. "You don't want to go hear that garbage." But I leave my hand on the doorknob, feeling a rebelliousness welling up. Even when I was little, Dadash's warnings used to seem overblown and arbitrary and only made me more determined to do the things he forbade.

Seeing that I am unconvinced, he sighs. A few weeks ago, he tells me, Niki was visiting and she saw a teenage boy peeping at her through the bathroom window. I raise my eyebrows, because Niki also sees jinns in the dark. Even if it is true, Nasser is just a kid, and he sings so nicely to the cows in the field that I could forgive him for his curiosity. I want to argue back, to tell Dadash I am old enough to decide for myself what is dangerous or not. I want to dash out the door and join the Kurds, whose voices are drifting across the garden. But Dadash is looking at me with such fatherly concern. It wouldn't be worth it to challenge him just to prove a point. Reluctantly, I kick off my shoes and go back into the bedroom.

Leila and Ammejun are sitting around the *korsi*. "Come sit," Ammejun says, patting the bedroll. "*Voh*," she says. "In the old days my big brother wouldn't even let me talk to male servants, let alone go into their houses. He used to say, 'Whatever you want, you tell me and I will tell them.'" She tells us a story about when bandits came to her village and all the women were locked into a neighboring fort so they wouldn't be stolen. They stayed for days, dancing and singing and telling stories. No men were around because they were all waiting for the robbers, and Ammejun says it was the most fun she ever had.

That night in bed I listen to the Kurdish music float in through my window. The singing and dancing are right outside, but I am bound not to go near. A girl cannot know men, cannot see or touch or hear them all through her growing up. But then one night a man who might as well have a tail and horns and hooves appears for her. That's how the jinns come, up through the toilet or in through the baths, using the underground water routes, those sunken toilets that are scary-looking even now. The jinn grabs the girl and jumps back down into the straight stone hole she's always avoided. That is what being a girl is. You have no contact; you are covered and hidden and sheltered and warned off. And then one day a total stranger comes in and takes off your clothes, and the alien world becomes the known.

Abu-bakr came for Ami like a jinn. When he first tells me this I don't believe him.

"I stole my wife," he says one morning as we are crossing alfalfa fields, with the rising sun casting an orange mist over the valley.

"What do you mean?"

"I was in Kurdistan and I saw her and I liked her. Her father didn't like me. I did *khastegari* and everything, but no matter many times I went he would not give me his daughter. So I stole her."

"Did she want to be stolen?"

He shrugs. "One day I told her I was leaving town that night and she could come with me or not. When it got dark I went to her house. It was snowing; the yard was this high with snow. I stood outside her window and she came down and I put her in a taxi and took her to my uncle's house. We hid for three days. Then the mullah came and married us."

"Really?"

He nods his head so seriously that I suspect he is lying.

"Why didn't her father want her to marry you?"

"He was a rich man. When I came to his house I had been traveling around for ten years. He said I had no house and no money, so why should he give me his daughter? After we got married he never spoke to her again. Neither did her mother. They refused to see her."

"She hasn't seen her parents in fifteen years? And they've never seen their grandchildren?"

He raises his eyebrows no.

"That's so harsh."

"Why? Her father was right, I had nothing. And I stole his daughter."

We hike across a field of wild poppies that give off a sweet, yeasty scent. Abu-bakr picks one and offers it to me, and the stem bleeds white milk that stains my fingers red. When we reach the river, he kneels down and pulls at a piece of string tied to a tree. A homemade net rises up slowly from the rushing water. "No fish." He lets the net drop back in, then looks up at me. "If anyone stole my daughter," he says simply, "I would kill him."

"Abu-bakr says he stole you," I say to Ami, expecting her to laugh.

"Yes, he did."

We are hanging laundry on the clothesline, and I peer at her from behind a sheet, trying to catch some expression of defiance or regret. But she may as well be talking about a childish prank. "Oooh, was my father mad! I made dinner that night and set it on the *sofreh* and slipped out the window. When they were ready to eat they called, 'Amineh! Amineh!' But I never came to dinner."

Two of her little girls who are listening cup their hands over their titters.

"*Halle-buru!*" she says in Kurdish, and they shrink behind a tree, pretending to be gone. "They shouldn't be listening," she says in Farsi. But the girls peek around from the other side of the trunk.

"Weren't you scared?" I say.

"Sure. I was scared my father would catch us and kill us."

"But weren't you scared to run away with Abu-bakr?" He would have been thirty years old then, a lean, sunburned man with a black mustache and coarse hands and charred, smoky breath. How could Ami have known that he would be good to her?

"I was ready to get married and my father wouldn't let me," she says matter-of-factly.

"And you really haven't seen him since then?"

"No." She takes the empty basket from me and throws in the extra clothespins. "I would like to see my mother and father. My heart is tight and I miss them." The little girls follow us back into Ami's house, big-eyed.

"So why don't you go see them?"

"Ooh, I'm too scared. Last year your uncle and aunt came with us to Kurdistan. Khanoum said the same thing. 'Go see your parents.' She said, 'I'll come and be there with you in case they get mad.' We were going to go, but then I got too scared." Ami lights the samovar for our tea and we sit down on the floor.

"You went all the way home and came back without seeing your parents?"

"Oh yes, I go all the time. I see my brother and his family, and I buy cloth to make Kurdish clothes. But I don't dare go to my father's house."

"But I went." Her son Mohammad's voice rises from the other end of the room where he is stretched out with a schoolbook. "Last No-ruz holiday. I stayed with my uncle and I went to lunch at my grandparents' house."

"Yes," says Ami in a voice filled with wonder. "They told my father he was a friend of my brother's son."

"So did you talk to your grandparents?"

He grins and tips his head up. "Hardly. I was too afraid. All through lunch my grandfather stared at me. That's what made me afraid. He didn't say anything; he just stared. Then after lunch he told my uncle what a good boy I was." His eyes shine and Ami alternately nods and shakes her head, enraptured, though she must have heard this story thirty times by now. "My uncle didn't tell him who I was. But later he said maybe my grandfather had a feeling about it."

"How brave you are!" Ami says, flinging her arms around Mohammad and planting a kiss on each cheek. "See, Taraneh-khanoum, what a brave boy I have?"

Leila-khanoum has cupboards full of herbs and potions and dried flowers that will cure almost any malady. She has a big bottle of oil for stomachaches and a big bottle of pills for headaches and other aches. When a village woman comes to the door with a sick baby, Leila waves a plate of burning rue over its head; the fragrant smoke curls around the room and in the morning the baby is better.

Leila can also sew just about anything. She offers to make me a cha-dor, so Dadash takes me and Arezou, the oldest Kurdish girl, to the ba-zaar in the neighboring town. We pick out a frivolous pink-flowered fabric that we would never wear outdoors, and, one at a time, we stand on top of the *korsi* as Leila drapes the cloth over our heads.

"*Bismillah-alrahman-alraheem,*" she says as she cuts my cloth. In the name of God, most benevolent and mericiful. "May you find a good husband."

"*Bismillah-alrahman-alraheem,*" she says as she cuts Arezou's cloth. "May you become a doctor."

"Hey," I say, "how come she gets to be a doctor and I just get a husband?"

"Well, you're already at the university," Leila says. "So you can become a doctor if you want." I suppose she also takes into account the fact that Arezou is only eleven and still has good chances for finding a husband, while my time is running out.

It takes two people to run the sewing machine—one to sew and the other to hold the cord together, so Arezou squats with one hand on the outlet and rummages through a pile of fabric scraps with her other hand. She pulls out a black chiffon sleeve attached to a black swatch of satin with a tiny gold buckle.

"What is this?"

Leila-khanoum smiles. "Those were evening clothes."

"For when we used to go out at night," I add, as if I had ever gone out at night.

But Leila gives me a knowing look. "Ah, what nights we had! We never worried that someone might come and catch us."

Arezou looks at her blankly, but Leila does not say anything else.

"All right, take off those cowboy pants and put on this skirt," Leila says, waving her scissors over a pile of old clothes she wants to alter for me.

I pull off my jeans. "Eh, how cute," she says, running a hand up my thigh. "Taraneh, for God's sake, go get Mehdi and bring him here and marry him."

I look at her, surprised. No one has mentioned my marrying Mehdi for years, not since the time Ammejun invited us over to dinner and then told everyone he hadn't accepted me. "Ah, he wouldn't come

here," I say. "All those people move to America and they never want
to come back."

"But you came back," she says.

"Yeah, but they like it better there." I picture Mehdi speeding up
the freeway in his Porsche, nodding his head to the Gypsy Kings as
the wind whips his hair. "They'd get bored here."

"Ah," Leila says. "Why do they think it's so wonderful there?"

"Maybe they don't know how good it is here." I wonder if, from
a Silicon Valley commuter lane, goat herding in the village would
seem appealing. It might sound like a nice break, a return to the land;
but more likely it would sound like a bore. I think about spending a
year here—learning to make cheese, learning to plant tomatoes and
bake bread and speak Kurdish. The pace of living would be so slow
that small events—a drive out to the flower-growing town to buy
seedlings for the garden; a discussion about whether or not to buy a
horse—would take on an importance that was lost long ago in the
big city. I think I would like that, at least for a year. But then, I am
more likely to try it out than Mehdi or most of my other cousins.
For them, the village is still something to get away from. Although
we are all only a generation removed from it, I, being half American,
am once more removed. I am less concerned with denying my "villagey" side than with finding it in the first place.

Leila pulls me over to the mirror and opens up a pot of cream she
has made from desert roots and honey. Her voice becomes low and
melodic.

> *Oh, wine-girl, pour the wine,*
> *For in Paradise you will not find*
> *The banks of the Rokhnabad*
> *And the hills of Mosallah.*

"That's Hafez," she says. "The Rokhnabad was a river and the
Mosallah was an area near his house. Hafez always said it is best to
stay by your own home. It was Saadi who liked to travel. Saadi said,
'The love of the motherland is very dear. But you cannot die in hard-
ship just because you were born here.' " Leila pauses to make sure I
have understood the words of Iran's most famous ancient poets.

"Well, Mehdi and those guys must be more like Saadi," I say.

Leila sighs. "Even Saadi didn't go to America for twenty years. If they came here we could find them wives."

"Yeah, like Reza," I joke.

"Eh, that was not a smart match. But Mehdi would be doing a good thing to marry you. You've both been in America, you both speak English and Farsi; you could understand each other."

"Ah well, it's too bad he doesn't want to come," I say teasingly. "Because Ami said if I got married here she'd do a whole Kurdish wedding for me, with henna on my hands and singing and dancing."

Leila claps ecstatically. "Wonderful, wonderful! We must arrange it." She smooths buttery lotion under my eyes and I close them and think about how easy it would be to fall into this life, to never again worry about looking for an apartment or paying rent or finding a job. I could automatically have a position, not as a secretary or a translator, but as a kind of Leila-khanoum, sewing chadors, gathering roses, and waving rue as I chanted the evil eye away.

But it would not be Mehdi I would marry. And do I really think I could bring some light-haired, green-eyed American boyfriend here and expect the Kurds to throw me a wedding? As if I didn't already appear strange enough without bringing more foreignness onto myself. An Iranian man can bring a wife back from anywhere—the old royal harems included women from China, India, Africa, and the Frankish lands; and the foreign-educated engineers of today still bring home adroit German and English wives who learn how to speak Farsi and cook just like Iranians. Strange women are accepted; strange men are not.

"Tell me about your wedding," I say, sliding under the *korsi* beside Ammejun.

She smiles involuntarily. "*Ya Ali,*" she huffs, pulling the quilt up around her legs. "Rub some of that cream into my shoulder." She pushes her shirt aside and I smooth the cream on, feeling her bones' fragility, the worn silk of her skin.

"I was ten years old," she says, knowing this will impress me. "They took me this way and that way, trying to let me see him. Finally they said, 'Come, come,' and I looked through the window and saw a thirty-year-old man in a courtyard, washing his face."

"What did you think?"

She smiles shyly. "I liked him very much. He was very handsome. Have you seen the picture of him from that time?"

"Yes, but how did you feel about getting married when you were ten?"

"Leila," Ammejun cries. "Bring that picture of your father, the one that's in the frame." Leila brings the picture and I see a man in a black cap and a dark wool jacket with a vest and a white collarless shirt. He has a straight nose and bright eyes. Above a five-o'clock shadow, the hint of a smile plays on his handsomely drawn lips.

"Isn't he good-looking?" she says. "I liked him so much, from the moment I saw him until sixty-five years later when he couldn't shave himself because he was too weak. Then I shaved his face. I washed him, I helped him go to the bathroom. Have you heard the tapes I have of him reciting Hafez? He does it so beautifully you can't believe it. Did you see the poem he wrote for me? In a frame, in my apartment? He wrote it halfway through our marriage and if you read it you will see how much we liked each other."

"But weren't you nervous about getting married?"

"Why should I be? What else did I have to do? Girls didn't go to school after they were ten. Girls didn't work. My wedding was the most exciting day of my life." She smiles and her eyes become watery. "My dress was light pink, like these roses, and it reached the floor. They embroidered it by hand—they didn't use machines in those days. Ah, and my shoes were so beautiful you wouldn't believe it, because they don't make such shoes now. Leather as shiny as mirrors, and high heels, and straps the color of saffron."

"You should have kept them," Leila says.

"For what? My feet wouldn't fit in them now." Ammejun points for me to keep rubbing her shoulder. "My nighttime dress was white, and embroidered by hand from the top to the bottom. And they came to get me in a car"—her smile widens—"the first car anyone had ever heard of coming to get a bride."

"Rummy?" Leila says, starting to flip out a worn pack of cards.

"And do you know what one part of my marriage contract was?" Ammejun says, frowning and putting her hand on Leila's wrist to make her listen. "If my husband ever left me he would have to give me one kilo of flies' wings."

"Why on earth would you want that?" I ask.

"Bah, that is not the point. They wrote that in the contract because how do you get one kilo of flies' wings? Even if he had wanted to—which he never did—my husband couldn't have left me."

I last saw Ammejun's husband at a Noruz picnic in California. He was in his nineties and nearly blind and deaf, but he had his arm around her, and he smiled blissfully as his hand fondled her breast. That was the arranged marriage at its best, with no distant husband and no reluctant bride. Ammejun never had to be a second wife like Aziz. She did not have to drop out of school like Homa-khanoum. Homa was among the last of her kind—her own sister Massi, just eight years younger, was allowed to finish high school and to veto the doctor her parents had picked for her. She even got to request that Zia, whom she'd met through her older brother, be allowed to come *khastegari* her.

But for Ammejun there was no high school to finish and no opportunity to meet dashing brother's friends. Ammejun's father drew up a marriage contract with lapis spires and liquid gold and the seals of the town elders stamped onto its parchment pages. It hangs in a frame above her dining-room table, next to her husband's love poem, testimony to the best thing that ever happened to her.

The moon sits like a pot of honey on the purple line of mountains. Outside the garden wall, Abu-bakr is burning a large pile of dried branches. We come out of the houses to stand around the red circle of fire as it dances and lights up our faces.

From the hut nearby we hear the sound of arguing, and we all look at each other and smile. This has been going on for a week, ever since the two old shepherds who share a hut got into a disagreement over the martyr Hossein. The first shepherd, who comes from a nearby village, is a Shiite and believes that Hossein's ride into Karbala was a noble sacrifice for Islam. But the Kurdish shepherd, a Sunni like the other Kurds, says Hossein was a rebel who deserved to get killed. The Shiite shepherd has threatened to quit over this, and none of Leila-khanoum's diplomacy has had any effect. In the meantime the sheep have been split into two sects that graze on different sides of Dadash's pasture, with each shepherd staring proudly off toward opposite ends of the mountain range.

The stars come out and Leila-khanoum's girlish voice rises up with a song about the brightening moon. The slender, white-trunked pop-lars swish above our heads. "Look up," Dadash says, "they're danc-ing," and Leila-khanoum smiles softly at him. A faint dead smell wafts in from far out in the desert where Abu-bakr shot a boar yesterday. Brown foxes bound over the tall grass and Leila-khanoum fills her pockets with wild cumin, its spicy scent mingling with the smells of flowers and fire and death.

Slowly everyone drifts indoors. I sit outside, waiting until the orange-and-black wood collapses into a pile of bright embers. And then, walking back to the house alone, I see a small ghost. I look hard to make sure. The breeze in the tree branches makes shadowy skeletons dance on the ground, but no, between the trees I see it again—a short, white-draped figure drifting toward me. I stop, trying to figure it out. One of the old shepherds, going out to sleep far from his nemesis? No, they are both tall. A poacher, disguised to scare off anyone who might see him? The apparition passes me, and I turn and follow it to the bottom of the garden, down to the pool of water.

Suddenly a billowing of white fans out. It is Ammejun, who has chosen this hour to come out and drape her sheets and underwear over the bushes.

"*Ai*, you scared me!" she says. "Where were you?"

"With the Kurds."

"Ha." She throws a pair of underwear up to a high part of the bush where she cannot possibly reach it again. "They are good people."

I take a chador out of the pile and toss it up.

"Not so high. It wouldn't do to have people see these things when they walk by here in the morning." She hooks the two arms of a large white bra over the naked branches. "You know, everyone thinks it was because of the smallpox that Wife-of-Agha Jan had no more ba-bies," she suddenly says, as if we had just been discussing it. "But what everyone thinks is wrong. Put that over here, where the wind will not take it. This is what happened to Wife-of-Agha Jan. Agha Jan used to go to Arak on business, and when he was there he used to visit the *zanhaye harja-i*, the women who go with everyone. He got a sickness from them. He took many baths in watermelon juice and prayed that his wife would not get it too, but eventually he realized that she had. For eight years they tried, but she never had any more babies." Ammejun throws the last scarf up and it ripples down to the bush. "Agha Jan had to take a second wife, so he offered to divorce his first wife and pay all her expenses for the rest of her life, but she said she would rather stay on with him, which made him very happy."

We walk back up to the house and Ammejun pats me on the shoulder. "Lock the door," she reminds me. But I stay outside a few minutes longer, staring up at the moon that has become a high white dot in the sky.

In America, first wives do not sit around to help raise the children of second wives. In America, if I heard about a grown man marrying a ten-year-old or kidnapping a teenager from her father's house I would consider him a criminal. But here in the village none of this is so clear. The act of leading seventy-two people out to die in the desert is revered by one side and scorned by the other. Abu-bakr will stay up all night tonight, hiking far up the mountain in his black rubber boots to direct the spring water to Dadash's land, the land that feeds his own children; but to the grandfather of those children he is a bad man. Ami misses her family, but when I ask her if she has any regrets she gives me a funny look. "Ooh no," she says, laughing at such a crazy thing. "How could I, when I like Abu-bakr so much? You leave your family, you go with your husband, you have your children. That's what life is, after all."

✥

"All this talk about old times makes me want to go see my father's fort," Ammejun announces at breakfast. Dadash stops stirring Nescafé into his milk and gives her a sharp look. "For fifty years I have not gone back," she says indignantly. "Taraneh wants to see it, and I want to go too."

I am surprised that in these fifty years Ammejun has never gone back to see the place where she grew up. She must have passed the road that leads there a hundred times. She does not drive; when she visits here Dadash takes her everywhere she wants to go—to the graveyard, to an old friend in a neighboring village, to the bazaar in the nearby town. Now, all of a sudden, she wants to go to her father's fort.

I have already asked Dadash about going there; he replied that he would not go driving all the way out to see a piece of land that is no longer his. But he cannot argue with the woman who is both his aunt and his mother-in-law. After lunch and a nap, he backs the car out of the garage. The farmhands gather around, wiping smudges off the car and checking the oil as Ammejun and Leila-khanoum and I put on our scarves and coats and find our purses. Agreen and Azadeh, the little Kurdish sisters, climb into the backseat to ride with us to the end of the village. Abu-bakr and the farmhands wave, and we slowly coast over the gravel and out the gate.

To hear Dadash describe it, Ammejun's fort lies several hours away over quicksand and lava. In reality, the drive takes forty minutes and the road is paved until the last turnoff. We drive along brick-red mountains dusted green at the base, with white veins running along the sides. Beyond these, a range of higher, jagged points lean and dip like dancers cloaked under a sheet. The clouds make ripples on the range; dark and light stripes of sun and shadow play with the distances. This was all Baba saw as a child, before Aziz moved the family into town. There was no city skyline, no view from an airplane, not even the images a movie theater could have brought to make his world feel small.

Ammejun gives a squeal. "Look! Ghaleh-e-Qanat!" Far off the road, a long, square building with four round towers glows bronze in the late afternoon light. Ghaleh-e-Qanat, the Castle of Aqueducts. "My father built that," Ammejun says grandly. I look at Dadash to see if he is listening—after all, it is his own grandfather's fort—but he is frowning and looking out the side window. And then I notice that the car is shaking.

"Flat tire," he says glumly. We roll to a stop in the gravel. Dadash lifts a spare tire out of the trunk and Leila and I watch him jack up the car for a few moments before we realize that Ammejun is running off across the desert, her sky-blue raincoat flapping behind her.

Dadash sighs. "You go after her, Taraneh." I take off over the tufts of desert scrub and soon the car is far behind.

"Do you think anyone will be there?" Ammejun says anxiously, her eighty-five-year-old legs striding toward the castle so fast I have to trot to keep up.

"*Enshallah*," I say. "Do you know who lives there now?"

She clicks her tongue no.

"Is this where you lived when you were little?" I ask.

"No, I never lived here. I lived in another fort. I would have lived here, but my father was killed right before he finished building it."

I want to ask more, but I don't want her to get in the mood where she snaps and says, "No more questions." So I hurry alongside her and wait for her to talk.

"For fifty years I haven't been here. And it was built thirty years before that. It is the same age as me, and see what good shape it's in."

"You're in good shape too."

"I take my medicines. *Bah, bah*, look at the walls." She shakes her head. "If only they had finished it a little sooner my father wouldn't have died." I look back to see if Dadash and Leila are coming but the car is a white spot in the desert. I hope they are not waiting for me to bring Ammejun back. I could as easily bring back the fort itself.

"What should I say?" she asks, her face flushed. "Should I tell them who I am? Or should we just say we're interested in old forts and we want to see the inside of this one?"

"Let's say that, and then later we can casually mention who we are."

"Yes," she says. "That's a good plan."

But when we reach the big front archway, the wooden door is locked. We pound, but no one answers.

"*Ai*," she says. "We have to get in." I walk around the whole fort, trying to find another entrance. But up close the walls are high and smooth, impossible to scale.

"*Akh*, how bad, how bad," she says. We look around the silent desert for some movement. Even the birds have flown from this place.

Ammejun turns to the only thing that interrupts the solid mud wall. "Look at how strong this old door is," she says. "Look at the bolts my father put in. And see, through this hole—my father put a carpet of stones in the entryway to welcome his guests."

Ammejun was just a year old when her father died. She only knows his name and the name of his mother and the name of his mother's father, who hunted zebras for Fath Ali Shah in what must have been around the 1820s. She was a whole generation younger than Agha Jan, her half brother.

"When my parents died, I went to live with Agha Jan and Wife-of-Agha Jan," she reminds me as we wait for Dadash and Leila to catch up. "But in those days before he married Aziz we just called her by her name, Ghamar."

Ghamar was the daughter of a servant to the Qajars, and she grew up playing with local Qajar princesses. She would have been thirteen or fourteen when Agha Jan came for her, himself only twenty but the son of a small landowner, and a man of rising fortunes. On the day before the wedding, the princesses took Ghamar to the bathhouse and stayed with her all day. They washed and waxed and perfumed her. They brought in a woman poet who used henna to write love poems up her thighs for her husband to read on the wedding night. "Then the princesses' mother, who loved Ghamar like her own daughter, called for her special box and pulled out her jeweled crown and placed it on Ghamar's head," Ammejun says. "They put her on a horse whose blanket was covered with so many rubies and pearls and amethysts that it shimmered like water. As the horse walked to Agha Jan's village, musicians and acrobats danced in front of it, and in each village the people came out to see the bride pass." The procession even detoured through an out-of-the-way village at the request of Agha Jan's father, who was feuding with it and wanted to show off the good connection his son was making.

"Take a picture of me, here, in front of this door." Ammejun stands still and stares hard at the camera until she hears the click. "Thank you," she says, patting her scarf. "What was I saying? Ah— Wife-of-Agha Jan. She was a very good woman. My brother liked her very much. I remember when it was cold and we didn't have heaters and the two of them would lie on the bed with all their clothes on and hold very tightly to each other to keep warm. Married people don't have to do that, after all."

"And so you must remember their children," I say tentatively, worried I am asking too much.

"Of course! How could I not? Their boys were my age, we played together. *Akh*, what handsome boys they were, straight and tall as cypress trees. Those Qajar princesses would send boxes of children's clothes, and they would wear them, each one a little taller, playing together in the matching black hats the princesses sent." Her voice gets small, as if she is talking to herself. "Three handsome little boys with hats. By now they would have been as old as I am."

"What were their names?" I ask.

"What were their names?" She tips her head and squints her eyes shut. "How could I not remember their names? I played with them every day." Her eyes snap open and she frowns. "Eh, how do I know? You think anyone can remember such things?" She purses her lips and I know I have talked too much.

The car jerks over the gravel and stops in front of us. Leila-khanoum and Dadash step delicately out.

"They're not home," Ammejun says, putting her chin up defiantly.

"You see," Dadash says, straightening his jacket. "We came all the way out here for nothing."

"No, not for nothing," she says. "I wanted to see it and so did Taraneh. And now we can find out who has the key."

"Hey, look!" Leila-khanoum is a few yards away, standing over a hole in the ground. "What's this?"

"That is the *qanat*," Ammejun says, hurrying over to make sure. "*Bah, bah*, look at what water it has." A few feet down, a stream runs clear over pebbles. It is part of a complicated, ancient system of underground tunnels that carry fresh well water for kilometers through the desert. "Still so clean," Ammejun says, suppressing a smile as she peers into the hole. "Eighty years after my father built it."

The *qanats* gurgle out into a large stone pool of water. "Ah, the guests used to stay here," Ammejun says. "Imagine, forty tents around this pool, under these trees, the men feasting and laughing out here all night. See how my father planted trees leading up to the fort?" She sweeps her hand toward the double row of gnarled trees that form a canopy over the road.

"But I thought your father was killed before he ever moved in," I say. "How could he have had guests here?"

"My father died one month before it was finished," she says. "They were just putting the plaster on the walls. But Agha Jan, my brother, had guests stay here later; those are the ones I remember sitting under these trees and playing the *tar*."

"So this isn't the house you grew up in?" Leila says.

"No, after my father was killed we stayed in our old house. The Ghaleh-e-Qanat stayed empty until later. Come, I will show you the house where I grew up." We follow her down a dirt path, past broken walls with crooked trees growing out of the tops. A white donkey chewing grass looks up as we pass.

"Are you sure it is this way?" Dadash says.

"Of course I'm sure," Ammejun says, glaring at him. "See where those two mountains meet? That is where the caravan would appear in the night, a train of white camels under the moon. Ha! Taraneh! This is it." She stops in front of a mound of dirt, and I follow her hand toward a row of eroding mud-brick walls, a run of arches that gape at us like open mouths.

"This was our fort! See, here was the room where we kept wheat, and here was the bread room." Her voice falls into a villager's cadence and I have to strain to understand her as we stumble over the rubble. "See how the rooms are connected? This was the women's room where I was a child. It was very beautiful, with walls painted red and white. See the fireplace? See the arches in the wall?" The edges of the recessed arches are still sharp and fine; the fireplace is still black with soot. I put my hand out next to Ammejun's and together we run our fingers over plasterwork that has survived a century of sun and rain and wind.

She cannot keep back her smile any longer. "This room was where the men brought the wood in; that room was for the wheat they loaded onto the camels. Everyone in the house would wake up to load them up. Why at night? So the robbers wouldn't come. Ah, you see, there were many robbers in those times."

Ammejun unties the knot in her scarf so it sits loosely on her head, threatening to slip off altogether. "And this hole in the wall—see? If we had to speak to the servants we would talk through this so they wouldn't see us. And look," she says, pointing up at a half-collapsed structure in the corner of the fort. "That is where they shot my father."

The tower is crumbled. Long tufts of grass grow out of the floor. But this is the lookout room that Baba used to tell us about, the tower that belonged to his white-bearded grandfather.

"When my father heard the bandits were coming he called out for his neighbors to come help him. Nobody came. So he climbed up to this tower to defend us . . ." Ammejun begins the story I have heard all my life, and I lean into her words, rubbing against them like a cat as she takes me through it again.

As she talks, I look around at the rich brown land covered with a green carpet of clover and shaded by fruit trees. This is the last scene my great-grandfather ever saw, standing alone in his crenellated tower, waiting for the bandits to gallop in from the desert. Their arrival came as no surprise—he had refused to give the bandit leader his "under the mustache" protection payment, and so his men were coming to take it anyway. This is why Agha Jan's father's house was a fort—with watchmen and guns and a slitted window through which he fired at the approaching horsemen, unaware that one of them had already entered his house.

"After they shot him," Ammejun says, "it turned out to have been a mistake. The bandit leader Rajab-Ali got very mad at his men and said, 'Why did you kill him, you fools? I only told you to take his wheat!' He even sent a note to Agha Jan, apologizing for his men going too far. Rajab-Ali said he respected Agha Jan's father; he had only wanted the same cooperation as he had gotten from the other landowners. Now he asked for cooperation from his son, and even provided a list of goods to be sent back with his messenger. Hah! Agha Jan told the messenger that the only thing Rajab-Ali would get from him was a bullet."

Two years later, when the great bandit was finally led up to the scaffold, tears ran down his face. He begged for forgiveness. *Az sar-e khoonesh migzaram* would have been all Agha Jan needed to say. "I will pass over this man's blood." Rajab-Ali scanned the faces and cried out, "I don't want to die!" and Agha Jan had an urge to step forward and save him. But then he remembered his father's eyes. He did not move. Rajab-Ali was hanged, and Agha Jan's reputation for strength and harshness was born.

"Salaam aleikum, how are you?"

A tall man in a fedora and loose, worn clothing steps out of the nearby gatehouse. Ammejun hurries up to him and we follow.

"We're well, thank you," Dadash calls out. "And yourself?"

The man lowers the wood-handled shovel he is carrying and nods to Ammejun, who has reached him first. "By the grace of God, I am well."

"We wanted to see inside that fort where the door is closed," Ammejun says, motioning for the rest of us to be quiet.

"Ah," the man says, turning slowly toward the intact fort, a long arm moving up to shield his eyes although the sun is behind him. "That fort. It isn't open."

"Yes, I know," she says, her voice shaking in her effort to match the man's slow way of talking. "But whose is it?"

"Ah, that," he says. "That fort is from the old times."

"Yes, yes," she says impatiently. "But whom did it belong to in the old times?"

"The old lords."

"The old lords." Ammejun rolls this over her tongue, holding back a smile. "Okay, and what was their name?"

He pauses to think and a chill runs down my spine. How many ruined villages must there be in these hills, how many broken forts? What if this is not the one she was thinking of? Or, even if this is the right one, why should this man know anything about it? He cannot be more than fifty.

Ammejun's fists are clenched inside the pockets of her blue raincoat. Dadash is frowning, his eyes riveted on the man. The man screws up his weather-beaten face.

"Haj Morad-Ali-khan," he finally says, pronouncing Agha Jan's full name.

"Ha!" The hands come out of the pockets. The frown widens into surprise. "And can you tell me," Ammejun says carefully, savoring the words, "what his father's name was?"

The man squints over at an old tree whose bare trunk rises like a rifle against the sky. "Haj Abdollah-khan."

"And where are they now?"

"*Vallah*, to be honest, I don't know. They moved to the city. Then we heard one of the daughters had gone to America."

This is too much for Ammejun, who has been trying hard to conceal her smile as the man finishes his sentence. "I," she says slowly and distinctly, "am the child of that Haj Abdollah-khan. Haj Morad-Ali-khan was my brother. I am that very daughter who went to America."

"*Ehhhhh?*" And she gets what she wanted—the man's face slowly opens, his eyebrows rise as if he's seen a mythical spirit, his hand goes to his heart in respect. Then his words pour like thick honey; he wishes he had the keys but they're in the hands of his children and

As she talks, I look around at the rich brown land covered with a green carpet of clover and shaded by fruit trees. This is the last scene my great-grandfather ever saw, standing alone in his crenellated tower, waiting for the bandits to gallop in from the desert. Their arrival came as no surprise—he had refused to give the bandit leader his "under the mustache" protection payment, and so his men were coming to take it anyway. This is why Agha Jan's father's house was a fort—with watchmen and guns and a slitted window through which he fired at the approaching horsemen, unaware that one of them had already entered his house.

"After they shot him," Ammejun says, "it turned out to have been a mistake. The bandit leader Rajab-Ali got very mad at his men and said, 'Why did you kill him, you fools? I only told you to take his wheat!' He even sent a note to Agha Jan, apologizing for his men going too far. Rajab-Ali said he respected Agha Jan's father; he had only wanted the same cooperation as he had gotten from the other landowners. Now he asked for cooperation from his son, and even provided a list of goods to be sent back with his messenger. Hah! Agha Jan told the messenger that the only thing Rajab-Ali would get from him was a bullet."

Two years later, when the great bandit was finally led up to the scaffold, tears ran down his face. He begged for forgiveness. *Az sar-e khoonesh migzaram* would have been all Agha Jan needed to say. "I will pass over this man's blood." Rajab-Ali scanned the faces and cried out, "I don't want to die!" and Agha Jan had an urge to step forward and save him. But then he remembered his father's eyes. He did not move. Rajab-Ali was hanged, and Agha Jan's reputation for strength and harshness was born.

"*Salaam aleikum*, how are you?"

A tall man in a fedora and loose, worn clothing steps out of the nearby gatehouse. Ammejun hurries up to him and we follow.

"We're well, thank you," Dadash calls out. "And yourself?"

The man lowers the wood-handled shovel he is carrying and nods to Ammejun, who has reached him first. "By the grace of God, I am well."

"We wanted to see inside that fort where the door is closed," Ammejun says, motioning for the rest of us to be quiet.

"Ah," the man says, turning slowly toward the intact fort, a long arm moving up to shield his eyes although the sun is behind him. "That fort. It isn't open."

"Yes, I know," she says, her voice shaking in her effort to match the man's slow way of talking. "But whose is it?"

"Ah, that," he says. "That fort is from the old times."

"Yes, yes," she says impatiently. "But whom did it belong to in the old times?"

"The old lords."

"The old lords." Ammejun rolls this over her tongue, holding back a smile. "Okay, and what was their name?"

He pauses to think and a chill runs down my spine. How many ruined villages must there be in these hills, how many broken forts? What if this is not the one she was thinking of? Or, even if this is the right one, why should this man know anything about it? He cannot be more than fifty.

Ammejun's fists are clenched inside the pockets of her blue raincoat. Dadash is frowning, his eyes riveted on the man. The man screws up his weather-beaten face.

"Haj Morad-Ali-khan," he finally says, pronouncing Agha Jan's full name.

"Ha!" The hands come out of the pockets. The frown widens into surprise. "And can you tell me," Ammejun says carefully, savoring the words, "what his father's name was?"

The man squints over at an old tree whose bare trunk rises like a rifle against the sky. "Haj Abdollah-khan."

"And where are they now?"

"*Vallah*, to be honest, I don't know. They moved to the city. Then we heard one of the daughters had gone to America."

This is too much for Ammejun, who has been trying hard to conceal her smile as the man finishes his sentence. "I," she says slowly and distinctly, "am the child of that Haj Abdollah-khan. Haj Morad-Ali-khan was my brother. I am that very daughter who went to America."

"*Ehhhhhh?*" And she gets what she wanted—the man's face slowly opens, his eyebrows rise as if he's seen a mythical spirit, his hand goes to his heart in respect. Then his words pour like thick honey; he wishes he had the keys but they're in the hands of his children and someone named Ahmad, who turns out to be the son of Ammejun's half sister, and then it turns out that Ammejun played with this man's mother when she was a girl. They talk for so long that Dadash takes off his jacket and Leila-khanoum drifts toward the side of the road where a field of wildflowers rustles in the wind.

"Do you remember your father getting killed?" the man says.

"No, how could I?" Ammejun says. "I was one and a half."

"Do *you* remember?" Leila-khanoum asks, standing up from where she has bent to pick flowers.

The man laughs. "My father told me the story. My father was a hundred years old." Ammejun looks delighted to hear this.

"Who lives in that fort now?" I ask.

"No one," he says.

"I wanted to see the inside," Ammejun says again.

"I know, mother, I know," he says regretfully. "What can I do? The keys are in the hands of other people and they are out of town. You come back in a week and the door will be open for you."

"Little Ahmad," she says, shaking her head. "The son of Shahrbanu-khanoum." She asks me for a piece of paper and carefully writes down her telephone number for the cousin she hasn't seen in half a century. "That's in Tehran. Tell him to call me." He takes the paper and she promises to return, although he has no phone to dial the number and she has no car to carry her back here.

"Ah, what water that *qanat* has," Ammejun says, looking out the window as we drive away. "You know, my father was a very smart man. Once a prince came and asked about the water and my father pretended it was not plentiful because he was afraid the prince would take it away."

No one says anything.

"What fools we were!" she sighs. "To sell it for nothing."

"Better that they sold it," Dadash says. "So that later it wasn't taken away."

"We did a very good thing to go see it," Ammejun says. "Did you see how that man remembered us? How happy he was to see us? He told me my brother's family were much better people than the ones they sold the fort to, the Sadeghis." She chuckles to herself.

"The Sadeghis' children are doctors in England," Dadash reminds her.

She ignores him. "He said everyone loved my brother and that he was the best landlord of any of the khans."

Seeing her excitement, I understand even less why she has never come here before. How could she have lost track of her own cousin, only a short drive away these fifty years? And why would Dadash have never been interested in coming to see the fort his grandfather built?

Ammejun's face glows all evening. For a special dinner, we grill kabobs in the fireplace and sit at the big table to eat them.

"Did I tell you how Agha Jan caught the bandit Rajab-Ali and watched him be executed?" she says.

"Yes," Dadash says. "*Bah, bah,* what kabobs!" He slides another oblong patty onto my plate, black and glistening.

"And you saw how much that man liked us?" she says.

"Yes." Dadash smiles in spite of himself. "It's true he remembered a lot about Agha Jan and your father."

"And you all saw the room in the tower where my father was shot?"

We nod and scoop fresh yogurt onto our bread.

"What was it your father said that made the men find him in the tower?" I ask.

"What did he say?" She frowns, remembering. "He saw the bandits coming and he told Ghamar to run and get the deed to the house and hide it. He was afraid if the bandits got the deed then he would lose the house. Then when he heard sounds behind him he thought it was Ghamar coming back, so he said, 'Did you get it? Did you hide it?' Of course, she had hidden the deed and was hiding herself, smart girl. But the bandits heard him and they came in and gave him the bullet in his head."

That night in bed I watch the clouds race like horses over the moon. I think of Baba as a boy, galloping up into those hills to hunt, secure in the life his father had built for him. Agha Jan's house sheltered his siblings, his wives and their relatives, and his children and servants. By the time Baba was born Agha Jan's hairline had receded and his stomach was round and all the villagers for miles around came to him for their needs. His dynasty had become part of the landscape, a dominion that could no longer be downed by a single bullet, or a greedy prince—or, in the end, by the Shah's land reforms. Even today, some of the older villagers still come to Dadash, asking him to "please accept this portion of our earnings and give your sisters and brothers their shares so that our profits will be *halal"*—clean and pure. And even today, a man barely old enough to remember Agha Jan remembers that he was once the lord, and that his father, Haj Abdollah-khan, was the man whose name went with that empty castle of aqueducts.

I look up at the high corners of the ceiling. Dadash built this yellow brick farmhouse thirty-five years ago, but it feels older, and not just because of the old-style colored glass windows and curved archways. The white plaster walls are hung with the dried wildflowers that Leila-khanoum gathers in the mountains and the solid wood furniture was made by local woodcarvers. The decor is elegant and calm, as I imagine Iranian houses were before gilt-edged European chairs and lacquered end tables made their appearance.

On the mantelpiece above my head, a young Agha Jan looks down from a wood-framed photograph. Dashing in a black Qajar fez and frock coat, he stands on a Persian carpet, his arm resting upon a false Grecian column, with a vague Parthenon sketched onto the backdrop. I look at his dark eyes, his brows curved like sabers, and I imagine him standing silently as his father's assassin was hanged; I picture him curling around his wife to warm her, and I see him watching his three sons die despite the doctors and the prayers. When only one son was left, Wife-of-Agha Jan begged God not to let him die of smallpox too; he died of whooping cough instead. By the time Agha Jan had reached his thirties, he knew it was fruitless to try to rearrange the stars of fate. It was what God wanted, he said when his wife became barren, and he said it again when Khosrow died, and again when the lands were taken away.

In imagining Iranians to all be terrorists and fanatics, Westerners do not always notice their submissiveness, although it is elemental to Shiism. Within the "fanaticism," within the willingness to be martyred and bend to the will of God, lies a simple desire to get from one day to the next without interference from the evil eye. It is not prudent to protest, to ask too many questions, to delve too deeply into the past or the future. Ammejun waited fifty years to be driven

down the road to her old home. Homa-khanoum refuses to look at
the date on her airplane tickets. Niki warns me not to marry outside
the family. Ask for too many details, look too far off, and surely you
will reel in some misfortune. Better to leave things to God.

And yet, once in a while, these same practicers of submission suddenly take to the streets, turn into Hossein in the desert, risk their
lives to give voice to their passions. Only fifteen years ago, there was
a revolution here. But sometimes it is hard to see where it came from.

❖

Omid, the younger Kurdish boy, is small and skinny, even for a
twelve-year-old. When he carries my bag out the door, his arm strains
under the weight.

"That suitcase has wheels," I tell him. "You can roll it."

He shakes his head manfully and we walk out toward the car where
Mohammad is filling the trunk with apples for Dadash to sell in town.

Omid heaves my bag up with one thrust. "Lucky you," he says. "I
wish I were going to America." He grins and rubs his hand against
the fuzz of his shaved head. "Can I come with you? In your suitcase?"

"Well, I guess you're not too heavy," I say, reaching for the zipper.
"Get in."

"No, really," he says. "Do you think I could find work in
America?"

"Yeah, probably, when you're a little older. But what if you didn't
like it there?"

"Oh, well, then I'd come back here," he says. "I just want to see
what it's like."

"How about you, Mohammad?" I say. "You want to come?"

"Nah," the taller boy says, tipping his head up. "What would I do
in America? The most beautiful place in the world is Kurdistan. As
soon as I have enough money I'm going back there. I'm going to
open up a shop."

"You don't want to stay here and open a shop?" I ask. "To be
near your parents?"

"Nah." He looks at the trees along the sunbaked wall and wrinkles
his nose.

"He doesn't like working for other people," Omid says.

Mohammad's face reddens, and he casts a quick glance at me. "I just want my own shop," he mumbles.

"So next time I'll have to visit you in Kurdistan. What kind of shop are you going to have?"

"Oh, a store that sells everything," he says, brightening. "Anything you want, I'll have."

"How about you, Arezou?" I say. "Will you come to America with me?"

Arezou gives a slight tip of her head—no—but I can't see her face under her scarf. She just started wearing it a few days ago, on her own, and her father keeps walking by and yanking it down to tease her.

"Kurdistan, then?" I say. "Or Tehran?"

She shakes her head. "My father and mother are here. Everyone I know is here."

"Well, what if your father and mother moved back to Kurdistan?" I ask. "Would you go with them then?"

She thinks for a few seconds, then shakes her head again. "I mean, I am Kurdish. But I'm from here now."

As I walk out of the house, Leila-khanoum hurries over with a tray. "Kiss the Qoran," she says and, murmuring a prayer, she holds the tray up for me to walk under three times. Then she lowers the tray, and I close my eyes and kiss the old copy of the Qoran that is sitting next to a bowl of water with a rose in it. As I walk out to the car I hear the splattering of water on the gravel—a good-luck ritual to ensure my safe return.

We do this all the time in America now. Neither Baba nor Mama nor any of us kids will go on a long trip without walking under the Qoran. We, who back in Iran never believed in religion or bad luck, are now willing to miss an airplane in order to run back and kiss an old leather book. Mama says if we didn't do it she would not be able to sleep; and even after we left home and moved to Berkeley, Ali and I would faithfully go to each other's houses before an early-morning flight to put a sprig of houseplant next to a Qoran and toss a cup of water down the stairs.

The bus pulls away from the town depot and my stomach lurches. I can still feel Ami's vigorous kisses on my cheeks and my forehead, and Abu-bakr's warm callused hand, hard as stone, shaking mine in farewell. I can hear the catch in Leila-khanoum's voice when she said goodbye and I can see Dadash in the bus parking lot, standing straight and alone in a silent gesture of communion as my bus passed through the gates. I want to jump off and run back to them. I want to assert my presence in this place that seems in danger of collapsing under so much abandonment. The village, once the center of life for so many, is now a vista of eroding fortresses. The children who grew up here are scattered all over the world; they might someday bring their own children from America or Canada to visit the farm, but they won't move back. Dadash and Leila-khanoum are the last members of our family still here, and no one is set to carry on after them. It is unbearable to think that their house could be sold to strangers or left to crumble after they are gone.

The bus trundles along through the narrow, quiet streets of the town, still cool and shadowy, with only a few blades of sunlight piercing between the low brick buildings. Yesterday at this time, I woke up early and wandered over the dewy fields to the next village. Like Dadash's village, it had no roads or cars or signs to announce it. Thinking myself alone, I stooped to collect a handful of the blue flowers growing along the cow path.

"Who are you?"

Three wrinkled faces peered down at me. Under their loose chadors and frizzy hennaed hair, six lizard eyes, bright and unblinking, fixed upon me.

"I am the older daughter of the youngest brother of Abdollah-khan," I said, pointing back toward the trees.

Three wavering voices repeated this to each other.

"Who is your father?" asked the middle one.

I said his name.

They turned to each other, grimacing, frowning, muttering Baba's name.

Suddenly one of the faces lit up. "Esfandiar-khan? The son of Haj Morad-Ali-khan?" The old woman put her hand on an imaginary child's head. "Esfandiar-khan," she said to the others. "From over the mountain." She pointed to the purple-gray peak to my left, the direction of Ammejun's fort. Three toothless mouths broke into smiles. "Ah, yes, the brother of Abdollah-khan, Haj Morad-Ali-khan's son, Esfandiar-khan—what a sweet little boy." The middle woman clasped my hand and pulled me in as if to kiss me, then pushed my hand back and put her own hand to her heart, smiling and nodding, her eyes moist with ancient memory.

What was it she remembered? Some distant day when Baba was driven through here; some village wedding where this woman noticed a little laughing-eyed boy and held onto the image for fifty years? Walking back along the river, I thought of that boy with his round shaved head and the mole on his cheek, and of the village women who used to stop him in the road to plant kisses on his head. It must have felt good to him to know that they knew him; to be seven years old and already have a place in the world. I knew it must, because it felt good to me. These women had never seen me before, but hearing the name of my father had brought tears of recognition to their eyes.

I bent down and trailed my hand in the cold river, letting my fingers sway like the roots of trees along the bank. This was the river I had walked along as a child, the river Baba had fished in, the river Agha Jan's first wife had crossed on the Qajar-jeweled horse that carried her over the hill to her new life. Our own new lives—Baba's and my own—strayed far from this river; but for those who stayed, life retained a continuity that cannot be found anywhere else. I can see it in their faces—in the wonder-struck eyes of Ammejun when she finds the son of her childhood playmate; in the pleased recognition in Ami's eyes when she pins her Kurdish clothes on me; in Leila's appreciative smile when she runs her hand up my thigh and tells me to marry Mehdi. All this touching between women bothered Mama when she was in Iran; she hated the way that after lunch the women would all go off and take naps together, massaging each other's sore legs, braiding each other's hair, plucking each other's eyebrows and smoothing on ointment afterward. She found those rituals intrusive —especially when coupled with the sexual jokes and insinuations that passed between giggling married women, jokes designed to be tantalizingly inscrutable to unmarried girls who might be listening. But none of this bothers me. I like the slightly bawdy banter among women in my family; I like the touching. It reminds me of the way I used to touch my friends and cousins before the sixth grader in

America warned me not to. Once in America, I forgot the pleasure of casually entwined fingers, of arms linked together in friendship. I strictly followed the rules of American adolescence and made it clear to my family that kissing me was no longer acceptable. Physicality became confined to romance, and it was many years before I began to remember the comfort that comes with owning, and being owned by, a large, affectionate clan.

Now, back in it again, I have the sense that it is not just me they are touching. Running her hand up my thigh, Leila-khanoum is also touching her own, remembered, self, and that is part of her pleasure. Every girl is a version of the woman, every woman a model for what the girl will someday be; and at the end of the day, when the sun has set and everyone has helped with the apple harvesting and the baking of the bread and the cooking of dinner, the candlelight flickers over the faces, and the differences are smoothed away.

If I were to stay here I would probably be only partly satisfied. I would always feel I belonged; I would always feel glad to run into those old ladies who remembered the child my father was. But being away from America, I might also start to feel more American, more trapped. I might become impatient with the old ladies' talk of marriages and deaths and old property squabbles, and start missing the other kind of old lady—the book-reading, hiking, and swimming old lady that I imagine my mother will be and that I want to be too. An old lady who might live far from Iran but would bring her grandchildren back here to discover the places from their past that don't change no matter who comes or goes. Fifty years from now, they would find the same cool river and the same smell of mountain grass. They would find a row of white poplars glowing in the sunset; and a husband and wife who laughed as they grabbed at each other under the cows; and, inside the house, a fire in the grate, a table laden with fresh cutlets and yogurt, and a basketful of mint from a rained-on garden.

At the front of the bus, above the driver's seat, a mirrored placard hangs beside the No Smoking sign. It is written in stylized calligraphy, and it takes me a minute to make it out. *Een neez bogzarad*— "This too shall pass." I smile, remembering Baba complain once about how when he was a boy he used to see this saying every-where—in shops, on taxi dashboards, on living-room walls. When in high school he asked his calligraphy teacher to write something he could frame and put up in his room, the teacher wrote, beautifully and meticulously (and to Baba, annoyingly), "This too shall pass." It is a Sufi proverb, a saying that is supposed to have the power to make you happy when you are sad, and sad when you are happy; a reminder that no pain or pleasure lasts. But I think it irritated Baba because instead of freeing people, it seemed like an excuse for paralysis. It was the submissiveness, the surrendering of one's life to fate, the giving up of the fight.

We stop at a speed checkpoint and the driver runs to a booth across the road to have his mileage chart recorded. As we wait for him, a cry rises up through the bus.

"Eh, eh! Eh, EH, EH!!"

A half-second of silence, then an earsplitting crunch. The bus in front of us, whose rear trunk is open, has backed up, and its trunk door has crushed our front windshield like an eggshell.

Immediately all the men jump out of our bus and all the men jump out of the other bus. I rise from my seat, along with the only other woman on my bus, an old lady in a black chador, and we stare out at a blur of punching, pummeling, and kicking. Men race over from other buses to join the fight or to yell from the sidelines.

"Get him! Hit him! That's the way!"

"Look out behind you!"

"No, no!" the old lady shrieks from the back of the bus. "My son! Morteza! *Ey,* God, don't let this happen!"

A face covered with blood appears at my window and I instinctively take a step back before it disappears into the crowd. From across the street the driver runs over to us, followed by a small, red-faced po-liceman who starts pushing the men apart. But they fall back on each other, grabbing at hair and shirt lapels, slamming each other against buses in an almost ecstatic frenzy. The policeman turns to a hand-some, amused-looking soldier who is watching from the side. He points at the soldier's machine gun and the soldier affably hands it to him.

The old lady shrieks and starts running up and down the bus aisle.

"They're killing my son! They're shooting my son! God protect him!"

"No, no," I say as the policeman runs screaming into the crowd, using the gun to swat at people. "See, he's just telling them to stop fighting."

"If you don't get back on your bus this second I'll use this the way it's meant to be used!" The policeman digs the gun butt into the men, herding them back onto the bus.

"Hey, I'm not from this bus," says a short, stocky man boarding our bus with his dress shirt ripped from shoulder to stomach.

"Well, then what are you doing here?" the policeman barks. "Get on your own bus or you'll be sorry!"

The men stomp down the aisle, patting each other's backs, handing around tissues. The driver's apprentice opens up a cooler and passes out bottles of Coke. The driver picks up a book from the dashboard and uses it to brush the shards of glass from his seat.

The driver from the other bus comes over and climbs up onto ours. "I'm very sorry," he says. "We didn't see you." He pulls out a wad of bills. "Here's money for the damage."

"No need," our driver mumbles dejectedly.

"Oh, please, take it."

"No, no, that's too much," our driver says, eyeing the wad.

"Don't shame me, please."

"Well, just to make you happy." Our driver takes the money and stuffs it into his pocket.

"Here is my phone number," says the other driver. "If it costs more to fix, call me."

"You're very kind."

They shake hands, and as the other driver leaves he stops to wave to us. "Go in good health," he says.

"*Alhamdollelah,*" the whole bus answers. Praise be to God.

So this is the balance. A busful of men who don't know each other jump up and risk their lives fighting another busful of men for no reason. Then, just as suddenly, they turn around and go back to their seats, waving goodbye to the other bus as it pulls away. The passion boils beneath the surface, erupts, and subsides.

Historians call Iran a flexible society. Iranians, they point out, have withstood centuries of military, linguistic, and religious onslaughts by accepting and incorporating what came their way. Iran has been invaded so much, the scholars say, that Iranians have just had to learn to be accommodating. According to that logic, the revolution should never have happened. But that logic is only part of the story. Because amid all the accommodating and all the fear of action, there is still an impulse for life; and that is what finally bursts forth, all the more powerful for having been kept down so long. After fifteen years of obedience, the dutiful daughter runs off on a snowy night; after eighty years of prayers the grandmother turns against religion. Perhaps that is what the revolution was—an awakening, a release of passion so urgent, so compelling, that it took a world of statesmen and historians by surprise.

"This too shall pass" is now tipped at a precarious angle. Everyone sits quietly as the driver flicks the last slivers of glass off his seat and covers it with a coat. We are more than an hour from the nearest town large enough to have another bus, and the entire front window is caved into a buckled spiderweb with its nucleus above the driver's seat.

"Now what do we do?" someone cries from the back.

"Call for a new bus!" someone else says.

"No, that would take hours," says a third voice. "And what if there is no other bus? Better to just turn around."

As the passengers throw out suggestions, the apprentice rolls up a blanket and props it up against the caved-in window. The driver turns on the engine. A chorus of whispers rises up—"*Bismillah-alrahman-alraheem*"—and we roll out onto the road. The windshield gives a deep groan and crumples further in toward the driver. "Better to go back right now and switch buses!" someone calls out. But the apprentice jumps out the door. We hear his footsteps thudding over the top of the bus, and soon a long wooden plank has been roped across the front of the windshield.

And then we are off, driving fast through the mountains, the wind whistling through the shattered glass as we cover our faces. Every now and then we hear a loud crack, and a little shower of glass rushes past our heads. "*Allahoma-salou-Allah-Mohammad-va-ahle-*

Mohammad," someone calls out, and the others repeat it once, twice, three times. "May God's peace be on Mohammad and the people of Mohammad." May God's peace be on us, may He get us there alive.

We round the top of a bend and start sailing down a hill. The wind grows stronger and the crackling gets louder and the apprentice holds his right hand over the driver's face to shield his eyes. *Allahoma-salou-Allah-Mohammad-va-ahle-Mohammad.* We pick up speed and fly down toward the desert.

This Other Night Inside

❖

SOMEWHERE OVER AMERICA, A WEB SITE PLAYS HOST TO A MEL-
ancholy community of Iranian exiles. The site posts anecdotes about
Iranian life in America; interviews with Shah-era Iranian pop singers,
and photographs of Esfahan, Persepolis, or a Tehran *joob* that reminded someone of home. Now and then I find essays or short stories
about first trips back to Iran. Written for the insider, they tend toward melodrama, but the authors' poignant expressions of nostalgia
could not be more sincere.

   They remind me of my own dislocation when I first flew back from
Tehran to Brussels, over two years ago. On my first day back I went
out for a long walk and lost my way. I forgot the number of the tram
I'd taken to work every day over the previous summer, and when I
asked two young men for directions they stared at me, baffled, as I
realized that what I'd meant to be French was coming out in rapid
Farsi. I longed for Massi and her watermelon juice. I missed the talkative taxi drivers, and the Shahrak women in raincoats and scarves
who knew just by looking that I was an ally and would warn me if

there was a *komiteh* checkpoint around the corner. In downtown Brussels I recoiled at the sight of policemen and gaped in shock at a man and woman holding hands in public, only to look around and realize that here I would find no silent bonds of solidarity, nothing of the watchful, comforting community I had grown so accustomed to.

Twenty times a day I reached up to my head, panicking when I didn't feel the scarf there; at home I fished it out of my suitcase, and the dark, slippery fabric felt soothing between my fingers. Flying out of Iran, I had sat down in my airplane seat with the other Iranians and feyly pushed my scarf off my hair and down to my neck. But at the end of my journey, whizzing in a taxicab down a slick Belgian highway, I grabbed at the scarf and pulled it back up, wanting it to cover me and take me back again. I held it to my face and inhaled, trying to catch a last, lingering breath of Iran. Then I shook it out and proceeded with the ritual I'd gone through every day for so many weeks—folding it into a triangle, tying it loosely at my chin, pulling the top sharply forward so that not too much hair showed. Going through the motions made me feel better, as if I was still participating in the life I'd left behind; and for a few nights, when I was missing Iran, I would wear the scarf alone in the bedroom like a secret vice.

Now, on the Web site and everywhere else where I find Iranians, I see a similar sense of displacement. Strangely, it seems strongest in Iranians my own age. Those young enough to have adjusted to America but old enough to still remember Iran seem to have the most difficulty choosing their cultural allegiances, perhaps because they were too young to have made their own decisions about staying in Iran or leaving. Their personal essays are particularly wrenching, and their entries in the Web site's "lost and found" corner make plaintive appeals to their prerevolution ghosts:

> I am looking for anyone that attended Arvand Elementary School in Ahvaz, located in the New Sight area. I was there till fall 1979 until that day when they told us to go home!! My teachers were Mrs. Ranjbar, Mrs. Jaffari, Mrs. Omidi, and my last teacher was Mrs. Ashourian.

I am looking for my friend Mohammad Reza whom I used to play with in my childhood. He was my neighbour, had three sisters; one of them died years ago in a car accident. He went to the States after his youngest sister. I used to call him Khan Dadash. He is almost 30 years old.

I am looking for Ebrahim Samii Zonouzie (the spelling might be incorrect). His family has not heard from him in 12 years. His mother is a very old and sad woman that wants to talk to her son. Thanks, countrymen.

Reading these messages, I see a world of people swirling past each other in a fog, hitting and missing, hoping the right person will notice their name on the screen. I see myself at twelve, perusing the "D" pages of the Portland telephone directory in search of my lost friend Pamela. I see myself at twenty-four, scrutinizing Shahrzad's Community School yearbook, trying to recognize the little black-and-white faces there; and I see myself with Ali, discovering that the Internet has an international yellow pages that can find people's addresses all over the world. We entered the Dars' names, elated and apprehensive. But every search of India and Sweden and the United States always ended in "No Match."

And then, one spring day, I am playing soccer in a Brooklyn park when I find someone I never thought to look for. A friend attending my old journalism school unzips his duffelbag and I spot the "face book" for this year's graduating class. Curious, I open it to a random place, and a face in the middle of the page catches my eye. Dark hair, pale skin, serious eyes, and a slightly uneven smile. "Hey, I know her," I say. "We went to nursery school together in Iran."

My soccer friend glances at the picture and frowns. "I don't know her," he says. "Are you sure it's the same girl?"

"Yes, of course." I can't explain why I am so sure. That face is looking out at me from across a twenty-four-year chasm, but somehow I know that however many Carla Powers might inhabit the world, this one is mine. I was only five when she and her parents and brother moved away from Iran, returning for only two short visits along a route of foreign countries I could not keep track of. But her name and face remained etched in my memory. She is my earliest friend, my most distant ghost, and here she is, magically resurfacing at my old school.

I don't have much time to find her—she graduates this week, and after that, judging from the long list of degrees and honors and traveling fellowships listed beside her photo, she could go anywhere. Even now, she is probably packing her bags to fly away to a new location with her new degree, far out of reach of any people-finder device. I hurry up to Columbia University and explain to the dean's secretary why I need Carla's phone number. The secretary gives me a withering look. "You haven't seen her in almost twenty years?" she says. "And you really expect her to remember you?"

The last time I saw Carla she was headed for Egypt. It was the early fall of 1978, and her family had hurried out of Afghanistan in the wake of the Soviets, carrying out all their belongings. Back in Kabul she and her professor parents had lived alongside a community of American hippies and diplomats. In the afternoons Carla and her friends from the American school would wander around the sleepy, low-rise city, honing their bartering skills and helping the bazaar jewelers sort lapis stones for necklaces. On Fridays, the Islamic day of rest, Carla would ride on the handlebars of her father's bicycle as he pedaled down into the darkest depths of the bazaar, emerging with a rolled-up carpet balanced on his shoulder. Friday nights the whole family would go down to the American Staff House for burgers and milk shakes.

One day, driving away from a school-sponsored Little League game, the family saw a column of tanks heading toward them. "Look, Mom, it's a coup," eleven-year-old Carla said, having just learned about coups in school. "Don't be silly, darling," said her mother. "It's a parade." But the soldiers' guns were loaded, and the following week the university apologetically informed her father that they had no work for him for the time being. After five months the Fulbright Commission, who had been sponsoring them, finally moved the family to a new post in Egypt.

When Carla's family stopped in Iran on their way out of Afghanistan, we were just getting ready to start our new life in Shahrak. We were dividing our time between Tehran and the Caspian Sea, watching the walls being plastered inside the Shahrak house, watching the cement-block skeleton being laid among the lush coastal trees for our small beach house. It must have been midweek, putting us in Tehran, when Carla's mother called from the Intercontinental Hotel to say they were in town for the night. And so that evening, on one of the last warm nights of the year, we took them to the German Club for dinner. Under the poolside canopy, at a table covered with a thick, deep crimson cloth, our parents lamented about Afghanistan. Carla's parents described how relaxed and un-Westernized it was, like Iran had been in the sixties; my parents reproached themselves for not visiting when they had the chance. As they waxed philosophical about unexpected turns of fate, Ali and Sufi and I led Carla and her brother out to play on the dark, cool lawn behind the restaurant. We invented a new kind of tag and played it all evening, running and shrieking ourselves into a warm exhaustion. The next day Carla went to Egypt and I never saw her again.

I dial her number hesitantly. As the phone begins to ring, I think again of the dean's secretary's comment. Why should Carla remember me? Just because I remember playing with her when we were five? For Snow White and the Seven Dwarfs we gave each other poisoned apples to bite into and sank to the floor in comas; for Doctor and Patient we pulled down our underwear and illustrated each other's bottoms with Magic Marker. But the only news I had of her after she went to Egypt was in a letter her mother sent to my mother, years later. Carla would be going to Yale in the fall to study drama, her mother wrote. For me, still in eleventh grade and struggling through chemistry lab, drama at Yale sounded glamorous and adult. I was far too intimidated to even think of writing Carla a letter.

"Hello?"

"Hi, is this Carla? I don't know if you remember me, but my name is Tara and I went to nursery school with you in Iran."

"Of *course* I remember you! I saw your name on the school alumni list and tried to find out where you'd gone . . ."

We make a brunch date for Saturday. When the day comes I dress nervously, checking the back of my skirt, changing my T-shirt twice, feeling as if I am about to meet a movie star whose career I have followed for years. It's not just the drama school, or the fact that she has already completed two master's degrees that make her out to look like a Middle East expert. It is also the myth of Carla herself. What will she be like? A taller version of her straightforward, inquisitive childhood self? A mature, self-possessed scholar who will expect me to discuss twenty-five hundred years of Persian history? Was that uneven smile in the face book hiding the wider smile of an old friend or masking the disdainful smirk of someone who will be disappointed in me? Will I dare to bring up the time we drew on each other's butts?

She is going to ring my doorbell; I'll go down and we'll go to breakfast. But even though I am expecting all this, the buzzer sends a jolt of panic through me. I take a deep breath and start down the stairs, and as I approach the front door of the building I can see her through the little square window, standing on the stoop, red-faced and smiling. Her fine brown hair is cut into a neat, professional bob, her eyebrows are raised tentatively, her heart-shaped face looks both more familiar and more strange than I imagined. I open the door and we hug awkwardly, unable to contain our smiles. Then we step back to look at each other. Something about her dark brown blazer reassures me and even makes me wonder if she too was nervous this morning; did she worry like I did about what to wear? If she did, I want to tell her that her baggy blazer, a size too large and slightly out of fashion, was the perfect choice. It makes her look both relaxed and vulnerable and it makes me like her at once.

I had worried that we wouldn't have things to say. But, sitting at an outdoor café on St. Mark's Place, we can't stop talking. Our omelets grow cold as we mirror each other's memories—of a nursery school Christmas party, of ballet classes on my mother's living-room floor, of Carla's pink sleeveless dress that we both thought looked so grown-up. "Of *course* I remember playing doctor," she says, blushing a little. We are equally nostalgic, equally pleased to find someone else who knows our own pasts so well.

"You know, you guys were a golden family for us," Carla says, picking at her cold eggs. "We made up songs about you that we would sing on car trips. And we also sang the songs you taught us."

"Really?" I say, pleased and surprised. "Like what?"

"Remember that game you and Ali made up? Primary School in Africa?"

"Of course," I say. "We played it all the time. But it didn't have music to it."

"Yes, it did." And putting her hands on the table for emphasis, she bursts into song. "PRI-mary School in AF-rica, it's the BEST School in AF-rica." We collapse into giggles, but at the same time I feel tears prick my eyes.

"You and Ali taught it to us that night you took us to the German Club," Carla says. "I remember—your dad was late to dinner because he was working really hard on your new house. He arrived looking all shaggy with his long hair, and I remember being so impressed that you guys had a father who actually went to work, because my dad had been out of work in Kabul ever since the Russians came. And I was also impressed that you had a real house that you were going to live in, because we were so used to moving from one place to another."

Families who move a lot have to be close. Nobody else sticks around—no neighbors or school friends or even other relatives—the brothers and sisters and mother and father have only each other as reference points. Without those anchors, the evidence of their past is in danger of floating away. But Carla's family sang our song long after we ourselves had forgotten it, and when she sings the words now I feel like I am hearing from a sister who disappeared long ago, carrying with her a little box of my life. She feels this too. "I can't believe you're real," we keep saying. "I can't believe you're sitting in front of me now, and that we like each other so much."

Later, I think back to the only comment Carla made that did not ring fully true for me. "Isn't it hard," she said, "to think about settling down here when you've grown up living the expat life?" I started to nod, but then I stopped. The expat life? After the last time I saw Carla she moved on exotically, to Cairo and Rome, making friends with foreigners who sat together at swimming clubs and embassy parties and returned home with crates full of antiques. Carla continued this life long after I came to America; she was old—a senior in high school—when her family finally flew back to St. Louis for good.

Even if I had stayed in Iran that long, I don't think I would have called my life "expat." The word evokes aloof, wealthy outsiders; white-suited diplomats and archaeologists; people to whom the place they live in remains foreign no matter how long they stay. It is the opposite of "immigrant," which implies large families crammed into small apartments, perhaps not legal, hampered by their foreign accents and their dark skin (expat skin is simply pink and peeling from the sun). Immigrants miss their own country—maybe they didn't want to leave it in the first place; expats love the adventure of being away. "Expat" can always go home again. "Immigrant" is close to "refugee."

My life in Iran was, of course, adorned with some of the trappings of the expat life. Our Americanness—both my mother's background and my father's education—was a ticket into an elite made up of anyone who bore the stamp of the West. It was reflected in our parents' choice of a plot in Shahrak, in our attending Community School, in Mama's working at CBS—even in Baba's job at the university, where a foreign education provided an extra mark of distinction. But that day at breakfast Carla illustrated my own expatness with a story I hadn't remembered, an indication of how separate, at the age of four, we already felt from those around us. One day we begged to dress up like Iranian women, so Mama bought a length of black cloth and made us two little chadors. We draped them over our heads and squatted silently against a wall the way we had seen Iranian women do in the street. We already knew we would never wear chadors in our real lives; no matter how many dark, draped women we passed on the sidewalk, we would end up in minidresses and tights like our mothers. Ours was an expat game. You don't see children of immigrants to America dressing up as Americans for a day; they make sure to dress American every day.

But despite all this, my family were not expats in Iran. We were growing up there, our relatives lived there; it was our home. When we saw the red-painted letters that spelled "Yankee Go Home," we did not turn the focus in on ourselves. Yankees were the apple-cheeked American military fathers who wore pirate costumes at the

Iran-America Society Halloween parties; Yankees were the wide-hipped midwestern mothers and the thin-lipped blond California mothers who complained about how the Iranian-made cornflakes just didn't taste as good as the real thing. When we saw those dripping red letters telling them to go home we shrugged, half agreeing that they should leave if they were that nervous, half surprised that they left so fast and easily. Our school closed and opened and closed again like an illness in remission, but we did not take it personally.

And yet, when we finally left, we were not immigrants to America either. Three of us had been born there; four of us spoke perfect American English. Landing in America, we went straight to Grandma and Grandpa's backyard swimming pool in the hills. But as soon as we arrived I began to miss what Carla calls the expat life. Abroad, our lives had been unlike anyone else's. We had not fit into any mold; compared to Iranian kids in Iran or American kids in America, we had had a sense of being untethered in the world. We had traveled all our lives; we were seasoned experts on jet lag and layover and the toy shops at London Heathrow. Our futures too were uncharted. With no model to follow, we could imagine ourselves anywhere in the world, and it seemed that in the end it was only a slight breeze that pushed one family toward Egypt and sent another back to America.

That day at the café, Carla told me she was living in London when bandits broke into her family's house in a small Mexican town called San Miguel de Allende. The regular townspeople knew the American family on the hill, but this was a fiesta night and these men were not from town. They beat up her father, who was there alone. The Mexican hospital assured Carla's mother that it was not necessary to fly in from St. Louis, but after eleven days she flew in to sit beside him anyway. The next day a blood clot traveled up to his heart.

Carla's family didn't go to San Miguel for adventure; they thought they were finished with wars and revolutions. Tired of always having to pack their bags and leave, they went to Mexico and bought a vacation home. What happened was a fluke, Carla says, and afterward she and her mother and brother said they bore the place no ill will, although they put the house up for sale. It happened just days after

I flew back to Iran, sometime during the week that I was trying to retrieve my confiscated passport. At that point Carla returned to America, where two years later I—another fluke—ran across her picture in a duffelbag.

Now Carla's mother comes to New York for her graduation and the two of them stop in to visit me. They joke about how her father must have arranged this. Up in heaven, with nothing to do, he saw that Carla and I were in the same city and fixed it so we'd find each other. Now he must be laughing.

As they say this, I want to laugh along with them, but I can't. My mind is fixed on a single image—sitting at the café breakfast table and seeing Carla's ash-gray eyes glisten with tears as she told me about her father. That day I walked home from the café shaking, feeling almost as if it had happened to me. I stopped to buy flowers, which I never do, and clutched them to my chest. Back in my apartment, I called California. Baba was home alone, working on the design for a new remodel, and I told him what had happened. Poor Dick, he said quietly. Poor Carla.

The tall white flowers sweeten my living room now, and I want to say something to Carla and her mother as they sit on my couch. But what? How happy I am to discover that they are so similar to us? How sad I am to hear about her father? Or something general, like how comforting it is to find that what you begin your life with stays with you, a series of familiar threads that you eventually return to no matter what else happens? Instead of saying these things I forget myself and start to talk about my father, wincing in the middle as I realize what I am saying. It feels unfair to still have him. But Carla doesn't flinch; in fact she talks about her father in the present tense, as if he is simply in a different town. This disturbs and reassures me, and I wonder if I would do it too, if that is how it is with loss—that you never really let go of the thing you are missing.

Carla's mother remembers more forgotten details of my childhood, including my early resistance to Iran. "You were always comparing everything to America. For some reason which I never quite understood, you identified with an American girlhood. It was as if you felt you were a princess who had been stolen away from her kingdom."

I blush, remembering the bossy little girl who insisted on hamburgers instead of kabob and who clapped her hands over her ears when anyone tried to speak to her in Farsi. But Carla's mother's description of me rings even more true when I think of what happened a few years later. Didn't I feel just as displaced when we left Iran; didn't I look back just as longingly at my old life and disparage the new one—the American public schools that could never provide the Renaissance lectures and science classes I'd left behind, the series of houses that would never live up to Shahrak, my parents' American jobs that were pale substitutes for the careers they would have thrived on in Iran. At age three I felt stolen away from one kingdom; by age eleven I had adapted so well to the new one that moving was like being stolen all over again.

Some memories come back only in the presence of other memories, like a series of locked doors. Opening one allows you to open another, which in turn opens a window through which to view your past. It was not until Carla began to talk about her last visit to Iran that I remembered, after seventeen years, the game we played at the German Club on that balmy, honeysuckle-scented eve of the revolution. I never played it again, and Carla did not mention it when I saw her; but being with her made me suddenly remember standing in the middle of the dark garden that night, making up the rules of the game. It calls for four people to stand beside four trees in a wide-open square of grass. The fifth one stands in the center, and at a signal we run, trying to switch trees without the middle person getting there before us. The pattern is circular and endless. After each run, someone is always left floating in the middle of the lawn. The floater cries out and the rest of us pick a direction and run blindly until we hit a tree and whip our arms around it. We stop with a jerk, breathless, relieved to be holding on to the solid trunk. And then we look around to see where we are.

Acknowledgments

❖

THIS BOOK COULD NOT HAVE BEEN WRITTEN WITHOUT THE family and friends who told me their stories and helped to shape mine, especially those who opened their lives to me in Iran and made me feel as if I had never been gone. They helped me discover a part of myself, and I am grateful for their love and generosity. To the extent that it is possible, I have tried to protect the privacy of people who never asked to have their personal lives made public, by changing some names and identifying details.

I am extremely lucky to have Barney Karpfinger as my agent. His unwavering championship of this book, his consistently sound advice, and his warmth and vision inspired me and helped keep my head above water. I also could not have asked for more dedicated support from Jen Unter, Joe Gramm, and Liv Blumer at the Karpfinger agency.

I am very grateful to my editor, Elisabeth Kallick Dyssegaard, who put her faith in this book and kept her faith in me. Her instinct for subtlety and her clearheaded editing persisted through this book's many incarnations, and her patience outlasted the long time it took me to complete it. I am also grateful to Elaine Blair, who spent many hours fine-tuning these pages, and whose sound judgment and good cheer were a great help.

Sam Freedman convinced me that I had a book to write, and did not let me back away from it. I thank him for his careful readings and for the advice and guidance that he continues to offer with such unstinting generosity.

Many thanks to Marvin Siegel for his humor and sincerity as well as his sharp, honest feedback. Also for calling up now and then to remind me that there is a world beyond all this.

To Leonard Michaels, who first made me realize that I wanted to write. Without his encouragement, I might have followed an entirely different path.

To Carla, Dalton, Elsa, Mimi, Natalie, Andreas & Marta, Persheng, Zia, and the Monday Night Writers' Group who read, listened, and offered valuable suggestions. To the friends, including Stephanie, who gave me extracurricular support, and especially to the soccer gang, who got me out of the house and into the mud and rain.

To Haithum, who was there for me through some of the most difficult parts, who gave me invaluable advice about writing and about life, and who will always be in my heart.

To Pamela, for finding me, and for proving that what you leave behind is not really lost.

To my two grandmothers, whose presence I often felt near me as I was writing this book.

To Hedwig, Muffy, and Liesl, who loyally watched over us in our various homes.

To Ali and Sufi, with whom it is just as fun to be big as it was to be little, and whose brotherly and sisterly love has lasted long after they figured out that the Good Brother and Sister Clubs were all made up. I am honored to be their sister.

To Brian, who carried many versions of this book around with him and took thoughtful care in reading each one. He pushed me to think through to deeper truths, and his instinct for clarity and harmony guided me through every page. More important, he teaches me to feel the present without forgetting the past, and every day I am grateful for his wisdom and his love, and for his reminder to cherish that butterfly.

Finally, I thank Mama and Baba, who endured countless long-distance interrogations and who gave up their own privacy in letting me write about our family. They shared their memories and insights with the same unconditional affection and dedication they have given me since I was a little girl. It is not possible to do them justice here; I can only thank them for always putting us first, for being my friends as well as my models, and for ensuring that our home was rich in love at all times, no matter where in the world we were.